For Judy

continuing success in

your care management endeavors'

Warmest regards

MW01002492

THE CASE MANAGER'S HANDBOOK

Catherine M. Mullahy, RN, BS, CRRN, CCM
President
Options Unlimited
Huntington, New York

AN ASPEN PUBLICATION®
Aspen Publishers, Inc.
Gaithersburg, Maryland
1995

Library of Congress Cataloging-in-Publication Data

Mullahy, Catherine M.
The case manager's handbook / Catherine M. Mullahy.
p.   cm.
Includes bibliographical references and index.
ISBN: 0-8342-0537-8
1. Hospitals—Case management services—Handbooks, manuals, etc.
I. Title.
RA975.5.C36M85   1994
362.1'1—dc20
94-21948
CIP

Editorial Resources: Amy R. Martin

Library of Congress Catalog Card Number: 94-21948
ISBN: 0-8342-0537-8

Printed in the United States of America

3 4 5

Table of Contents

Foreword

This handbook arrives on the case management scene at a time of maximum growth in both the number and diversity of case management practitioners, when other health care professionals have a need to know what to expect of and how to relate to the range of practitioners.

With its thrust toward quality health care, cost containment, and managed competition, the case management industry has suddenly become the focus of considerable hope and attention. Having proven itself in the areas of workers' compensation, elder care, home care, social services, and group health, it now holds a prominent position on the national stage. Case management's performance will impact each one of us over the next several years.

The number of case managers has risen from an estimated five to ten thousand in 1985 to a total of fifty to one hundred thousand today, and this explosive growth will undoubtedly continue. The character of case management has also matured from competitive to collaborative. The industry has assumed responsibility for credentialing, thereby establishing nationally recognized standards of practice so long needed. Permitting case managers to practice with greater clarity of purpose and integrity, ethical and legal issues are more clearly defined than ever. Educational programs are more abundant and contribute toward forging a standard of case management. But how is the art of case management to be communicated?

By the time-tested method: from one person to another, from a mentor. Someone willing to come alongside, to share not only what he or she knows, but also to convey workable strategies on acquiring ever-changing information—the "stuff" of case management. The mentor's role is even more important when it comes to the essence of case management: the care, the passion for quality, the art of the business. This book is one such link between mentor and learner, written by an author who has experienced and developed case management at its finest and who shares not only the "stuff," but her heart.

It was through a mentor-learner relationship that I first came to know Cathy Mullahy. A few years ago, half a continent away and in the midst of working cases, she offered the expertise I required to take what I had learned in other areas of case management and transfer it to the group health experience. It was during our crucial conversations that I discovered her knowledge and her vision of case management. Well versed in the ins and outs of claims, the nuances of benefits language, and the clinical and operations management of various reimbursement systems, she provided insight and direction. More importantly, she cared about people—the patient, the family, the provider, and the payer—and incorporated that concern into case management.

I have known Cathy when the status of her business was incredibly good and when it could not have been worse. It was in those "worst of times," when the desire and determination to make her case management vision work were about all that was left, that I came to recognize and respect her uncompromising ethics and values. In a number of ways she has been, and continues to be, a mentor and has also become a coplanner, coconsultant, copresenter, and friend. All of this is to say that I can commend the author of this handbook as a trustworthy communicator and adviser, a teacher who has carefully crafted a significant part of case management practice. From her years as a staff nurse in emergency room and other critical care settings through the establishment of her own case management company, she has consistently applied new techniques and innovations, making her a leading case management professional and a well-received lecturer and commentator.

As you refine your own manner of case management delivery, you will be involved in a three-part pursuit: gathering medical and clinical expertise, learning the industry, and fulfilling your personal goals. This practical book, written by a pioneer who has creatively and compassionately addressed patient, provider, and payer needs via case management, will enable you to achieve peak collaborative performance in your practice setting, on behalf of your clients and in conjunction with the other professionals serving them. I believe you will find that its content will wear well over time, through the tests of a changing health care system, and that it serves as a rich reference. Using this major tool prepared for practiced and novice case managers alike, you will be introduced to the basics and subtleties of one mentor's vision of truly meaningful case management.

Jeanne Boling, MSN, CRRN, CIRS, CCM
Executive Director
Individual Case Management Association
Little Rock, Arkansas

Preface

Case management can help resolve one of the paradoxes of the current health care delivery system: Our technologically advanced medical facilities are staffed by highly skilled and trained professionals, yet we fall short in our efforts to provide optimum care to individual patients, especially those afflicted with multifaceted, problematic, chronic diseases or disabilities. Patients enter a high-performance health care system so specialized and organ-specific that treatment is often fragmented and the overall quality of care is diluted. Serving as a vital connection linking all the private and public associations, agencies, disciplines, and practitioners within the delivery system, case managers are catalysts and communicators, advocates for patients, providers, and payers. They help focus the system for each person, facilitating the delivery of more individualized, coordinated care.

While working toward improved quality of care and better patient outcomes, case management professionals have also become recognized for their abilities as good financial managers. Case managers have become good financial managers simply by fulfilling the role and function of their profession. However, it is both incorrect and unconscionable to equate case management with cut-rate health care. Finances should not drive case management systems, but the pressure for cost containment and some hefty greed has led to the creation of several large financially focused case management groups. There are case managers who earn a base salary plus a bonus determined by the reduction of care costs. Applying case management solely to cut costs is just not an acceptable strategy.

Committed individuals, adhering to ethical case management principles, *will* deliver more cost-effective health care. Once case management methods of coordinating medical services are put in place, cost-effectiveness becomes assured, as do quality and improved outcomes.

The discipline of case management is evolving as you read this. Because the need is so great, the escalation of medical costs so swift, and the application of case management strategies so effective in maintaining high standards of care while cutting expenses, case management has become an industry "overnight," although it has been practiced for years. It is an industry that is changing in response to modifications in the health care delivery system even as it influences those modifications. Accepted as an integral element in the health care system, it is attracting increased recognition as well as generating demands for a consensus on standards of practice. Some who have only a rough idea of the nature of case management are claiming they are case management practitioners regardless of their expertise and the appropriateness of their interventions. This is one unfortunate result of the industry's youth. As long as we lack established operating systems and professional guidelines, we risk being viewed as obstacles to the provision of medical care rather than as providers of independent assessments designed to reinvigorate and support care delivery.

Fortunately, a credentialing process for case management professionals has been developed under the guidance of the Certification of Insurance Rehabilitation Specialists Commission (CIRSC) in Rolling Meadows, Illinois. Announced in September 1992, the credential of Certified Case Manager (CCM) brought into existence a nationally accepted standard for case management practitioners.[1] The outgrowth of intensive research, review, and preparation, the CCM may be earned by case managers who satisfy specific educational and employment criteria and successfully complete the CCM examination. The exam, given for the first time in May 1993, encompassed laws, public regulations, and a comprehensive understanding of case management services as delivered in the United States. The definition of the case management designation, CCM eligibility criteria, and exam content were designed and coordinated by the CIRSC using input from a number of case management specialists, including representatives from the Individual Case Management Association; Foundation for Rehabilitation Certification, Education and Research; Association of Rehabilitation Nurses; American Association for Continuity of Care; Case Management Society of America; American Medical Association; American Hospital Association; American Nursing Association; Blue Cross/ Blue Shield Association; National Association of Social Workers, as well as the Workers' Compensation Case Management and Liability Case Management departments of prominent insurance firms.[2]

Growth in the case management industry will be spurred by various sectors. As the number of insurance companies in the health care business decreases, due to mergers and acquisitions, and the trend among employer groups toward self-funded benefit programs increases, we will see more case management organizations within larger corporations. Smaller companies and entrepreneurs, realizing that claims administration services that lack cost-containment mechanisms do little to ease the burden of health care payments in the long run, will begin to self-administer their programs, relying on case managers to coordinate care delivery. Sensing case managers are true advocates, individual consumers and communities will call on them directly for help in navigating the channels of health care support services, from selecting a suitable head trauma center or obtaining family counseling for those living with a terminally ill loved one to representing the estate of a disabled individual in court.

Before case management professionals will be accepted as part of the mainstream of advanced medical care, a change will need to occur in current thinking regarding human resources and medical benefits. Case management must become a standard element in the administration of benefits. The concept driving case management is so straightforward, and the results of case management so positive, that it is difficult to believe we are still in the process of educating other medical professionals, insurers, corporations, communities, and politicians regarding its benefits rather than simply implementing its procedures.

For years, it has been known that the greatest portion of health care costs is generated by the 3 to 5 percent of the patient population that are at high risk, critically injured, or suffering from a chronic disease. As an example, from January to October 1992, one client firm spent over $1.8 million in health care benefits for its employees and their dependents (2,520 covered lives). Fully one-half of that dollar total was distributed to 30 individuals (4 percent of the employees). This means that one-half of the benefit dollars spent, over $900,000, was focused on 1.1 percent of the total covered population. Twenty-two employees spent $588,702, meaning that 3 percent of the employees accounted for 32 percent of the group's total in paid claims. When one considers the covered lives, the figures are more remarkable: 0.8 percent or *less* than 1 percent spent 32 percent of the dollars.[3]

By developing systems to identify and manage cases from day one, case management promotes quality care and contains costs. By wrapping the case management approach around all lines of medical coverage, case managers can be appropriately attentive to potentially problematic cases, more creative in problem solving, and better able to address spiraling expenses before they take off. As a byproduct, case management also tackles three other problem areas that push up employer costs and concerns: employee morale, decreased production, and absenteeism. A case manager's professional intervention and guidance improves employee morale by providing direct communication and personal attention, helps return employees to the job more quickly, and helps eliminate repeated occurrences of the same afflictions.

Case management, in conjunction with such programs as preadmission review, utilization review, claims administration, and health care education for individuals and their families, can smooth the path of health care delivery. Patients and their families do not have to feel that they are being abandoned in the middle of an overwhelming and confusing system controlled by inaccessible authorities. Health care providers will rest assured that the individuals they treated will be tracked through home or hospice recovery and that fewer cases will be readmitted due to complications that could have been prevented. And insurers can put the brakes on escalating health care claims by using backup data on where dollars are needed and where dollars are being spent.

True, money is pouring into our health care system. But improved treatment and services are not flowing out at the same rate. Case management is one needed catalyst to push performance to more cost-effective levels. Although patient responses and cost-benefit analysis sheets are proof positive of top-level treatment and bottom-line results, we must continue to address the misunderstanding and misuse of case management procedures and to demonstrate how the common-sense approach of case management can improve a potentially successful health care system that appears in danger of running into the ground. Our challenge is to maintain the high standards of care and commitment, backed by expertise and performed via repeatable and verifiable procedures, and the industry we are creating will become standard operating procedure.

This handbook is designed to define good case management, examine the case management process in its entirety, and present practical procedural information. It reviews case management's current business applications and also discusses future possibilities as well as the expanding opportunities for professional case managers.

Capitalizing on my experiences, I have created a how-to manual. I had to learn through a great deal of trial and error because there was no Case Management University, no place to study the kind of case management that exists today. There was no case manager's reference guide to consult. Much of the information contained in this manual was developed through my own "pilot projects." I have shared my experiences, including my failures. Hopefully, these experiences will keep other case managers from repeating my mistakes. The manual is filled with instances where I was left with a dilemma because I did not think things through in advance or I did not plan sufficiently. It also incorporates methods that started as trials and became tried-and-true approaches to care and claims management.

Each person can do exactly what I have done. Given experience and time and grade in the health care business, much of what is contained in this book has immediate application. It can serve as a resource or inspiration when something that you have done does not quite work, when you are looking for an alternative. That is why I like including anecdotal information. Case management is not a perfect science. It is filled with individuals and systems, some of which function, some of which are so fraught with disaster that when you prepare a final report on a case, you wonder how you managed to promote anything good. This handbook was written to serve as a reference on those days when you become convinced there must be another way, a different approach. My answer will not always be the right answer, but it may provide a new perspective just when one is needed.

The Case Manager's Handbook can be used as a training guide for new case managers or a teaching tool for client groups. It stands apart from other case management references, in that it is partly designed to function as a tool for *the business world.* Case management, besides improving health delivery outcomes, is also a financial and human resource tool that more businesses should be using. There are some strong examples in this book to help persuade and educate business executives who might be inclined to incorporate case management practices as a way of serving their employees better, containing the expenditure of benefit dollars, and getting more value for the dollars they do spend.

Other special features of this book include examples of usable forms, letters, and dialogues, tools that with modification may make sorting information, collecting data, or presenting material easier. Some will simply be ideas holding the seeds for new methods. You may look at a paragraph in the book and say, "Well, that's good, but . . ." These concepts have worked for me; they can be improved upon by you.

Because so much of case management is specific to a patient, an insurance plan, the community where a patient lives, the providers one works with, some of the examples are not going to be useful to all readers. The information in the manual is based on my own experience and may not have universal application. Case management is utilized in so many arenas today, it is difficult to give examples that fit every criterion. If you are a case manager, not everything in this book is going to be immediately appropriate for you in your current employment setting. However, the handbook will have something to offer for virtually every case manager. Is it the definitive book for case managers in a rehab facility? No, it is not. But are there some methods discussed that a rehab facility case manager is going to be able to apply? Yes, there are. If you are a provider-based case manager, your reports perhaps are not going to be useful to a claims department, but you will still have to justify the amount of money that someone spent in your facility, maybe to another case manager so that she will continue to refer people to you. So, when I talk about presenting a cost-benefit analysis report to an employer group, this does not mean that employers are the only audience for CBAs. Many of the issues discussed have several different applications, and while the focus in a particular chapter or paragraph may be for one kind of case manager, another will be able to redirect it to her advantage.

I did not set out to write the all-purpose case management handbook. I never intended to try to incorporate all the answers in one manuscript— *that* would take a lifetime. I know there will always be new challenges for case managers, new hurdles caused by changing health care policies and programs. My goal was merely to create a compendium of knowledge for now and a vision for the future. What this book offers is the nuts and bolts of case management and a sense of where it can go. I want to empower the industry and the individual. I hope the work I have done and shared will encourage other case managers to create and be the difference in their health environment rather than waiting for someone else to incorporate them into the mainstream.

Author's Note: Because the majority of case managers are women, I have used the feminine pronoun throughout this book. No offense to our male colleagues is implied or intended.

NOTES

1. Deborah K. Jensen, "CIRSC Announces New Case Manager Certification at ICMA's Medical Case Management Conference in Nashville." Press release. (Little Rock, Ark.: Individual Case Management Association, October 1992).
2. Tom Strickland, "National Case Management Task Force," *The Case Manager*, Spring 1991, 47.
3. *Cost-Containment Analysis and Recommendations* (Huntington, N.Y.: Options Unlimited, 1992).

Acknowledgments

The idea for this book took form two years ago, and since that time many people have been involved in making it a reality. I especially want to thank Deborah Jensen, a superb writer and editor, for her invaluable insight, encouragement, boundless energy, and vision in all phases of this huge undertaking. To Jeannie Boling, my heartfelt gratitude and appreciation for her inspiration and continuous support from the earliest days of this project through ongoing reviews and changes and for sharing her knowledge and experience of case management as a friend and colleague. To Alice Casey Meadows, a wonderful friend and teacher, for imparting her claims administration expertise so generously over the years.

To these three women in particular I express my deepest appreciation. They shared their talents, their strength, their vision, their warmth, and, most importantly in such an endeavor, their humor. They offered their personal support of me and what I hoped to—and with their help was finally able to—accomplish.

There are many others whom I would like to acknowledge. I would like to thank Jack Bruggeman, at Aspen Publishers, for his belief in this project and his continued support. I would also like to thank the dozens of people who reviewed the manuscript for content and accuracy, among them Eda Holt, Chief Executive Officer of CIRSC; Art Steinberg, MD, Vice President, Medical Operations and Member Services, AETNA Health Plans; and Gary S. Wolfe, President of CMSA and Vice President, Managed Care for Staff Builders.

I express profound gratitude to my staff at Options Unlimited for their understanding and support while this book was in development, and to Linda Mercurio for her assistance in preparing the manuscript. I also want to thank our client companies, our patients, and their families for according us the privilege of working with them, and to all the many case managers who have been my colleagues and friends and the inspiration for this work, you too were part of this endeavor.

And finally I want to express my deepest appreciation to my husband, John, for his love, unfailing enthusiasm, and belief in me, and to my children, Michael and Aileen, my parents, family, and friends, who encouraged and allowed me the time to complete this handbook.

Profile of a Case Manager

1

The Case Manager as Catalyst, Problem Solver, Educator

Case management is not for the faint at heart. It is not for those seeking to avoid the stress of a hospital setting or the stretch of working with patients and families in distress. Providing intervention on behalf of the patient, medical provider, and payer (insurer), a case manager must place herself at the center of the confusion in today's health care delivery system and be willing and able to ask the tough questions. Is that surgical procedure appropriate and necessary? Can we do better on the pricing for the TPN (total parenteral nutrition) infusion or the MRI (nuclear magnetic resonance) testing? Can we honor this patient's wishes and enable him to live his last days at home? And because case management is a process, a case manager must have commitment to go the distance, offering ongoing, on-site, individualized services and becoming involved in finding medical treatment alternatives, monitoring results, solving problems, and revising the treatment plan as needed. A case manager is the catalyst who sifts through the array of possible paths, selects the most appropriate plan, and then coordinates the expertise and support of other professionals, family members, agencies, and suppliers. Case managers are concerned with every detail, from the minute (is there room for the oxygen tanks in the patient's bedroom at home?) to the major (can the family member, home health aide, or registered nurse in attendance handle a patient emergency?). It is not an easy professional specialty, but it is a tremendously rewarding one.

As a discipline, case management requires an understanding of how various medical, insurance, government, and corporate mechanisms affect the health care delivery system. Each of these areas influences the type of care available and how it will be administered. It is the case manager's responsibility to know the distinctions between acute hospitalization, subacute care, and specialized chronic care; the results and impact of federal legislation; and the coverage offered by different lines of insurance.

It is also the case manager's responsibility to make assessments and recommendations on an objective basis, having no vested interest in which rehabilitation facility or infusion service is selected. If it seems that case managers are held accountable not only for their academic credentials and work history but for their personal ethics as well, it is because they are. Often functioning without peer support or direction from an immediate supervisor, case managers must bring their own motivation, moral strength, independence, and confidence to each case. This is the personal profile needed to oversee a wide spectrum of activities with the sole focus of ensuring the best possible outcome for a patient in the most cost-effective manner.

THE CASE MANAGER'S ROLE

Case managers are not the claims police. Ensuring cost-effective treatment does not mean that case managers are overrated number crunchers who review treatment alternatives simply to find the cheapest scenario. Case managers are coordinators, facilitators, impartial advocates, and educators. Their roles are as varied as the sites where they are employed and the job titles that designated their position in the past.

The case manager in a home health agency may have been called "Supervisor, Home Health Services" a few years ago. In head injury facilities, the "Program Coordinator" or "Coordinator of Patient Services" may now carry the title "Case Manager."

Case managers in hospitals, rehabilitation facilities, home health agencies, and infusion care companies are in the provider sector of health services and may include nurses and social workers. They may oversee treatment while a patient is in a particular facility or receiving a certain type of service, such as infusion therapy, but not be involved with that same patient's care once the patient moves on to a different center or care program. Depending on the employer, a case manager may never make a home visit or manage care outside of a particular facility.

In the payer sector, case managers work for employer groups through third-party administrators, self-administered programs, health maintenance organizations, or major insurance carriers. In these settings, case managers identify and track all hospital admissions and other events where there is a likelihood of costly or high-exposure conditions. Although employer emphasis may seem to be on reducing overall costs, these case managers are also dedicated to assisting employees and their dependents in the utilization of services. While all forms of case management are valuable, provider- and payer-sector case management differ significantly from independent case management.

Independent case managers are needed. Because of their lack of affiliation with insurance companies or providers of services, independent professionals are outside both the medical care provider and the claims payer system. They have the opportunity to make totally objective assessments and to coordinate a program of care. With no vested interest in the companies selected to provide this care, independent case managers can remain impartial advocates for their clients.

The focal point of case management in all of its roles is to empower patients, giving them and their families access to a greater understanding of their disability or disease, a larger voice in the delivery of their care, and more personalized attention to their particular needs. Obtaining data on the particulars of each patient's case, case managers enable patients and their families to make informed decisions. Through their role as advocates, they help patients deal with the complexities of the health care system.

CASE MANAGEMENT IS NOT EQUIVALENT TO MANAGED CARE

Managed care and *case management* are not interchangeable concepts. Managed care is a system of cost-containment programs; case management is a process. A global term, managed care consists of the systems and mechanisms utilized to control, direct, and approve access to the wide range of services and costs within the health care delivery system. Case management can be one of those mechanisms, one component in the managed care strategy.

Based on the use of cost-containment programs that include guidelines and criteria for health care delivery, managed care incorporates health maintenance organizations (HMOs), preferred provider organizations (PPOs), direct contracting (in which an employer contracts directly with a hospital or other health care facility), bill audits, utilization review, preadmission authorization, concurrent review, retrospective review, second surgical opinions (SSOs), independent medical exams (IMEs), and case management. While managed care programs strive to involve all potential users of health care services, case management focuses on certain individuals—the 3–5 percent of the patient population responsible for 60–70 percent of the expenditures in any health plan.[1] Case management is a personalized process that aims to identify high-risk or high-cost patients, assess treatment options and opportunities to coordinate care, design treatment programs to improve quality and efficacy of care, control costs, and manage patient care to ensure the optimum outcome. Concentrating for the most part on catastrophic or chronic cases, case managers are called in to consult for diagnoses such as head injury, multiple trauma, cancer, AIDS, organ transplants, cardiovascular disease, stroke, burns, spinal cord injury, premature infants, and high-risk pregnancy.

In the third annual National Executive Opinion Poll conducted by *Business & Health*, company executives were asked to rank health care programs that have been effective in cutting costs. The results, published in July 1992, compare case management to utilization review, preadmission authorization, self-insurance, second surgical opinions, HMOs, and PPOs, among other health care plan components. Case management led the list, with 69 percent of respondents agreeing as to its efficacy.

MEDICAL CREDENTIALS AND EXPERTISE

Agreed-upon credentials and criteria for what makes a good case manager and the level of preparation required to handle the usual responsibilities have recently been established as part of the development of the Certified Case Manager (CCM) credential. Predictably, the criteria caused an outcry from some individuals who claim to offer case management but discovered they are worlds apart from those case management practitioners who are eligible for certification. For example, there are individuals currently working as case managers who have no more training than one year of school and a certificate. Case management as a practice setting demands critical thinking skills, clinical knowledge, and experience within the health care delivery system, and case management as a profession requires higher standards if it is to grow and develop as an industry.

Today's case managers come from diverse educational and clinical settings, many with broader backgrounds than a strict hospital environment. Generally, they are nurses, social workers, or rehabilitation counselors, and a number of them have had experience administering workers' compensation and disability cases involving catastrophic injury. No longer intent only on helping an individual recuperate and return to work, case managers now address everything from tertiary neonatal cases and premature babies to geriatric cases and stroke victims. There is a need for higher levels of clinical knowledge, which is causing subtle shifts among case management practitioners.

Social welfare caseworkers, involved with programs like Medicare, originated some elements of case management procedures. They developed and perfected the skills involved in connecting people to their community resources and obtaining financial aid from federal and state agencies. Social workers will undoubtedly continue to make up a substantial portion of case managers. Although considerable supplementary training and experience might be required before they could manage complex medical cases, such as ventilator-dependent babies or an individual requiring infusion services, social workers with medical backgrounds can handle stable cases and provide assistance to our fast-growing "gray" population. And combining social workers and RNs in medical case management teams has already proven very effective, enabling speedier identification of solutions to patient problems. As professionals with a different focus, rehabilitation counselors have also become valuable members of such teams, with their emphasis on recuperation and the return to work.

Because of the medical problem-solving and coordination responsibilities inherent in the case management role, the kind of experience and education that nurses possess becomes important. In addition to basic educational preparation—associate degree, diploma-school, or baccalaureate-level college—life experience counts for a great deal. But case management demands a greater depth and intensity of involvement than traditional nursing, as well as more advanced medical, psychological, and sociological training. Therefore, a case manager's educational process should be ongoing and, through continuing education studies or postgraduate work, should be directed toward achieving a master's degree in a clinical specialty, for example. Because continuing education is not mandated for updated RN certification in many states, a number of practicing case managers neglect their obligation to remain current in their field. Those selecting case management as a career owe it to their patients, their profession, and themselves to read, attend conferences, and sit in on seminars and lectures so as to broaden their knowledge base. The CCM designation requires case managers to take advantage of continuing education to maintain their credential status.

The kind of clinical experience of greatest value is that of a generalist. While there are case managers with a single practice area, such as those who specialize in high-risk neonates, head trauma, organ transplants, oncology, or hematology, most case managers should have experience with various age groups, treatment facilities, and medical conditions. The majority of case managers will receive referrals requiring knowledge of a wide spectrum of medical practice specialties, and they will need to acquire a diversified clinical background to meet the challenges. Ideal clinical preparation includes in-depth exposure to medical-surgical treatments, intensive care, critical care, home care, psychology, obstetrics, pediatrics, and neurological care. Case managers must be able to distinguish good care from bad care, understand potential complications, and evaluate lengths of stay. Working in one hospital unit for one year does not provide the range of cases and insight required of a good case manager. Even comprehensive hospital experience alone is insufficient preparation. In most hospitals, equipment and supplies are readily available. Leaving the safety and support systems of the hospital environment, we can appreciate how vulnerable our patients can become when necessary services are fragmented. Further, case management requires self-direction, critical thinking, and independent functioning and judgment, skills honed more readily in nontraditional health care settings. Experience in home health care, walk-in clinics, and occupational health nursing can provide a beneficial view of community health care options.

Because the work requires financial savvy, a business background is also helpful. Hospital nurses do not have to meet expenses, but independent case managers are aware of the importance of financial accountability. If they cannot demonstrate the positive impact of case management to corporate and political America, they undermine the whole industry. They need to know, for example, the cost of ventilator equipment so they can refuse payment on a padded invoice. Forget that they can help improve employee morale, can help a disabled person get back to work faster to continue a rewarding career, can locate an appropriate facility 10 miles from home rather than 550 miles away for a child with a head injury—if they cannot combine their healing skills with practical business skills, they will lose the opportunity to practice.

Case management work often places individuals in situations in which patients and their families are devastated by health-related problems. Beyond facilitating health care decisions on behalf of other human beings, case managers also face the type of intense social/dynamic family issues that never become "easy" to handle but can be approached with more empathy and grace by practitioners who have become acquainted with the emotions encountered in marriage, divorce, illness, and death. Nurses fresh out of school are likely to have difficulty appreciating the significance of such issues. Five or more years of clinical experience helps develop a maturity and depth that makes it easier to relate to patients and understand their emotional state.

Finally, case managers need personal stamina and strength. Most caseloads include tragic cases. Case managers cannot make a terminal illness fade away. They cannot fully empower a patient if the family is too broken to accept the necessary responsibility. Case managers therefore need personal resources and support from friends and family to meet the challenges each day will present.

A DEFINITION OF CASE MANAGEMENT

CIRSC, the credentialing agency selected by the National Case Management Task Force in February 1992 to develop the case management certification process, defines case management as follows:

Case management is a collaborative process which assesses, plans, implements, coordinates, monitors and evaluates the options and services to meet an individual's health needs, using communication and available resources to promote quality, cost effective outcomes.[2]

In the broadest sense, a case manager is the person who makes the health care system work, influencing both the quality of the outcome and the cost. In our country, health care delivery is fragmented and complex. Providers range from the walk-in clinics to exclusive provider organizations and centers of excellence, and care settings run the gamut from a patient's own bedroom, up through rehabilitation facilities, outpatient facilities, specialized long-term care sites, and nursing homes, to hospices, subacute care facilities, and hospitals. It is no surprise patients are confused.

Working as an advocate for the patient (always searching for and moving toward the most medically appropriate solution), an empowering agent for the family, and a facilitator of communication among the patient, family, care providers, and payers, the case manager is a sentinel for quality assurance and cost-effectiveness. Perhaps the case manager can effect an earlier discharge, negotiate a better fee from a medical equipment supplier, or encourage the family to assume responsibility for a portion of the day-to-day care the patient needs. She can be a catalyst for change by seeking solutions that promote improvement or stabilization rather than simply monitoring patient status. If the case manager performs all these functions well, quality assurance and cost savings fall into place as a matter of course, prolonging the life of benefit dollars for individuals and helping to free up health care monies for the 37 million uninsured and the 80 million underinsured in the United States today.

CASE MANAGEMENT ROLE AND FUNCTIONS

To be effective, case managers require broad-based knowledge. They need to be part general practitioner, part social worker, part psychologist, and part minister or rabbi. Even if the case management role never requires going beyond the boundaries of this specialty, a case manager needs to be aware of the psychosocial, environmental, family, economic, and religious dynamics that can impact patients. She also must have a diverse medical background; being a clinician is not enough.

In mid-1992, more than 20 specialists representing various areas of case management met at CIRSC's offices in Rolling Meadows, Illinois, to adopt a comprehensive role and function study "based on the literature and research currently available in the case management field." This meeting provided the basis for developing the educational and experience criteria for the CCM.[3] The skills the specialists identified as necessary for the case management practitioner included the ability to

apply problem-solving techniques to the case management process; assess variables that impact on health and functioning; interpret clinical information and assess implications for treatment; develop an individualized case management plan that addresses singular physical, vocational, psychosocial, financial and educational needs; negotiate competitive rates to maximize available funding for individual's care; understand insurance policy language; present various health care options; document case management activities; maintain confidentiality regarding the release of information according to legal and ethical requirements and guidelines; and maintain familiarity with disease processes, available resources and treatment modalities, assessing their quality and appropriateness for specific disabilities, illnesses and injuries.[4]

Areas of general knowledge and the understanding of health care treatments and systems required by case management practitioners were encompassed in the same report. Suggested general knowledge included theories of family functioning; the characteristics of various stages of physical and psychosocial development; the traits of functional and dysfunctional coping and their implications for health; and resources, eligibility for services, and referral procedures. In the area of health care, the preliminary CCM credentialing report called for comprehension of "home health resources; strategies to access medical records; medical terminology; pharmaceuticals and pharmacological management; levels of care in acute and rehabilitative treatment; adaptive equipment and assistive devices for various disabilities and illnesses; issues involving experimental treatments and protocols; and competitive cost for medical and health care services, aftercare and independent living resources,"[5] in addition to other health care factors.

Because of the case manager's role as a communicator and liaison, she must also be familiar with certain elements within the insurance, legal, and vocational disciplines. For example, to interact successfully with insurance and funding sources, a case manager must be facile with insurance terminology, the preparation of cost-benefit analyses for payers, the reporting requirements of various health care reimbursement and government agencies, disability compensation systems, extended medical or indemnity payments, and the coordination of benefits. To practice ethically and safely, a case manager should also be familiar with legal terminology, liability issues, use of depositions, confidentiality laws, and the accepted procedures and requirements for releasing or sharing information. And finally, vocational and legislative protocols will govern care options and benefit plan dollar availability for some individuals. These areas of knowledge will encompass resources for re-entry into the labor force, work evaluation processes, job accommodation principles, affirmative action, the philosophy of workers' compensation, the Americans with Disabilities Act (ADA), Medicaid and Medicare provisions, and the rights of individuals under federal and state law (both the state a case manager practices in and the state a patient is undergoing treatment in).[6]

All this said, it must also be noted that case management is not a hands-on role. Case managers are not actively practicing nurses, clinicians, or caregivers. They do not diagnose an ailment, prescribe a medication, or set the course of treatment. Case managers do offer their observations on a patient's status and use their expertise to plan and suggest alternative care options. Using on-site visits as fact-gathering missions, a case manager can make sure a noncompliant patient is following the treatment plan outlined by the physician or note the possible complications from the medication recommended by the patient's ear-nose-and-throat specialist but never mentioned to his or her cardiologist. Case managers are consultants, advisors, and facilitators.

Although case managers do not offer hands-on care, neither can they be truly effective if they act in a totally hands-off manner. Telephone work, which is a part of case management, is necessary for keeping open the lines of communication without driving up costs. It is particularly effective for preventative and case-screening measures as well as for tracking low-intensity patients or patients whose conditions have improved to the point where in-person case management is no longer needed. However, strict telephonic case management, in which all the communication between the case manager, patient, family, physician, and payer occurs over the phone, can lead to major oversights in care, especially in cases where the patient is noncompliant, undereducated, or poor. The vulnerability of the patient, any patient, combined with the legal and monetary exposure of the case manager, provider, and payer, necessitate on-site interaction.

Case managers fulfill a role not provided for elsewhere in the health care system. They become the eyes and ears for others, a resource for physicians, insurance groups, employers, and particularly families. Because people tend to picture described situations in terms of their own experience, they tend to make incorrect assumptions. A telephonic case manager might envision a patient's "home" as complete with a stocked refrigerator, adequate room for the respirator, and clean sheets on the bed. During an on-site home visit, a case manager will be able to note the empty refrigerator, the two toddlers careening around the couch and bumping into the infant's oxygen supply, the unopened medication bottles, and the family in need of respite. Beyond the medical aspects lies another whole dynamic of an illness, the logistics of coping, which might require putting a caretaker's job on hold or a home up for sale. Here is where a case manager can help fill a void in the system, by assisting the well persons in the family to deal with practical matters. The coma patient does not need hand holding, but the caretaker in the family might—or might need guidance from a person who can fully explain treatment options, a safe person to share emotions with, or someone to fill out the forms and help file the claims. When the claims department returns a form marked "incomplete," there is no note describing what information was omitted. Unfiled claims cannot be reimbursed, and the case manager can be the person to help pull the details together, to get the burned-out caretaker some part-time assistance, or to call the bank and request a payment plan for the home mortgage.

Again, once a basic assessment of the patient's condition and family and home setting has been completed and the case manager has established her role with the patient, treating physician, and nurses and set up the services to match the resources and needs of the patient and family, then the telephone can become a tremendous resource. The moment a case manager hears something during a telephone conversation that sets off an internal "red alert," an on-site visit should be made.

A CASE MANAGER'S EDUCATION, CLINICAL PREPARATION, AND LIFE EXPERIENCE

The most useful guide to the kind of education, clinical preparation, and life experience that will most benefit a case manager is the list of "Criteria for Eligibility" contained in the *CCM Certification Guide: Certified Case Manager*, available from CIRSC, 1835 Rohlwing Road, Suite D, Rolling Meadows, Illinois 60008; 708 818-0292.* The list includes the education and employment criteria that applicants for the CCM credential must satisfy prior to sitting for the CCM examination (see Appendix 1-A).

There are a total of six categories for certification within the CCM credential, three for registered nurses holding current licensure within their state and three for applicants who "hold a current professional license

---

*The *CCM Certification Guide* is periodically updated. For the most recent version, please call CIRSC at 708-818-0292.

(other than nursing) or national certification in a health and human services profession." The RN categories are distinguished by length of experience: Category A1 requires "a minimum of 24 months of acceptable full-time case management employment experience" whereas Category A3 requires "a minimum of 54 months of acceptable full-time employment experience of which 6 months must be case management experience, and 48 months must be clinical experience."

Applicants who have their licensure in professions other than nursing may be certified under a similar range of categories. Category B1 of the CCM credential calls for "current professional licensure or national certification in a health and human services profession" and "a minimum of 24 months of acceptable full-time case management employment experience." Clinical experience is a prerequisite for Category B2 and Category B3. The latter requires "a minimum of 54 months of acceptable full-time employment experience of which 6 months must be case management experience and 48 months must be clinical experience" in addition to "current professional licensure of national certification in a health and human services profession."

According to the *CCM Certification Guide*, for employment experience to be considered acceptable, the job description must include patient advocacy, support, and empowerment (see Appendix 1-B). Applicants for the CCM credential must submit verification of employment that reflects direct contact with the individual recipient of case management services. Acceptable clinical experience is defined as "direct experience in a professional clinical setting; that is, any combination of direct patient care in a specialty area and work setting." The specialty areas and work settings noted are home health care, general clinical, hospital facility, private practice (consultant), government-funded institution, psychiatric mental hospital, industrial nurse, and community or nationally sponsored entities.

NOTES

1. Catherine M. Mullahy, "'Insurance' for Self-funded Employers," *The Self-Insurer* 9, no. 5 (1992): 18.
2. *CCM Certification Guide* (Rolling Meadows, Ill.: CIRSC/Certified Case Manager, 1993), flyleaf.
3. Dorothy Sager, "From Need to Reality," *The Case Manager*, Summer 1992, 81–86.
4. Case Management Expert Panel, "Case Management Role and Function," prepared for Certification of Insurance Rehabilitation Specialists Commission, July 27, 1992.
5. Case Management Expert Panel, "Case Management Role and Function: Knowledge of Health Care," prepared for Certification of Insurance Rehabilitation Specialists Commission, July 27, 1992.
6. Case Management Expert Panel, "Case Management Role and Function: Insurance/Funding Sources, Legal, Vocational," prepared for Certification of Insurance Rehabilitation Specialists Commission, July 27, 1992.

APPENDIX 1-A

Eligibility Criteria for Certification as a Case Manager

SECTION 3: CRITERIA FOR ELIGIBILITY

To be eligible for voluntary certification as a case manager, an applicant must meet **ALL** of the licensure or certification requirements and employment criteria described under **ONE** of the categories shown in this guide.

The *Category A* licensure or certification requirement applies only to persons who are currently licensed as Registered Nurses. The candidate's licensure status must be one of "good standing" in the state of residence.

Category B applies to those individuals who currently possess a professional license or national certification in a health and human services profession. To qualify under Category B, your license or certification must be based on a minimum education requirement of a Bachelor's degree in a field that promotes the physical, psychosocial, and vocational well-being of the persons being served, and the license or certificate that is awarded upon completion of the program must be obtained by passing an examination in your area of specialization.

All applicable licensure or certification and employment requirements must be fully satisfied by the application deadline (January 15 for the May examination or July 15 for the November examination). The Commission considers licensure to be a process by which a government agency grants permission to an individual to engage in a given occupation provided that person possesses the minimum degree of competency required to reasonably protect public health, safety, and welfare. The

14

Commission considers certification to be a process by which a government or a non-government agency grants recognition to an individual who has met certain predetermined qualifications set by a credentialing body.

Please read the eligibility categories carefully. **REMEMBER, THE $125 APPLICATION FEE IS NONREFUNDABLE.** A handling fee of $20 will be assessed for any check returned for non-sufficient funds.

All requested documentation must be submitted before an application can be reviewed for eligibility.

Category A1

Licensure/Certification:
Registered Nurse (RN)—Current licensure in your state (good standing).

Employment Experience:
A minimum of 24 months of acceptable full-time case management experience (see Section 4A).

Category A2

Licensure/Certification:
Registered Nurse (RN)—Current licensure in your state (good standing).

Employment Experience:
A minimum of 36 months of acceptable full-time employment experience of which 12 months must be case management experience, and 24 months must be clinical experience (see Sections 4A and 4B).

Category A3

Licensure/Certification:
Registered Nurse (RN)—Current licensure in your state (good standing).

Employment Experience:
A minimum of 54 months of acceptable full-time employment of which 6 months must be case management experience, and 48 months must be clinical experience (see Sections 4A and 4B).

Categories B1, B2, B3

These categories are designed for applicants who hold a current professional license (other than nursing) or a national certification in a health and human services profession. To qualify under Categories B1, B2, or B3, your license or certification must be based on a minimum education requirement of a Bachelor's degree in a field that promotes the physical, psychosocial, and vocational well-being of the persons being served, and the license or certificate that is awarded upon completion of the program must be obtained by passing an examination in your area of specialization.

Category B1

Licensure/Certification:
Current professional licensure or national certification in a health and human services profession.

Employment Experience:
A minimum of 24 months of acceptable full-time case management employment experience (see Section 4A).

Category B2

Licensure/Certification:
Current professional licensure or national certification in a health and human services profession.

Employment Experience:
A minimum of 36 months of acceptable full-time employment experience of which 12 months must be case management experience and 24 months must be clinical experience (see Sections 4A and 4B).

Category B3

Licensure/Certification:
Current professional licensure or national certification in a health and human services profession.

Employment Experience:
A minimum of 54 months of acceptable full-time employment of which 6 months must be case management experience and 48 months must be clinical experience (see Sections 4A and 4B).

Source: Reprinted from *CCM Certification Guide,* pp. 2–3 with permission of Certification of Insurance Rehabilitation Specialist Commission, © 1993.

Acceptable Employment Experience for Certification as a Case Manager

SECTION 4A: ACCEPTABLE EMPLOYMENT EXPERIENCE
CASE MANAGEMENT

As a service, Case Management is intended to help clients coordinate and gain access to needed medical, psychiatric, social, educational, psychosocial, and other services essential for meeting basic human needs. The major components of case management include: 1) case management concepts and services; 2) medical and psychological factors; 3) return-to-work systems and services; 4) cost analysis methods and containment strategies; 5) referral coordination and community resources; and 6) principles of wellness and empowerment.

As a valid fulfillment of the employment criteria, all positions shown on the application must be full-time paid work or its equivalent in part-time work. Part-time employment will be calculated on a pro-rated basis of 37 hours per week. Internship, preceptorship, practicum, and volunteer activities are **NOT** considered acceptable employment experience.

For employment to qualify as acceptable, each place of employment must be verified on the form that will be sent to you with the application acknowledgment (following the Commission's receipt of your application and application processing fee). The verification form for case management experience must be completed and signed by your supervisor/ employer. It must also be accompanied by an official job description signed by the supervisor/employer who signed the employment verification form. **INCLUDE YOUR NAME/CCM ID NUMBER ON ALL VERI-FICATION DOCUMENTS.** For a place of employment to be considered acceptable, the official job description must reflect your provision of advocacy, support, and empowerment services to the client as well as direct client contact within the six areas described below.

All employment experience submitted on the application must reflect direct contact with the individual receiving case management services. Refer to Section 12 for definitions of "assessment" and "clinical experience."

1. Case Management Concepts and Services

This area encompasses a broad range of topics from the role of the case manager through specific case management techniques and areas of service. Acceptable work activities would involve the following:

- Documents services and outcomes.
- Evaluates effectiveness of the case management process.
- Identifies available treatment modalities and establishes treatment goals.
- Understands case management philosophy and principles.
- Communicates case management objectives.
- Assesses clinical information to develop treatment plans.
- Establishes working relationships with referral sources.
- Makes referrals for assessments and acts as an advocate for the individual's health care needs.

2. Medical and Psychological Factors

This area includes the medical and psychological characteristics of various disabling conditions as well as the identification of appropriate treatment protocols and resources. Acceptable work activities would include the following:

- Understands standard treatment protocols for psychiatric illnesses.
- Understands treatment resources for chemical dependency.
- Understands levels of care required in the acute phase.
- Understands disease process of medical illnesses.
- Understands characteristics of illnesses.
- Determines respite needs of individuals.
- Understands principles of health care maintenance.

3. Return-To-Work Systems and Services

This area addresses a wide range of topics such as job accommodation principles and their applications, federal legislation affecting persons with disabilities, and the philosophy of disability coverage. Acceptable work activities would include the following:

- Understands job accommodation principles and their application.
- Plans for the client's vocational service needs.
- Understands techniques for re-entry into the labor force.
- Understands philosophy of workers' compensation systems.
- Identifies resources that can improve the client's earnings capacity.

4. Cost Analysis Methods and Containment Strategies

This area encompasses a number of financial strategies including assessments of benefit value to cost, indemnity payments, and coordination of benefits. Acceptable work activities would include the following:

- Understands cost analysis procedures and determines cost-effectiveness.
- Prepares accurate, timely cost/benefit analyses.
- Uses service negotiation techniques and assesses extra-contractual coverage.
- Uses cost containment strategies that maximize an individual's access to extended medical payments.

5. Referral Coordination and Community Resources

This area focuses on topics such as service eligibility and referral procedures in both the public and private sectors. Acceptable work activities would include the following:

- Understands eligibility requirements for services in the public and private sectors.
- Understands referral procedures in the public sector.
- Understands community-based funding resources and Medicaid provisions.

6. Principles of Wellness and Empowerment

This area addresses topics that range from principles of self-determination and theories of personality through evaluations of an individual's use of and response to medication. Acceptable work activities would include the following:

- Understands theories of personality and family functioning.
- Understands principles of group dynamics and relationship building.
- Understands principles of self-determination and empowerment.

SECTION 4B: ACCEPTABLE EMPLOYMENT EXPERIENCE— CLINICAL

Clinical experience is defined as direct experience in a professional clinical setting; that is, any combination of direct patient care in a specialty area and a work setting as follows: 1) home health care; 2) general clinical; 3) hospital facility; 4) private practice (consultant); 5) government-funded institution; 6) psychiatric mental hospital; 7) industrial nurse; 8) community or nationally sponsored entities.

For clinical experience to qualify as acceptable, each place of employment must be verified on the form that will be sent to you with the application acknowledgment (following the Commission's receipt of your application and application processing fee). The verification form for clinical experience must be completed and signed by your supervisor/ employer. It must also be accompanied by an official job description signed by the supervisor/employer who signed the employment verification form. INCLUDE YOUR NAME/CCM ID NUMBER ON ALL VERIFICATION DOCUMENTS.

Source: Reprinted from _CCM Certification Guide,_ p. 5, with permission of Certification of Insurance Rehabilitation Specialists Commission, © 1993.

2

The Case Manager's Universe

IMPORTANT CONTACTS AMONG HEALTH CARE PROVIDERS

The list of health care providers a case manager needs to know is as varied as the places these individuals work. Among a case manager's major contacts are physicians, surgeons, medical specialists, physical therapists, psychiatrists, pharmacists, discharge planners, rehabilitation nurses, rehabilitation and job counselors, nurse case managers, social workers, home health aides, family counselors, and medical equipment and service providers. The range of facility resources includes hospitals, hospices, subacute care facilities, skilled nursing facilities, outpatient rehabilitation centers, nursing homes, and facilities offering illness-specific, chronic, or catastrophic care.

Case managers must be conversant with providers of specialized care, including, for example, neonatal teams that treat high-risk newborns at hospitals offering tertiary-level care. Centers for Excellence, which are designated areas within major university centers or other facilities that insurers have approved as providers of treatment, also offer specialized care. Also among a case manager's vital resources are specialized hospitals. There are, for example, fully accredited pediatric care facilities such as Stanford Children's Hospital in California, Children's Memorial Hospital in Chicago, and Schneider Children's Hospital in New York. The Mayo Clinic is noted for its team approach to diagnostic work-ups, while Memorial Sloan-Kettering Cancer Center in New York City is renowned for its cancer research and treatment. Located in Denver, National Jewish Hospital/National Asthma Center is a diagnostic, research, and education facility that specializes in the treatment of asthma and pulmonary conditions, offering both adult and pediatric programs. Other specialized centers include Joslin Diabetes Clinic in Boston, Patricia Neal Stroke Center in Knoxville, Rusk Institute for Rehabilitation Medicine (New York University Medical Center), Bascom Palmer Eye Institute in Miami, and the M. D. Anderson Hospital and Tumor Institute in Houston.

Beyond acute care centers, case managers need to maintain an updated database listing facilities with accredited expertise and specialized programs for rehabilitation following head or spinal cord injury, burns, amputation, loss of sight or hearing, and other disabilities and diseases.

In recent years, postacute or subacute care facilities have gained recognition as lower-cost alternatives for those medically complex cases that do not require the depth of service offered by a hospital or specialized care center but demand more than home-based recuperation. Individuals who might benefit from treatment at a subacute facility include patients needing short-term care following surgery, patients with a chronic illness who require intravenous pain control and/or nutrition, patients needing extended or respite care due to permanent debilitating injuries, and patients in a transitional stage of rehabilitation therapy after a fracture, stroke, or amputation. Subacute care centers are designed for medically stable patients and generally offer services such as wound management, infusion therapies, respiratory care, nutritional management, dialysis, TPN, and physical, occupational, and speech therapy.

HMOs AND PPOs

HMOs and PPOs are often perceived as standing facilities, buildings in which health care services are provided. However, they were originally developed as alternative health care delivery systems, cost management strategies in which services are packaged for a group of insureds. The hope was that by shifting from a fee-for-service system to the use of payment schedules for packaged services, providers would have greater incentive to consider the appropriateness and costs of care when suggesting treatment.

In the HMO arrangement, the physicians or practitioners within the HMO group agree to provide set benefits as needed by voluntarily enrolled members for a fixed dollar amount per member. Generally taking one of a few forms—staff model, group model, network model, or independent practice arrangement (IPA) model, an HMO usually offers members the choice of a primary care physician or other specialist from among those participating in the HMO. This primary physician will then coordinate all the individual's medical care as well as any needed referrals to specialists and hospitals. The group HMO physician is usually employed by the HMO or receives most of his or her patients from the HMO. Staff-model HMO physicians limit their practice to the HMO and are salaried employees. In the IPA model, the HMO arranges contracts with physicians who also maintain their fee-for-service practice and who are paid a blend of fee for service and fixed fee.[1] In a network model, two or more independent physician groups contract with an HMO to supply medical services. The HMO pays an established fee per employee per month, and the physicians or physician groups determine how those fees are split.

Most HMO services are generally covered in full or subject to copayment. Limitations, restrictions, or nonreimbursement provisions come into play when services are sought outside of the HMO's geographical region of coverage or when medical treatment is obtained from nonparticipating providers. Waivers are usually granted if care given by a nonparticipant was received following an accident or the sudden acute onset of a life-threatening disease. The HMO will then retrospectively review the nonparticipant services and may provide coverage if the appropriateness of the care can be verified.[2]

A PPO basically consists of a "limited provider panel," health care providers selected for their cost-effective style of practice. These providers also agree to lower their fees for services provided to PPO members. PPOs can be sponsored by medical providers, investors, or insurers. Some large national employers have created PPOs (and HMOs and HMO-PPO mixes) as nationwide networks of health care providers for their employees.[3] In a PPO, members can choose to receive care from a provider outside of the PPO network, accepting reimbursement at levels similar to those received from traditional insurance coverage. (Network services may be provided with no deductible or for a lower copayment than traditional insurance-covered services. Nonnetwork services may be subject to a deductible and higher coinsurance.) Nonnetwork emergency needs may be reimbursed at rates comparable to those for network services.[4]

MANAGED COMPETITION

Managed competition, a recent buzzword in the health care delivery industry, refers to the very real competition HMOs, PPOs, and other managed care entities face in getting and maintaining business. Managed competition introduces new criteria for health care decision making and price evaluation and puts control back in the hands of the purchaser. Within the last few years, the availability of outcomes data has made it possible to review and select a health provider facility based on quality of service and patient outcomes as well as pricing. It is no longer good enough to be price competitive; service providers have to demonstrate effective pricing and good outcomes without sacrificing the satisfaction of patients and their families.

When the term *managed competition* was first coined in the late 1970s by Alain Enthoven, he mentioned "sponsors," agencies that acted as brokers by examining all the health plan possibilities in the field and negotiating with those plans to help a client get the best mix of care and price based on the client's needs. More recently, the term *health insurance purchasing cooperative (HIPC)* has gained acceptance as a way of referring to brokering organizations that serve small employers and individuals. (In some managed care models, there is only one HIPC per geographical region, and all individuals purchase health insurance through that HIPC.)[5] HIPCs and sponsors relate to that version of managed competition that is still in the theory stage. Yet managed competition is already here in some form.

Managed competition is growing today because of the existence of managed care organizations. The PPOs that are successful are the ones that are able to deliver quality and good outcomes while holding down costs. The biggest HMOs are the ones that are able to penetrate the market. Some argue that HMOs benefit from adverse risk selection, that healthier people usually opt for HMOs based on a belief they will not need catastrophic coverage. They are attracted by the lower premiums or have young children whom they can take to the doctor for a small fee per visit—a prime concern during the winter chickenpox-sniffles-and-strep school season. The sicker people stay in the indemnity plans, which offer the most freedom of choice regarding physician selection but have fewer people watching costs. Even so, I believe we are already in the midst of the move to managed competition. Employer coalitions and business alliances are buying services and getting discounting arrangements from providers of prescriptions and durable medical equipment or from local rehab facilities. They say, "We'll send all of our people to you. What can you do for us?" Employers and insurance carriers and brokers and TPAs *are* managing care and cost; they are being aggressive negotiators because of the law of supply and demand.

These changes signal the total management of the health delivery system, where the purchaser is now more in control. Even when risk, which influences the payments an employer group makes, is a consideration, the employer group will still have an edge. For instance, if a company has a high incidence of a particular disease, that is factored in to how the company is rated and the premiums it will have to pay. But the company now will have an ability to choose from a variety of health insurance programs and health providers and facilities, whether its health insurance network includes an HMO, a PPO, or whatever.

ALTERNATIVES

Case managers also need to know about alternative treatment facilities and programs, such as residential and experiential programs for teenagers. Aspen Achievement Academy in Southern Utah combines an outdoor therapy program with traditional mental health therapeutic interventions for 13- to 18-year-olds that suffer from psychiatric, emotional, and substance abuse disorders. Working with emotionally disturbed youths aged 10 to 17, the Eckerd Alternative Treatment Program blends reality therapy, behavior modification, individualized mental health services, group therapy, and problem-solving sessions in a wilderness camp setting.

Other resources case managers need to be aware of include nursing services, home health agencies, infusion and respiratory care companies, counseling centers, surgical supply firms, and a host of local, state, and federal agencies and associations targeting problems such as aging, learning disabilities, and physical disabilities. There are national organizations for most major diseases, and it is the case manager's responsibility to know about them. As an example, the National Head Injury Foundation will send on request a state-by-state listing of facilities treating head injuries at various levels, from the catastrophic stage through transitional stage to rehabilitative care. National organizations are invaluable for their assistance in another area: education. The American Lung Association and the American Heart Association are two prime providers of free educational materials. The YMCA runs a healthy back program and is willing and able to provide informational pamphlets.

Where can a case manager begin to locate these legions of specialists, services, and support personnel? The *Case Management Resource Guide*, updated annually, includes information on mail-order pharmaceutical companies, pediatric home care, hand rehabilitation centers, hotlines for physical and mental disorders, and auto remodelers who can fit a car for a wheelchair ramp. A national guide, it is divided into four regional volumes and is available for purchase from the Center for Consumer Healthcare Information, 400 Birch, Suite 112, Newport Beach, California 92660; 714 752-2335.

Other resource volumes include the *HCIA Guide to Hospital Performance 1992* (HCIA, Baltimore, MD, 800 568-3282), *The Best in Medicine: Where To Find the Best Health Care Available* (by Herbert J. Dietrich and Virginia H. Biddle, Harmony Books, a division of Crown Publishers, 1990), and *Best*

Hospitals in America (by Linda Sunshine and John W. Wright, Henry Holt & Co., 1987; paperback published by Avon, 1989). Another facility resource is *Health Care U.S.A.: Where To Find the Best Answers for Your Family's Health* (by Jean Carper; Prentice Hall Press, 1987). Also check for regional volumes. *The Source Book: Social and Health Services* (Oryx Press) is a compilation of health care resources in the metropolitan New York area.

As a case manager weighs the best solution for an individual, she must remember to examine all alternatives the patient is entitled to as well as possible overlapping resources. For example, if the case manager can refer a patient to one of the Lighthouse sites supervised by the Association for the Blind in the state, dollars may be conserved for insurer-provided care.

For additional information on medical facility and service directories, please refer to Appendix A at the end of the book.

STANDARDS OF CARE

How does one distinguish the professionals from the we-do-that-toos? One method of evaluating an organization is to check whether there is a governing body or written standards of care. For instance, rehabilitation facilities are accredited by the Commission on Accreditation of Rehabilitation Facilities (CARF). When there are no recognized standards of care or when an individual is being evaluated, the best strategy is to combine available performance criteria information with a personal critique. Some case managers create their own facility or individual review form to separate core quality from showcase dressing. Questions might include these: How does the specialist or medical facility director answer questions—directly or by responding with his or her own questions? Is the facility truly open to sharing information on its programs or reciting the five-minute marketing speech? Is a request to attend a team conference met by resistance or a welcome? An individual or a group trying to control access to or hide background information should set off an alarm. The case manager should begin to suspect that getting complete reports on a patient's progress will be an onerous task.

Individual specialists should be board certified in their field, have teaching experience, and have a strong hospital or facility affiliation. Because there are bogus boards and subpar credentials, check the certifying agency. In New York, the Medical Society of the State of New York has published a medical directory that lists credentialed practitioners in a number of specialties. National medical societies can offer guidance on how to verify credentials. Whether reviewing a person or an agency, ask for names and phone numbers of references. If a home health agency provides dated information—case managers it last worked with when an actor was in the White House—question its capabilities. If a physician is unwilling to give references, question his or her reliability (the same goes for an agency).

Another way case managers can educate themselves on the appropriate levels of expertise and service to expect from providers and suppliers is to become a member of local and national associations. Meetings planned by professionals working within separate disciplines and condition- or illness-specific conferences are excellent sources of information and resources. At conferences with exhibitors, case managers should talk with adaptive equipment vendors, marketers of oxygen-supply devices, prosthetics designers—and ask every question that comes to mind. Then, when reviewing bids from suppliers, they will have enough background to spot the inclusion of unnecessary equipment or overzealous billing.

NOTES

1. William S. Custer, "Strategies for Health Care Cost Management," in *Driving Down Health Care Costs: Strategies and Solutions 1992* (New York: Panel Publishers, 1992), 3–4.
2. Alice C. Reynolds-Meadows, "Managing Case Management," presented at the Individual Case Management Association Medical Case Management Conference III, Dallas, September 1991.
3. Custer, "Strategies for Health Care Cost Management," 5–6.
4. Reynolds-Meadows, "Managing Case Management."
5. Custer, "Health Care Reform: Managed Competition and Beyond," EBRI Issue Brief no. 135, March 1993: 4–7.

CHAPTER

3

Insurance Providers and Administrators

When considering the world of insurance, including insurance companies, reinsurance companies, indemnity providers, self-insured firms, and self-insured/self-administered corporations, case managers are tempted to ask, "Who *are* those guys? What are the differences in their services and why is it important for me to distinguish between them?" Good question.

The role of the case manager becomes more complex the larger the company that is insuring and the larger the group that is being insured. Size and type of both the insurer and the insurance administrative arm will impact the autonomy of the case management role, influence (if not dictate) the format and frequency of communications, and affect the case manager's ability to obtain approval for allowances or exceptions in coverage should the need arise. In a CIGNA or Travelers fully insured plan, a company customarily pays premiums based on expected case incidences and outcomes. Conversely, case managers often work with patients whose needs are not considered in the typical premium structure. Further, when employer groups are blended into larger groups (PPOs, multiple employer trusts, or business alliances, for example) to increase their purchasing power, case managers find themselves layers away from the decision makers—the CEOs and employers, who sometimes can help speed the approval process when plan dollars need to be utilized in a nontraditional fashion. A case manager might have more flexibility and success working with local or regional insurers and employers because of

28

the closer contact with those capable and willing to make decisions regarding reimbursement.

Insurance companies vary in how they work with case managers. Some firms have in-house or affiliated case management capabilities (e.g., CIGNA has Intracorp, Travelers has Conservco). Other insurers contract with several case management entities across the country, using one for all cases in the Northeast, for example, and another for cases on the West Coast. The larger the insurer, the less likely it will employ an independent case management provider, unless the insurer is sophisticated and already has an in-house regional coordinator for case management services.

Are the insurer's operations contained within one state or does it have national capabilities? Because the activities of case managers are largely mandated by both federal and state regulations, it is the case manager's responsibility to know the effect of state regulations on different health insurance benefits. A state might require that x number of mammographies per year be covered for women in a certain age group as part of the regulations companies must follow if they want to write insurance in that state. (Under ERISA [Employee Retirement Income Security Act of 1974] guidelines, companies that self-insure are not compelled to hold to those same minimum benefits regulations and provide equivalent benefits. For example, employer groups can choose to limit their fiscal responsibility for HIV-related treatments over a claimant's lifetime.)

In the majority of cases, case managers will be employed by the payers, the insurers, and their work will be governed by the group, department, or agency carrying the fiduciary responsibility for the benefit plan. This entity defines what will be covered and when coverage will be cut or phased out so as to ensure that no one person or group of persons makes excessive claims that consume all the benefits dollars in the plan. As the plan or insured group becomes larger, the efforts to provide appropriate, timely, cost-effective care can become convoluted. With numerous layers of fiduciaries, insurers, administrators, and claims adjustors to contact for approval, the patient's experience is often over before a decision is reached.

BASIC INSURANCE AND ADMINISTRATIVE COMPANY PLAYERS

In traditional insurer-client relationships, a company or individual pays an annual premium to an insurance firm. The cost of any particular benefits plan is determined by the breadth and length of coverage that will be provided; the age, sex, and health of the individual at the time the plan is drawn up; and the statistical likelihood the individual will suffer from a disease or disability. Generally, group plans, in which insurers cover a body of employees or associates in the same industry along with their dependents, are available at a lower premium than plans for single individuals. The entire administration of the benefits plan is managed and handled by the insurance company. For example, when an individual makes a claim against his or her insurance plan, the claims department within the insurance firm will process the paperwork and will arrange for full or partial payment or will deny payment. Similarly, it is the insurance firm's responsibility to invest and manage the premium dollars it takes in to ensure its ability to pay claims.

In response to rising insurance costs, many businesses have pursued alternative financing methods, such as self-insurance. The switch to self-funding does result in a significant initial reduction in health care benefits costs for individual companies. *Business & Health*, in its 1992 annual survey of business executives nationwide, reported that 65 percent of respondents found self-insurance helped streamline company operations and offered better control over where their health care dollars were used. In self-funding, companies assume dollar-for-dollar responsibility for employee health care and avoid the spillover of financial responsibility previously included in their premiums to cover other clients an insurer might be carrying. However, self-insured firms run a risk. By narrowing the universe of contributors to their health benefit fund (by eliminating the old insurer's other clients), companies also limit their payout capabilities. Financial liability is spread among a smaller group, often without the application of support systems, such as preadmission authorization, utilization review, claims review, or case management, to help manage the benefit program. A few catastrophic claims, such as for a premature infant, an organ transplant, childhood leukemia, a head trauma, or a burn or cancer patient, can sap a plan's resources and eliminate any bottom-line savings.[1]

With the appearance of self-funded plans, two other types of service companies became more prominent, third-party administrators (TPAs) and firms offering administrative services only (ASO) contracts. TPAs and those insurers or companies providing ASO contracts take on the administrative responsibility of handling claims for self-funded groups. They will process claims, answer claimant questions, and act as the liaison between the offices and officers of the payer and the health care provider groups. There are a number of TPAs and ASO companies that, at the request of their self-insured employers, have begun to render claims management services (e.g., educating client company employees via wellness programs, assisting with medically fragile cases, tracking high-cost cases, and providing comprehensive cost-control programs). They provide these services by subcontracting with a case management or utilization review firm or by setting up an in-house case management or utilization review group. Some self-funded companies elect to self-administer their plans as well, processing all claims through their own claims group.

To handle an unexpected rise in health care costs or a number of catastrophic or chronic claims, self-insured employers often invest in excess or surplus lines of insurance such as reinsurance or stop-loss coverage. Premiums are paid to a reinsurance firm, establishing a plan that commits the reinsurance firm to step in and cover health benefits payouts in the event that claims should surpass a set dollar limit. In its annual nationwide health care benefits survey of employers, A. Foster Higgins & Co. (a benefits consulting firm based in New York City) reported that 64 percent of respondents with 1,000 or more employees self-funded their plans and bought some type of stop-loss insurance in 1993.[2] "Specific" stop-loss protection becomes activated when an individual's claims reach the deductible level selected by the self-funding group; such protection usually covers up to one million dollars per lifetime per employee. "Aggregate" coverage, which kicks in when a self-insurer's total group health claims outstrip 125 percent of its annual estimated claims costs, is another form of stop-loss protection that is available.

Too often, employer groups assume that their insurers "know the business" and settle into a false sense of security. Granted, today's insurers are astute in the business of setting premiums and designing benefit plans, but they may not be well versed in the business of properly managing available health care benefit dollars and the broad array of health care claims. Regardless of the size of the company and its method of insuring and administering health benefits, it is the case manager's responsibility to know the allowances and restrictions of the benefit plan. A case manager subcontracting with a TPA might find that of the TPA's eight clients, three are fully insured and the others are self-insured, each with a unique benefits plan design and claims administration package. Although working in-house with a major insurer and responsible for helping to manage the insurer's own employee benefits, a case manager might have to coordinate her work with the TPA overseeing payment of all claims. A large regional firm with thousands of employees and dependents might be self-funded but contract with an insurance firm for the administration of its plan.

In addition to the setup of the plan, a case manager needs to know the relationship of the referring party to the claimant. Was the request for case management the result of a red flag sent up by the stop-loss insurer, was it made by the utilization review staff within the insurance firm, or was it the suggestion of a human resources manager within the employer company? The referral source will affect how the case can be managed and the amount of autonomy the case manager will have. Being in a position to ask direct approval to change a treatment plan from a corporate CEO is a far cry from taking a call from the claims department at a TPA—already once or twice removed from the benefit plan decision maker—on a case where the claimant is covered by an insurer who does not offer reimbursement for case management services. Likewise, if a case manager needs allowance to spend a slightly higher portion of benefit dollars now to prevent spending a substantial amount of money for repeat hospitalizations for complications later on, the CEO of a self-insured firm looking at that scenario might be better able to appreciate the case manager's point of view than the three owners of an HMO, who see dollars spent on case management as an expense that directly diminishes profits because of the way the HMO's profit base is structured. The utmost in cost control and practice autonomy occurs in the self-insured, self-administered employer group that has hired its own medical administrator or case manager to track all stages of the health benefit process, from plan design through claims processing.

ADMINISTRATIVE AND CUSTOMIZED SERVICES

Along with the paper pushing involved in claims payouts, many insurers, TPAs, and ASOs provide specialized or auxiliary administrative services. These may include claims adjustment, claims analysis, risk control services, design and creation of PPOs, utilization review, and case management. Case managers can contribute effectively to each of these offerings.

Because of their clinical medical experience, case managers can evaluate a claims run, ascertaining those areas where claims are excessive and perhaps indicating special needs (e.g., the need for an employee wellness program). Case managers can also analyze specific claims for use of services. Risk control requires a system to identify possible high-care, high-cost cases so they may be properly managed each step of the way. Again, case managers have the experience and expertise to review an employer's or insurer's covered lives and establish an appropriate "grading" system—not to pull out individuals for restricted coverage or treatment but to provide early warning so that each case receives the attention it needs.

The same skills make case managers particularly effective when an employer seeks or an insurer designs an HMO, a PPO, or a blend of the two. Using a geographical or medical services–based strategy, a case manager can help develop the provider profile most appropriate for the characteristics of the employer group being covered. Utilization review, rather than the lower service fees typically associated with HMOs and PPOs, is the ingredient that leads to reduced expenditures, although it has come under fire as a "gatekeeper" strategy that can prevent individuals from getting the care they need. In developing a utilization review program, case managers, because of their medical background and their tradition of managing each case individually, are in a position to elucidate the importance of establishing a treatment path for each patient. Putting the individual back into the care picture enhances the benefits of utilization review for both the patient and the payer.

THE CASE MANAGEMENT DELIVERY SYSTEM

Employer groups are now beginning to see the health benefit system as it truly is, but there is still a need for more comprehensive employer education. The system is undoubtedly complex, and given the expanding numbers of providers and payers, it is not growing any simpler or more streamlined. Education remains an uphill struggle. When they discovered that their health benefit premiums were often higher than the coverage or reimbursement their employees received in return, many employers turned to self-funded plans, and the first- and second-year savings were substantial. On the flip side, any catastrophic case within the employer group became more keenly felt than before. As for controlling that risk, some employers have responded proactively by acquiring reinsurance and others have taken the unwise position that the money saved through self-insuring will cover any big cases that come along.

Payers, on the other hand, want to know how successfully a case might be handled through case management prior to giving the go-ahead for its application. So current standards lump all cases together. Any patient claim exceeding a specific dollar limit or falling into a specific diagnostic category is earmarked for case management. But what of the situations that lend themselves to case management more readily than the diagnoses would indicate? A pregnancy experienced by a healthy 22-year-old differs from that experienced by a healthy 14-year-old or 45-year-old. Because there is often little leeway in the standards set by payers for case management intervention and there are numerous restrictions on how and when case management can come into play, many opportunities to provide high-quality, cost-effective care are lost.

Case managers have created a win/win scenario; patients and payers are both well served. Instead of routinely spending $50,000 on a treatment, employers, providers, payers, and case managers manage that money, putting it to its best use. However, case management has a distance to go before it is integrated as a routine element of a benefit plan rather than as an alternative treatment applied to specific cases upon request. Case managers need to expand their communication with employers and decision makers. When they work directly for an employer group, case managers have a greater opportunity to review medical care and benefit dollar protection issues thoroughly and to position case management as a solution to escalating health care costs. There are case managers holding in-house positions now (predominantly registered nurses with teaching backgrounds), but only a few case managers are involved in marketing the service to CEOs and relatively none in the benefit plan design and decision-making loop. The next step in educating insurance providers and administrators is to convince these companies to put case managers in more pivotal positions.

NOTES

1. Catherine M. Mullahy, " 'Insurance' for Self-funded Employers," *The Self-Insurer* 9, no. 5 (1992): 19.
2. Deborah Shalowitz Cowans, "Stop-loss Remains Popular, Prices Moderate," *Business Insurance* 28, no. 6 (February 7, 1994): 20.

CHAPTER

4

Insurance Lines and Health Benefit Plans

What is the health benefit plan? And why does it matter? Often, what a case manager can accomplish and the positive impact she can effect upon a patient's outcome are dictated by the terms of the benefit plan under which an individual is covered. It is vital that case managers understand what their role is relative to the type of coverage in question. Some plans contain no provision for case management services, leaving case managers struggling for approval to implement alternative treatment strategies at the eleventh hour—with answers at hand but no means with which to put the care-at-home or subacute care scenario into action. In the optimum situation, case management services are covered by the benefit plan, enabling case managers to make the best use of one of their assets— the ability to respond quickly to complex problems.

In all cases, a case manager must know a policy's caps on dollars or duration, service exclusions, and any specific treatments that may or may not be covered. Basic coverage terms of a plan are available in the summary plan description, an easy reference guide written in lay language that describes the benefits. However, the master contract—called the plan of benefit or the policy of insurance—prevails in any matter. A plan of benefit is a technical and legal contract containing definitions of the terms within the text, all eligibility requirements, and a list of treatments that are not covered.

WORKERS' COMPENSATION

Unlike group medical, long-term disability, or short-term disability insurance, where a master plan is written for a national company and health benefits will be the same whether the employee of a California company lives in California, Minnesota, or New Jersey, workers' compensation falls under the guidelines of the state in which the policy is written. Workers' compensation regulations therefore vary from state to state for companies with coast-to-coast operations. Similarly, a case manager's activities will also be dictated by each state's workers' compensation process. The benefits an employee in Arkansas is entitled to will not match those for an employee in Delaware. Wage replacement funds may range from $150 to $400 per week, and rates and medical benefit exposure for the employer will differ as well.

The state workers' compensation guidelines also take precedence over the funding source. Employers must provide employees with the level of benefits the state mandates, not the level of benefits they can afford. Regardless of whether a company is self-funded, self-administered, or utilizing a traditional indemnity plan, workers' compensation cases fall under the jurisdiction of the state workers' compensation commission, whose laws and regulations set the limits and extent of coverage. A liaison or intermediary agent between the claimant, employer, insurance carrier, and funder, the state workers' compensation commission acts as an advocate for the claimant. It determines the level of benefits, the obligations of the employer, the responsibilities of the employee, and the level of capability and performance that constitutes "rehabilitation." In some states, the workers' compensation board may list those doctors individuals may utilize.

Bound by a greater degree of legislation than group medical coverage, workers' compensation cases tend to be more legally involved and litigious than group medical cases. In order to sell group medical insurance, an insurance company must include certain benefits and coverage as designated by the state. Under ERISA guidelines, self-funded companies are exempt from meeting those same mandates for levels and provisions required of insurance firms covering companies paying premiums for benefits. This is what allows for the elimination of medical benefits or for top-dollar caps on medical treatment for AIDS or psychological problems in some employers' group health plans. But workers' compensation cases are different. If state guidelines require that an out-of-work person be reimbursed for medical expenses at 100 percent of cost and for lost wages at 80 percent or two-thirds of preinjury salary, even self-funded employer groups must provide that level of benefits.

Case managers are also bound much more by legislation in state-by-state workers' compensation cases than in group medical cases. Those who have only worked group medical insurance cases need to be aware that in workers' compensation, most insurance companies and employers face a double exposure. Although states have varying levels of benefits, insurers and employer groups are mandated to reimburse both medical costs and lost wages. Therefore, a carrier not only is interested in optimizing the results from medical care but also wants the patient back to work as soon as possible. As a result, case management professionals may find themselves asked to achieve inconsistent goals—medical health vs. a timely return to the work force. It pays to be aware that an employer's first and only concern might be the return-to-work time frame because the replacement of salary is a greater expense than the actual medical care.

For example, imagine a case involving a back injury. The employee might see a doctor once every few weeks without undergoing any major surgical procedure or complex medical care, such as a laminectomy or extensive physical therapy. Nevertheless, the employer is getting hit and hit heavily by salary replacement benefits. In a group medical case, an employee either has sick leave or disability leave, but the employer is not paying a salary indefinitely. In most workers' compensation cases, the employer is required to keep the job open. Added to the employer's constraints is the fact that in workers' compensation cases, employees are more inclined to hire attorneys if they feel they are not getting the benefits they are entitled to. The involvement of an attorney is sometimes perceived by a claims examiner or an employer as a roadblock: "Well, this guy has an attorney, so why bother with case management now?" However, this might be the juncture where case management is most needed. In fact, one case manager, Jan Woods, Claim Quality Consultant, Claim Quality Implementation Team for the St. Paul Companies (an insurance firm), established the St. Paul's Liability Case Management services program. Noting that her case management services team had "a tough group of liability folks to convince," she now gets the message from the same group that they "will never give these services up due to the enhanced ability to evaluate and control the damages associated with liability claims." Woods believes liability is the next big arena for case managers.[1]

Recapping, the payer's exposure in a workers' compensation case can be much greater than in a group medical case, even though the illness or injury is less severe, and the involvement of attorneys sometimes complicates the situation. Complying with the regulations of different states compounds the difficulty for case management professionals, especially those working for a nationwide insurer. Other variables contribute to the challenge. In mandated rehabilitation states, patient report formats must follow stringent guidelines; case managers must also file specific forms for billing. Further, there are more players in workers' compensation cases. In addition to the claims department and medical rehabilitation professionals, there are administrative law judges, vocational counselors, and vocational rehabilitation boards. Working on such cases can be a nightmare for independent case management companies as they try to keep abreast of changes in workers' compensation regulations in all the states they serve.

On the other hand, coordinating care and benefits under a single group medical plan is basically the same state to state. An independent case management company with licensed nurses in multiple states can work group medical cases in several states fairly easily. To be effective, a case manager almost has to decide beforehand whether to tackle the workers' compensation arena or stick with group medical.

AUTO INSURANCE

Like workers' compensation regulations, auto insurance policy regulations vary state to state in terms of medical coverage limits and lost-wage replacement. Some states pay medical costs (in auto policies, this is called PIP [personal injury protection]) from the day of the accident. In New Jersey, there is medical coverage up to $250,000 and no duration cap. New York policies generally cover individuals for $50,000 or three years, whichever comes first. There are states with very low caps, where auto policies have perhaps $5,000 maximum medical exposure. Where does an individual go when that $5,000 is exhausted? To a group medical plan. Those states with generous medical coverage sometimes provide minimal salary replacement coverage. Because these variations can create incentives or disincentives for individuals to get medical problems resolved quickly and return to work, case managers need to be aware of the fine points of auto insurance coverage. There are states where, as long as an employee can demonstrate some level of impairment, he or she can continue to remain off the job. This type of provision leads people to tend toward prolonging the recovery process.

Every case manager needs to know the terms of coverage for the line of insurance, the state regulations, and any other plans covering an individual to make the best use of time and dollars. As discussed, workers' compensation and no-fault auto insurance policies vary state to state, but they also differ in structure. In a given policy, does the term *state* refer to the location where the accident occurred, or where the employee resides, or where the corporation has its headquarters office? For example, I have case managers working a case in Arkansas under New York state regulations. A truck driver from Arkansas was injured in an accident in New York, where his company has its headquarters. The driver is recuperating in Arkansas, but the case is being treated as a New York workers' compensation case, not an Arkansas resident compensation case.

INDEMNITY PLANS

The meaning of *indemnity* is determined by its usage. In general, *indemnity* refers to a traditional insurance plan where reimbursement or compensation for loss or personal injury is provided via a contract. A company or individual pays premiums for a policy that outlines a contract of benefits and entitlements. The formation of HMOs, PPOs, and the applications of self-funded plans were responses to the escalating costs of traditional indemnity plans.

Indemnity can also be used to describe legal exemption from liabilities—the "hold-harmless" clause.

GROUP MEDICAL PLANS

While workers' compensation plans use terms such as *degree of disability* and *causally related* and auto policies refer to PIP portions, group medical policies contain a different terminology: *caps, limitations, copayments, coinsurance, pre-existing, exclusions.* Aside from knowing the exact meaning of these terms, a case manager needs to be apprised of the source of funding that backs a group medical policy. If it is a fully insured plan, the plan may have to meet certain conditions on a state-by-state basis. Is it a premium-rated plan or is it self-funded, PPO backed, or HMO backed? Because employees are able to choose the plan they wish to belong to, one employer group can refer to a case manager individuals in any number of plans: fully insured plans, HMOs, PPOs, and so on. Some of these plans will have case management provisions written in; some might not utilize case management.

In my experience, employers tend to be less involved and less interested in the administration of fully insured plans. Some employers continue to pay the premiums and consider themselves done, paying little attention to wellness programs, cost containment, and management of claims. For these reasons, a case manager might find less flexibility for alternative care arrangements when working within a fully insured plan. On the other hand, I believe case managers will be utilized more and more in the managed care entities such as HMOs and PPOs.

Case managers should be aware that the group medical benefit structure often changes as an individual moves from one level of employment to another. Is the patient an active or retired employee? A retired employee who has COBRA coverage and is now at the age of Medicare eligibility? On disability and moving into retirement? Adjustments may be triggered by the employee's age as well. A case manager working with a 63-year-old active employee who suddenly retires must have an answer to the question, How does retirement change the patient's coverage?

For example, under the Consolidated Omnibus Budget Reconciliation Act (COBRA), the employer must offer terminated employees an 18-month continuation of benefits under the plan the employee had been covered by during tenure with the company. Coverage extends for 36 months to a spouse and all dependents on the policy at the time of termination. If the employee was disabled at the time of termination—an unlikely scenario—coverage continues for 29 months. The employee is responsible for meeting the premiums.

The extent of medical benefits, in terms of length of time, is subject to the determination of the employer group or union contract. Some companies only provide coverage to their active employees. Others will offer benefits to retired employees for a specified period; if an individual had been with the company for five to ten years of continued service, he or she might receive an additional three years on the medical plan. The larger the firm, the more likely it is that retirees will leave with their benefits intact—because of management loyalty to senior staff. For those hired at a later date, and therefore younger, the benefits structure might have been revised to meet the expense constraints of the times.

DISABILITY PLANS

Disability plans can be very specifically worded according to the desire of the employer group or single employer. Self-employed individuals can hold disability policies on themselves. Short-term disability (STD) plans can transition into long-term disability (LTD) plans carrying a different level of provisions. Varying in terms—the policy definition of short-term, long-term, and total disability; the portion of salary replaced; the number of months or years covered—disability plans require individual review by a case manager.

Within a LTD policy, there are two major distinguishing provisions: HISOCC (try, "his occupation") and ANYOCC (a.k.a. "any occupation"). Under HISOCC, a person must be totally disabled from performing any and all aspects of his or her job. Even if the person can perform three out of four job functions, that one missing function entitles him or her to the replacement of salary. HISOCC usually carries specified time limitations, ranging from one to five years. In general, a HISOCC plan might state that a person totally disabled from performing any and all aspects of his or her job is entitled to receive x amount of dollars for no more than five years but no less than one year. LTD plans may also be group specific. Physicians and other professionals, for example, tend to establish well-worded policies and will often "layer" their coverage, purchasing several policies to provide the salary protection necessary should illness limit their earning power. These multiple disability policies are designed to take effect as claims escalate, and because some higher socioeconomic groups readily pay the more expensive premiums necessary to fund such coverage, the entitlements are generally more generous than other ANYOCC or HISOCC plans.

The other portion of an LTD plan, the ANYOCC clause, is where the rubber hits the road. Under ANYOCC, an individual may not be able to perform all aspects of his or her previous job but may well be able to perform the tasks required in other occupations. Most LTD policies cover individuals up to age 65 totally disabled from performing any and all aspects of their jobs and provide perhaps two-thirds of their salary. These policies are expensive, and employer groups are trusting the law of averages and an actuary that while all employee premiums are paying into the LTD plan, only a small percentage of the employees will require coverage under it. Therefore, when a patient has improved to the point of moving from HISOCC status to ANYOCC, LTD carriers get very aggressive. Often, case managers are not involved in any type of intervention until the end of the HISOCC stage, when a carrier feels, "Okay, it's been a year now" (or three years or five years), and takes a closer look at the particular circumstances of the case.

Case managers, rehabilitation managers, and anyone else competent to intervene should know that sometimes STD and LTD policies are strictly wage-replacement plans and lack provisions for medical services. Obviously, it is much more difficult to work cases without that medical arm to put to good use. Despite knowing medical treatment could improve a patient's situation, a case manager might be stymied because medical benefits have been terminated or used up and the patient continues to linger on LTD. To cut short their losses, other LTD carriers are much more willing to be creative and bend the rules. Such carriers, looking at risk management as well, will buy the motorized wheelchair or electrify the employee's van in order to move toward a solution. Carriers concentrating on vocational rehabilitation are more likely to pursue these alternatives.

As an example, when working with a major corporation that had self-funded all its lines of insurance for employees, I could call the benefits manager directly to arrange funding for medical treatment on behalf of an LTD employee. The benefits manager and upper management were familiar with case management and could see that such medical support would make sense.

In contrast, a fully insured employer might have Travelers or John Hancock as its LTD carrier while buying its major medical coverage from Blue Cross/Blue Shield or Aetna. Coordinating two different carriers adds levels of approval and discussion that hinder the case management–medical intervention process. I could get an LTD case and know exactly what needs to be done medically, but if the medical plan does not cover the intervention and the LTD claims examiner cannot see the need for it, I must make a very convincing argument for a medical course. This is where the financial planning capability of case managers comes into play. Depending on a carrier's exposure—the amount of money it is responsible to reimburse under the plan—the carrier can be willing to stretch provision boundaries to include medical treatment when a case manager can demonstrate that once x dollars are spent on medical treatment, an employee could be off LTD and back to work. Carriers are especially willing to look at a creative case manager's ideas when the employee is a heavy-hitting physician with LTD receipts ranging in the thousands of dollars per month.

POINT-OF-SERVICE PLANS

Originating approximately six years ago, point-of-service (POS) managed care plans include a range of customized care plans most often offered by larger companies. They evolved from PPO plans as companies sought to combine employee choice, cost reduction, and efficient utilization. The most successful POS arrangements are characterized by effective providers, limited network size, and provisions requiring health care providers to share a portion of the payer's risk, making for a more realistic plan design. These plans run the spectrum from open-access HMO plans to gatekeeper PPOs. HMOs with open access tend to incorporate smaller network panels and to be more rigid in their procedures. Consequently, employee resentment is more likely to occur when an employer moves from a traditional insurance plan to an HMO-based plan. POS networks based on gatekeeper PPO models generally include broader network panels, impose fewer restrictions on patients and providers, and allow more range in plan design. Responsibility for overseeing a POS plan falls to a network manager within the company. The key feature differentiating POS plans from PPO arrangements is that a higher level of benefits can only be accessed if care is provided through a primary care provider, such as a pediatrician, an internist, or a family practitioner (OB-GYNs are the exception to the rule).[2]

According to a survey of 1,057 randomly selected public and private companies with 200 or more employees conducted by KPMG Peat Marwick and reported in the December 1992 issue of *Managed Healthcare*

News, 55 percent of the employees were enrolled in a managed care health plan. As a portion of that managed care plan pie, POS plan enrollment increased from 3 percent in the spring of 1991 to 8 percent in the spring of 1992, making POS plans one of the fastest-growing options in managed care, along with PPOs. *Business Insurance* (February 14, 1994) noted a study by benefit consulting firm A. Foster Higgins in which 15 percent of all large employers (with 500 or more employees) reported offering a POS plan in 1993. Among employers of all sizes, POS enrollment was up from 6 percent of employees in 1992 to 9 percent in 1993. A 1993 KPMG Peat Marwick survey of 1,003 employers (with 200 or more employees) showed that POS plans experienced a lower rate of health care premium increase than staff or group model HMOs. As covered in the December 1993 issue of *Business & Health*, the increase in POS rates from 1992 to 1993 was only 4.9 percent, as compared with increases of 8.3 percent and 8.2 percent for HMOs and PPOs, respectively.

Case managers working cases that fall into the POS category need to ascertain the type of POS the employee is enrolled in—open-access HMO, gatekeeper PPO, or a hybrid falling between the two. To be in a better position to make a case in favor of an alternative treatment, a case manager should also be aware of which party within the network is responsible for what portion of the risk. Is the employer, provider, or payer most exposed to financial risk?

DIAGNOSIS-SPECIFIC BENEFITS

There are conditions and diagnoses that may allow for additional funding through federal, state, and local programs. The availability of programs varies from state to state. A preemie baby with developmental delays, like those caused by cystic fibrosis, may be eligible for state early-intervention programs. (For example, Mississippi has a liberal program whereas Arkansas has no provision for cystic fibrosis.) Medicare automatically becomes the primary fund source for patients with end-stage renal disease, even those who are active employees, after 18 months of dialysis treatment, but only for services related to the renal condition.

For those with physical limitations or disabilities, such as the legally blind, there are also federal and state programs that help stretch fund dollars. Easter Seals aids those with muscular dystrophy; the Shriners have funds available for burn victims. As citizens and taxpayers, patients are entitled to the offerings of these and other programs. (Unfortunately, most case managers do not take as much advantage of these alternative sources as they could. This is an area where case managers need to expand their activity.)

Admittedly, utilizing these funds is not always easy or straightforward. Working with state or federal funding sources is often more difficult for case managers because of the bureaucratic layering. In any state-operated or federally funded program, the rules are sometimes so stringent that they allow for no flexibility at all, even when it would seem that a more cost-effective solution is available. For example, some regulations force case managers to spend more money. Case managers are mandated to use only Medicare-certified agencies in some state Care at Home program cases despite the fact that such agencies may be as much as 50 to 100 percent more expensive than another home care agency. In its effort to protect both those people who might not be able to fend for themselves and the taxpayers, Medicare has adopted rules that are not always in anyone's interest.

Further, case managers will find that government billing and report formats are entirely different than those used in the private sector. Case managers with a high overhead might not be able to afford to handle mostly Medicare cases because of the significantly lower profit margins. In addition to generating an increased number of diverse reports and tracking down agencies that are delinquent in payments, case managers will have to contend with a high turnover rate among government staff (necessitating reintroductions to case management), regulatory changes, and midstream program cuts.

TRADITIONAL INSURANCE VERSUS SELF-FUNDED PLANS

In working with a number of major insurance companies that provide traditional insurance (a.k.a. indemnity plans and premium-based plans), I have found that there appears to be less willingness to be flexible with benefit alternatives. This may be because the premiums have been set based on known experience (the history of health benefit usage for that type and number of employees) and an anticipated projected cost for that employee group over time. The insurer has been investing or managing the premium income to make certain there will be enough funds to cover employee claims. A change in the benefit payout—even if it lessens the payout—is perceived as a disruption to the system. There also seem to be rigid constraints on adopting options that, even at first and second glance, appear sound from a business-management perspective. When case management might result in an extra expense or administrative cost that the insurer will have to absorb at the year's end, a traditional insurance company almost requires a guarantee of projected savings neatly spelled out, which is brought back to the employee group for review at a multitude of levels prior to taking action.

With one major insurer, I had to complete a cost-benefit analysis immediately following my initial evaluation before the insurer could determine whether it felt case management would be viable in each particular case. Instead of being able to blend our experiences, pulling on the volumes of past history, I had to justify case management again and again. While the reams of documentation were prepared for the claims managers and everyone else in the approval process, we were missing opportunities to help the patient and save benefit dollars. During the three to four weeks it took for all levels to decide that case management might indeed be a good idea, we missed *more* opportunities. I have no problem with the demand for a round-figure estimate of potential cost savings, but in these instances it seemed that the carrier was asking case managers to become actuaries.

The approval process itself is too convoluted, too enormous to be successful, fraught with so many players and layers, and "we have to talk with legal," that case management options become too big a "problem" to be resolved. The "problem" is twofold: getting to the decision maker and presenting the information.

If case managers could go directly to the group paying the premiums and tell them their options and alternatives, they could snap the trap and get their jobs done. But case managers dealing with traditional insurance most often talk first to agents, then brokers, and case management reports are finally presented by marketing managers or claims managers instead of the case managers, who are of course closest to the issues. There seems to be insufficient education and preparation by case managers as to what case management can accomplish and an inability on the part of large insurers to take a successful pilot case management project and make the transition to a successful corporate-wide program.

For example, suppose a case manager is assigned a case by a large carrier, a case that had been directed to the carrier by its preadmission/concurrent review contractor. By the time the case has come to the attention of the insurer and has been determined to be appropriate for case management, several days have passed. The patient has cancer and is in the hospital *now*. The insurance contract has an absolute limit on home health benefits, no more than 30 visits per calendar year, but unlimited dollars can be spent in hospital care. Other than a hospital, it seems there are very few places where this patient could be cared for—at a skilled facility or perhaps at home with multiple support services. The indicators seem to dictate that the person remain in the hospital.

After seeing the patient on-site, the case manager follows up her visit with a verbal report to the insurer's in-house case management contact. The patient would like to go home, and the case manager would like to move him out of the hospital as soon as possible. Such a move will not threaten his current medical status or recovery. The insurance contact has to discuss the plan with her manager, then bring it to the service representative, who reviews it with the service manager to see if a plan exception can be made. The service manager would like to speak with legal counsel, and then there is the meeting of the trustees next week, where they will see if they can do something about it. Meanwhile, alternative care is in place, the patient is poised to go home, but the contract will not allow it. The case manager needs an exception but cannot get a decision, and the hospital charges are adding up.

Now, consider the same basic scenario but where the insurance is provided by a self-funded employer group that has a TPA administering its claims. The benefit plan contains the same language limiting home health visits to 30 per calendar year and providing unlimited hospital benefits. Through the same process of identification—via a preadmission/concurrent review contractor—the case is red-flagged in the claims department of the TPA. Knowledgeable about case management, the claims adjuster contacts the TPA's case management contractor. Returning from her on-site visit, the case manager talks directly with the employer's service representative and the claims department within the TPA, outlining the alternatives for the patient, who requires support services and really wants to go home or at least into a less intensive care setting. With case management, a program can be constructed that results in the best care for the patient and saves the plan substantial benefit dollars.

The TPA's service representative contacts the fiduciary or controller of the benefit plan, who sees the economic sense of adopting the use of case management. (Fiduciary responsibility obliges the controller not only to meet the needs of the individual but to safeguard dollars for the needs of the entire benefit group). By deciding for case management in this instance, the controller creates a win-win scenario—quality of care is increased and cost is decreased. The recommendation and decision take a few hours, as opposed to the days needed in a large insurance firm.

This is not to say all TPAs have seen the light and welcome case management with open arms. The issue really centers on a level of sophistication and the willingness to make decisions and assume a controlled risk regardless of the insurance benefit system. In general, the larger the organization, the more tortuous the decision. TPAs tend to be small and local; insurance companies tend to be larger and operate nationally from a central location.

I believe my frustration with the convoluted decision-making process within some larger insurance firms remains an industrywide frustration. When I have the opportunity to work one-on-one with an employer group or a small group of payers, whether within a claims department or a TPA—or when I speak with CMs in a large company—and show them what a smaller firm has been able to achieve for patients and payers, their eyes light up. If we can restrict the players in traditional-insurance decision making to the key people, we have a chance at success. The difficulty of working with a larger complex bureaucracy provides a strong argument for becoming self-funded—it is the control of decisions and dollars that make case management programs work. Case managers need to spend more time taking their successful scenarios and pilot projects and bringing them to the marketplace. Education and proof of case management's viability will make case management a more readily used medical- and business-management tool.

STOP-LOSS INSURANCE PLANS

Because of their position in the insurance industry, stop-loss insurance carriers (reinsurance carriers) are of special interest to case managers. They can see more clearly the positive effects of case management. Many employer groups, whether utilizing traditional premium-based insurance or a self-funded plan, will set a threshold over which the financial responsibility for health benefits will be borne by a stop-loss carrier. Handling only the big-cost cases, stop-loss carriers absolutely see the benefits of case management. Customarily, a reinsurer will request a specific limit report—notification when a claim reaches 50 or 75 percent of the set threshold. At that point, the carrier might intercede and put case management in place or have written into the stop-loss agreement that a case manager be automatically assigned by the company when a claim hits its specific limit. In fact, many stop-loss insurers will mandate cost-containment measures, agreeing to write reinsurance only if the company puts preadmission review, case management, and other managed care strategies in place.

Reinsurers are looking closely at how they can best protect their layer of coverage from exposure to financial catastrophe. A company might have health care benefits of a million dollars per covered life, with a threshold set at $100,000 with a reinsurer. This means there is coverage for patients for claims of $150,000 or $250,000, but the company only pays the first $100,000 out of its group coverage and is reimbursed dollar-for-dollar by the stop-loss carrier for any costs over the threshold up to $1 million. Therefore, reinsurers are very interested in using case management to keep benefit payouts beneath the level of stop-loss. If a case manager can help manage health care and costs, keeping benefits payouts from moving upward into the stop-loss range, the firm saves not only in its fiscal year but also in the next year, since premiums are based on claims experience. Just as the stop-loss carrier uses case management to protect it from high dollar losses, the employer group itself should be seeking the same protection.

Using this information, case managers can create opportunities by "creating the need" for case management (i.e., identifying the need and demonstrating it). When I talk to employer groups, I tell them that for many groups, stop-loss coverage can be hard to sign. The premiums can become so costly that company managers are forced to raise the group's threshold—the amount of money the company is responsible for—higher than the firm can actually carry. However, if an employer group can tell a reinsurer that it already has case management and other cost-containment strategies (preadmission review, concurrent review) in place in the first layer of coverage, the reinsurer might be more inclined to write coverage for the group, more assured that high numbers of catastrophic cases will not reach the stop-loss layer.

MULTIPLE-EMPLOYER BENEFIT PLANS AND TRUSTS

Prior to the passage of Taft-Hartley in the 1950s, there was no mandated health care coverage for individuals who worked for multiple employers during the course of the year. Unlike the office workers employed year-round by a single firm, the organized laborers employed annually by various contractors (carpenters or painters who worked out of a union hall) had no single organization sponsoring a health benefit plan. The Taft-Hartley federal labor law included a number of citations, among them a provision allowing for the establishment of multiemployer benefit trusts (a.k.a. welfare funds). Funded by multiple employers, a trust of this type is regulated by a board of trustees (with union and employer positions equally represented), which determines the operative and administrative rules. As in a pension fund, the monies are gathered and placed in a trust overseen by a welfare plan administrator. The manager at ABC Building Co. will send in a monthly statement listing the individuals employed by ABC, the hours worked, and the amount ABC owes to the fund on the workers' behalf. There is then a pool, the "Carpenters Health and Welfare Plan" pool, for instance, from which health benefits can be drawn.

Case managers with patients who are covered by a multiemployer trust should ascertain the name of the welfare plan administrator (or health and welfare officer) for assistance in clarifying benefits. Eligibility for these trusts is complex and can fluctuate from quarter to quarter. The hours a carpenter works in the first quarter will be applied to his or her coverage for the second quarter. If the carpenter does not have the required hours of employment to cover plan participation, he or she might have to self-pay for a quarter to maintain eligibility.

NONTRADITIONAL POLICIES

There are also a number of nontraditional supplemental policies currently available that, although not necessarily recommended for purchase, are often selected by individuals seeking more comprehensive coverage.

Disease-Specific Policies

Cancer Policies

While working on behalf of one patient, I discovered he had paid for a cancer insurance policy due to the high incidence of cancer in his family. This policy allowed for greater benefits than his health plan or an LTD policy would have provided. To receive the entitlements of a cancer policy, an individual must have a confirmed diagnosis of cancer as described in his or her policy. Although a broad number of cancer policies have been purchased, they are not recommended to the general public because of the limitation of the coverage. People are usually encouraged to put the money they might spend on a cancer policy toward expanded health plan coverage instead.

Alzheimer's Policies

These are seen as very limited and costly policies. The stated qualifications for nursing home coverage—a key issue with this type of policy—generally preclude any history of Alzheimer's within a family, eliminating the patient group most likely to benefit.

Specified Disease Policies

Covering a broad range of terminal diseases (including, but not limited to, cancer), such plans provide benefits upon a confirmed diagnosis of the specific disease by a physician.

Occupation-Specific Policies

AIDS and HIV policies are sold to law enforcement officers and fire fighters, who, because of their occupation, are at a high risk of exposure to HIV infection through lifesaving efforts, resuscitation procedures, or hostile bites.

Long-Term Care and Nursing Home Policies

Long-term care plans are now being perceived as an insurance vehicle that everyone in our society needs to look at and consider for themselves. While case managers may not be seeing high numbers of these policies now, they probably will in the future. Meant to meet the bulk of expenses for unexpected catastrophic events, such as a head injury, long-term care policies fill the gaps in a plan that might not cover custodial care or other treatments no longer considered part of a traditional health care plan. As employers look for ways to protect themselves from long-term health care responsibilities, medical policies—whether traditional indemnity plans or ERISA (self-funded) plans—are becoming more stringently worded. As an example, a group medical plan might cover 30 days of inpatient rehabilitation. However, if someone claims that this amount of rehabilitation is not sufficient to restore a patient to his or her prior degree of function or capability, the group medical response will likely be, "That's not restorative you're requesting, that's long-term custodial care, and we don't pay for that."

The long-term care policies being offered by some employer groups to employees and their immediate family or dependents do respond to a tremendous need in the health care marketplace. Unfortunately, even these policies are so narrowly written that they bar a great number of people from access to care or limit the actual length of care to be covered. The industry is just now seeing a gradual move toward more consumer-friendly long-term care policies.

Medigap Policies

Similar to long-term care policies, Medigap plans were devised as a safety net for those areas of coverage where Medicare stopped short. A Medigap policy is an independent policy purchased by individuals through an insurance agency to augment Medicare coverage. Launched in the marketplace with a great deal of hype, some Medigap policies are actually less than they appear. Guidelines on items that should be included in every Medigap plan can be obtained from the federal Department of Aging or the Department of Health and Human Services.

Dental Insurance

Dental insurance policies are currently popular in the marketplace. Further developments in this product line include a shift toward PPO networks and POS arrangements as alternatives to "indemnity" dental plans.

RIDERS TO LIFE INSURANCE POLICIES

Accelerated Benefits

Additional funds for terminal illness care may be obtained through a rider to a life insurance policy. Should a policyholder develop a terminal illness (as validated by a physician statement that the person is likely to die within a year), the person can gain access to approximately one-half of the life insurance policy's benefits.

Accidental Dismemberment Clause

Also written as a rider to a life insurance policy, this clause has not come into common use. It provides for a flat dollar amount to be paid, regardless of the medical care delivered and its cost, if a person loses an arm, a leg, or his or her vision or suffers multiple losses.

COORDINATION OF BENEFITS

When there are two or more coverages on a claim—perhaps a wife and husband both work and are covered by their employers, a no-fault auto policy, or Medicare—there are rules governing which of the plans is primary and pays first and which pays second. In an "intact" family, an employee's plan pays first on that employee. When the claim is for a child covered by both parents' plans, the "birthday" rule comes into play. The plan of the parent with the earlier birthday, by month and day, not year, is utilized. If Mom's birthday is April 12 and Dad's birthday is August 20, Mom's plan is primary. (In the past, Dad's plan was always primary; some plans still hold the male parent as primary.)

Medicare is primary if a person retires on pension and his or her spouse is not an active employee with coverage as an active employee. However, an employer group health plan is *always* primary vis-à-vis Medicare. A 74-year-old active employee is entitled to Medicare, but his employer plan is primary. That same plan is primary for his 69-year-old spouse named on the plan, as well. If an employee is disabled but still covered by an employee group plan, Medicare is the secondary payer.

To clear up any unknowns and prevent future confusion, a case manager should always ask about all insurance in effect during an initial visit or telephone call. The source referring the case might not have all pertinent information on file. All findings regarding multiple coverage, coverage origin, plan sponsor, and who is insured under each plan should be recorded. In divorced families and step families, coordination of benefits becomes more intricate, as custody and court-order issues may be involved.

Coordination of benefits is always specific to the types of plan involved in a case, and a coordination of benefits statement is customarily included in each plan.[3]

NOTES

1. "Profile: Jan Woods, R.N., C.I.R.S., *The Case Manager*, Summer 1992, 62–74.
2. Lawrence B. Leisure, "Point-of-Service Plans," in *Driving Down Health Care Costs: Strategies and Solutions 1992* (New York: Panel Publishers, 1992), 143–153.
3. Alice C. Reynolds-Meadows, "Managing Case Management," presented at the Individual Case Management Association Medical Case Management Conference III, Dallas, September 1991.

CHAPTER

5

Legal Responsibilities of the Case Management Profession

To serve as an advocate for individuals in today's massive, intricate health care delivery system, a case manager needs to know the laws governing patient rights and entitlements as well as the criteria determining "fair treatment" under the law. This does not mean that case managers must have each minute detail of workers' compensation legislation committed to memory, but they do need to understand policies to know when it is appropriate to file for COBRA coverage or set an appeals process in motion. For self-protection and protection of her employer, a case manager must also be aware of any recognized standard of practice by which her work will be judged. Like nurses, physicians, social workers, and physical therapists, case managers now have protocols (practice guidelines) that are becoming the established benchmarks for appropriate case management services.

PATIENT BILL OF RIGHTS AND PATIENT CONFIDENTIALITY

Every hospital has a patient bill of rights that outlines the individual's prerogatives regarding care, including the right to emergency aid, the right to diagnosis and prognosis information, the right to unbiased treatment, and the right to voice grievances. Prominent among the items covered are the right to privacy and the right to confidentiality of all patient records. (Exhibit 5-1 is a sample patient bill of rights and Exhibit 5-2 is a patient bill of responsibilities, a list of corresponding duties a patient is expected to fulfill.)

Exhibit 5-1 Patients Bill of Rights

As a patient in a hospital in New York State, you have the right, consistent with law, to:
(1) Understand and use these rights. If for any reason you do not understand or you need help, the hospital MUST provide assistance, including an interpreter.
(2) Receive treatment without discrimination as to race, color, religion, sex, national origin, disability, sexual orientation or source of payment.
(3) Receive considerate and respectful care in a clean and safe environment free of unnecessary restraints.
(4) Receive emergency care if you need it.
(5) Be informed of the name and position of the doctor who will be in charge of your care in the hospital.
(6) Know the names, positions and functions of any hospital staff involved in your care and refuse their treatment, examination or observation.
(7) A no smoking room.
(8) Receive complete information about your diagnosis, treatment and prognosis.
(9) Receive all information that you need to give informed consent for any proposed procedure or treatment. This information shall include the possible risks and benefits of the procedure or treatment.
(10) Receive all the information you need to give informed consent for an order not to resuscitate. You also have the right to designate an individual to give this consent for you if you are too ill to do so. If you would like additional information, please ask for a copy of the pamphlet "Do Not Resuscitate Orders—A Guide for Patients and Families."
(11) Refuse treatment and be told what effect this may have on your health.
(12) Refuse to take part in research. In deciding whether or not to participate, you have the right to a full explanation.
(13) Privacy while in the hospital and confidentiality of all information and records regarding your care.
(14) Participate in all decisions about your treatment and discharge from the hospital. The hospital must provide you with a written discharge plan and written description of how you can appeal your discharge.
(15) Review your medical record without charge. Obtain a copy of your medical record for which the hospital can charge a reasonable fee. You cannot be denied a copy solely because you cannot afford to pay.
(16) Receive an itemized bill and explanation of all charges.
(17) Complain without fear of reprisals about the care and services you are receiving and to have the hospital respond to you and if you request it, a written response. If you are not satisfied with the hospital's response, you can complain to the New York State Health Department. The hospital must provide you with the Health Department telephone number.

Source: Courtesy of Nassau County Medical Center, East Meadow, New York

Exhibit 5-2 Patient Bill of Responsibilities

The Nassau County Medical Center recognizes the primary role its patients play with regard to their care, their safety and the safety of others, and the safeguarding of the rights of other patients and staff.

A bill of patient responsibilities describing this role is set forth below in the interest of promoting a safe, comfortable environment in which the best possible care may be rendered.

Patient Responsibilities:

NCMC patients shall be responsible:
1. To provide, to the best of his/her knowledge, accurate and complete information about present complaints, past illnesses, hospitalizations, medication and other matters relating to his/her health.
2. To report unexpected changes in his/her condition to the responsible practitioner, as soon as possible.
3. To make it known whether he/she understands a contemplated course of action and what is expected of him/her.
4. For following to the best of his/her ability the plan for medical care as recommended by the physician primarily responsible for his/her care.
5. To keep appointments and when unable to do so, to notify the hospital with sufficient time to reschedule.
6. For his/her actions if he/she refuses treatment or does not follow the practitioner's instructions.
7. For assuring that the financial obligations of his/her health care are fulfilled as promptly as possible.
8. For following hospital rules and regulations regarding patient care and conduct.
9. For assisting in the control of noise and the number of visitors.
10. To comply with the No Smoking Policy as posted and assist Medical Center staff in their efforts to provide a smoke free environment for all.
11. For being respectful of the property of other persons and of the hospital.
12. For being considerate of the rights of others.
13. To fill out the patient evaluation form to provide feedback to the hospital.

Source: Courtesy of Nassau County Medical Center, East Meadow, New York

In its 1988 *Accreditation Manual for Hospitals*, the Joint Commission on Accreditation of Healthcare Organizations identified privacy and confidentiality as two patient rights, entitling a patient to the following:

- to refuse to talk with or see anyone not officially connected with the hospital, including visitors, or persons officially connected with the hospital but not directly involved in the patient's care;
- to wear appropriate personal clothing and religious or other symbolic items, as long as they do not interfere with diagnostic procedures or treatments;
- to be interviewed and examined in surroundings designed to assure reasonable visual and auditory privacy;
- to expect that any discussion or consultation involving the patient will be conducted discreetly and that individuals not directly involved in the patient's care will not be present without the permission of the patient;
- to have the medical record read only by individuals directly involved in the patient's treatment or in the monitoring of its quality, and by other individuals only with the patient's written authorization or that of a legally authorized representative;
- to expect all communications and other records pertaining to the patient's care, including the source of payment for treatment, to be treated as confidential;
- to request a transfer to another room if another patient or visitor in the room is unreasonable, disturbing the patient by smoking or other actions; and
- to be placed in protective privacy when considered necessary for personal safety.[1]

As health care professionals, case managers are ethically charged to maintain the maximum amount of confidentiality possible on matters of health and finances on behalf of patients. Confidentiality touches on a number of issues and relationships. Regardless of the health plan and their health status, patients are equal. The getting of information is not an arbitrary and capricious procedure. It can be argued that providers, payers, case managers, and patients all have rights, and in fact they do, but in particular cases the rights of one group will override those of another. Each member of a health plan enjoys the same right to know about his or her condition, and the same protection must be given to the privacy of any member. A cancer or HIV-positive patient has the right to keep his or her health status from being known by anyone else; an employer requesting such particular information from a case manager is out of line.

However, some patients need to be educated on how far they can push their right to confidentiality. A case manager cannot forge a document or fudge a claims report, altering the diagnosis, treatment, or medication, for example, to cloud facts about an illness because it might be a tip-off to the patient's condition. Although claims forms generally include a patient's name, social security number, age, and illness, patient codes are utilized to help protect the patient's identity on reports that might be sent to a corporate office, such as cost-benefit analysis reports.

Jeanne Boling, the executive director of the Individual Case Management Association (ICMA), assembled information on confidentiality issues that case managers typically must deal with. The material was adapted from "Confidentiality: An Issue CMs Must Understand," handouts developed by Susan Scheutzow. Case managers will ask themselves two very basic questions to clarify confidentiality concerns: When must information be disclosed? When must information not be disclosed?[2]

Following the principle that the sensitivities of patients must be respected while facilitating the truthful and complete disclosure of information necessary for proper health care determinations, Scheutzow says that information must be disclosed when a patient requests it (as qualified by state law). Many states have statutes requiring that any patient be given access to his or her medical records except when the content might be damaging to the patient. In the absence of statutes, courts generally hold that patients must be allowed to see their medical records.

Varying from state to state, statutes may require that the following events be reported: births; deaths; child or elder abuse and neglect; violent injuries; animal bites; contagious, infectious, and occupational diseases; certain conditions of newborns; abortions; impaired health care professionals; and breath, blood, and urine testing for alcohol and drugs. Federal law mandates the reporting of certain adverse transfusion reactions, certain misadministration of radioactive materials, and certain medical device defects and failures. According to Scheutzow, case managers have a duty to warn authorities in cases of communicable diseases or violent inclinations of the mentally ill. They are also compelled to respond to subpoenas and court orders; if information is privileged, a case manager should request a signed consent from the patient and consult a lawyer.

When can't case managers share information? When it comes from a drug or alcohol abuse treatment provider or a patient's mental health records or when it concerns AIDS or a sexually transmitted disease. As an example of why case managers should consult legal counsel, the list of confidential matters includes cases of abortion, in direct contrast to state statutes that might require disclosure of abortion. To help clarify such issues, Scheutzow recommends that case managers have a strict, well-defined confidentiality policy, operate with the informed consent of patients, and get adequate and valid releases or consent authorization forms for all disclosures of confidential information.

CONSENT/DISCLOSURE AND CONSENT AUTHORIZATION FORMS

Empowerment derives in part from awareness. Therefore, a case manager, as patient advocate, must have utmost respect for a patient's right to knowledge. During a well-conducted assessment, the case manager will discover just how much the patient understands about his or her condition and prognosis. In most instances, not enough background has been provided to enable the patient to safely manage his or her illness or injury. The wife or husband or eldest child perhaps knows a few more details, but the patient remains in the dark. There must be a free disclosure of information so that an informed decision may be made.

When a case manager begins working with a patient, she should have in hand a consent authorization form (Exhibit 5-3), signed by the patient or the person authorized to act on the patient's behalf, whenever arranging for an alternative care location or provider, considering an optional medical procedure, or developing a case management plan. This docu-

---

Exhibit 5-3 Consent Form

CONSENT

Date:_____

To assure appropriate medical case management services, I _____

_____, authorize any physician, hospital, or other professional involved in my treatment to disclose medical, hospital, vocational, or related information. I authorize that the information may be shared with other professionals, agencies, or insurance companies who may be involved in the provision or payment of necessary services.

A copy of this authorization may be accepted, if necessary.

Signed _____

Guardian _____

Witness _____

Courtesy of Options Unlimited, Case Management Services Division, Huntington, N.Y.

---

ment provides for the release of information to the case manager and certifies the patient's permission to review case information with the treating physician, other health care providers, the payer, the employer group, and so on, when some data must be shared to further the case. In essence, it safeguards the patient–case manager relationship, noting who the case manager is, those people she will need to speak with, and the records that will be discussed. In a group medical plan, consent forms are not strictly required, but in a workers' compensation or no-fault case, especially in situations more prone to litigation than others, they are a necessity. A consent form can be very specifically written or broad-based to cover a number of medical situations, but it should authorize access to information for the duration of the case. A copy of the consent form is kept on file and accompanies all case management reports sent to a physician, lawyer, claims examiner, and so on. For long-term cases, a consent form should be signed annually.

A case manager might think, "John is in the hospital and I need to see him." So off she goes, driving 45 minutes to the hospital. But John feels that case management intervention is not necessary and certainly does not want to sign any consent form. There is no other family member present. The case manager has now trekked to the hospital and gotten nowhere because she was not prepared. It would have been better to have moved a little more slowly, but thoroughly, through the case management process. Perhaps the case manager is planning on seeing a man who is on life support; she needs to review his hospital records. The man's wife, authorized to sign for him, cannot meet the case manager at the hospital. The case manager may send the consent authorization form by mail or fax and have a signed copy with her when she visits the hospital.

Perhaps the patient is in an intensive care unit. She has spoken with the doctor and the family; both parties think case management is a great idea. The case manager arrives at the ICU and a family member says, "Oh, we have an attorney. You'll have to show this to him." Unable to speak to the patient without the counsel's permission, the case manager is back to square one. To prevent this, the case manager will want to ascertain whether or not the patient is represented by an attorney. However, she will want to be careful not to put herself in the position of inadvertently "suggesting" that the patient needs an attorney. Instead of saying, "Do you have an attorney? I need to know because I will need his or her authorization as well," the case manager can call, explain her role, mention the use of a consent authorization that will enable her to speak to the doctor, and ask as an "afterthought" if there is anyone else who the patient thinks she might need to contact. The patient may retort, "Well, my lawyer already told me that I can't sign anything, so you'll have to talk to her." In this way, without asking directly, the case manager finds out an attorney is involved.

In some cases, a consent form is not critical but is used to give the patient confidence. When a case manager gets a referral from an employer group or an insurance carrier and the patient's diagnosis is AIDS, a consent form offers the patient an assurance of confidentiality. (There is extra anxiety in the case of a diagnosis of AIDS, and justifiably so, as insurers and companies have been known to cut benefits or employment for individuals with AIDS.) In response to this growing concern, some states have imposed additional mandates to ensure the confidentiality of HIV/AIDS status. I send a consent form with a brochure on my services and a note requesting the patient's signature so I can speak to the doctor, the therapist, and others, to help them work with the patient. With such a form, there is a record that a case manager is working in tandem with the patient and the doctor and that sensitive patient information will not be disclosed to a boss or an insurance representative.

Many case managers have difficulty with consent forms, feeling that as soon as they have to ask for a signature the patient will respond negatively. It is true that many people are intimidated by anything requiring their signature. What I basically do is follow rules of full disclosure, explaining the authorization and telling the patient that it is good for his or her protection and for my protection. Often case managers will call a doctor on the telephone for details of a treatment plan. Sometimes broader background must be gleaned from patient records, or assistance is needed on an emergency basis. How can a case move forward if the patient must be contacted for each and every release? I tell each patient that the document is a simple statement showing that he or she is aware of what is going on, that it is similar to the form signed upon entering the hospital or when a doctor wants to forward patient records to someone else for review. I also explain that my ability to help might be severely compromised without the authorization. When the patient understands all this, consent is customarily given readily.

In her comments regarding consent and disclosure issues, Scheutzow outlines the process of informed consent:

- Give the information verbally and in writing.
- Offer an opportunity for questions and answers to clarify patient understanding.
- Witness the signing of the consent form and retain the current consent in case management records.
- Recognize the two legal standards for disclosure: Disclose the information that a reasonable medical practitioner would disclose under

the same or similar circumstances, and disclose all the background needed to make the decision-making process meaningful.

When there is a question of a patient's competency (legal judgment rendered by a court after hearing evidence) or capacity (the patient's functional ability to understand the diagnosis, treatment, risks, and alternatives), the case manager should involve family members in the case management plan and also recommend that they seek legal help for purposes of establishing power of attorney, durable power of attorney, or guardianship.

MEDICAL RECORDS

Case management files are considered medical records and consequently must be retained for the period of time mandated by state and federal statutes. In most states, this period is five years or the period of time in which lawsuits may be filed, whichever is longer. Children's medical records must be kept until the children reach legal age, as defined by the state.

THE RIGHT TO KNOW VERSUS THE NEED TO KNOW

When case managers work directly with employer groups, especially self-funded employer groups, the issue of an employer's right to know (as opposed to need to know) comes to the forefront. Involved with the bigger, more expensive cases, charged with tracking a company's stop-loss ceiling, on facing an employer who can, if it is dedicated to the search and illegally sorts through reams of paperwork, identify a particular employee by matching a benefit claim to the corporate checkbook register, case managers find that their fiduciary relationship with patients can be compromised. (A fiduciary relationship is the legal relationship of confidentiality that exists when one person relies on another, as in the case manager–patient relationship.)

Despite the risks of a lawsuit, an employer will ask for specific information on a patient. Citing pending layoff, promotion, or management decisions that need to be made or the responsibility to protect dollars now that it self-funds and administers its health package, the employer might assert that it has the right to know which employee is costing the most. A CEO might say, "Before I can approve that home care alternative, I need to know who we're talking about here."

It is true that the boss does need to have a broad perspective on employee problems, but the "who" must be protected to the greatest extent possible. Without naming an employee or dependent, the case manager can respond in generalities. Cost-benefit analyses and other reports can give credible but not identifiable narrative data. John, the 45-year-old drill bit specialist who works in the machine shop, becomes a "middle-aged man." Further, the case manager can explain to the employer that it is in the employer's best interests *not* to know exactly who John is in the event of an unlawful discharge or workers' compensation lawsuit.

DISCLOSURE ISSUES

Issues of disclosure and confidentiality are not as clear-cut as they once were. Susan O. Scheutzow noted how changes in the ways in which society, the government, and the courts perceive these issues impact on a case manager's responsibilities and liabilities. At "Confidentiality: How a Case Manager Can Protect It," a session given at ICMA's 1993 Medical Case Management Conference, she included these comments in her conference materials:

> The issue of disclosure of information includes mandatory reporting of information to the government, disclosure of information to protect third parties such as when there is a duty to warn third parties about the illness of a patient, and disclosure of information pursuant to judicial or quasi-judicial process. Information may be required to be released in these instances even if there is otherwise a general legal requirement to keep information confidential.
> Generally there has been a trend to increase mandatory disclosure of information. The physician-patient privilege, which generally came into being in many states over 100 years ago and protected confidential communications from release pursuant to judicial process, is largely inadequate today. The physician-patient privilege generally is limited to communications made to physicians. With the proliferation of licensed health care professionals rendering care in today's health care system the physician-patient privilege is inadequate to protect health care communications.
> The laws requiring confidentiality and requiring disclosure of medical records are on a collision course for health care providers as providers are increasingly required to release information to comply with the law yet are subject to liability for errors in making such disclosure.[3]

Given this environment, it is still the case manager's responsibility to protect the rights of the patients she is working with by keeping medical (as well as financial and emotional) information confidential unless required by law to disclose it. In questionable instances, case managers should consult legal counsel for advice.

ADEQUATE INFORMATION

Because they may be held legally responsible for their decisions, it is important that case managers make certain the information they use is accurate and adequate. Second-hand information, unless it comes from a reliable source, might not be good enough. Long-distance telephonic case management, conducted without on-site or in-person visits, can be dangerous if an element of the treatment plan is overlooked. In all cases, the case manager should document decisions, medical sources, transitions from one care facility to another, and so on, to support the selected case management plan.

CONTRACTS AND LETTERS OF AGREEMENT

Case managers working in-house for insurance carriers, HMOs, TPAs, and so on, will not have to consider this question, but those working independently as case management consultants should review the use of case management service contracts. As Thomas K. Hyatt pointed out in a presentation titled "Contracting for Case Management Services" given at the 1993 Medical Case Management Conference, the decision whether to utilize a formal business contract must be based on legal and practical considerations and the case manager's working relationship with the client. How frequently are cases referred by this payer or client? What is the range of services the client is expecting and how much responsibility will the case manager have?

If a written contract or letter of agreement is used, Hyatt recommends that it include the following:

- A "due diligence" section. Basically, this section includes the practices, conduct norms, documentation, and so on, that both parties can reasonably expect from each other. As an example, the payer will expect the case manager to document his or her credentials and qualifications. The case manager will expect to receive the benefit plan (summary plan description) and all amendments applicable to the beneficiary. The case manager should review the insurance contract for a statement giving the insurer the authority to perform case management and to delegate this function to an outside entity.
- Evidence of the payer's professional liability insurance. Does the insurance cover case management services and for how much?
- Specific terms, if any, between the payer and a TPA or any TPA terms for case management intervention.
- Written releases allowing the case manager access to confidential medical information.
- Any applicable medical protocols.
- The payment structure.
- A clear delineation of the duties of the payer and the case manager.

- Confidentiality protection.
- Physician and patient consent.
- Professional liability insurance protection.
- Compliance with laws.

A case manager's ability to negotiate with a large payer might depend on her specialty, the needs of the payer, and a host of business circumstances, Hyatt suggests. In my mind, the most important requisite for negotiating is that the case manager adopt the firm position that she is a health care professional working to achieve a positive outcome for all parties. This stance enables the case manager to pursue the contract she deserves and to turn away contracts that are inadequate.

In his session materials, Hyatt also notes that case managers should read carefully any prepared written agreements presented by a payer and should not sign anything they do not fully understand. It is appropriate to line through any provisions that are unacceptable even if the agreement is subsequently signed and returned to the payer. If a payer rejects the need for a written agreement, Hyatt says, the case manager should consider developing a letter stating her understanding of the business terms and the case manager–payer relationship, including the case manager's duties, the payer's duties, compensation (per hour, per day), and the payment schedule (payment within 30 days of receipt of the case manager's invoice), insurance coverage and indemnification (e.g., a "hold harmless" clause to protect the case manager from claims, liabilities, damages, etc.), and the length of the term for case management services (for one particular case, a group of cases for five years, etc.).[4] (See Appendix 5-A for the sample written agreement that Hyatt included in his presentation handouts.)

LEGAL ISSUES IN CASE MANAGEMENT

In her main session comments at the 1993 Medical Case Management Conference, Alice G. Gosfield noted, "Case managers are at the fulcrum of where the care management aspect of the health care delivery system currently is focused, and a great deal of what you do is going to get much more scrutiny as years go by. The concept of liability and accountability for the outcomes of care is not just going to be competitive but is increasingly going to be based on whether patients are harmed as a result of the choices that are made in this changing system." This means that case managers will not only need to document "controlled costs with appropriate outcomes demonstrated on the basis of data" but also that a case manager's recommendations for care might have to stand up in court.

Following is an overview of case management and the law. The basis of this section is a reference document compiled by Jeanne Boling and titled "Legal Issues in Case Management." This document is revised regularly to keep it current, and it has been incorporated into "Case Management Practice," the core curriculum for the CCM credentialing process offered by the Foundation for Rehabilitation Certification, Education and Research. In her brief, Boling succinctly captured the range of diverse elements that may legally impact on a case manager's practice.

The first focus is on a case manager's competence, noting that it must be and will be measured against accepted standards of care in the industry. Among the existing formal standards of care pertinent to case managers are those developed by the Association of Rehabilitation Nurses, the National Association for Social Work, the National Association of Rehabilitation Professionals in the Private Sector, The National Association of Geriatric Care Managers, the National Institute on Community Based Long Term Care, the American Nurses Association, and the Steering Committee of the National Case Management Task Force (incorporated into the CCM credentialing process), as well as nurse practice acts developed by individual states. Also appropriate are the Guidelines for Health Benefits Administration (a joint effort of the American Hospital Association, American Medical Association, American Managed Care and Review Association, Blue Cross and Blue Shield Association, and Health Insurance Association of America), the Care Maps™ developed by The Center for Case Management, located in South Natick, Massachusetts, and the clinical practice guidelines being created by the Agency for Health Care Policy and Research (see Chapter 7). Currently relevant certifications available to case managers include the Certified Case Manager (CCM), Advanced Competency Continuity of Care (ACCC), Certified Rehabilitation Registered Nurse (CRRN), Certified Insurance Rehabilitation Specialist (CIRS), Occupational Health Nurse (OHN), and Certified Rehabilitation Counselor (CRC).

Beyond these protocols and certifications are the basic educational curricula and degrees for the various health care professions, continuing education credits, and the more informal standards of care "set" by peers in case management practice and other health care professionals. Taken together, such standards will be used as criteria to ascertain whether a case manager has the background and experience to practice case management. From a legal standpoint, what are the questions of liability that may arise?

Case managers may be held liable for negligence in the form of malpractice. Malpractice includes any professional person's wrongful conduct, improper discharge of professional duties, or failure to meet standards of care that results in harm or undue costs to another person. There are a few relevant cases that help illustrate the implications for case managers regarding liability and malpractice. Marilou M. King, the executive vice president and CEO of the National Health Lawyers Association based in Washington, D.C., has noted that while some of these cases do not "involve the activity of case management per se, they do involve the activity of utilization management generally, thus they are instructive for case managers."[5]

Discharge

The first four cases reviewed here concern issues that arise with regard to patient discharge. The first, *Wickline v. State of California* (1986, 1987), is one of the more widely known cases with elements pertinent to case management practice. Alice Gosfield summarized the basic message of the *Wickline* decision as follows: Anyone can be held liable for damages or harm to a patient when (1) services being provided in the utilization management environment are not in accordance with standards of care, (2) the attending physicians disagree with the utilization management function, or (3) appeals on a medical decision are not pursued or are arbitrarily ignored or denied.[6] For case managers in particular, these implications follow:

- Case management is a reasonable activity.
- Case managers can be held accountable when something bad happens to the patient.
- Case managers must meet a reasonable standard of care.
- Case managers must not conduct their activities in a way that corrupts medical judgment.
- Case managers must act within the scope of their licensure and their own competence and education.
- The case manager's role is as a consultant to clients and physicians (who make the final medical decision).
- Case managers should not practice medicine and should not interfere with the doctor-patient relationship.
- Alternative treatment plans should be placed in writing as much as possible and be signed off on by the physician.

In light of the legal ramifications and consequences, case managers must act on complete information. If contradictory information exists, it is the case manager's responsibility to determine what is true. The case manager should consider carefully whether sufficient information can be gathered over the phone or whether an in-person meeting is necessary. At a minimum, the case manager should work from a claims history and all available medical records, and the case management plan should be based on data that a competent professional in the case management role would deem sufficient for clinical decision-making purposes.

Because they may be held responsible for the patient's care, case managers should not comply with unreasonable third-party payer limits without written protest. Case managers are patient advocates foremost and the courts demand that a patient's interests come first. Also, if employees make treatment decisions based on payment mechanisms or a fear of denial rather than on what is appropriate for the patient, the company may not be protected.

Protection against liability claims when dissent from a treatment plan exists requires that the case management review process be conducted by adequately qualified reviewers using valid medical criteria and include a thorough review of medical records and a discussion with the treatment team. If discharge is called for, the review should incorporate an assessment of the risk of discharge.

Another high-profile case with discharge issues at its center is *Wilson v. Blue Cross of Southern California and Blue Cross Blue Shield of Alabama and Western Medical Review* (1990). This case involved the premature discharge of a patient from a psychiatric hospital. At the time of discharge, the physician had written in his notes that the patient was discharged on the recommendation of the utilization review company. The patient went home and committed suicide. The family did not sue the physician or the hospital; they sued the insurer and the utilization review company that had suggested the discharge. In court, the insurer and utilization review firm held that they were not responsible for the decision to discharge the patient and that the attending physician was responsible for making his own decisions and, if at all concerned, should have appealed the decision for discharge. The jury felt that the insurer violated three of the four elements of the case, and only held back on finding the insurer guilty of a "bad faith denial of claims." Because all four elements against the insurer did not hold up in court, the insurer was not held liable in this particular case. (Alice Gosfield commented, "Some in the industry now say, 'Oh good, we can't be held liable.' My view is that this was a squeaker and somebody better start paying attention to the processes by which these judgments are going to be made.")[7]

As for the implications for case managers, there are two. First, case managers should check benefit plan contract language. Does it include coverage for case management? Has the insured authorized case management? If not, the case management entity can be charged with interfering with the insured's insurance contract and perhaps with liability for any harm resulting from that interference. Secondly, it is critical that a case manager's treatment plan have the approval of the treating physician and the patient or family.

Two additional cases of record with lessons for case managers are *Hughes v. Blue Cross of Northern California* (1989) and *Linthicum v. Nationwide Life Insurance Company* (1986). In *Hughes*, as noted by Marilou King, an appeals court upheld a trial court's award of $700,000 in damages, finding that there was a "defective determination of medical necessity because only a part of the beneficiary's medical records were reviewed by the utilization reviewer." This case also contained some "bad faith" implications for case managers. When a case management plan denies a patient access to the benefits of an insurance contract, it is usually the result of intentional and outrageous conduct, but to avoid any problem in this area, a case manager should thoroughly review and/or discuss contractual obligations with the insurer, should formulate a recovery plan or plan of care in concert with the treating physician and patient, and should ensure that it is satisfactory to them.

In *Linthicum*, the insurer was held liable for failing to consult the treating physician. The implications for case managers are as follows: All medical records must be reviewed and reflected in case management reports and recommendations, and a case manager must consult the treating physician. Consult the treating physician? Sounds like very basic advice, but someone somewhere along the line at Nationwide forgot and was held accountable.

Negligent Referral

The next legal area to be considered is negligent referral. When referring a patient to a facility or provider, case managers have a responsibility to act in good faith in the best interest of the patient, investigate the competency and qualifications of the facility or provider, and use reasonable care in making the referral. The more choices a case manager offers the patient or physician, the less her risk of being held liable for that referral.

When considering a practitioner or facility for referral, a case manager should examine current licensure and accreditation, the outcomes of cases similar to the one under consideration for referral, billing practices, insurance coverage, and the records of any previous pertinent malpractice judgments. (The National Practitioner Data Bank in Camarillo, California, 1 800 767-6732, retains information on all malpractice judgments and settlements, catalogued by practitioner and institution. Although there is a recommendation currently under consideration to open these records to all inquiries, only those nurses and physicians with cases on file and hospitals can retrieve their own data. Thus, an independent case manager would have trouble checking a physician's record through the data bank.)

Case managers should document their continuous inquiry into the credentials and performance of the practitioners and facilities to which they refer patients, offer the patients and families a choice of practitioners and facilities, and always follow up with patients who are referred to review their status and response. Further, a case manager should disclose any problems to the patient and physician for their informed consent and obtain the patient's and physician's consent in writing, keeping it on file in a case management report.

Relevant case law citations include the nationally publicized case of *Bergalis v. CIGNA Dental Health Plan* (1991). Kimberly Bergalis of Florida sued her dentist for allegedly infecting her with the AIDS virus and also sued CIGNA for $20 million on the basis of a negligent referral to this particular dentist. According to Marilou King, "The claim is not that CIGNA knew the dentist had AIDS but that CIGNA should have undertaken a reasonable investigation to discover if the dentist to whom CIGNA referred patients had a disease that could be communicated like AIDS."[8]

Another case, *Moshe v. Rush–Presbyterian St. Luke's Hospital* (1990), alerts case managers to the fact that utilization review and case management activities may be interpreted as inhibiting the ability of physicians to render care. Therefore, in making a referral, a case manager must use a reasonable process for determining that the referral is in the patient's best interest, give complete referral instructions, and, if the agency or facility is providing questionable levels of care, take corrective action immediately.

This issue of access to care is also seen in *Nazay v. Miller*, a 1991 Pennsylvania case, where the original court ruling supported a retiree who did not comply with PreCert/UR requirements and was subsequently penalized for noncompliance by the plan. A subsequent ruling reversed that decision. Even in a cost-containment environment, denial of access to care is a very sensitive issue. A case management plan should always be proactive and in the patient's best interests.

LEGISLATION

In addition to tracking case management protocols and practice guidelines, case managers need to monitor local and national legislative and regulatory changes and statutes to make certain their practice is in line with current regulations. This task can appear daunting. Major pieces of pertinent legislation include the following:

The Employee Retirement Income Security Act (ERISA) of 1974 governs the majority of nongovernmental employee benefit plans. It exempts companies that self-insure from meeting the same minimum benefit regulations that govern insurance companies.

The Tax Equity and Fiscal Responsibility Act (TEFRA) of 1982 amended the Social Security Act and made Medicare secondary to employer group health plans for active employees 65 to 69 years old and their spouses in the same age group. It also revised the Age Discrimination in Employment Act (ADEA) of 1967 by requiring employers to offer active employees age 65 to 69 and their spouses the same health benefits as those made available to younger employees.

As a result of the Social Security Amendments of 1983 (Title IX), Medicare reimbursement shifted from reasonable costs to DRGs (diagnosis-related groups). The amendments also clarified professional review organization (PRO) functions.

The Consolidated Omnibus Budget Reconciliation Act (COBRA) of 1986 eliminated the age cap of 70; made the employer's plan the primary payer for all active, Medicare-eligible employees and their spouses regardless of age; mandated the extension of medical plans after termination from a job and after a person becomes ineligible under medical coverage; required employers with health care plans to provide health care coverage to former employees, divorced or widowed spouses of employees, and former dependent children of employees at group rates over a fixed amount of time.

The Omnibus Budget Reconciliation Act (OBRA, or, *oh boy,* regulations *a*gain, with a nod to Alice Gosfield) of 1986 made private employer health plans primary and Medicare secondary for claimants who were permanently disabled and were covered dependents under a working spouse's health plan or for claimants who returned to active employment.

The Health Care Quality Improvement Act (HCQIA) of 1986 established the National Practitioner Data Bank mentioned earlier.

The short-lived Medicare Catastrophic Coverage Act (MCCA) of 1988, which was repealed in 1989, mandated the largest expansion of Medicare since its introduction in 1965: a cap of $1,370 for personal expenses for physicians' services; elimination of all cost sharing for inpatient hospital care after the deductible; and revisions in skilled nursing, home health, and respite care benefits.

AIDS-related legislation passed in 1988 by Congress provided funds for research, education, HIV testing, and home health demonstration projects.

The Omnibus Budget Reconciliation Act (OBRA) of 1989 and 1990 included updates to HCQIA and required states to extend Medicaid coverage to all pregnant women and children up to age six with family incomes less than 133 percent of the federal poverty level.

The Agency for Health Care Policy and Research (AHCPR) was created as a result of OBRA of 1989. The agency has recently developed the Office for Forum on Quality and Effectiveness to publish and disseminate national clinical practice guidelines.

The Americans with Disabilities Act (ADA) of 1992 required that employers not prevent employees from returning to work even if they can no longer perform 100 percent of their jobs.

The Civilian Health and Medical Program of the Uniformed Services (CHAMPUS) gives all active and retired military personnel and dependents access to treatment at any Department of Defense medical facility. Retired military personnel, dependents, and dependents of deceased personnel are compensated by CHAMPUS if they are not eligible for Medicare.

The Federal Employees Health Benefits Program (FEHBP) provides health insurance coverage for federal government employees. The coverage is voluntary and includes variable benefit and premium levels and a choice of competing health plans.

DAY-TO-DAY PRACTICES

There are a number of areas in case management practice where common sense and thinking ahead will help case managers prepare for liability claims (see also Appendix 5-B). As mentioned throughout this handbook, discussions and decisions regarding the case management treatment plan should be documented. If a patient, family member, or physician resents or is unhappy with case management intervention, this too should be documented, along with memos on steps taken to resolve any concerns or problems. Routine patient and provider satisfaction surveys will help monitor quality assurance and serve as an indicator of responsiveness to patient needs (see Chapter 7).

In practice, follow the agreed treatment plan. Noncompliance with the plan can be construed as mismanagement. In any publicity or marketing efforts, avoid puffery or claims that case management guarantees better outcomes or cost containment. In contract making, be very cautious of any type of incentive compensation arrangement with a payer or provider. Again, remember that case management is administrative in nature (except in rural areas, where a nurse–case manager might provide hands-on care because she is the only medical practitioner in town). Consequently, case managers should not insinuate that they are in any way determining the medical treatment plan.

Case managers should keep suspicions, conjectures, and allegations out of their correspondence and reports; these documents can be subpoenaed. A situation can be objectively covered in a report without accusation and without giving legal weight to either side in court. It is enough to record a patient's verbalized wish to return to work, and the missed job interviews as well, letting the judge decide the motivations behind the actions. Similarly, a case management report can mention that a patient has stated his or her benefit payments have been significantly delayed, causing hardship; that the patient has been directed to contact a claims examiner; and that the case manager has undertaken to relay this information to the claims examiner—end of story. Case managers should consider what might happen if "the other side" sees the report.

Further, case managers may be requested by either party in a court case to appear as witnesses. (While nurses are rarely called, certified rehabilitation counselors and vocational counselors can and do serve as witnesses in court.) If requested to appear in court, a case manager should consult with the client and a lawyer.

To defend her own interests, a case manager needs to remain involved in a case. If taken off a case ("We don't need you now; the home health company will take care of it"), the case manager should document the situation in an accurate and objective manner. The report might include language such as this: "Despite our suggestions that we continue to monitor this case actively and despite our concern for the patient, which was communicated to our client, the client has decided to end case management involvement in this case." Further, the case manager should file copies of the written notices to the patient, the medical provider, and all other members of the treatment team informing them that she is no longer involved at the client's request, not because the case manager thinks there is no need. The case manager should also make certain the patient knows whom to contact—the physician, therapist, claims examiner, and so on—if a problem arises.

ETHICAL CONSIDERATIONS

Closely connected with questions of legality are questions of ethics or morality. It is not illegal for a case manager to accept a finder's fee from a durable medical equipment supplier, but neither is it ethical. There is no law prohibiting a case manager from taking the season football ticket from a rehabilitation center contact, but it does cloud the objectivity of the relationship. Whether self-employed or working in a health care setting or insurance firm, case managers have to make clear decisions regarding their ethical standing.

Money is shifting to case management. Providers understand the purchase power case managers wield and their ability to refer to one facility over another. It is an accepted marketing strategy in the medical industry for providers and pharmaceutical houses to wine and dine physicians and others who might recommend their institutions or products. Given the relative newness of case management and its professionals (e.g., nurses just entering the field from hospital settings), such perks are unexpected and they look very good. To avoid the criticism that case managers have become just another part of the "fat" medical bureaucracy (and, even more important, to avoid the possibility of litigation), case managers must rely on their inner conscience to remain free from associations where objectivity can be questioned.

There are ethical dilemmas on the patient side of case management as well. John appears fit, is begging to return to work, and has mentioned his readiness to his employer, who is eager to have him back in the machine shop at his old station—the only job station that is available to him at this time. However, John has not been able to control a hand tremor completely, which will jeopardize his safety at the drill. Does the case manager fudge her report on his capabilities and release him to work?

Jane, while recuperating from a skin graft, has returned to a drug habit she had kicked three years ago. Her employer and family are unaware of the problem. Does the case manager keep this "secret" to herself or take steps to enroll Jane in a drug rehabilitation program?

Mary has made it clear to her family and the case manager that she does not want her life prolonged by any artificial means under any circumstances. The treating physician has authorized the insertion of a feeding tube and family members are reluctant to challenge the MD's authority. Does the case manager raise the issue or let it pass?

Case managers have access to a great deal of information. What will be the decision regarding the disclosure of someone's substance abuse or HIV status when the choice involves either compromising one's principles or losing a client?

Case managers sometimes stumble across legal or ethical problems. Among those things a case manager has an ethical responsibility to report are patients who are potentially or habitually dependent on their medication, who are overmedicated or overtreated by multiple physicians, or who are lying to their physicians regarding compliance. If a patient has not been receiving the treatment that claims are filed for, if an occupational therapist is treating a patient outside practice guidelines, or if a physician inappropriately refers a patient to a center he or she has a financial interest in, the circumstances should be reported to the plan administrator, the treating physician, or a peer review organization. A case manager must develop a knowledge of professional ethics, standards of practice, and the appropriate code of behavior and report through proper channels whatever is intolerable or fraudulent or abusive in hospital or private practice.

A case manager needs a network of people to bounce around ideas on ethical challenges. Perhaps there is an ethicist at a local college or other case managers not in direct competition who can act as sounding boards. The unexpected case will arrive, and case managers need resources for ethical counseling. In addition to books such as Kenneth Blanchard and Norman Vincent Peale's *The Power of Ethical Management*, there are magazine and newspaper columns that address the issues of professional ethics. John D. Banja is a medical ethicist specializing in disability concerns and an associate professor of rehabilitation medicine at Emory University School of Medicine. His column "Ethics" appears regularly in ICMA's magazine *The Case Manager*. Books that are helpful in exploring ethical issues include *Ethics on Call* (Nancy Dubler and David Nimmons, Vintage, 1992), *The Crisis in Health Care: Ethical Issues* (edited by Nancy F. McKenzie, Meridian, 1990), *Ethics and Law in Nursing* (K. Fenner, Van Nostrand, 1980), *Ethics at the Bedside* (M. Fowler and J. Levine-Ariff, Lippincott, 1987), *Tough Decisions: A Casebook in Medical Ethics* (John M. Freeman and Kevin McDonnell, Oxford University Press, 1987), and *Ethical Issues in Health Care* (M. Froner, Mosby, 1981).

GETTING LEGAL INFORMATION

No case manager has to be a lawyer, but it is important to be current regarding case management professional guidelines. There are conferences specifically for case managers, training seminars, a host of national conferences relevant to case management, and magazine coverage of pertinent issues. *The Case Manager*, for instance, includes a column written by attorney Marilou K. King, who has case management law expertise. Other publications, such as the *Wall Street Journal, Rehabilitation Nursing Journal, Caring,* and the *American Journal of Nursing,* also carry articles on medicolegal issues.

Unfortunately, much of the law that will eventually affect case management practice is currently in the process of creation. While waiting for a clear code of conduct, case managers should do the following:

- Work within the guidelines that already govern case management practice settings.
- Develop a risk-management mentality. ("How do I protect myself, my company, and my patients against lack of knowledge?")
- Act according to their best judgment and keep apprised of changes in the profession. ("Is this how another prudent person in this profession would act in similar circumstances?")
- Use common sense and instinct. (If something does not feel right, it probably is not. Network and ask questions of peers.)

- Get a lawyer who is knowledgeable about case management.
- Document case management activities and decisions in an objective manner.
- Purchase professional liability insurance in the form of a personal or corporate policy.

For more extensive coverage of legal issues in case management, consider attending "Case Management Practice," a two-day seminar sponsored by the Foundation for Rehabilitation Certification, Education and Research (708 818-1967).

NOTES

1. Jeanne Boling, "Legal Issues in Case Management," in *Managing Case Management Seminar Manual* (Little Rock, Ark.: Individual Case Management Association, 1991), 183.
2. Jeanne Boling, "Legal Issues in Case Management," prepared for the Individual Case Management Association, January 1994. (The material was adapted from "Confidentiality: An Issue CMs Must Understand," handouts developed by Susan Scheutzow for a presentation at ICMA's Medical Case Management Conference IV in Orlando, 1992.)
3. Susan O. Scheutzow, "Confidentiality: How a Case Manager Can Protect It," in *Medical Case Management Conference V Manual* (Little Rock, Ark.: Individual Case Management Association, 1993), 323.
4. Thomas K. Hyatt, "Contracting for Case Management Services," in *Medical Case Management Conference V Manual*, 395–398.
5. Marilou M. King, "Liability for Negligence," in *Legal and Risk Management Issues in Case Management Seminar Manual* (Little Rock, Ark.: Individual Case Management Association, 1991), 87.
6. Alice G. Gosfield, "Clinical Practice Guidelines and Managed Competition: Legal Implications for Case Managers," prepared for the Individual Case Management Association Medical Case Management Conference V, Orlando, Florida, September 1993.
7. Ibid.
8. King, "Liability for Negligence."

Written Agreement: Some Typical Provisions

Caveat: While these provisions have been prepared by a professional attorney, they should not be used as a substitute for legal counseling in specific situations. Readers should not act upon the information contained herein without professional guidance.

1. *Recitals.*

This Agreement is entered into by and between _____ (Payer), a _____ corporation and _____ (Case Manager), an individual residing in _____.

Whereas Payer has entered into an agreement with one or more employee health benefit plans (the Plan) and thereunder has agreed to provide case management services to beneficiaries of those plans; and

Whereas Case Manager is a registered nurse licensed in _____ _____ and certified by _____, who desires to perform case management services to beneficiaries of the Plan, as appropriate;

Now, therefore, for adequate consideration, the receipt and sufficiency of which are hereby acknowledged, the parties agree as follows:

2. *Duties of Payer.*

(a) Payer authorizes Case Manager to perform services defined in Section 3 for beneficiaries referred by Payer to Case Manager pursuant to _____.

(b) Payer shall provide to Case Manager current, accurate and complete benefit plan information pertinent to beneficiary and shall cooperate with Case Manager in explaining terms of such benefit plans and in supplying Case Manager with any information.

(c) Payer shall provide to Case Manager all necessary waivers of confidentiality for release of medical information which it warrants are valid for beneficiary.

(d) Payer represents and warrants that plan documents are sufficient to authorize the performance of the case management services to be performed by Case Manager pursuant to this Agreement.

(e) Payer represents and warrants that it shall maintain professional and general liability insurance coverage in the amount of _____, which shall provide primary coverage for any claims arising from the acts of Payer pursuant to its agreement with the Plan and this Agreement.

(f) Payer represents and warrants that it shall make and communicate to beneficiary all benefit determinations regarding beneficiary's health insurance coverage and that Case Manager's reports and recommendations shall be advisory to Payer and may form the basis, in whole or in part, of Payer's benefit determinations. Case Manager shall have no responsibility to make or communicate benefit determinations.

(g) Payer represents and warrants that as part of its benefit determination program it has in place an appeals process that complies with the Guidelines for Health Benefits Administration published by _____ _____.

3. *Duties of Case Manager.*

(a) Case Manager shall receive referral of beneficiary by Payer pursuant to _____.

(b) Case Manager will review beneficiary's coverage as supplied by Payer and necessary waivers of confidentiality. If this information is incomplete or inadequate, Case Manager shall contact Payer and shall not take any further actions until such information is complete and adequate.

(c) Case Manager will obtain pertinent medical information from beneficiary, facility or primary or admitting physician(s) as necessary and shall devise an alternative plan of treatment for beneficiary. Case Manager shall provide beneficiary and physician(s) with alternative plan of treatment and thoroughly discuss plan with same. If physician(s) and beneficiary competently agree with the alternative plan of treatment, Case Manager will obtain their written consent thereto. Thereafter, Case Manager will contact providers of such alternative treatment and secure rates.

(d) If agreeable to beneficiary and physician(s), Case Manager shall facilitate beneficiary's access to alternative treatment. Case Manager shall report in writing to Payer within _____ business days its recommenda-tions and outcome with originals of all written consents by beneficiary and physician(s).

(e) If not agreeable to beneficiary and physician(s), Case Manager shall report in writing within _____ business days to Payer its recom-mendations and outcome. Thereafter Case Manager's responsibilities with regard to said beneficiary shall end.

(f) Case Manager represents and warrants that it shall maintain pro-fessional liability insurance coverage in the amount of _____, which shall provide primary coverage for any claims arising from the acts of Case Manager pursuant to this Agreement.

4. *Compensation.*

For the duties performed by Case Manager under this Agreement,

(a) Payer agrees to compensate Case Manager at a rate of $_____ per hour, which shall include travel time as necessary.

(b) Payer shall pay Case Manager within thirty (30) days of its re-ceipt of invoice from Case Manager.

(c) [Penalty for late payment.]

(d) [Additional fees for expenses of Case Manager such as supplies and xeroxing.]

5. *Relationship of Parties.*

Payer and Case Manager mutually agree that there shall be no rela-tionship between them other than an independent contractor relation-ship, and nothing herein shall be construed to create a principal-agent, employment or partnership relationship. Payer shall neither have nor ex-ercise any control or direction over the methods by which Case Manager performs its duties under this Agreement. Case Manager recognizes that Payer shall not pay or withhold on behalf of Case Manager any sums for income tax, unemployment insurance, social security or any other with-holding requirement of any law.

6. *Indemnification.*

(a) Payer agrees to indemnify Case Manager and hold it harmless from and against any and all claims, losses, liabilities, suits, damages and expenses incurred by Case Manager, including court costs and attorney's fees, to the extent such claims, losses, liabilities, suits, damages, and ex-penses arise out of any acts or omissions of Payer, its officers, agents or employees, or arising from any breach or default on the part of Payer in the performance of its duties under this Agreement or under the Plan.

(b) [Only if Case Manager has to, insert corresponding indemnifica-tion of Payer by Case Manager.]

7. *Term and Termination.*

This Agreement shall commence on ____(effective date)____ and continue for a term of one year. Thereafter, this Agreement shall automatically renew each year for successive one-year terms. Either party may terminate this Agreement without cause upon _____ days prior written notice to the other. In the event Case Manager is in the process of performing services hereunder for referred beneficiaries at the time of termination, Case Manager shall complete such performance even if to do so extends past the date of termination. The right of Case Manager to be paid for services already performed hereunder shall continue past the date of termination of this Agreement.

8. *Miscellaneous.*
  (a) Choice of law/venue;
  (b) Assignment;
  (c) Compliance with applicable laws;
  (d) Entire agreement/amendment; and
  (d) Other.

In witness whereof, the parties hereto have caused this Agreement to be executed on _____, 19_____.

Payer   Case Manager

Name: _____   Name: _____

Title: _____   Title: _____

Date: _____   Date: _____

_____
Source: Reprinted from *Medical Case Management Conference V Manual*, pp. 399–404, with permission of ICMA and Thomas K. Hyatt, Esq., © 1993.

Legal Issues in
Case Management Checklist

COMPETENCE OF THE CM

❑ 1. Are you properly trained and licensed? Have all qualifications been checked and documented?

❑ 2. Are you working toward the highest appropriate credential license or certification? Are you maintaining appropriate continuing education units to support the existing credential/license?

❑ 3. Are you first a client (claimant) advocate? Does your CM practice reflect this standard?

❑ 4. Are your case management plans created in concert with treating physician and client?

❑ 5. Are you familiar with your company's Job Description and Organization Chart and Policies and Procedures?

❑ 6. Is there anything in your current operations that seems inconsistent with existing formal standards for CM? (If so, discuss with your supervisor and/or legal counsel to resolve.)

CONSENT/DISCLOSURE

❑ 1. What consent form and written materials explaining case management services are you using? What is required? (Discuss any concerns about appropriate procedure or materials with supervisor and/or legal counsel.)

❑ 2. How do you explain CM services?
—by phone?
—by brochure?
❑ 3. Is your explanation consistent with staff, appropriate, and accurate?

CHANGE OF PROVIDER

❑ 1. Is your CM role empowering/facilitating to physicians and clients? Are you directing care or transfer without physician and/or client agreement? (If so, stop. Rethink and revise your role.)
❑ 2. Are you always acting within the scope of your licensure, your own competence and education? (If not, focus your CM practice on your area of competence and/or obtain additional supervision education or experience to support you in an expanded role.)
In reviewing referral policy procedures
❑ 3. How are practitioners/agencies/facilities evaluated?
❑ 4. Is a continuous inquiry into credentials and practice of the above documented?
❑ 5. Is patient/family offered a choice? Are pros and cons reviewed with family appropriately? Is referral in patient's best interest?
❑ 6. Have you followed up after referral to assure good care?
❑ 7. Are referrals with knowledge of benefit/funding structure?

CONFIDENTIALITY

❑ 1. Do you know state legislation relating to confidentiality and reporting concerns which apply to your CM practice?
Check Areas of Applicable Legislation
❑ Patient right of access to medical information
❑ Abuse/Neglect—Child and Elder
❑ Contagious/Occupational Disease
❑ Alcohol Treatment
❑ Chemical Abuse Treatment
❑ Mental Health Treatment
❑ AIDS/Sexually Related Disease
❑ Abortion
❑ 2. Do you know and/or have you reviewed and are you complying with your company's confidentiality policy? (Review and revise if necessary with legal counsel.)
❑ 3. Are you clear about the appropriate path of medical information in your office to assure confidentiality is protected?
❑ 4. Are discarded medical records shredded?
❑ 5. Are faxed medical records handled so that only seen by appropriate people?

❑   6. If CMs have field files away from office, are they locked at all times in car or home? Are they safe? Who might have access?

❑   7. If electronic records, are they accessed only by appropriate people?

❑   8. If information returns to employer, is it "sanitized" so individuals cannot be identified? Who sees this information?

❑   9. Are CM files retained according to state law then destroyed as medical records? (Adults 5–7 years; Children, to age of majority)

❑ 10. Is documentation concise yet complete for CM assessment, plan, implementation, follow-up, and outcome?

❑ 11. Do you know clearly how to handle medical information with employers, self-insureds, families of competent clients, others requesting access to your files?

CONTRACTING

❑   1. Are contracts or letters of agreement (LOA) in place for all major referring accounts?

❑   2. Are these contracts or LOA reviewed by legal counsel before signing?

❑   3. Do contracts clearly define
   • your duties
   • payer's duties
   • your compensation and time of compensation
   • insurance coverage and identification
   • term for performance

❑   4. Do agreements/contracts avoid incentive compensation (or waste) arrangements? (May cause appearance of over-emphasis on financial arrangements corrupting judgement regarding your primary responsibility of client advocacy.)

❑   5. Do the entities referring cases to you have the authority to authorize you to perform CM services? Do they *warrant* that fact?

❑   6. Do you understand the benefits and restrictions of different payer/reimbursement systems? (i.e. group health, indemnity HMO, PPO, reinsurance, COBRA, work comp, liability, Medicaid, Medicare, CHAMPUS, military, FELA, etc.)

CLIENT CARE NEGOTIATION

❑   1. Does state insurance law allow you to proceed with quality and cost negotiation for client care and services?

❑   2. Do quality issues always supersede cost issues?

❑   3. Are you operating in concert with the primary physician and client? With their understanding and support?

❑ 4. On major decisions, do you have client and physician written consent?

❑ 5. Have you documented referral data on all options being considered?

❑ 6. Is there a direct contract in place which establishes a rate? Is this non-negotiable?

❑ 7. How and to whom will the agreed upon quality and cost of care be documented? Monitored? Concluded?

CUSTOMER SERVICE/RISK MANAGEMENT

❑ 1. What's your company's **Incident Occurrence Reporting System**?

❑ 2. What is your CM quality assurance program? Do you keep routine patient satisfaction surveys as a quality assurance monitor?

❑ 3. Are all advertising/marketing materials and procedures fair and appropriate? (not overstated)

❑ 4. Is staff consistent in offering information describing CM services and CM company?

❑ 5. Are written materials and policy reviewed by legal counsel?

❑ 6. Who communicates benefits decisions? (Never communicate a payer benefits decision unless the payer indemnifies you for it.)

❑ 7. What are your corporate, personal liability, medical malpractice, and errors and omission policies? Do you review them regularly with the carriers?

❑ 8. Do you keep current by
  • reading journals, medical, and general literature?
  • attending seminars, conferences in your area of practice?
  • networking with peers on local, regional, and national level?

❑ 9. Are potential clients transported by CM? (Be sure liability insurance is in place to support.)

❑ 10. Is there a policy regarding staff protection when there is possible exposure to violent and high risk neighborhoods?

Source: Developed by Jeanne Boling, MSN, CRRN, CIRS, CCM for the "Case Management Practice" Seminar and used with the permission of the Foundation for Rehabilitation Certification, Education and Research, © 1994.

PART

II

Case Management Procedures

6

The Case Manager's Role in Making Case Management Part of the Medical Mainstream

If case management is truly to become an integral part of the medical mainstream, it is essential that new dialogues and heightened levels of communication be achieved. Case management is a person-to-person service, and open pathways must be laid for good interaction. More focused and conscious communication is needed between case managers and physicians, patients, families, payer sources, and related legal entities. To communicate effectively with each of these groups, case managers must recognize the obstacles to communication and strive to overcome them.

I think it is also important for case managers to make their letters, phone calls, and reports useful to the people they are addressing. It sounds simplistic, but it is appalling how many case managers totally ignore this basic rule of communication. Case management nurses in particular, more than rehab professionals or vocational counselors, tend to offer explicit medically oriented information to individuals who have not the foggiest idea of what the terms mean, that this blood gas is saturated or unsaturated, elevated or unelevated. The data may be of some use to another nurse or physician, but they are of no help to an adult child of a patient or to a claims examiner. This does not mean that a case manager should never attempt to produce a professional-looking report or should never use medical terminology when speaking with a claims examiner, but I would suggest combining the medical terminology with remarks to educate the referral source or recipient as to its meaning.

COMMUNICATING WITH PHYSICIANS

Working against positive communication between case managers and physicians are stereotypical judgments long held by each group about the other. In many ways, the stereotypes derive from the personality traits that cause an individual to become a physician or a case manager in the first place. Physicians tend to be results oriented, trained to "diagnose and treat," with only episodic patient involvement. Case managers, who usually come from traditional caretaker professions such as nursing and social work, maintain ongoing patient contact to perform their functions. Therefore, from the onset, case managers tend to view physicians as being less interested in their patients, whereas physicians tend to regard case managers as being overly involved.

A second obstacle to case manager–physician communication is the health care system itself. Churning with change, it is unwittingly pitting health care professional against health care professional. Despite a common cause (the well-being of patients), physicians and case managers are becoming adversaries in an eroding system where territorial struggles run rampant. With the bureaucracy collapsing around them, physicians view case managers with a wary eye, wondering, "Are they going to take my patients away?" or "Are they going to try to tell me how to treat my patient?"

In addition to issues of care control there are issues of cost control. Misperceptions and misunderstandings stem from the emergence in the 1980s of cost containment as a factor influencing health care delivery. Necessitated by advancing medical technologies with advancing price tags, a longer-lived population requiring care, and a shrinking pool of dollars funding both general and high-tech treatment, managed care practices have placed case managers and physicians in "uncharted territory." Neither group of professionals is accustomed to considering, much less negotiating, the cost of care.

Mistrusting them as "claims police" who deny patient access to needed care (and confusing them with "gatekeepers" who sometimes deny care based on computer software programs), some physicians perceive case managers as a threat to their medical judgment and their income. For example, when RNs began assuming clinician roles, establishing clinics in rural areas or in disciplines less attractive to MDs, the traditional physician-nurse relationship remained unchallenged. Nurses were making medical decisions and advising patients on their treatment plans, but there were no physicians in the picture. When case managers, on the other hand, began to be accepted by corporations, insurers, and the public and play an active and high-profile role in devising care plans, some MDs felt their medical opinions were being second-guessed.

Case managers can address both the stereotypes and the stresses of a shifting health care system by opening up positive dialogues with physicians. With a new case comes both the responsibility and opportunity to take a proactive stance and begin promoting better case manager–physician relations. The initial phone call is an example. It is important to communicate the purpose of that call—concern for the patient. Certain cases, by nature of their circumstances, may automatically cause a physician to be on guard regarding the case manager's intent. For example, a case manager may be called upon to intervene on behalf of a patient who has been in an acute care setting for three weeks and for whom new health care settings are being explored. The case manager needs to relay that there is a concern over the patient's limited policy and that she would like to work with the physician to make better use of the patient's benefit dollars so that funds will be available for a longer period of time. The communication is upfront and professional and the case manager's role is clearly defined.

This kind of direct communication should not be confused with taking a militant or overly aggressive attitude. Too often, case managers starting out mistakenly believe that in speaking with physicians they need to validate their role—by emphasizing that they are representatives of a large insurance company, for instance. However, they soon learn that, instead of causing physicians to acquiesce, this approach alienates them. The more secure case managers are in their role, whether speaking with physicians, hospital discharge planners, social workers, or patients, the better able they are to convey their objectives and all necessary information.

Because of the changing working relationship between case managers (nurses, social workers, and counselors) and physicians, the transition to full collaboration is often awkward. Involved are differences in orientation, training, spheres of influence, and recognition of each group's expertise. Generally, society conceives of physicians as being at the apex of medicine. Buying into this mythical pyramid, nurses, along with other health care professionals, have failed to recognize their own contributions to the system. Caught in their traditional roles by their own and others' perceptions, case managers are sometimes seen as "simply" nurses or assistants. As a result, nurses may not be confident in dealing with physicians and have difficulty assuming anything more than a secondary or tertiary function. Also hindering the establishment of a collaborative alliance with physicians is the so-called sacred physician-patient relationship and physicians' perceptions of their legal responsibility to protect confidentiality. This impediment too can be hurdled by empowering case managers to recognize the value of their role and understand what their abilities have brought and can continue to bring to health care management.

Case managers have the kind of knowledge and insight into patients' needs that derives from a tradition of 24-hour patient attendance. Most also come with strong medical credentials and experience. Taking on a role that MDs were less inclined or less able to assume due to time constraints, case managers honed their skill in locating and recommending alternative treatment facilities and suggesting options for the provision of care via community services and resources. Some now feel their income and status as professionals are being jeopardized by MDs who are challenging their role in health care delivery and by medical directors at insurance companies and HMOs who do not appreciate or fully understand their contribution to care. It is difficult for case managers to have to confront such resistance and to feel they are being denied entrance into the "inner circle" as widely recognized medical professionals.[1]

In working with physicians, case managers need to make it perfectly clear that their first and foremost concern is for the patients, that their interest is in ensuring the highest quality of care and the best possible outcomes. Additionally, physicians must be assured that the case managers are not there to control or dictate patient treatment plans. Instead, the communication between the two groups should create an atmosphere of cooperation and collaboration. Case managers, after all, posses a different knowledge base than physicians (e.g., an understanding of the patients' insurance policies as well as information about various community resources that may be accessed to effect better outcomes).

In short, what must be conveyed is, "We are all focused on our patient." This statement not only sets the stage for a unified effort but also communicates that the case manager will assume an integral role in the care of "our patient."

To facilitate physicians' receptivity to and cooperation with case managers, exchanges should occur in a certain order. First, case managers must clearly state who they are representing. Since case managers come from diverse practice settings, ranging from within an insurance company to health care provider or corporate entity, they must establish who they represent, the organization's interest, and what can be offered in the way of services. A waiver of confidentiality or consent from the patient or guardian should be presented to permit the physician to legally share the necessary information. This introduction should also include an explanation of the line of insurance involved, which will shape the case manager's objectives.

If the case manager comes from a payer group (e.g., an employer group, a Medicare/Medicaid plan, a company's premium or indemnity plan, or a workers' compensation carrier), it is important that she state, for instance, "I am the case manager representing John's employer group working within his workers' compensation plan. John was injured on the job, and my goal is to help your patient get the best possible results and return to work in the shortest period of time, as medically comfortable as possible. If he can't return to his previous type of work, I want to help him find other suitable employment."

Especially given the current chaos in the health care system, including the confusion between case management and managed care, it is critical that this complete introduction and communication of intent is done at the outset. Remember, not every call a physician has received from a case manager has been a positive one. The last "case manager" dealt with may in reality have been a clerk in the utilization review department of an insurance carrier. This individual may have called the physician to say that the carrier's software tracking system indicated that her patient's condition should only require a three-day hospital stay rather than the five days she authorized. Understandably, the physician may recall the experience with anger. Because of the possibility of this kind of scenario, the case manager may want to try to establish rapport with the physician's nurse or office administrator in order to pave the way for better communication. This person will also be a tremendous resource in maintaining ongoing communication with the physician.

TIMING THE INITIAL PHYSICIAN CONTACT

The means by which a case manager acquires a case often dictates the order in which the exchanges with a physician will proceed. Some insurance companies do not permit involvement of a case manager until case management has been approved by the treating physician. This is akin to putting the cart before the horse. It is also unfortunate, since most physicians, once knowledgeable about case management, welcome the case manager's intervention at the earliest possible stage of treatment. In addition, it is probably unethical, since patients, unless incompetent, should be empowered by the case providers to make decisions on their own behalf.

Typically, the case manager will first contact the patient or family, then the treating physician. In making the initial contact with the patient, and hopefully winning over that individual, the case manager can gain valuable information that can later be passed on to the physician. The preliminary contact can also be used to confirm the identity of the patient's physician and determine his or her schedule for visiting the patient. The case manager can enlist the patient to alert the physician to expect her call and to tell the physician, "I think it might be helpful to have you and this case manager working together." This plants the seed with the physician that the patient has accepted the case manager and supports a joint effort.

If a patient is in the hospital setting or critically ill with no family members in attendance, the case manager may need to contact the treating physician first (or concurrently with attempts to reach relatives). The first outreach to the physician should be well planned and well executed.

It is important to take into account that, like all professionals, physicians have their own work schedules and daily priorities. A surgeon's day, for example, may consist of morning rounds at a hospital, followed by surgeries, then time spent at the office for patient appointments or paperwork, and finally a return to the hospital for postoperative rounds. The case manager should be cognizant of this regimen and acknowledge it when contacting the physician's office. The case manager might say, "I understand Dr. Jones is very busy and may not have time to meet with me during his office hours. Would it be possible for me to call him after hours? Is there a particular time that is better for him?"

Once someone in the physician's office understands that the case manager is aware of the physician's busy schedule demands and is trying to be accommodating, he or she will usually be helpful in coordinating a meeting or telephone contact.

The information gleaned by the case manager in the initial exchange with the patient will also influence how time-sensitive the physician communications must be. The case manager may have uncovered relevant information that the patient neglected to tell the physician and that may alter the treatment plan, but it is essential to use common sense in determining the appropriate urgency of the call. By understanding the importance of effective physician contact and properly timing dialogues, the case manager is more likely to make a real contribution toward a successful outcome for the patient.

Finally, in establishing good communication with physicians, case managers should not agonize over their knowledge of a particular medical specialization. Although some large insurance companies or provider organizations may have case managers who concentrate on pediatric or elder care, oncology or cardiac cases, head injuries, and so on, many very effective case managers are generalists. There is nothing wrong with saying to a physician, "I am really not that familiar with your patient's particular treatment plan. Would you explain it further?"

On the other hand, many nurses have had the opportunity to work with very fine physicians, renowned in their fields, and have in-depth experience in specialized areas. Drawing on these resources to gain better insight into a particular case can only serve to equip case managers for more effective partnerships with physicians.

When I started my case management company, I was asked to handle a case involving an infant with a brain stem aneurysm. He had survived an extremely intricate surgical procedure but was left with multiple problems. His neurosurgeon, highly respected and also a clinical professor in a university hospital, was very much in demand and maintained a full schedule. The family was insistent that the physician be involved in all aspects of their child's care. I realized that to gain their trust, I needed to establish a good relationship with the physician.

In trying to reach him, it seemed I was jumping through one hoop after another and getting nowhere. I eventually ended up calling him at his office on a Saturday morning and arranging to meet him the following week after his office hours.

When we met, he was very relaxed and helpful in providing information. He even took the time to draw medical diagrams to clarify his points. He was also outwardly appreciative of my involvement and admitted he did not really understand case management. In fact, he opened up and expressed some of his own difficulties. He said that he entered neurosurgery because of an infinite fascination with the brain, never considering that some cases would require him to give advice regarding a patient's long-term care. He helped me to see that, like many physicians, he just did not have the time or even the preparation for this type of case, one that called for ongoing participation on a number of levels. I, in turn, proved my value by recommending a state-funded early intervention program for the child. The neurosurgeon and I visited the facility and, along with the pediatrician, attended team meetings together. He soon became convinced that this program, by affording the right care and social interaction for the child while alleviating much of the family's stress, was the best alternative. Ultimately, he helped convince the family, who were initially reluctant to remove their child from a home care setting. In that case and others to follow, the physician became a strong ally. This example underscores how a free-flowing and solid case manager–physician relationship facilitates effective communication between the case manager and the patient or family.

PRACTICAL STEPS TO A WIN-WIN RELATIONSHIP BETWEEN CASE MANAGERS AND PHYSICIANS

Here are some practices case managers can put into play to better their working relationships with physicians and improve the standing of the entire case management community.

1. Develop an understanding of the physician's practice setting. When is the physician in OR? When is the best time to call the physician's office? Who is the best contact in the office? Sometimes a nurse or receptionist can provide a quick answer if you frame a clear question over the phone.

2. Go in as a pro. Send the physician credible information on you and your role. Include your credentials.

3. Use your business card. Giving out your card facilitates Rolodex® reference and supports your presentation of yourself as a professional.

4. Assure the physician that you will not be talking to him or her every day about every patient. Present yourself as a collaborative partner, a right-hand associate.

5. Reassure the physician that you will never presume that you can put a better treatment plan into action. You care about license liability and patient outcome as much as he or she does. State that you recognize the need to back up your assessment, and plan to review your findings, concerns, and suggestions with the physician.

6. Never drop in on the physician unannounced. Confirm all your appointments. Emergencies arise.

7. When you attend a meeting with the physician, state how much you appreciate the time being given. Time is a valued commodity among physicians.

8. Make it easy for the physician to give you the information you need. Often, physicians lack the time to meet in person. Type a questionnaire requesting specific information and enclose a self-addressed stamped envelope for the reply. Include a copy of an appropriate signed release of information from the patient. In preparing your questions, remember that you are trying to avoid responses that will have to be dictated to a receptionist and typed, delaying a prompt response. Do everything you can so all the physician has to do is generate clear answers. (See the introductory letter and questionnaire samples in Chapter 7.)

9. Attend the physician's hospital visits. It underscores your dedication and gives you the opportunity to directly ask the physician, "How can I help you?"

10. Let the physician know you are a resource: "I have this brochure with specific and clear information on open-heart surgery. Would you mind if I pass it along to Mr. Jackson?"

11. Express your recognition of excellence and a job well done. A brief note (with copies sent to the insurance carrier and the patient, if appropriate) can make a big impact. Writing such notes tells the physician that you value expertise and effort and communicates to your client company that you and the physician are working well as a team.

12. Make it clear that you are also a resource for referrals. After a successful effort on behalf of a patient, let the physician know that you are aware of and value his or her care and concern and that you will certainly make patients in similar straits aware of his or her skill and manner.

13. Get to know the physicians in your community and develop a good relationship with a support person in each office.

14. Do not trust your memory. Maintain a physician database to document specialty areas, preferred communication patterns, and previous experience.[2]

15. You know how to problem-solve with other case managers, so use the same techniques in your associations with physicians. For example, every case manager and every physician struggles with patient compliance, so let physicians know you will be their eyes and ears to ensure that treatments are carried out. For a broader perspective, attend a physicians' conference or pick up publications written for physicians, such as *Physician's Management*.

16. Maintain the collaboration. Offer to give the physician an update after your house call or hospital visit.

17. When apt, provide the physician with copies of your case management report, enclosing an authorization release. Such updates can be particularly helpful for the physician seeing a patient on a consultation basis.

18. Hone your diplomacy skills and try to handle any problems in an ethically and morally responsible manner. Perhaps you discover a patient is taking medication that has an adverse effect in combination with another pill. He may be using over-the-counter medication or have forgotten to mention a drug he has been on for ten years. Make it clear that you are interested in the best outcome, not in pointing a finger, when you uncover a bad situation. Document your concern as a partner, without laying blame, unless you are confronted by overt negligence.

19. Do not undermine a physician's position in front of patients. Request a moment in the hall or office afterward.[3]

MAINTAINING COMMUNICATIONS WITH PATIENTS AND FAMILIES

The timing of a patient's referral to a case manager will describe how her role should be introduced and explained to the patient or family. For instance, consider this workers' compensation case. The patient has left the hospital, has completed a physical therapy program, and is now involved with various follow-up services. He has not returned to work, prompting the case to be referred to a case manager. Understandably, the patient may view this intervention less than positively. In fact, all parties may have been better served by earlier involvement of the case manager. Helping to educate clients as to the ideal time for case management intervention should be a constant objective of all case managers. However, since case managers cannot always influence when a case is referred, they must learn how to establish good patient communications regardless of the circumstances. Empathy is the key.

Case managers should put themselves in their patients' shoes. For instance, a case may have been referred within 24 hours of a catastrophic event—a massive stroke, an explosion, or the severing of a limb. Or perhaps a patient has just entered a rehabilitation center or experienced a difficult or dangerously premature delivery. To facilitate the best possible exchange, the case manager needs to have as many facts as possible about the patient and the reasons for the referral. The case manager should be aware that the patient and family may be experiencing much more than a medical crisis and take the time to consider the patient's and family members' feelings. The medical circumstances may have created financial difficulties, marital problems, role reversals, and so on. Knowing this, the case manager should not simply pick up the phone and dial.

The person receiving the call may be waiting for news from the treating physician or the hospital. The case manager may be calling the wife of a patient who was involved in a head-on collision and is in a hospital 300 miles from home. Consider the impact of a call by a case manager who begins by introducing herself as a representative of the insurance company for the driver whose car struck her husband. The case manager must understand that there will probably be negative feelings and low receptivity and try to surmount these obstacles by using good communication skills.

Similarly, if it is a workers' compensation case and a patient was injured on the job, the case manager should recognize that management–employee or management–union relations may affect the patient's response to the case manager. The individual may have been injured in a plant recently cited for hazardous working conditions. If the patient was a new employee, he or she may be somewhat threatened and skeptical of the employer's position, fearful that management is questioning the veracity of his or her accident report. Conversely, a key senior employee of a company may have none of these concerns owing to his or her more secure position and possibly positive experiences relating to past insurance claims.

Something as simple as whether or not a company has sent flowers and cards to an injured worker can also influence how the case manager will be received. While some organizations act in a humane way toward employees—sending gifts, calling on family members to express their interest, and setting up a "sunshine organization" to help maintain contact—others do not. The case manager should bear this in mind and try to get a sense of the company's corporate culture before calling on an employee. Especially in programs where the case management service is new, the case manager might wish to make a joint contact with the claims department or the employer benefit department to help ease patient concerns.

After introducing herself, the case manager should ask, "Is this a good time to talk?" The case manager must appreciate the suffering going on and offer support by asking how the family is, what information they have been given by the hospital, and so on. It is not a good strategy to assume family members know everything about the case and launch into the specifics of changing the treatment plan before giving them time to accept the involvement of someone new in an emotional and intense family crisis. If the case manager flounders, she can lose the family's good will before she begins her work.

Group medical cases also introduce special challenges to patient communication. Consider a patient who was just diagnosed with brain cancer. He comes from a rural community and was transferred to a major metropolitan hospital for optimum care. His family is distraught, shocked by the news. Family members may be completely out of their element, not knowing what to ask or whether they are making the best decisions. When the case manager comes on the scene, they may believe she is there to control things or keep down the high medical costs. She is looked upon as an unwanted intruder. Particularly in such situations, it is imperative that the case manager make a timely introduction and state something like this: "It may be possible, after we have spent a little more time talking and I've visited with your husband, that my assessment will be that he is receiving the best possible care and we will not be suggesting any changes. My role is to act not as a hands-on provider of care but as a coordinator of medical services and a resource for additional alternatives. Your insurance company (or employer) does not require you to accept case management. It is totally up to you."

Communications with a family are as important as those with the patient. There is a saying in case management, "If you lose the family, you lose the patient." It's often a good idea for case managers to give the patients and family members examples of how they have worked with other people in similar circumstances. This helps families perceive case managers as caring human beings and not just additional bureaucrats in the health care system.

THE PATIENT COMMUNICATION CHAIN OF COMMAND

Communications between a case manager and a patient should ideally follow a certain sequence. However, many factors can alter this sequence. Today's society has introduced new family units, including step-, common-law, gay, and multigenerational family units, creating different hierarchies for patient communications. The case manager needs to remember that communications with the patient and family might affect and be affected by numerous other people. Generally, the patient communication chain of command is as follows:

1. patient (if of legal age)
2. spouse (if married)
3. parent or legal guardian (if patient not of legal age)
4. oldest child (if patient widowed or divorced)
5. significant other (if patient has an alternative lifestyle)
6. individual with power of attorney (if patient is incapacitated)

A caveat exists in regard to the "significant other" category. Although new legislation has begun to clarify the legal rights of close companions, it is important that case managers adhere to what society and the legal community recognize to be the significant other on behalf of a patient. Also, in many workers' compensation or auto cases, although the referral may come from the carrier or the employer group, if the individual is represented by an attorney, the attorney, not the individual, is contacted first. For legal reasons, the case manager must explain the role of a case manager and obtain the permission of the attorney before contacting the patient.

Elder care cases in which only one sibling is represented or cases involving children whose parents are divorced may also have a skewed communication sequence. The oldest child in a family might not be the most appropriate child to assist a needy parent, being too distant physically or emotionally or being simply unable to take on the responsibility of making a life-and-death decision. At some point, the case manager might want to suggest that the on-site child contact any brothers or sisters for additional support in dealing with a parent who is critically ill.

WHEN THE FAMILY BECOMES A PATIENT

Many medical cases, particularly those of a catastrophic nature, will devastate a family. In tough medical situations, all attention is focused on the ill or injured person, even though the caretaker or family member might be hanging from a thread. Case managers must understand that their role includes advocacy for the families. Family members should be encouraged to say what is on their minds and be reminded to ask for help if they need it. Keeping a family intact through a difficult period can ultimately be one of the case manager's greatest achievements in managing a particular case. The case manager should communicate to the family that she is there to assist in any way possible, whether that means helping the family sort through accumulating bills or prepare for the patient's return home by providing information about special equipment or home care services.

Case managers have to meet people where they are. One of my very first cases—and probably one of the biggest challenges to communication that I have had in case management—involved a gentleman who was injured in an automobile accident and rendered a quadriplegic at a C-4 level. He was on a respirator. His daughter, a nurse on a neurosurgical unit in a major metropolitan hospital, worked over one hundred miles away. Although she was absolutely devastated by the situation, as the nurse in the family she had a great deal of responsibility thrown at her. All the relatives were asking her all their questions. She felt that she had to make all the decisions, and she was having tremendous difficulty dealing with the pressure. Although she probably was very capable, she was beset by conflicts. What if she chose wrongly? She remained confident in making determinations for her own patients, but in this case she was a daughter and not simply a nurse on the case.

Many of the medical professionals supposed that since she was a neurosurgical nurse on a unit, she knew everything she needed to know. They were talking to her not as a family member, but as a peer. I, as the case manager, became the claimant's advocate and his daughter's advocate as well, making it easier for her to be just the daughter in this particular situation. I acknowledged that she had certain expertise, but I did not make further assumptions regarding her knowledge and skills. For example, when we were researching rehabilitation facilities for her father so he could go into a weaning program and eventually get off the respirator, I gave her detailed information. I did not presume that she knew what a respirator was or could distinguish the benefits of one rehabilitation program over another. I put myself in her place—and now I've been in that place.

Last year, my mother had a massive coronary and was rushed to the hospital at 3 AM. The family looked to me to make all the decisions, especially since I had worked as a nurse in a coronary care unit. I had not been as intimately involved with the intricacies of coronary care for a while, and I would have liked to have had someone who could reassure me. Yet my family said, "You're the expert. Tell us what's going on." I was panicked, I was panicked to death. Some case managers might assume that they can take less of a role in such situations because of a family member's medical background, but I would alert them to the possible need for more tailored assurance and support.

With the C-4 case, I spoke to the physicians involved and reminded them that this nurse was a daughter first, that she had doubts and questions and required shoring up. This intervention was effective and in fact became very important because this was a liability case. The father had been struck by a municipal vehicle that was being used for something other than official town business. I was referred by the insurance carrier that represented the town, so I was on the absolute opposite side, giving the daughter and her family a reason to doubt my intentions. But because I was able to work nurse to nurse and person to person, I helped her see that I really was not there just for the town, just to cut dollars; I was interested in maximizing the auto policy resources. There was a limit to certain of the benefit dollars, but there was also a huge lawsuit involved. While communicating with both parties and both parties' attorneys, I kept myself from taking a side. It was a difficult situation, but if case managers keep their goals straight and remember exactly what they are contributing, they can handle such challenging cases successfully.

THE QUESTION OF CONFIDENTIALITY AND THE QUESTION OF COST

In their communications, case managers must assure patients and families that their discussions will be held in confidence. Certain diagnoses (substance abuse–related illnesses, cancer, AIDS, etc.) in particular cause patients to worry about others' knowledge of their condition. Although case managers must tell patients whom they represent (an employer's group medical plan, workers' compensation, etc.), they must also make it clear that certain information will not be communicated to employers or supervisors.

Along with issues of privacy, there may also be worries about the cost of the case manager's involvement: "I don't have the money for this. Who's going to pay for this help?" The case manager should explain how the intervention is being funded and indicate that it will not represent another bill to the patient or family. In most lines of insurance, case management is a claims administration expense and the cost is not deducted from the patient's benefits. Regardless of how the service is being funded, some patients will consider it unnecessary. They may also sense that the case manager's involvement reflects another agenda (that of the insurance carrier, workers' compensation plan, etc.) and be wary.

Some referrals may in reality be thinly disguised requests for case managers to serve as medical investigators. Soul searching is in order here. Case managers have to decide whether these assignments are really the ones they want to take on and recognize the consequences of their decision. Particularly in smaller communities, where everyone knows everyone else, being regarded as the individual who interrogated the local grocer about his back injury can definitely cause future patients to become close-mouthed, preventing effective communication and case management. It is appropriate to tell a potential client that claims investigation is not a case management role.

DOCUMENTING THE PATIENT CONTACT

Case managers should document all of their patient communications, whether in-person or telephonic, regardless of the patient's acceptance or refusal of services. Beyond chronicling a case manager–patient exchange, correspondence can be used to reinforce important messages. For instance, the document may highlight certain aspects of the conversation, such as the statement that the services will not cost the patient anything, thereby offering reassurance to the patient and family.

Communication should flow between case managers and patients and families whenever appropriate: at the time of referral, after the referral, and when new information becomes available. Case managers should write to keep lines of communication open—to reassure an invalid parent's adult child who wants to remain in the loop or to document a change in treating facilities. Sometimes a case manager needs merely to send a simple reminder, "I'm writing to confirm that I will accompany you when you go to therapy next week." Letters can help establish consensus among those involved in caring for a patient and create the impression that the case manager, far from being an intruder, is one of the team.

Form letters can be used, but they should be personalized. Easily produced using word processing, the customized letter projects a personal interest rather than one governed by routine. The case manager might include words that focus on the patient or family: "I hope your husband is recovering comfortably from his back injury by the time you receive this letter." Or "I just wanted to elaborate on our discussion. I know we covered a lot of information about burns in a short period of time. I thought this might be helpful." Throughout their communication with patients and families, case managers should strive to position case management as apart from the medical bureaucracy.

The case manager–patient correspondence should document the patient's acceptance or refusal of case management services. In the case of refusal, it should note patient and family concerns and their reasons for declining the service, address them, and leave the door open for future dialogue and possible reconsideration.

The correspondence should reinforce and redefine the role of the case manager. It should explain who is being represented and how the services will be paid for, and it should underscore the point that the purpose of case management is to facilitate a positive outcome for the patient. The case manager might well include some promotional material that is user-friendly and helps the patient better understand case management's role and objectives. The initial letter might close with a statement such as this: "I am sending you this letter and brochure to better acquaint you with our services. I will call you in a few days when, hopefully, we can further discuss some of your concerns." Or: "I look forward to seeing you again at the hospital with Dr. Johnson and your husband. In the meantime, one of our brochures is enclosed to give you a better idea of our services." The letter should indicate that the referral source has been provided with a copy.

COMMUNICATIONS WITH PAYER SOURCES

Each payer source or line of insurance (whatever entity is referring the case for case management) places certain restrictions or obligations on the case manager. For instance, workers' compensation in one state may mandate that a case manager perform stipulated duties in a set time period, use specific forms, apply stated criteria in an evaluation, and charge only a fixed amount. In other cases, the case manager has to listen very closely to what the payer is requesting and not begin a program that she considers ideal. Specifically, what does the payer expect? What are they asking for? The semantics of the communication must be clarified at the outset.

Following referral, a group medical carrier usually wants to know how big the case is going to be. Is this long-term, is this short-term? If it is a plan with stop-loss insurance, another umbrella of insurance coverage, is it likely to reach the stop-loss threshold? If so, maybe the group medical carrier is required by the nature of the policy to advise the stop-loss carrier when the accumulated benefits reach 50 percent of the threshold figure. Part of the case manager's responsibility might be to predict when that will occur.

For each of the various lines of insurance, the case manager needs to be able to help the referral source to know which are going to be the big cases in terms of time and dollars and what case management can do to improve the situation. Can the case manager get John out of the hospital sooner, move him into a more aggressive rehabilitation program, or work with his employer to modify his job site according to his needs?

In their communications, case managers need to make the effort to tell the whole story and illuminate the issues that do not come across on a piece of paper or a claims form. I think case managers too often report major problems and think the job is done. They say, "Oh, this is horrible," without saying, "Listen, you have a problem case here, but I really think we can make this a better scenario" or "I've found the patient is giving us more to work with than we might have thought initially."

For example, if a patient is getting reimbursement for disability care or income replacement, the physician might not distinguish in his or her reports between stages of disability. My office handled a disability case where the individual had a diagnosis of postmeningitis syndrome. Month after month, the doctor continued to rubber stamp "totally disabled" on the claims form. Well, the guy was totally disabled for his job at the time, but he was absolutely desperate to go to work again. Nobody knew that, nobody took the time to make a telephone call, and when our case manager went out and saw how motivated this guy was and how hard he was trying, we got him into a computer training program. He made arrangements for his own transportation and attended classes like clockwork. All we needed to do was to get out there and see him and bring back the unknown information. Prior to that, the diagnosis was that his disability was forever, based on the lack of knowledge within the claims department. He had gotten lost in the system, he was labeled "postmeningitis" and "neurological disorder," and everyone assumed his condition was permanent.

Group medical cases are the same. It may well be a horrible situation, but the family members are very supportive, they really want the patient home, services can be put in place, and some serious cost containment and positive results can be achieved simultaneously. Again, case managers must realize they are problem solvers. They must not cut short their communications with payer sources by saying, "Just let me know what you want." They do a disservice to the patient, the payer, themselves, and the case management industry.

Below is a list of typical challenges for case managers in communicating with payer sources:

- Because of prior experience with case management services, a payer might have assumptions about what case management can and cannot do.
- Lack of medical knowledge within a claims department can slow a case manager's progress. This is where the role of educator is vital.
- The line of insurance might present problems. A fully insured plan can be more difficult to work with than a self-funded plan, due to restrictions prohibiting some of the more creative interactions between the referral source and the case manager.
- Sometimes the size of the company can be a hindrance. I often find the bigger companies are not willing to explore the what-ifs of case

management, to take a risk. They say, "We've always done it this way and that's it."

COMMUNICATIONS WITH LEGAL PROFESSIONALS

Attorneys are rarely called on for case managed group medical claims, with the exception of certain HIV cases, but are frequently contacted in workers' compensation and short- and long-term disability cases and sometimes contacted in auto liability cases. Above all, a clear explanation of the case manager's intent and role, along with an honest and straightforward manner, goes a long way toward overcoming an attorney's concern regarding case management intervention. Anticipating questions, all communications should underscore the case manager's proactive involvement in a complex delivery system.

During the early years of case management, case managers allowed attorneys to state the case for case management to clients. Intimidated by attorneys (as some still are), case managers had no comfort level for butting heads with a lawyer who portrayed case managers as out to find fault. When legal counsel said no to case management, there was little further discussion. Today, case managers are more apt to use a negative response as an opportunity to begin a brief public relations campaign. "Why are you denying case management on behalf of your client? I'm really surprised. Most attorneys I know have no problem with the service."

The reasons behind a refusal might have merit. Perhaps the carrier has acted in bad faith; perhaps the client's lost-wages payments or a physician's invoices are being held up unreasonably. If the case manager can resolve the problem, she should, demonstrating to the attorney that case management can be a catalyst for positive change.

There are some attorneys who do not understand case management or who will be aggressive and challenging. Case managers have to be articulate and assertive in return. The more comfortable they are with their role, the better job they can do as case managers. If they do not challenge a refusal and transform it into an assent, they are walking away from work and very possibly from a career.

There are stereotypical judgments on both sides. Some lawyers think case managers are claims investigators in disguise, and some case managers see lawyers as litigation hounds. And of course there *are* less-than-professional case managers and lawyers, both. On the other hand, there are law firms that are interested in case management and how it can benefit their clients. We need to move past the us-versus-them mindset. Attorneys want patients to get the best from the health care system and that is what case managers want too. They want patients to be able to go back to productive lives; so do case managers.

In some instances, the time frame in which a case manager is contacted can confuse communications. When a case manager is brought to a case early on, patients and lawyers alike tend to view case management intervention as more beneficial, and some of the long letters of introduction and initial lawyer–case manager meetings can be avoided. If an insurance carrier refers a case one year after the fact because the individual is still not at work and the care costs are piling up, a case manager might have more difficulty portraying the payer as truly concerned and herself as an objective advocate. The claimant is likely to ask, "Where were you six months ago?" and an attorney would be smart to ask, "Why weren't you offering help when John had his accident?" A more wary lawyer might question the case manager's intent: Is it advocacy or investigation? Case managers must be aware of politics; the carrier might well intend to tap her for information (e.g., What is the HIV status of the ill employee? Is she an alcoholic?). Is this a case the case manager wants to take? Can she be credible when the payer's motives are so suspect?

In another scenario, an attorney, unbeknownst to the carrier, might become involved several weeks after an accident. The case manager should obtain the attorney's written permission to work with the patient before continuing on the case.

Case managers will want to maintain ongoing communications with attorneys involved in their cases. Especially when a case manager has a particular concern about a claimant, an attorney can be quite helpful (by obtaining, for example, better cooperation from a patient who insists on drinking or smoking in direct opposition to the doctor's recommendation). By sharing information with and giving credit to attorneys, case managers make them a part of the care team.

As with contracted medical services, the case manager should track whether or not the claimant is well served by his or her attorney. Many attorneys are cooperative and interested, others are aloof and detached. If the claimant voices a concern regarding the attorney's representation, the case manager can suggest that there are alternatives but should stop short of recommending specific replacements, just as she should not name a certain physician as the best choice.

COMMUNICATION SUBTLETIES

Not everything a case manager communicates is verbal or written. The case manager's overall demeanor projects a message to patients, physicians, and social workers. For instance, many nurses in the habit of wearing comfortable clothing in the hospital environment adhere to the same dress code in their role as case managers. They might wear a skirt and blouse with sneakers rather than pumps. Or they might go to the extreme of wearing a warm-up suit. At the other end of the spectrum are case managers who don the complete "corporate look" (tailored suit and briefcase) without considering that it could intimidate a patient. Minor modifications, such as not wearing the jacket and walking in with an envelope rather than a briefcase, can soften the image and signal a more approachable individual.

Case managers also need to know their audience. When visiting a patient whose home is in a low-income neighborhood, it is preferable not to march in dressed to the hilt in designer labels and expensive jewelry. For appointments with physicians or corporate representatives, the power look not only is appropriate but also places the case manager on a par with other professionals, affording greater credibility.

Demeanor also extends to behavior. Upon entering a patient's home, a case manager should remember that he or she is a guest. Extending courtesies such as complimenting the decor, taking note of photographs, or kneeling down to greet a young child communicates a genuine interest. Commenting on a patient's new level of skill (such as moving from wheelchair to walker) further assists in projecting the image of a caring professional. When meeting a physician or human resources manager, it is a good idea to express awareness of how busy the office seems to be or to request literature regarding the practice or company.

THE RIGHT MINDSET

A positive attitude and confidence in one's role are essential for good communication. Case managers who are motivated and even proud of their role as catalysts for change will convey the value of case management. Those who chose the profession merely to escape a battered existence in another health care role are likely to suffer from low self-esteem and be ill equipped to meet the challenges that case management presents.

The case manager's role can be extremely difficult and, depending on the motives of others involved, quite disheartening. In fact, certain lines of insurance will present case management assignments that may be layered with bureaucracy and rifts between medical personnel, payer groups, and legal entities. Such cases cause some case managers to be timid and even apologetic. Case managers who feel powerless may resort to an opposite tactic. Rather than withdrawing and becoming subservient, they ride roughshod over patients or others, drawing their "authority" from what they perceive to be the powerful "big business" or insurance company. This approach only serves to alienate people, creating barriers to effective communication.

Case managers need to accept the fact that their job will not always give them warm feelings and provide professional satisfaction. They also need, however, to keep feelings of frustration and disappointment in check, particularly when communicating with patients. Usually, the difficulty with making certain calls to patients will lessen as a case manager's experience builds. Moreover, if a case manager views each case as a new opportunity to improve a situation, communication can become a more agreeable aspect of providing assistance.

COMMUNICATION AND CARING OVERLOAD: BURNOUT

Simply because of the nature of the work, most case managers' caseloads consist of tragic cases. Many are life-and-death situations; the bulk of them have no happy ending. Yes, the high-risk pregnancy often results in the birth of a healthy infant, and getting a partially disabled person well situated in a new job is especially rewarding, but the balance between success and tragedy that exists in more traditional health care delivery roles is not part of case management. Often case managers deal with people who are angry at the system, at God for allowing this terrible thing to happen, at themselves for not handling it better, and at the patient for getting ill in the first place. Angry patients and families tend to voice their opinions to case managers rather than physicians. Case managers who try to distance themselves emotionally by totally walling themselves off from the pain their clients feel will lose their ability to be effective because they will stop interacting with those clients. They must create for themselves a balance between success and tragedy by finding an appropriate level of involvement.

There is a fine line between "I have no hands-on role" and "I am totally responsible for this person," and case managers must be able to walk it by knowing where the function of case management begins and ends. They must take on enough of the responsibility to help fix problems while acknowledging their limitations. In their former roles as practicing nurses, many case managers were able to offer a quick solution to pain; the proper medication "made it better." But case managers cannot deter a terminal illness or make a dying child well; they cannot keep contracted services or equipment from failing; they cannot absorb everyone's woe. Despite the day-to-day challenges, case managers need to maintain their equilibrium and a strong sense of their role; otherwise they will become overwhelmed and burn out.

When a case manager begins to blow up at associates, dreads the next call or any further involvement in a case, is unable to see any positives in her work, and grinds through cases that appear completely hopeless, she needs to step back and get help on the cases that seem overwhelming. Usually, a case manager is burned out on a few cases rather than on the job as a whole, unless she has pushed herself long beyond the point where she needed to take a break.

One way to avoid taking on too much responsibility for a case's progress is to draw on the knowledge and experience of peers, even peers in another state. By calling, putting thoughts and concerns out in the open, knocking ideas around and getting feedback, it becomes easier to see a situation clearly. Perhaps there is a personality clash with the patient, or maybe the case manager has simply run out of ideas for a successful intervention. Sometimes a case has to be given over to an associate or back to a supervisor. How can a case manager turn over a case to someone else and not lose face with the client? Nothing works better than honesty. Some cases benefit greatly by another's expertise in an area; sometimes all that is needed is a better patient–case manager match.

To prevent burnout, a case manager would do well to understand the parameters of the job and not glamorize it. An RN trying a utilization review or case management role needs to prepare for the role's requirements. Many professions have hazards, and recognition of them is three-fourths of their solution.

One problem is isolation. Case managers are often on their own, enjoying minimal interaction with other case managers. They are no longer on the nursing team, and they are not physicians, claims adjusters, or rehabilitation specialists. They interact with all these specialists, but their work places them outside the "inner circle" of an office or professional group. This can lead to a lack of input when facing a problem and a lack of recognition for a job well done. There may be few or no peers providing the "safety valve" of shared laughter or griping. Case managers can combat the isolation by creating a case management "team." They can talk to their contacts in the claims department about their lives and interests. They can make an effort to observe and discuss improvements in patient abilities with the family, choosing to dwell on the joy of progress after all the time spent on the tougher aspects of an illness.

Case managers also need to get out of the case management cycle. The job allows for flexibility, and because the job includes great tension and stress, it is vital for a case manager to use some of that flexibility to provide "fueling up" time. Instead of writing all the necessary reports during the 9–5 workday, the case manager might take time off to attend a child's scout meeting, visit a museum or park, water the garden, or exercise, completing the reports in the evening or on a Saturday morning. Regularly going out to lunch, taking no-work-allowed coffee breaks, and attending at least one annual case management conference are the types of activities that can help keep burnout at bay.

NOTES

1. Catherine M. Mullahy, "Working Associates, Not Adversaries," *The Case Manager,* Spring 1992, 63–69.
2. Ibid.
3. Catherine M. Mullahy, "Ten Ways You Can Improve Your Working Relationship with Physicians," *Case Management Advisor,* June 1992, 81–82.

CHAPTER

7

The Case Management
Work Format and Process

When a case manager receives an assignment, she will make a series of contacts, including contacts with the patient and family, the treating physician(s) and medical facility staff, the employer, and, if the patient is involved in or considering a lawsuit, an attorney. The information gathered is reported in writing, and planning is coordinated with the payer. The process of case management can be broken into categories: case finding and targeting, gathering and assessing information, planning, reporting, obtaining approval, coordination or putting the plan into action, follow-up, and evaluation. Each step of the case management process involves medical, financial, behavioral/motivational, and vocational management activities. It is vital at each phase that case managers analyze and not simply record or report their findings. (See the case management flow chart presented in Figure 7-1.)

CASE FINDING AND TARGETING

Case finding and targeting encompasses the determination of eligibility and the identification of high-risk or high-cost clients. The way in which a case manager approaches a new case is influenced by the referral source (generally the payer) and the line of insurance. The referral source might be an insurance company with clients covered under workers' compensation, auto, or group medical plans, a TPA that is paying claims for a client company, a hospital discharge planner, a corporate human resources

Figure 7–1 Case Management Work Format Flow Chart

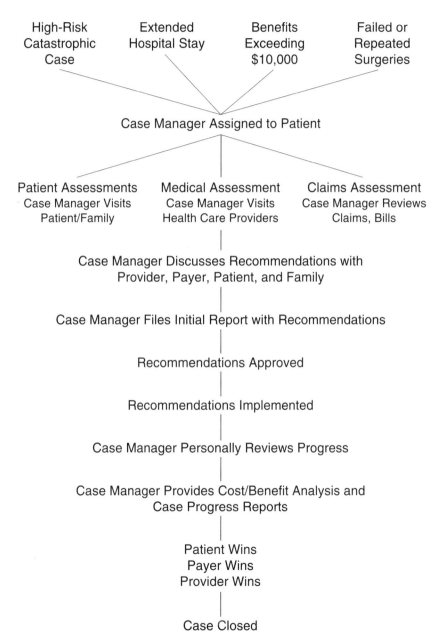

High-Risk Catastrophic Case   Extended Hospital Stay   Benefits Exceeding $10,000   Failed or Repeated Surgeries

Case Manager Assigned to Patient

Patient Assessments
Case Manager Visits
Patient/Family

Medical Assessment
Case Manager Visits
Health Care Providers

Claims Assessment
Case Manager Reviews
Claims, Bills

Case Manager Discusses Recommendations with
Provider, Payer, Patient, and Family

Case Manager Files Initial Report with Recommendations

Recommendations Approved

Recommendations Implemented

Case Manager Personally Reviews Progress

Case Manager Provides Cost/Benefit Analysis and
Case Progress Reports

Patient Wins
Payer Wins
Provider Wins

Case Closed

Courtesy of Options Unlimited, Case Management Services Division, Huntington, N.Y.

manager, or a home health services agency. It might be a state Medicaid office with case management services within a line of insurance or a population segment, such as high-risk newborns or children who are dependent on technological medical assistance. In today's growing and diversified market, cases may also come directly from consumers. An individual might contract elder care services and request that a case manager evaluate a family member's capabilities and needs. For the independent case manager, the case might be referred as a "trial run" by a new client she has been soliciting.

Within some larger case management, insurance, TPA, and employer firms, computer software programs are utilized to flag potential cases appropriate for case management intervention. For example, system software can be programmed to pull out every individual with claims totaling over $5,000 or $10,000, each individual with claims bearing the ICD-9 or CPT codes indicating a certain type of illness or condition, or each patient experiencing three or more hospitalizations over a set period of time. (*ICD-9-CM: International Classification of Disease—Clinical Modification*, one of the ICD-9 code reference books, is published by the Commission on Professional and Hospital Activities, Ann Arbor, Michigan. *CPT: Physicians' Current Procedural Terminology* is published annually by the American Medical Association.)

Other artificial intelligence systems screen cases through a series of reviews. Generally, on the first review level, nurse reviewers answer ten standard questions regarding a patient's file. If any of the ten questions is answered yes, the computer system presents a series of new questions to help single out those cases needing immediate case management attention. The system is making its "decisions" based on data taken from interviews with specialists in various medical fields. The system operator, usually a medical review specialist, answers the computer's questions. Cases are forwarded for case management by the system itself and by the system operator.[1]

Computer software can be of significant assistance in finding and targeting cases for case management intervention, but it should not be the sole instrument for reviewing claims. It requires the support of a personal interview with the patient, knowledge of the patient's prior history, or an independent professional judgment regarding the data. In other words, the use of computer software should be regularly combined with the efforts of an on-site case manager.

The variety of referral sources is enormous, as is the variety of backgrounds in case management referral sources may have. A company recently mandated to offer case management services might be referring its first case and have little or no understanding of case management. A claims examiner might have been told to refer the case and have scant knowledge of what type of report or data to request from a case manager. The source of the case might be another health care professional. Large companies and insurance carriers often have in-house medical directors who refer patients for case management. The referral may come from a senior claims person, a physician, or a nurse familiar with case management who coordinates all vended-out services. The source and his or her background will partially determine the information requested, expected, and provided. Case managers must take clues regarding assessment and reporting from the referral source.

GATHERING AND ASSESSING INFORMATION

The accuracy of the entire case management process depends on the information gathered. The process of collecting information might include scheduling a conversation with the referral source (payer), determining policy limits and coverage, interviewing the patient and family, interviewing the physician(s) and the key members of the medical treatment team, reviewing the medical records, holding discussions with employers and attorneys as needed, and determining the availability of community resources.

I always suggest to case managers that they go out to do assessments as a reporter first and then as an analyzer of the information. Too many nurses and other case management professionals have functioned like journalists, writing wonderful documentaries about patients but not really telling and selling the role of case management. Because of this, too many client companies and organizations see case managers as observers of care rather than contributors to the care plan. All case managers must be observers, but they must be much more as well. If they never looked beyond "what is wrong with this picture" to "what can I do to improve this," if they never envisioned the contributions they could make—to better the patient's condition, support the family, stretch the dollars, tighten up the treatment plan, coordinate the activities of the providers—then they would be merely a group of reporters who call themselves case managers. With the various functions of case management in mind, case managers should approach each case with an open mind and an eye for problems that must be addressed.

THE R.I.P. METHOD OF CONDUCTING INTERVIEWS

This approach is presented in the seminar Case Management Practice, conducted by the Foundation for Rehabilitation Certification, Education and Research, the parent organization of CIRSC, in a section entitled "Interpersonal Skills for Case Managers."

R is for rapport, the essential connection made by the case manager with the person being interviewed. That connection, which can last 10 seconds or 30 minutes, might take the form of a brief and pleasant introduction, a quick statement of purpose, or a warm comment or observation about the individual or his or her home or busy schedule.

The *I* in R.I.P. refers to information, the purpose of the communication, be it approval for a previously submitted case management plan, permission for a hospital discharge, or knowledge of the specific medication a patient is receiving. The case manager must focus on the objective of the contact and maintain the contact until she has the background needed to continue the case management process.

Even if the involvement of the interviewed party will be minimal, the conversation should not end before that individual completely understands the next step in the process or the plan (*P*). The case manager might conclude by saying, "Thank you for letting me visit with you in your home. My report goes to the insurance company shortly, and I'll call you with their comments in two weeks." To a physician, she might say, "Thank you for your time, Dr. Reynolds. I'll confirm your approval by letter and do everything I can to assist you in making certain John follows his treatment plan."

TALKING TO THE REFERRAL SOURCE

Prior to beginning an assessment of a case, a case manager will provide a clear definition of assessment and a description of the report she plans to file based on the needs of the referral source (claims examiner, vice president of human resources, corporate CM department head, etc.). Not every client will want the same type of initial needs assessment, nor will every client have the same document in mind when an "initial needs assessment" is requested. Because responsibilities for administering claims within an insurance policy will be different, client requirements will be different. The case manager might work for a company which considers an initial evaluation an on-site personal contact with the claimant, an on-site personal contact with the employer, and an on-site personal contact with the treating physician—a three-point on-site contact. Another company's "initial evaluation" may be either an extensive phone call or an on-site contact visit with the claimant only.

What is the referral source being asked to do? What is the problem that case management might have a role in solving? Perhaps the case will not merit case management intervention. There is no plain vanilla case management and no plain vanilla initial needs assessment.

Depending on the case manager's type of employment—whether working for an insurance firm, within a TPA, or self-employed as an independent CM, for example—and the kinds of clients served, request-for-service referral forms may be forwarded for completion. Some case managers have developed their own forms, but corporations often have a "Directive for Service" that is mailed to the case manager to utilize at the outset of a case. Perhaps the case manager works in a branch office of a company with national accounts, providing case management services for a large client group. The company might have its own referral intake sheet incorporating very specific data regarding past medicals, file numbers, and so on. A form designed and used by an independent case manager might also function as a marketing tool and include information on the range of services.

Referral form data can be taken in person, by phone, or sent by fax. Again, there are numerous variations that influence how and what information is obtained.

In a workers' compensation case the payer might ask, how extensive is this injury? What is my exposure in terms of dollars? How long is this individual likely to be out of work? If the client is paying medical costs and replacement of salary and is also handling liability issues, there may be multiple concerns, with the medical portion being the least important. A case manager accustomed to delivering an intense discourse on clinical aspects of the case will be preparing an initial assessment report that is of little use to this client.

In other situations, the case manager might be called in as an intermediary, perhaps to confirm the status of a case. In an auto liability case, a client might request that the case manager call two doctors or visit the hospital to determine the extent of an injury. If the policy carries $50,000 in benefits and the injury is so severe that the patient will be in an intensive care unit for two months at $1,000 per day, the benefits dollars are already spent. The client may decide that there is no action a case manager could take to save any money at this juncture. In a disability case, the client may have little interest in the course of medical treatment but be especially concerned with whether the disability will be permanent. Therefore, the case manager may be asked to conduct a telephonic assessment rather than make an on-site visit.

Imagine a situation where a case manager works for a company that has a set policy on procedures and a referral comes in regarding a workers' compensation case:

Case Manager: Kate, you've asked for an initial evaluation of John Jones. Does that mean you want us to visit John, his employer, and his treating physician or are you just interested in a visit with John?

Payer: We'd like you to conduct a visit with John only.

Case Manager: All right. Are you interested in our customary initial evaluation with a claimant, Kate? It includes a medical history, a current medical status, a vocational history, and a financial profile. It's fairly extensive. I anticipate that it will take me an hour and a half or two hours, and John is an hour away. [If John is represented by an attorney, there is a whole new angle and additional time required for an initial assessment.] Is that what you're interested in?

Payer: No. All I want you to do is go to the hospital and find out what's going on right now. Write it up and get me a report.

Case Manager: OK. Do you have a time limit, Kate, on when this needs to be done, or a specific format for that report? Do you want just a phone report, do you need a letter, or do you want this to be a full report? Do you have any benefit limits? What are you really looking for here? [Again, the case manager needs to find out the desires of the particular client and get as much of the client's agenda on the table as possible. The first case from a referral source is a key case: If the case manager messes it up, she perhaps may not get another referral from that payer. If the case manager goes on and on about what "we always do" but the payer has different requirements, the case manager runs the risk of losing the opportunity for future work. She should not make the assumption that *she* knows what's best for the client; the *client* is buying her services.]

Case Manager: Does the report need to be completed in 72 hours? Do you have to reserve dollars on this case? Is your home office looking for this information quickly?

Payer: As a matter of fact, I need to get someone out on it right away.

Case Manager: I'm sorry, the staff that I have right now that's closest to John already have appointments. If you can wait a little while, I can get one of our other case managers to do it, but it won't be until the end of the week. [A case manager should never, just to get that first case, make a promise that cannot be fulfilled. A broken promise will definitely destroy any hope of future referrals.]

Payer: Well, I'm sorry, Jessica. I'll have to get someone else, but we'll give you an opportunity another time.

Are there any limits on travel time? The call may come from a regional office in Atlantic City: "I hear you do great work in New Jersey. I need you to send somebody out as soon as possible on this person." Maybe the case manager has a representative in Paterson, New Jersey. She should say, "We can take that, but are you concerned about travel-time expenses? This particular case is three hours away from our office. Do you have a problem with that?"

Or a client may request a particular case manager for the case: "I want Jack to work this case. He did a great job for me on a head injury three months ago." The fact that he lives two hours away and his travel time will be factored into the case management fee might not matter to the client, but the case manager ought to verify this.

All business details—fees, how much is charged per hour, what service elements are charged (travel, phone, fax, postage), what service elements are not charged (report copies), the length of status reports—need to be clarified. The case manager might give a synopsis: "Our initial evaluation with these parameters probably will take from six to eight hours. Is that in the ballpark of what you would expect?" The payer may feel that is agreeable or excessive. The payer might have been expecting to be charged for four to five hours tops or might say, "We never pay for travel time" or "We only pay half the rate for travel time." The case manager must then decide whether to work within those guidelines.

It may be that the case manager is busy working a broad client base and may choose not to reduce any of her fees, including those for travel time. It may be that the case management company is big enough, good enough, that it does not need to compromise on prices. The response could be, "Listen, I'm sorry, but our expenses are such . . ." or "In this part of the country costs are such . . ." The case manager would then close with a request that the payer keep the firm in mind for other cases. On the other hand, the case manager might have been looking for the chance to work with that individual or payer company and say, "Our fees for this are $75 an hour. I understand that seems a little bit high, but I'd like you to see what we do. If you like what we do, maybe we can negotiate a lower cost another time."

Fees can be discussed on a case-by-case basis or can be set, for example, through the establishment of a two- or five-year contract. The important thing is to discuss fees openly at the beginning of the relationship and, if rates are raised over the course of the relationship, to communicate that as well.

A case manager should make certain that she is comfortable delivering the type of job a client is requesting. If the case manager feels incapable of completing an accurate and objective assessment of a particular case via the telephone, for example, or thinks there might be liability concerns with a particular assessment issue, the concern must be broached ("I only conduct on-site assessments" or "I've found that all physicians on a case must be consulted for an assessment"). When the criteria are clear, then information gathering may begin.

Prior to beginning an assessment, eligibility for coverage under the specific line of insurance paying for case management should be defined. The case manager needs to discover the client's responsibility on this case, for this individual, under this policy. Often, eligibility has not been ascertained, so the case manager must ask, "What is the line of insurance?" and "Is this individual covered under this policy?" Suppose the case manager works in the preadmission and concurrent review department of a large company and receives a call that James Jones is in the hospital with multiple injuries. James is named on the policy of his father, employee John Jones, and covered under the company's medical plan. But in talking to John Jones, the case manager finds that James was involved in an auto accident or hurt at work. Therefore, James is not eligible for benefits under his father's group medical plan, because it is an auto insurance or a workers' compensation case.

In the event that a child is covered under a parent's policy, other questions arise. Many insurance policies include a "birthday rule," a clause that states that the insurance of the parent whose birthday falls earliest in the calendar year will be considered the primary coverer and the other parent's plan will be used as secondary coverage. Perhaps James Jones fell off a ladder while putting up an antennae on the roof of his parents' house. John Jones's birthday is in August and his wife's birthday is in March. In this instance, the wife's coverage is primary and John's is secondary. John's company may have referred James's case to the case manager under the illusion it was the responsible carrier. During a preassessment review, the case manager discovers the correct status and refers the case back to the wife's insurer.

At the outset of a case, the case manager will ask, "How long has the patient been ill?" or "When did the accident or injury occur?" to review the case for the potential of high-risk or long-term cost factors. In general, the more severe the event is in terms of injury, accident, or illness, the more likely the case will be long term. Rarely does a person in a coma wake up in a day or two and go about the normal business of life. Based on diagnosis alone, a case manager can outline short- and long-term needs. Even if the referral source has little information other than "it's a spinal cord injury" or "it's a traumatic brain injury," the case manager can ascertain that this is a complex case and prepare the referral source for long-term case management involvement. For the short term, the case manager will identify those actions that can be taken immediately. Then, once the likely scenario becomes clear based on the present state of the individual or illness, the case manager can evaluate the long-term impact of case management on the situation. The line of insurance and the dollars available may determine what can be done. The case manager may devise an appropriate long-term plan but be unable to actualize the plan because of insufficient funds.

Therefore the next question is, "What dollars are available to this individual within the policy?" For example, an individual holds an auto policy with only a minimal amount of coverage ($10,000). He has multiple injuries and multiple problems and has been in a hospital intensive care unit for three days. Would case management be effective in controlling costs? No. The claimant's injuries are severe, he requires high-level care, and all medical treatments being delivered are necessary. The benefit dollars have been spent but spent wisely.

On the other hand, a group medical plan providing up to $50,000 worth of rehabilitation care may not stipulate that those dollars have to be spent in an inpatient setting. If the claimant has had a stroke, the case manager will look at the available dollars and determine how to maximize benefits while containing costs.

In addition to the dollar amounts, a case manager must ask about limits and restrictions on types of care, care facilities, and lengths of stay. Is there $10,000 or $100,000 for medical coverage? Is coverage limited to one year or is it open-ended until a cap of $300,000 is reached? Are there restrictions on the number of days the individual will be covered for hospital care? Perhaps the individual is in a coma in an acute care hospital. The case manager should then ask, "Are there any limitations on inpatient rehabilitation? What are the benefits for a skilled nursing facility?" A benefit cap of $1,000,000 may appear adequate to cover all needs, but the policy may dictate very specific ways in which those dollars may be spent.

There are times when case managers can foresee an unsuccessful intervention despite a policy generous in dollars and services. A case manager may not be able to make a meaningful impact because of the limits of a line of insurance; because a number of attorneys have become involved with a case that is in litigation, requiring the case manager to obtain the approval of each lawyer prior to speaking with the patient and in some cases to have the lawyer present for each conversation; or because of a pre-existing condition. Case management is undertaken on a voluntary level; a patient pleased with the medical services he or she is receiving may not be interested in any changes. Sometimes a patient is so heavily invested in a particular team of physicians that he or she discourages or even refuses case management involvement.

Beyond the type of policy, line of insurance, dollars, and limitations, the data that case managers request from referral sources will vary slightly depending on the line of insurance. In a workers' compensation case, the case manager needs to know not only the date of the injury but the employee's "time and grade," the length of time the individual has been an employee at the company, and his or her position and job responsibilities. How vested is the company in this employee? The founding fathers of a firm may be more likely to make special allowances for a key employee than for a short-term employee with under a year at the company—less is known about him and his contribution.

Salary and the person's status as a union or management employee also become issues in workers' compensation cases, and the case manager needs to be aware of this aspect of finances. Workers' compensation salary replacement regulations vary from state to state. Further, every union negotiates its own salary replacement. A union may dictate that an injured worker receive full salary for a year. This type of financial arrangement will impact a person's motivation and inclination to return to the workplace. Receiving 100 percent of normal salary can be a strong disincentive, even when the person is well enough to perform a portion of his or her job or work half-days. Lack of income will also influence a person's decision to return to work. Perhaps the individual on disability gets full salary for a month and then goes on state disability and receives only two-thirds of salary. This may be financially devastating for the family, to the extent that the person might attempt to return to work prematurely. Premature return to a hazardous environment is of as much concern to case managers as individuals who draw benefits for too long. Not everyone reacts the same way to financial stress, and not every family faces the same amount of stress. Some employees are the sole support, and others have partners who work full or part time. In the latter case, a role reversal often takes place, and the partner assumes the role of sole support for a time, easing the financial problem.

One question a case manager needs to ask in a workers' compensation case is, "How did the injury happen?" The idea is not to launch an investigation into who was at fault or to elicit background information for use in court but to prevent a recurrence of the incident. Sometimes an employee will say to a case manager, "I told my boss that this piece of equipment was falling apart" or "I knew the belt on that sander needed to be replaced and I reported it." This may be the third worker injury at that job station in two years, causing the case manager to go back to the claims examiner and urge that a risk management team be sent to the job station before another employee is disabled.

There may be litigation pending or in place. If a claimant begins to volunteer information, the case manager must stop him or her from inappropriately discussing the case. The case manager can acknowledge the claimant's anger, state that she cannot get involved in the legal issues, and put the focus back on the case management program. However, certain circumstantial questions may be appropriate. Has the injury impacted the individual's mental comfort level with his or her job? Is the individual concerned about safety back at the sander belt? Seeking answers to these types of inquiries, the case manager can then help put services or worksite modifications in place that will help the patient overcome his or her fear.

Some worker's compensation issues can hinder the case manager's ability to be effective on behalf of the patient and the referral source because they point to hidden agendas being played out. The mentality that leans toward suing and retiring on the proceeds is an obstacle to successful case management intervention, as is a lawsuit involving a piece of equipment or a manufacturer. The case manager might know from the get-go that a company is mistreating its workforce and that the patient's anger is such that the case manager's efforts will be sidetracked. If the role is to minimize the disability and improve the return-to-work outlook, the case manager needs to take an objective look at the situation, realize its lack of potential, and discuss with the referral source whether the continued use of case management is appropriate.

In group medical plan cases, case managers are only responding to medical care issues; there are no return-to-work or lost-earnings-replacement issues. A carrier will not be asking, "When can I expect John back in the office?" Again, key points will be the type of policy, the dollars available, the dollar limitations, the services included in the plan, and the plan's flexibility. Some group medical plans are very, very generous, incorporating provisions for home care, skilled nursing facilities, rehabilitation facilities, and rehabilitation, especially when provided outside of an acute care facility. On the other hand, other policies may include generous benefits for inpatient care and hardly any language supporting an alternative setting. Such limitations may dictate a case manager's degree of success. If the case manager uncovers these limitations as she is collecting information from the referral source and begins to see the intended care plan unraveling, what are the options? Work with half the case management plan? Work the case any way possible? The case manager might go ahead with the full assessment and offer options after ascertaining that there are decision makers who would consider covering benefits that are not outlined in the policy but that are more appropriate to the case and potentially less expensive as well. In group medical plans and fully insured plans, there is often less flexibility, as plan language has been set in stone because it is formulated based on group experience (e.g., premium rates are assigned based on age, sex, and lifestyle). With self-funded or employer-funded plans, even though the plan language may not include provisions for alternative care, there may be more willingness to consider other possibilities.

Like workers' compensation cases, auto insurance and disability insurance cases are governed by state regulations. When taking notes on an auto policy case, a case manager should request information on medical and lost-wages provisions, the amount of dollars available, the covered years, and whether the carrier has direct control of the policy. Is an individual covered for any medical treatment wherever it may be administered? If the auto accident happened out of state, which state's laws will take precedence? It may be the state in which the injury occurred, the state in which the policy is written, or the state where the employer's headquarters office is located. In short- or long-term disability cases, the extent and framework of the policy must be known before the case manager can begin an assessment.

A Wrap-up of Referral-Source Communication Steps

1. A referral call to the case manager is made.
2. The case manager gets the appropriate business details and confirms the needs of the referral source (e.g., expectations, fees, format, time frame for reports, etc.).
3. The case manager requests case background (e.g., the status of the patient, the diagnosis and prognosis, the type of insurance coverage, the patient's eligibility under the policy, the policy benefit limits, the plan's flexibility, the restrictions on care, etc.).
4. The case manager confirms the initial assessment and report parameters in writing to the referral source and/or payer.
5. The case manager makes a follow-up call to review the confirmation letter.
6. The case manager documents all conversations.

TALKING WITH THE PATIENT

Following the initial conversation with the referral source, the first person the case manager will interview is the patient. The object is to obtain an overview of the patient's current medical history, the particular individual, and the situation. The case manager must be proactive and non-threatening, perceived as an advocate and viewed as a benefit. The case manager must also encourage the patient to be participatory, which is done by being supportive and not being overly presumptive or controlling. Because the first contact is the key to future success, the case manager must take the time to lay the groundwork. To set up the first meeting with the patient, the case manager should telephone or, in cases where the patient has no phone or contact number, send a letter (see Exhibits 7-1 to 7-5).

Telephone Call to Patient To Set Up Initial Visit

Case Manager: Ms. Williams, this is Ann Sanders and I am a rehabilitation nurse [medical case manager, nurse case manager, counselor, etc.] here in the Brown-

Exhibit 7-1 Sample Letter to New Client Who Does Not Have a Telephone

---

Mr. John Williams
132 E. Main Street
Brownsville, TX 84362

Dear Mr. Williams:

I am a rehabilitation nurse [case manager] and I have been asked by your insurance company [name] to meet with you and see if I can be of assistance in your recovery from your injury [present illness]. In the information that was sent to me, I did not find a telephone number for you, and I need to talk with you so that we can arrange a convenient time to meet.

When you receive this letter, would you please call my office collect at the above number. If I am not in the office, please leave a message that you called and also a telephone contact number where I may reach you.

I am looking forward to working with you and I hope to hear from you in the next day or two.

Sincerely,

Angie White, R.N.
Medical Case Manager

Source: Reprinted from "Interpersonal Skills for Case Managers," *Case Management Practice,* with permission of the Foundation for Rehabilitation Certification, Education & Research, © 1993.

---

ville area. I work with people who have had serious illnesses or injuries. Your workers' compensation carrier [health insurance carrier, etc.] asked me to visit with you to see if I can be of assistance during your recovery. How have you been feeling today?

Case Manager: It sounds like you're still having a few problems. I am going to be out in the Hampton area next Tuesday morning. Would around 10:00 A.M. be a convenient time for me to drop in and visit with you for a few minutes? [I'm planning to be at the hospital around 9:30 tomorrow and will plan to visit you. As far as you know, will that be a convenient time for you?]

[If the patient seems hesitant or has questions about what the case manager will be doing in working with her/him, the case manager should briefly explain her role but try to direct the greater portion of her answers to the personal visit. A good rapport can be developed much better in person.]

Exhibit 7-2 Sample Letter of Introduction to Insured for High-Risk Pregnancy Management

August 16, 19xx

Dear Ms. _____:

I enjoyed speaking with you today and, as promised, this letter is to re-explain what my call and our services are all about.

As discussed, _____ is a private consulting firm used by Third Party Administrator on behalf of your employer group to provide assistance to individuals who may experience difficulties with certain medical conditions.

Diabetes can *sometimes* make a pregnancy difficult and what we want to insure is that you and your baby come through it healthy and happy. Our nurse case managers work with patients, their physicians, and families in coordinating the necessary care and services that may be necessary both now and in the future months.

This service is at no cost to you and is provided through the benefit plan. It again is not a "hands on" service, nor is it intended to interrupt or interfere with any care you are now receiving.

In order to determine just how we may be of assistance, one of our nurses would like to meet with you at your home. Because they are often out visiting patients, we ask that you call COLLECT at (999) 999-9999 so that we can put her in touch with you.

Please accept my personal assurance that every effort will be extended on your behalf and our best wishes for a happy, healthy pregnancy and a very healthy, happy baby for you and your husband.

If you have any questions or concerns, please feel free to contact me at any time at the above number.

Warmest regards,

Case Manager

cc: Claims Department

Courtesy of Options Unlimited, Case Management Services Division, Huntington, N.Y.

Case Manager: OK, fine, I'll plan to see you next Tuesday around 10:00 A.M. Let me give you my telephone number so if your plans change, you can just call me collect at my office. If I don't hear from you, I will look forward to seeing you next Tuesday.

Exhibit 7-3 Sample Letter of Introduction for Services Requested for Insured's Child

Date

Mr. xxxxxxxx
xxxxxxxxxxxx
xxxxxxxxxxxx

Dear Mr.xxxxxxxx:

Please allow this letter to serve as an introduction and explanation of services that have been requested on behalf of your son, Anthony, by _____ Managed Care Services, Group Health Insurance. *Case Management Company* is a private consulting firm utilized by Third Party Administrators on behalf of their insureds who may be experiencing difficulties with a variety of medical, psychiatric, and other complicated situations.

These services are provided at no cost to you and are offered to provide assistance and coordination of services that will be necessary both now and in the future. Our role is not intended to interrupt or interfere with any care or therapies that your son is now receiving, nor will our nurse consultants be providing any direct counseling or "hands on" care. We work with physicians, therapists, the family, and patient, in order that the best outcome is obtained in a manner that is caring, appropriate, and cost-effective.

In order to determine just how we may help, would you please call us COLLECT at _____. One of our consultants would like to arrange an appointment to meet with you, your son, and physician, if available.

Enclosed, please find one of our brochures which describes our services further. Please accept my personal assurance that every effort will be extended on behalf of your son and we look forward to working with you.

Thank you very much for your time and anticipated cooperation.

Very truly yours,

Courtesy of Options Unlimited, Case Management Services Division, Huntington, N.Y.

Case Manager: I have your address in my file but let me get directions to your house. I sometimes get lost if I don't have real good directions.

Case Manager: Those are good directions, thanks. Mary, I've enjoyed talking with you and I'll see you next Tuesday morning.[2]

Exhibit 7-4 Sample Letter of Introduction for a Workers' Compensation Case

---

Date

Dear Mr. _____:

Please allow this letter to serve as an introduction and explanation of services that have been requested on your behalf by _____, the Workers' Compensation Administrator for your employer. _Case Management Company_ is a private disability management consulting firm that works with individuals such as you who have sustained injuries in the course of employment.

This is not a "hands on" service, nor is it meant in any way to interrupt or interfere with the care you are currently receiving. The role of our consultant is to work with you, your physicians, therapist, and other health professionals who may be involved to insure that you derive the best results from these efforts. Our goal is to assist you with a return to a medically stable, comfortable, and productive lifestyle in an employment situation.

In order to determine just how we may be of assistance, one of our consultants, _____, R.N., would like to meet with you at your home. If you have not heard from our consultant, would you please call us COLLECT at _____ in order that we can put her in contact with you.

Enclosed, please find one of our brochures which describes our services. Should you have any questions or concerns, please feel free to contact me directly.

Mr. _____, we look forward to working with you and please accept my personal assurance that every effort will be made on your behalf.

Very truly yours,

Courtesy of Options Unlimited, Case Management Services Division, Huntington, N.Y.

It is often advisable to send a brief letter, postcard, or handwritten memo to remind the patient of the case manager's pending visit, especially if considerable travel time and mileage are involved.

Initial Visit

At the initial visit, the case manager's first questions will center on the patient's comprehension of his or her medical condition. What does the patient see as the problem? The patient might say, "My doctor told me I had a heart attack." The case manager can then elicit further information

Exhibit 7-5 Sample Letter of Introduction for Services Provided through a Third-Party Administrator

---

January 15, 19

Dear _____:

    Please allow this letter to serve as an introduction and explanation of services that have been requested on your behalf by _____ of Third Party Administrator (TPA) which is the company administrating the health care benefits on behalf of your employer, _____.
_____ is a private consulting firm utilized by TPA on behalf of their insureds to assist them with the problems resulting from a variety of medical conditions. This service is at no cost to you, and is a benefit provided by the company.

    Our nurse consultants work with you, your family, and treating physicians in coordinating whatever care and services are necessary in order that you may receive the best results possible. This intervention is not intended to interrupt or interfere with any care you are currently receiving, nor is this a "hands-on" service.

    In order to determine just how we may be of assistance, one of our consultants, _____, would like to meet with you at your home. Because our consultants are frequently out of the office, would you please call us COLLECT at (999) 999-9999 in order that we can put her in touch with you.

    Enclosed, please find one of our brochures which further describes our services. Should you have any questions or concerns, please feel free to contact me directly. Please accept my personal assurance that every effort will be extended on your behalf.

Very truly yours,

Case Manager

cc: Claims Department

Courtesy of Options Unlimited, Case Management Services Division, Huntington, N.Y.

---

by asking, "What do you think that means? Will it change your lifestyle?" By encouraging the patient to use his or her own words, the case manager can get a reading on the patient's level of understanding and acceptance (or denial) of his or her situation. Perhaps the patient minimizes the illness. The referral source may have told the case manager that the patient has a malignant tumor that has already metastasized to other organs. But the patient says, "Well, I had a growth and the doctor removed it and he said that I should be fine now." It might be that the referral source, the physicians, and the case manager all know the patient's true medical condition but the patient and family do not have a clue. Perhaps the family wants to isolate and protect the patient from knowing his or her true health status. It is the case manager's job to ascertain the reality of the situation by speaking to the treating physician and family members and by getting documentation from the referral source.

A case manager should never assume a patient has the ability to accept a diagnosis. Some of the most brilliant medical professionals are uncomfortable hearing about their own health problems. Patients and their families can block out information or deny the obvious. Case managers must take each person where they are at the time of the assessment and explore his or her view of the situation. Does this particular patient understand that he has had a serious or a minor illness? Does he understand how it is impacting his life now and will impact it in the future? Does he have any knowledge about that part of his body? If surgery was performed, does he understand why? Has his doctor been communicating with him? If he is on medication, does he know what it is for? If he is in the hospital and about to go home, is he knowledgeable about his discharge plan and what he needs to do? What does he need to be watchful for? Does he understand any specific limitations he may have now? Does he accept these? Many patients intellectually grasp such limitations but do not take them in emotionally.

A patient might say, "Yes, I've had a heart attack and I understand that the major wall of my heart was involved." When the case manager asks, "Do you think you can resume all your regular activities?" the response might be, "Oh, yeah, no problem." But the case manager knows that this is not the case. The patient has heard a portion of the doctor's answer, has been selective in listening, and does not have a total grasp of what he or she needs to know to be a cooperative, compliant participant in his or her health care plan.

Whereas some patients may be in denial, others are overly dramatic and intent on being a long-term part of the health care system. Some patients who have relatively minor problems try to boost them into life-threatening disorders. Having a major illness allows them a respite from life's burdens.

The ideal patient, after having been given good information about his or her condition, would accept that information and be realistic about possible treatments and likely outcomes. Unfortunately, the typical patient in the kind of cases that case managers tend to get may be physically or emotionally overwhelmed as a result of the severity of the condition.

The patient might be a poor historian, might be unable to recall information, might be on a life-support system and unable to communicate easily, or might be very young. In a pediatric case, even though family members will be making the "life-and-death" decisions on treatment alternatives and surgical recommendations, the case manager will want to know what the child understands. It is part of the case manager's role to make sure every patient has all the information he or she wants and needs about his or her case.

Because past medical history may impact the present, the case manager must also ask leading questions about other medical conditions that might, from a medical management perspective, affect recovery. This is best done by example, as the patient may not perceive how another condition (one that seems minor or that the patient has lived with for years) might influence treatment. For instance, the patient might decide his or her high blood pressure is "nothing" and never mention it. In the case of a patient about to undergo surgery to repair multiple fractures to a leg bone, the case manager might ask, "Have you ever had problems with your circulation, any bone disease or diabetes? Is this a recurrence of an old injury? Have you had prior surgeries or prior hospitalizations?" A person with a healthy, active lifestyle suffering a first injury should be able to recover in a reasonable amount of time given good medical care. An individual who has been through it all before, especially with a knee or back injury, or even one who's suffered similar work-related injuries with the same employer, might experience delays in recovery.

Another important query centers on medications. This area is crucial, and too little attention is paid to it by all members of the medical delivery system, including case managers. A case manager should ask a patient to bring out all the pills and medications being taken, including over-the-counter medications and herbal vitamins, whether or not the patient thinks they factor into his or her condition. There is a gap between what a patient perceives as a problem and what the medical profession knows is a problem.

I was working with a gentleman in New Hampshire who was diagnosed with cellulitis and thrombosis. Recently starting a new job as a security guard, this 275-pound man had been given a brisk physical and had been hired with this pre-existing condition because no one really looked at his legs. A member of an HMO plan, he had been seen by a different physician every time he had an appointment, and no one was tracking his needs and care. My role was to evaluate his status as a short-term disability patient.

At my on-site home visit, I found him living alone in a filthy house where he had just shared a can of stew with the cat. One leg was propped up on a chair and the other was on an ottoman. I asked if he had any other medical problems. The answer was no. I then requested that he show me any pills or medications he took.

He pointed to a shoe box filled with bottles, "Well, I've got these water pills here and my sugar pills . . ."

"What are these for?"

"My diabetes, but that's nothing. I've had it for years." In fact, he also had been diagnosed as having hypertension and emphysema in addition to the diabetes, was supposed to be on a low-sodium diet, and had just consumed a high-sodium lunch.

"And what's this bottle for?"

"I take those when I feel my blood pressure is high."

"How do you know when it's high?"

"Sometimes I get a headache."

It seems that when he was diagnosed as having hypertension, the presenting problem was his headaches. In his mind then, he had high blood pressure on the days he got a headache. In other words, high blood pressure was not a serious condition he felt he had, but a minor problem that might occur on one day or another. We repeated the question-and-answer scenario until we had reviewed all the bottles in the box.

People tend to follow their own rules for taking medications. Case managers need to ask not only "What are you taking for this diagnosis?" but also "Are you taking any other medications?" And as I found from experience, the question needs to be pursued. I might note a medication in the physician's report. When I ask the patient if she's taking it, she will say she is not. Why not? She does not like the way it makes her feel, she doesn't want to become dependent on it, she doesn't want to be taking it forever, or she simply got tired of taking it. Has she told her physician this? No, but she will tell him when she sees him. Her next appointment is scheduled for six months later.

In good situations, the medication manipulation has no unfortunate consequences; however, the ill effects of overmedication or lack of medication can be harrowing. Even if the patient appears to be progressing well, it is important for the case manager, as an individual charged with preventing patients from slipping through the cracks in the medical delivery system, to check this aspect of the care profile.

Another part of a case manager's assessment centers on socioeconomic and psychosocial factors. What are the family dynamics at work? Is the patient a child or an adult, married or single, single and living alone? A person with many contacts, active in the community and church, might have a vast network of coworkers, family, and friends who can become caretakers for a time. A single person new to an area is more isolated and will need, for example, an entirely different medical support system for home care.

What is the patient's vocational status? An active, valued member of a company tends to want to resolve any medical problems as soon as possible. A person recently fired or with a bleak economic outlook will react to treatment differently. An upbeat, optimistic, well-adjusted patient is more likely to follow a treatment plan. A person whom life has beaten about the head and shoulders could be on disability or workers' compensation for years, electing a "disability mentality" in which the illness becomes his or her job and social life. It is also important to find out about the patient's prior jobs in the event the patient is not able to return to his or her most recent type of employment.

Avocational interests and hobbies will also influence a patient's recovery curve. If a patient enjoyed a number of active physical pursuits, such as skiing, golf, and horseback riding, but can no longer engage in them, the case manager will want to help the patient develop other ways of expressing an interest in those pursuits and remain mentally stimulated during recovery (e.g., an avid golfer might be encouraged to read the biography of a golf pro). Generally, those with the most avocations are more likely to be responsive to treatment. People who are not participatory by nature sometimes have to be encouraged to take charge and fight for their health.

Prior to closing the personal meeting with the patient, the case manager should obtain a signed consent form (Exhibit 7-6) from the patient or the patient's guardian. Required to review medical records and to share information with the patient's physician(s) and attorney if the case is in litigation, a consent form allows the case manager access to medical data regarding the patient.

TALKING WITH THE FAMILY

After talking with the patient (when possible), the case manager will interview the family for their perception of the situation. Again, it is essential to explain the role of case management, citing examples of activities with other patients in order to help illustrate the case manager's potential contribution.

Owing to the stress of an illness or injury, particularly in long-term cases, the family will undergo role changes, dependency shifts, anxiety, anger, and an inability to make decisions. Therefore, the case manager must get a clear picture of the family structure and function prior to and after the illness.

When meeting with a patient and his or her family, it is important to observe the personal dynamics. As an illness progresses, some family members may foster a mentality of dependence on the part of the patient. Although well intentioned, they are so frightened by what has happened

Exhibit 7-6 Patient Consent Form

AUTHORIZATION

I, _____, HEREBY REQUEST AND AUTHORIZE ANY HOS-
PITAL, PHYSICIAN, OR OTHER PERSON WHO HAS ATTENDED OR
EXAMINED ME, OR WHO MAY HEREAFTER ATTEND OR EXAMINE
ME FOR _____

_____

_____

TO DISCLOSE ANY AND ALL INFORMATION OBTAINED THEREBY,
RELATIVE TO THIS INJURY OR ILLNESS, TO OPTIONS UNLIMITED. I
FURTHER AUTHORIZE THAT THIS INFORMATION MAY BE SHARED
WITH OTHER PROFESSIONALS, AGENCIES, OR INSURANCE COMPA-
NIES WHO MAY BE INVOLVED IN THE PROVISION OR PAYMENT OF
SERVICES THAT MAY BE NECESSARY.

_____   _____
        (Date)   (Signature of Party)

_____   _____
                                 (Signature of Guardian)

Witness: _____

Courtesy of Options Unlimited, Case Management Services Division, Huntington,
N.Y.

---

that they become overprotective. They no longer allow the patient to participate in conversation; talk goes on around the patient as if he or she
were not even there. "He needs to eat more." "She feels uncomfortable."
Sometimes this is the fault of the health care system. Assuming that a
patient is too weak or tired or medicated, professionals and family talk
about but not with him or her. The patient lies in bed and is discussed as
if lacking the will or desire to be involved in his or her own care. Such
behavior, rather than protecting a loved one, is dehumanizing. If the patient cannot converse, of course, another person becomes the historian,
but if the patient can communicate, the case manager really needs to involve and empower him or her. In no way would a case manager want to
demean a family member or friend, but it must be remembered that the
patient *is* the patient.

One object of the initial assessment is to determine how family members perceive their roles. If a case manager sees that one person seems to

be taking over the conversation and correcting other family members, some questions must be directed at that person. Perhaps this person has a completely different understanding of the problem than the patient; perhaps the physician has talked at greater length with him or her. If this person will be the prime caretaker at home, he or she might feel a responsibility to be the spokesperson for the family.

The case manager needs answers to the following questions. What was the prime caretaker's role in the family prior to this illness? Did the prime caretaker run the household? Hold down a job? Does the caretaker still have those responsibilities in addition to caring for the patient? Will the caretaker's job be jeopardized by this illness? How is the caretaker reacting to the illness? Will he or she be a willing participant or be frightened by the disease? What is the caretaker's intellectual and emotional capability? The caretaker might understand the situation intellectually but be emotionally devastated and barely able to cope.

Referral for case management intervention might come three months or three years after an accident or the onset of an illness, and the case manager might be confronted at the initial assessment with a family member who has been handling stressful physical, emotional, and financial aspects of an illness every day and is now burned out and about to walk out the door. (It is not uncommon for the spouse of a person with multiple sclerosis, after managing the disease for years, to suddenly cave in and leave the marriage.) The family member has used all his or her personal resources and unless someone does something soon, the case manager will no longer have an intact family with which to work.

The case manager needs to look at all the members of the family and determine their physical and emotional health. If children are involved, how has the situation affected them? Is there an older child who is now going to have to assume the responsibilities of one parent, perhaps taking time off from school to help? Are the children really worried because mom or dad may be dying? Is a brother or sister irrevocably injured to the extent of being unable to resume his or her prior place in the family? Depending on their age, children may develop symptoms or illnesses or engage in emotional outbursts as they try to come to terms with the changes in their lives. Even very young children, unable to talk, will sense that some acute changes have occurred and will react in some way.

The case manager should ask the family members about their own health as well as the patient's health. Especially if the case manager anticipates that a family member might become the primary care provider at home, even if that possibility has not been discussed, questions regarding this person's medical status are in order. Is the person healthy enough to assist or overwhelmed by his or her own illness? The case manager should also compile a "medical family tree." Are parents and grandparents still alive and well? Do they have medical disorders? In talking to a 42-year-old man recovering from a heart attack who says, "Well, yeah, my father died from heart disease when he was 53," the case manager will know that this individual is not only dealing with the fact that he now has a problem but is also facing his own mortality because of a strong history of cardiac disease in the family.

All these elements—the illness or injury, present condition, medical history, current medications, family dynamics, vocation, and avocation—help point up the pluses and minuses of the treatment plan and help the treating team do their best work on behalf of the patient.

TALKING TO THE TREATING PHYSICIAN

To set the stage for a good working relationship with the treating physician, the case manager should explain the role of case management and communicate a desire to work with the physician to ensure the best outcome for the patient. The physician should be made to realize that help is available for dealing with any problems with the patient that may occur. The more a physician understands about case management, the more collaborative the partnership can be.

Finding a good time for a personal meeting with the treating physician can be a challenge. A case manager can attempt to reach the physician at the hospital when he or she has just met with the patient or can telephone the physician's office to set up a visit. To smooth the path, it is a good idea to become friendly with a receptionist or nurse in the office.

Initial Phone Contact with Physician's Office To Set Up Personal Consultation

In setting up a consultation with the physician, it is best to address the receptionist or nurse by name if possible.

Case Manager: Good morning. My name is Sandi Miller, and I am a case manager [rehabilitation nurse, rehabilitation specialist, etc.]. I'm calling in reference to Dr. Brown's patient, John Fuller. I've been asked by Mr. Fuller's insurance company, U.S. America, to develop a rehab plan with him. To make sure my plan for him is appropriate, I need to schedule a brief personal meeting with Dr. Brown. [OR: I wonder if you can help me. I'd like to speak with Dr. Brown regarding Mr. Fuller today or tomorrow if at all possible. What would be the best way to contact him?]

[At this point, the receptionist or secretary advises that Dr. Brown does not see rehabilitation nurses and she requests that a letter be submitted.]

Case Manager: In some cases, a letter is adequate for a rehabilitation plan. However, in Mr. Fuller's situation, his medical care is very complex, and there are several issues that I just can't adequately resolve by letter. I understand that Dr. Brown's time is valuable but it's critical that I have about five minutes of his time.

Case Manager: I am willing to flex my schedule as much as possible to get this consultation. Would late afternoon be my best possibility?

Case Manager: Well, since Thursdays are better for you for these kinds of meetings, could I come in about 3:00? I promise I will keep the meeting brief and to the point.

Case Manager: Fine, I appreciate your help. I will be in next Thursday at 3:00. I'll be mailing you a confirming letter with a medical release for Dr. Brown's file. Could you give me your name please?

Case Manager: Jill, thanks again for your help.[3]

Initial Phone Contact To Schedule Phone Consultation with a Physician

When the case is medically less complex or the physical distance great, a phone conversation with the treating physician will be sufficient. Again, it is unusual to reach a physician by phone on the first call, so developing rapport with the office personnel can speed the establishment of a phone consultation date and time.

Case Manager: Good morning, this is Sandi Miller and I am a rehabilitation nurse. I'm calling in reference to Mr. John Fuller, who I believe has been a patient of Dr. Brown's for the past four months.

Case Manager: I'm putting together a long-term care management plan for Mr. Fuller, and I have several medical questions I need to discuss with Dr. Brown as soon as possible. Would I be able to speak to Dr. Brown this morning about Mr. Fuller?

Case Manager: Let me check my calendar. I'm going to be out of the office this afternoon after 3:00. If I called around 4:00 tomorrow, would that work?

[Next day]

Case Manager: Yes, Jill, good afternoon. This is Sandi Miller. We spoke yesterday regarding Mr. Fuller, and you asked me to call back at 4:00 for Dr. Brown. Is he available to talk?

Case Manager: Yes, I'll be glad to hold for a minute. I appreciate your time.[4]

The case manager needs to know the physician's orientation to the patient. How long has the physician been treating the patient? Is this a recent illness or has the physician been overseeing the treatment plan for some time? Is the physician new to the patient or does he or she have a longstanding relationship as the family practitioner? The physician may have cared for a brother, sister, mother, or father and thus have some insight into the health needs of the patient. Is he someone who is trusted by the family or is he, as in many cases today, a consulting physician who saw the patient for the first time in the hospital and does not yet have a feel for the patient and family? Maybe the physician had an assistant conduct the patient history interview and physical, and perhaps has not really been all that involved in the case.

The case manager should hear the patient's status in the physician's own words. I encourage case managers to pursue details by saying, "Doctor, I am going to be asking you some questions that I've already asked your patient. Although you believe you have already done a thorough job of explaining his condition to him, we find that when it all settles in, the information retained is very selective. Patients understand some elements and let others drift away. I need to find out in your words what his problem is. What have you told him? What do you think he understands?"

If I am able to reach the physician prior to speaking to the patient, I explain my reasons for asking about what has been said. "I need to know what you've told your patient for my own information and because, after speaking with you, I plan to talk to your patient and I don't want to tell him anything that you have not. If you feel he has a certain understanding, and when I speak to him I find that it seems to be lacking, I hope you don't mind if I call you. I feel it might be important. Sometimes we find that patients minimize their disease or choose to 'forget' the parts they can't cope with. This will impact your treatment plan. I want to make sure that we're all speaking the same language—that he has all the information you need him to have to be able to cooperate and follow your care plan for him."

Of course, it is important to ask, What is the diagnosis? What is the treatment plan and prognosis? What do you think is going to be the outcome for this individual, both in the short term and long term? Do you anticipate any complications? Is there anything you feel you might need assistance with—patient information, lifestyle changes, diet modifications? The whole physician–case manager introduction process should focus on eliciting and sharing of information and jointly establishing the best way to provide proper care.

The physician also needs to know how the case manager fits into the picture. "I represent the workers' compensation carrier," "I represent the employer group," or "I represent the employer group's insurance carrier for the medical plan, and I wanted you to know that the patient really has limited benefit dollars for inpatient care. Let's make those dollars stretch for the long term. May I suggest alternatives to you? You may be more comfortable with one rather than the others. Do you have any alternative-care ideas you'd like to suggest?"

When the case manager knows upfront there is a limit on care dollars, he or she has a responsibility to make the physician aware of the limit and share in the goal of using the money in the best way. Although some care options may be ideal, the expenses connected with them make them poor first choices. An alternative plan may not be the ideal, but it will not pose any risk to the patient and may buy care and services over a longer period of time. It also helps to give the physician examples of the kind of work case managers do and to suggest alternatives in a professional but noncombative manner. "These are the kinds of things I have done with other doctors before to help them with patients and they have appreciated it. It is not the patient's fault that there are limits on his benefits dollars. To ignore that reality is to deprive your patient of an alternative that will provide care over the longer term."

Sample Doctor Contact Script[5]

Introduction

"Hello, Dr. Brown." (Shake physician's hand, comment about office.) I'm the Medical Case Manager working with Mr. Fuller. I saw him for the first time on Tuesday and he seemed to be:

- getting along well."
- having trouble with his medication, his diet, restrictions on his activities. . ."
- anxious to return to his work doing construction, tree trimming, tennis instruction. . ."

If case manager has met with another doctor, briefly review conversation. (Case manager should offer specific information. If possible, offer it in a way that compliments the doctor's treatment.)

"In order to plan appropriately with you for Mr. Fuller's recovery [return to work, most comfortable and fullest quality of life], I need your direction. I'll be brief; I know you are quite busy. I just have a few questions."

Current Medical Status

"How do you see Mr. Fuller's current medical status? Where are we now with him medically?" (Case manager should listen for projected treatment plans and current limitation/abilities, filling in answers to as many questions as possible.)

Future Treatment Plans

"What are your future treatment plans for him [medication, length of treatment, surgery type and timetable, physical limits and duration, etc.]?"

Long-Range Prognosis

"You would anticipate maximum medical recovery when?"

Vocational Issues

"Mr. Fuller's job has been _____. He needs to be able to [case manager describes physical requirements of job]. His employer will let him return with half day/full day/limited activity [describe]. I'd like to set a target date when that might be possible. Would [date] be realistic?"

Residual Disability

"At this time, do you anticipate any permanent disability from the injury? If you anticipate permanent disability, what is your estimation of the percentage of this disability after maximum medical recovery?"

Long-Term Disability

"I will continue to stay in touch with you through his recovery process."

Closing Comments

"That answers all my initial questions. Is there anything else you can think of that I may have overlooked? Is there any way I can be of assistance to you with Mr. Fuller?

"What is the best way for me to contact you [phone, day of week, time of day, through nurse/receptionist]? Thank you for your time."

Letters of Introduction and Physician Questionnaires

Exhibits 7-7 to 7-10 consist of sample letters of introduction to a physician, several of which are designed to be sent accompanied by a physician questionnaire, a good tool for obtaining information for an initial needs assessment, as well as for follow-up reports. Exhibit 7-10 includes an attached physician questionnaire, Exhibit 7-11 is a blank physician questionnaire, and Exhibit 7-12 is a completed physician questionnaire.

When there is more than one treating physician, the case manager needs to touch base with all those having an active and ongoing role. The case manager might also discover during the family interview that there was a prior treating physician who may have some very valuable information that even the current medical team does not know.

Exhibit 7-7 Sample Letter of Introduction to Physician (Neonatal Case)

August 19, 19

Dr. _____
Neonatology
Smith Street
Morristown, NJ 07960

Re:
Insured:
S.S.#:
Employer Group:

Dear Dr. _____ :

As per our previous conversations, I would like to take this opportunity to express my appreciation for your input with regard to the above referenced infant. As you are aware, I am the Nurse Case Manager that was following his mother prior to her delivery. I would further appreciate a few moments of your time to become familiar with Case Management Company.

The services of Case Management Co., a private medical case management firm, were requested by the administration of Mr. _____'s group health policy to assist this family with any problems or needs experienced during the course of this high risk pregnancy. This benefit also extends to the infant that was delivered as a result, especially in light of his premature birth.

My role as the case manager is not to interfere with but to complement your prescribed plan of care. Having a neonatal nursing background, I can certainly appreciate the complications attendant to a premature birth. By coordinating with you, should the discharge plan include home services of any type, I would be able to arrange for those services while not creating additional stress for the family, and in many cases with minimal out-of-pocket costs to them.

I realize that at this time, it may still be premature to discuss the discharge plan, though a periodic update will enable me to anticipate possible needs and be prepared to implement ways of meeting those needs. As I believe that our mutual goal is to help this family and infant achieve the most optimal level of well-being available, your professional expertise and opinions are greatly appreciated.

I also realize that your time is at a premium, and am grateful that you have made it possible for me to obtain the updates from your office. It would be very helpful for further communication to occur as discharge be-

continues

comes imminent so that any posthospitalization care could be put in place in as expedient a fashion as possible.

I thank you for your assistance with this case, and appreciate that you have taken the time to consider the information in this letter. I am enclosing a copy of our brochure to further explain our services, along with my business card. Should you have any questions about this material, or concerns about your patient that you feel we need to discuss, please feel free to contact me at (999) 999-9999.

Very truly yours,

Case Manager

cc: Claims Department

Courtesy of Options Unlimited, Case Management Services Division, Huntington, N.Y.

INDEPENDENT MEDICAL AND SECOND OPINION EXAMS

In some cases, an independent medical exam or a second opinion exam will be requested. A case manager's involvement is linked to the type of exam performed (see Table 7-1). An independent medical exam is generally utilized by insurance carriers to determine the diagnosis, the need for continued treatment, the degree of disability (partial or total), the duration of a disability (temporary, long-term, or permanent), and the patient's ability to return to work. Customarily arranged by the carrier (see Exhibit 7-13), it is often seen by the patient as an exam he or she is required to undergo. The physician most often remains in a nontreating role. Depending on the circumstances, a rehabilitation nurse or a case manager may assist in setting up the exam and may accompany the patient, but in most instances neither the nurse nor the case manager will be present at the exam.

When should a case manager expect an independent medical exam to be requested? Such exams are used routinely by some carriers when treatment appears excessive (e.g., prolonged duplication of services, such as physical therapy or chiropractic manipulation), when the recovery time from an accident or injury appears overly extended, or when there is a delay in the patient's return-to-work schedule. They are also employed upon request to authorize surgery, expensive equipment, or unusual diagnostic testing or when there is an increase in the number of treating professionals. Certain diagnostic conditions (e.g., stress disorders) might also signal use of an independent medical exam.

Exhibit 7-8 Sample Letter of Introduction to Physician To Be Sent with Questionnaire

Date

_____, M.D.
_____ Pediatric Association
P.O. Box 5
417 State Street

_____

Dear Dr. _____:

Claimant:
Insured:
Employee #:

I have been asked by _____ Companies to provide medical case management services to the above named patient and to assist with any needed medical services. I met with Mrs. _____ and _____ at their home in _____ on July 11th for an initial evaluation.

My business card and brochure describing *Case Management Company* and our services are enclosed, in order to better describe my involvement with the _____. Mrs. _____ referred me to you on details regarding _____ past and present illness, as she was unable to recall specific details.

For your convenience, I have prepared and enclosed a questionnaire which I ask you to complete, along with a stamped and self-addressed envelope. Enclosed, you will find a signed release of medical information form.

Thank you very much for your time and assistance in answering these questions. I look forward to working with you and the _____ and assisting with any needs or services that may become necessary, both now and in the future.

I extend my sincere appreciation for your time and valuable input and I look forward to our future contact. Should you have any questions or concerns, please feel to contact me at _____.

Very truly yours,

_____, R.N.
Rehabilitation Consultant

XX:xx
Enc.

Courtesy of Options Unlimited, Case Management Services Division, Huntington, N.Y.

Exhibit 7-9 Sample Letter of Introduction to Physician To Be Sent with Questionnaire

Dr. XXXXXXX
10 Smith Street
Chicago, IL 60611

Re:
S.S.#:

Dear Dr. XXXXXXX:

Please allow me to introduce myself as the case management consultant, with _____, who is currently following the progress of your patient, _____.

The services of _____, a private medical case management firm, were requested by the administrators of Mr./Mrs. _____'s group health policy, on his/her behalf, to assist him/her with any problems or needs that he/she may experience during the course of his/her illness.

My role as Mr./Mrs. _____'s case manager is not to interfere with but to complement your prescribed plan of care. This is accomplished through my interactions, not only with this patient, but with you, his/her physician, as well as all other health care providers involved with his/her care.

I believe that our mutual goal is to help Mr./Mrs. _____ achieve the most optimal level of well-being available to him/her. To do so, I must anticipate his/her needs based on available medical data and physician input. Your professional expertise and opinions, on behalf of this patient, would be greatly appreciated.

Would you kindly take a few moments of your time to complete the enclosed questionnaire? Please return this to me, at your earliest convenience, to _____, in the enclosed stamped self-addressed envelope. Also, please find a signed release of medical information.

If you have any questions regarding this matter, please do not hesitate to contact me at _____ at (999) 999-9999.

Thank you for your anticipated cooperation.

Very truly yours,

Medical Management Consultant

Courtesy of Options Unlimited, Case Management Services Division, Huntington, N.Y.

Exhibit 7-10 Sample Letter of Introduction to Physician with Specific Questionnaire Attached

Date

Dr. _____
____ East 37th Street
New York, NY 10016

Re: Claimant

Dear Dr. _____:

As I explained to you in an earlier conversation, I am the Nurse Case Manager who is working with _____ at the request of _____, the third party administrator of his health care benefits. As his case manager, I have followed him now for approximately nine months. In that time, I am aware that he has recently had a liver biopsy and is presently awaiting the results. Because of this, and also as he has informed me that his T-Cell count is at 56, I am enclosing a questionnaire that I would ask you to complete. I feel that the time for additional information may be coming and in order for me to be as effective as possible, it is important that I have some additional information.

Because of the sensitive nature of this diagnosis, I am also including a copy of the authorization that the claimant signed enabling me to obtain such information. You will also note a copy of the _____ brochure, which I hope will help to answer any questions you may have with regard to my role, is also enclosed. Should you have any questions, I would welcome hearing from you.

I thank you very much for your time. I know that your time is a very valuable commodity. I trust that this information will help me in assisting _____. I also hope that this letter will provide an introduction for you so that you will contact me when I can be of assistance to both you and _____.

Should you have any questions or need to reach me with regard to my interventions on behalf of _____, please contact my office at _____ and leave a message. I will contact you as soon as possible.

Very truly yours,

_____

cc: Claims Department

continues

QUESTIONNAIRE

1. What is Mr./Mrs. _____'s specific medical diagnosis and extent of metastases?

2. In your medical professional opinion, what is the anticipated progression of this cancer?

3. Is his/her condition terminal in nature? As Mr./Mrs. _____'s case manager, I am responsible for providing qualitative yet cost-effective services when needed. This will help to reduce the family's stress levels as well as keep their out-of-pocket expenses to a minimum.

4. What types of therapies are being planned to treat the patient's disease?

5. In your opinion, is Mr./Mrs. _____ a candidate for any home therapy services, i.e., chemotherapy, pain management, hospice care?

_____   _____
Dr. XXXXXXXXXX   Date

Courtesy of Options Unlimited, Case Management Services Division, Huntington, N.Y.

Sometimes ordering of an exam results from one of a few administrative practices. Many examiners work selected cases using a "diary" system, where files are reviewed once monthly. In the third or sixth month, they schedule an independent medical exam if the case is still active. Similarly, if a workers' compensation hearing is scheduled, an independent medical exam is often automatically ordered.

Also used to determine a diagnosis, a second opinion exam is often performed to help clarify a complex medical picture or to prepare alternatives to the current or proposed treatment (see Exhibit 7-14). It is typically presented to the patient as a proactive exam, and the insurance nurse or case manager who arranged for it is usually in attendance. In group medical plans, a second opinion exam is often required prior to certain surgical procedures that the carrier or the latest utilization review statistics show

Exhibit 7-11 Sample Physician Questionnaire

---

1. What is the primary diagnosis?

2. Does the patient have any secondary diagnoses?

3. Do you think the patient might benefit from a cardiac rehabilitation program as an outpatient?

4. What are the prescribed medications?

5. What is the specific diet of the patient?

6. What, if any, are the limitations or restrictions?

7. What are your further plans for the patient regarding his rehabilitation period?

8. What is the prognosis?

_____   _____

                                             Date

Courtesy of Options Unlimited, Case Management Services Division, Huntington, N.Y.

---

to have a high usage rate (e.g., hysterectomies, hip replacements, cardiac bypass, disc surgery, etc.). Often the physician conducting a second opinion exam will become a treating physician.

A second opinion exam is called for when there is a conflict between potential treatment plans (surgery versus conservative treatment), when the patient requests one, when there is a multilayered medical scenario or a questionable treatment underway, or when the existing treatment plan

Exhibit 7-12 Completed Physician Questionnaire

Claimant:
Insured: (Mother)
Employee #:

QUESTIONNAIRE

1. Original date of diagnosis:
   A. Noonan's Syndrome: 10/11/84
   B. Growth Hormone Deficiency: 10/11/84
   C. Osteochondrosos, left knee: 9/86
2. The initial date of growth hormone replacement: 11/28/84
   Date and treatments (if any) for Noonan's Syndrome: None
3. Height and weight when the initial diagnosis of growth hormone deficiency was made: 132.3 cm   37 kg
   Height and weight now: 146.0 cm   51.5
   Have you been pleased with _____'s response to growth hormone therapy?
   Response is to double her growth rate at least.
   Off therapy growth only about 3 cm/yr, on Rx #16 cm/yr.
   Has been off a lot.
4. How long would you expect _____ to continue with growth hormone therapy?
   Maximum probably 2 years most likely 1 year if response slow or poor.
   Are there are alternative plans for treatment for growth hormone deficiency or Noonan's Syndrome?   No
5. When might you expect a plateau of bone maturation for _____?
   Bone age is 15 yrs at chronological age 16¹⁰. Thus not a lot of growth left and puberty is progressing.
6. Do you feel there is a psychological component to _____'s condition, and if so what would your recommendations be?
   Will definitely be very very short as adult. He will need to work with this. He is quite immature and probably treated as younger because of height of 12 year old.
7. What, if any, diagnostic tests and other treatments are planned for _____ in the future?
   I'm not sure of emotional or intellectual abilities. Both of these perhaps should be evaluated to help for placement or job recommendations.

_____   _____
XXXXXXXXXXX, M.D.   Date

Courtesy of Options Unlimited, Case Management Services Division, Huntington, N.Y.

Table 7-1 Comparison of Independent Medical Exams and Second Opinion Exams

Independent Medical Exams	Second Opinion Exams
Utilized by carriers to determine: 1. diagnosis 2. need for continued Rx 3. degree of disability (total, partial) 4. permanency of disability (temporary, total) 5. ability to return to work	Utilized to: 1. determine diagnosis 2. clarify a complex medical picture 3. propose alternatives to current or proposed treatment
Would prefer this physician remain in non-treating state.	Often becomes treating physician.
This physician often becomes involved as expert witness once litigation occurs—and appears *for* the carrier.	This physician often *refuses* to do exam if testimony may be requested.
Often viewed as "ordered" exam by the claimant.	Presented as proactive examination.
Rehab nurse often will not attend (depending on circumstances, however, may assist in arrangements and may accompany claimant). Usually arranged *by* the carrier.	Ins. nurse/case manager will usually attend and, in fact, arrange this exam, obviously with carrier approval.

Courtesy of Options Unlimited, Case Management Services Division, Huntington, N.Y.

is not achieving the expected outcome. The diagnosis may call for a second opinion exam, as when the need for a physician with more or different expertise is indicated. In some cases, a second opinion exam is ordered if a treatment is deemed inappropriate or excessive (e.g., when multiple drugs have been prescribed and all of them have the potential for abuse).

To get the most benefits from independent medical and second opinion exams, a case manager should thoroughly understand the purpose of any exam ordered and be specific as to what should be addressed in the physician's report. The physician most appropriate for the diagnosis or the patient should conduct the exam; a general orthopedist is not the most

Exhibit 7-13 Sample Letter to Physician To Arrange an Independent
Medical Exam

March 3, 1994

Robert Jones, M.D.
42 Amsterdam Avenue
New York, NY 10002

RE: James Williams
INSURED: ABC Woolens
CARRIER FILE #:   110-24
DATE OF ACCIDENT: 2/2/93

Dear Dr. Jones:

Please allow this letter to serve as confirmation with Jane in your office today regarding the above captioned claimant.

World Insurance Company is the Workers' Compensation Carrier for ABC Woolens where Mr. Williams is employed as an assistant manager in the Shipping Department.

He sustained an injury to his back on 2/2/93 and has been in treatment with a number of physicians and therapists. Surgery has been performed, followed by a course of physical therapy. For your review, I am enclosing reports from his treating physicians, hospital records, and diagnostic studies. Mr. Williams will also be bringing with him various X-rays and CAT scans pertinent to this event.

We are at this time one year post-injury requesting that you examine this claimant and note your findings with specific attention to (1) current status; (2) objective findings; (3) subjective symptoms; (4) need for continuance of PT and massage therapy and enrollment in a health spa.

You will also find enclosed a copy of a Job Analysis by our medical management consultant. Please note as you review this that the claimant has a mix of sedentary and physical labor, and the owner can accommodate some restrictions in activity. Following your examination of Mr. Williams and review of the Job Analysis, could you comment on his ability to perform in this job? For your convenience there is enclosed a physical capacities form which may be useful in your determination of his actual ability to perform the various tasks.

I have advised Mr. Williams of the scheduled date of his appointment, March 30th at 10:00 A.M., and have requested that he confirm this with your office.

Thank you very much for your assistance and I look forward to receiving your report.

Very truly yours,

Jane Ellis
Workers' Compensation Examiner

Courtesy of Options Unlimited, Case Management Services Division, Huntington, N.Y.

Exhibit 7-14 Sample Letter to Physician To Arrange Second Opinion Exam

---

June 2, 19

Adam James, M.D.
Director of Orthopedic Surgery
Long Island Central Hospital
New Hyde Park, N.Y. 10021

RE:	James Williams
INSURED:	ABC Woolens
CARRIER FILE #:	110-24
DATE OF ACCIDENT:	2/2/93

Dear Dr. James:

After discussion with your office today, I am referring Mr. Williams to you for a "second opinion" evaluation and consultation. The appointment is scheduled for June 20th at 1:00 P.M. With your permission and with Mr. Williams' approval, I will attend this appointment.

As a medical management consultant working with this man at the request of World Insurance Company (the Workers' Compensation Carrier for his employer), I am in the process of developing a plan to assist Mr. Williams with a return to a productive and comfortable lifestyle once again.

To date and following an injury to his back on 2/2/93, he has been receiving treatment and testing from a number of professionals, including an orthopedic surgeon, neurologist, chiropractor, and his family doctor.

He has received conflicting opinions as to the suggested course of treatment, including a recent one for a laminectomy. Mr. Williams has, as would be expected, questions and concerns regarding surgery which he feels were not explained to his satisfaction by his doctor.

As a medical management consultant, it is not our intent to interfere with or interrupt current medical care; however, we do assist individuals in obtaining sufficient information in order for them to make informed decisions about their treatment.

I am enclosing prior to our visit copies of various medical reports and diagnostic tests.

Thank you very much for your kind assistance and I look forward to meeting you.

Very truly yours,

Vivian Campagna, R.N., C.I.R.S.
Medical Management Consultant
VC:lm

Courtesy of Options Unlimited, Case Management Services Division, Huntington, N.Y.

appropriate physician if the claimant is using an acknowledged expert in hip replacement or needs specialized treatment. The examining physician should be provided as much information as possible, including operative reports, diagnostic test reports, x-rays, CAT scans, treating physician reports, and other independent medical exams, and be given enough time to review all the data prior to the actual exam. When appropriate, the case manager should arrange to discuss findings with the physician in person or over the phone following the exam. After reading the physician's report, the case manager should again speak to the physician if the report is not specific and responsive to the initial request for information.

TALKING TO OTHER PROFESSIONALS

In addition to the treating physician, the case manager may need to contact facility staff nurses, attorneys, therapists, and other professionals involved in the patient's care. If the role of any individual is not understood, the case manager should ask questions. In all cases, the case manager should introduce herself and explain her relationship to the patient.

Initial Phone Contact with Medical Professionals To Set Up Personal Consultation

Case Manager: Phil, my name is Angie and I'm working with your patient [Dr. Smith's patient], Ann Simpson, in developing a rehabilitation [case management] program.

Case Manager: I met with Ann last week and she told me that she was seeing you two times a week for physical therapy [occupational therapy, speech therapy, etc.]. I would like to meet with you briefly to get a better understanding of her current treatment program. Your input is very important in developing a recovery plan.

Case Manager: Ann said it would be fine if I met with you, and I'll have a signed consent form for your file. Would there be any possibility of meeting with you either next Tuesday or Wednesday, preferably sometime in the morning? I would only need about ten minutes of your time and I promise to be very brief.

Case Manager: Next Wednesday at 9:30 would be fine. I'll put this time on my calendar and if there is any change, I will let you know. Please do the same.

Case Manager: Thanks again for your time. I'm looking forward to working with you.[6]

After the appointment is set, the case manager might want to compose and send a brief letter, postcard, or handwritten memo as a time-efficient way to reinforce the date of the meeting and help ensure the medical professional will be there.

Part of the case manager's role may involve a review of hospital medical records. To facilitate this, the case manager will need a consent form signed by the patient or the patient's guardian. Next, the case manager must determine the hospital's procedure for medical record review. Some hospitals are very formal, requiring that all medical record reviews be completed through the medical records department. Many are more informal and merely require that identification and a signed consent form be presented to the primary nurse, head nurse, or hospital contact. If the case manager meets any challenge to her right to examine the patient's medical records, she should ask to speak with supervisory personnel or the hospital administrator. Case managers do have the privilege of reviewing medical records if they have a signed consent.

In an acute care hospital, the case manager should ask to speak to the primary or head nurse, introduce herself, offer a copy of the signed consent form and her card, and ask about the patient's current condition and any concerns or key issues. The case manager should then request to review the medical records. In a rehabilitation facility, the contact person may be the social worker on the case, a discharge planner, or the primary nurse.[7]

Staff nurses are good sources of information. Physicians have one window; nurses see the patient from a different perspective. They can be good historians. "Yes, we know John says he can test his urine to monitor his sugar level for his diabetes but he really doesn't do it. He's noncompliant. His family brings him treats and we see him sneaking things." Realizing the extensive demands made on RNs, case managers should make it clear to the nursing staff that they are available for use as resources for the nurses.

Another person to contact is the discharge planning coordinator, who is responsible for posthospital patient services and timely discharge. The case manager should let the discharge planner know that she is involved with the case, will be arranging for the patient's home or rehabilitation facility services, and will get coverage approval from the payer for those services. This frees the discharge planner to devote more time to other cases. Social workers involved with the family can also make a contribution by adding valuable background to the patient profile; they might even have a completed profile already prepared.

In workers' compensation or disability cases, the employer is a chief contact for the case manager. What does the employer know about the patient? How secure is the patient's job? Will the patient have a job to return to? Is the employer willing to modify the work site? Will the employer allow the patient to return on a part-time or reduced-hour basis? What is the employee's value in the eyes of the employer?

To obtain answers to these questions, the case manager should call the employer. If it is fairly clear that the patient's limitations will prevent a return to work, it may not be necessary or appropriate for the case manager to spend time arranging and attending a personal consultation. If the case manager feels that there is a reasonable possibility of a patient taking up a previous or modified job with the employer, a personal visit should be requested. In asking for time to meet with an employer, the case manager should never give the impression that she is coming to try to force an injured worker back to the job.

Initial Phone Call to an Employer

Case Manager: Mr. White, my name is Cathy Simpson and I have been asked by your health insurance carrier [name of company and/or adjuster] to assist Mr. King in his recovery and then back to work. The records that I have show that Mr. King had been working for you up until March 12th and that he has not returned since his injury. Does this sound about right?

Case Manager: I'm in the process of completing my initial evaluation and I would appreciate having your input on some work-related matters.

[for a personal visit]

Case Manager: I am going to be in the Lakewood area next Tuesday. Could I see you for just a few minutes while I am in town?

Case Manager: OK, what would be a better day? I'll see if I can rearrange my schedule.

Case Manager: I really appreciate your help with this. I'll see you next Wednesday at 1:00 P.M.[8]

An employer can also be part of the treatment plan. The case manager might request the employer's assistance for a patient facing a long recovery process. Fellow workers are usually great at sending flowers and cards at the beginning of an illness; can some contact mechanism be established to help maintain morale over the long haul? Is there an employee newsletter that the patient can receive so he or she will feel involved with the company? Does the company have a sunshine fund, a program that reaches out to injured employees so they do not lose touch with fellow workers?

In some cases, particularly when workers' compensation, disability, or liability claims are at issue, an attorney will also be contacted. (Case managers working a group medical case rarely see an attorney involved in the case before getting in touch with the patient.) In some states and among some employer groups, lawyers are called on regularly for minor cases—a neck sprain or a knee injury and the talk is lawsuit. Some attorneys are very hesitant to allow case management involvement; others approve the service right away. The concern stems from the fact that a case manager representing the employer or insurance carrier might pursue a hidden agenda and quiz or interrogate the client regarding his or her accident or illness.

Lawyers can deny a case manager the opportunity to work on a case, approve the case manager's involvement but refuse personal access to the patient, or allow access but deny full cooperation, setting strict stipulations for case management intervention: "You may only talk to him about medical issues, and you may not discuss his job." Or "Every time you make a phone call, you must call me and get my permission first." Or "Every time you have a meeting, I'm going to be there and we're going to tape it."

Obviously, the case manager's contact with attorneys is critical. Regardless of the injury, any time there is an attorney of record on a case, the case manager must contact that attorney and state very clearly who she is, who she represents, and the purpose of her involvement. It is very important to position case management as a proactive service and to make it clear that the case manager's role is not to investigate the accident, not to find out who is at fault, nor to discuss the circumstances and details of the accident with the patient. (Obviously, it follows that during an assessment the case manager will steer clear of questions regarding the circumstances and events leading up to an accident and avoid trying to establish who was at fault.) The object of case management is to assist with the patient's recovery and eventual return to a productive lifestyle. It is often helpful, prior to calling the attorney to answer any questions he or she might have, to send a letter clearly stating the case manager's role (she is not a claims investigator or a hands-on provider of services), along with a brochure describing case management services and a copy of the authorization the patient will be asked to sign.

Initial Phone Contact with an Attorney

Case Manager: Mr. Anderson, my name is Sarah Craig and I am a case manager [rehabilitation nurse, rehabilitation counselor, etc.] with Professional Case Management. I'm calling regarding your client, John Roberts. I have been asked by American Insurance Company, the company carrying his workers' compensation [or auto insurance], to visit with Mr. Roberts to see if I can be of assistance to him in his recovery. I'm calling to ask your permission to contact him and proceed with an assessment of his condition.

Attorney: What's the purpose of your service? What do you plan to do to help John?

Case Manager: My meeting with him and my initial assessment would be to determine if his recovery is proceeding well, if there are any additional medical services which may be of benefit, or if we can provide for his needs in a more efficient manner. I'm not really able to tell you anything specific at this point as I have not had a chance to meet with him and discuss his current medical status. Hopefully, after I talk with him and review the various medical reports that I have, I will be in a better position to determine what services he might need to maximize his recovery. I know you also share this goal.

Attorney: I don't see why his doctor can't handle his medical treatment.

Case Manager: His physician is certainly the one in charge of his treatment plan. However, because I work in his community, I can assist the doctor and help him to fully understand Mr. Roberts' special areas of need in regard to follow-up treatment, his home environment, the type of work he's done, his family support system, and things of that nature. I am part of the physician's team, and we all work to provide the best recovery possible.

Attorney: I want a copy of every report you make.

Case Manager: That's fine. I'd like you to be aware of my work with your client. I'll be glad to check with the insurance company; it's not usually a problem to copy a patient's attorney on our reports.[9]

Sometimes attorneys will request copies of a case manager's reports to the referral source before they will approve case management involvement. When this happens to me, I tell the attorneys that the reports belong to the referral source. If that company or insurer allows reports to go out, I will ask them to forward a copy of the report or I will send a copy from my office given the go-ahead. However, I would suggest that case management companies or departments working with lawyers always first give the report to the client (i.e., the carrier group or the employer) and let the client review it before making the final decision on whether to send it to the lawyers. This is because there might be something in the report that is not as objectively stated as it might have been or that perhaps compromises the client's position. Attorneys should never automatically receive a copy of a case manager's reports; they should be forwarded only with the client's approval. Case managers practicing in states with mandatory rehabilitation programs may have to follow specific requirements in reporting to attorneys.

An attorney may ask a case manager to sign a statement that the case management reports will not be used against the client in a court of law. Such stipulations should be referred to the carrier. It is the carrier's role to agree or disagree with the attorney's terms before case management involvement continues.

If an attorney questions a case manager's qualifications, the case manager should respond to this issue and perhaps ask for a brief personal visit to discuss the role of case management. There are some attorneys who really have not heard of case management before, have no idea what case managers do, and need an overview of the profession. The case manager should outline her experience and education, provide examples of case management work with other attorneys, offer to send literature on case management along with a personal resumé, inform the attorney that a refusal of services is very unusual, and address any objections.

The case manager might ask if the attorney would like to be present at the initial meeting of the case manager and the claimant; sometimes this allays fears that the case manager has an unwritten agenda as an investigator. When an attorney insists on being present at any case management meeting, the attorney's office can be used as the meeting place unless the patient is confined to a hospital or another care facility, is homebound, or needs to be seen by the case manager in his or her work environment. If a meeting time and place can be agreed upon, the case manager should let the attorney know that the initial interview may require up to two hours. The attorney may demand that he or she be present at every single meeting. This may not be possible given the case manager's schedule, nor be conducive to the most honest exchanges with the claimant.

In one case I had, the first such meeting was not very productive. The attorney stopped the patient every time I asked a question. The second meeting was a repetition of the first. At the third meeting, the lawyer had a tape recorder running with a microphone attachment. He continually interrupted my conversation with the patient. When I asked how the patient was feeling, the lawyer said, "Don't answer that!" I knew that we were getting nowhere. Because the atmosphere, due to the attorney's level of involvement, was no longer supportive of an effective case management intervention, I suggested to the referral source that we close the file. I believe case managers can meet lawyers more than halfway, but they cannot work around the obstruction created when patients are being coached on their answers.

If case management services are denied by an attorney, the case manager should try to find out the specific reasons behind the decision and address them. If further consideration is refused, the case manager should thank the attorney for his or her time and close the conversation. Some law firms have a reputation for sending patients to certain physicians and therapists, allowing no other involvement.

To keep all lines of communication and participation clear in a legal case, the case manager should document any acceptance or denial of service in a brief but specific letter to the insurance carrier or payer and the employer group. Additionally, the attorney should be sent a letter either acknowledging appreciation for his or her approval of case management involvement or noting his or her refusal. In the instance of a denial, the case manager should document for the record that the attempt to institute case management was a good-faith gesture on the part of the employer or carrier. This demonstrates that help was offered, and it also may alert the workers' compensation board that they may be dealing with an uncooperative attorney.

In my letters, I begin by reiterating the lawyer's refusal of case management services, along with the reasons given, noting that of course I will abide by the decision (see Exhibit 7-15). To make a point, I will include direct quotations: "You said you 'believe our involvement will jeopardize a fair hearing,'" or 'I never work with case managers.' I'm not courting a lawsuit myself, so I am careful in my use of quotation and synopses. If someone slams down the phone in my ear, I may write, "You abruptly terminated our conversation despite the fact that I assured you that I was contributing medical expertise to the case and was not a claims examiner." I also include an example of how I have worked successfully with an attorney in the past.

I have also started sending the claimant copies of letters of approval or denial that go directly to the attorney in workers' compensation, auto, or other liability cases. Several times, once an attorney's concerns or agendas were addressed (or the attorney was no longer on the case) and I was able to speak to the claimant, the claimant asked, "Well, where were you when I needed you two months ago?" I was there two months ago, trying to get in touch with him or her, but the claimant never knew because the attorney did not relay the information. Not every attorney shares everything with his or her clients. I feel that if it is the client's insurance policy, he or she has a right to know that case management is being offered; the client deserves access to information that can directly impact on his or her physical well-being.

The attorney should be sent copies as well, giving him or her an opportunity to clarify any misunderstanding regarding the refusal of case management services on behalf of his or her client.

When an attorney denies case management intervention in a particular case, this does not close the door on an association with a case manager in another case. Case managers are wise to inform attorneys about the range of their work. For example, case managers with expertise in life care planning are often sought by attorneys looking to settle a claim on behalf of a

Exhibit 7-15 Letter to Attorney Who Has Denied Case Management Services

---

Mr. John Smith, Esq.
456 Main Street
Buffalo Grove, IL 34678

Re: William Jones

Dear Mr. Smith:

Please allow this letter to serve as a confirmation of our telephone conversation today and your declination of services that have been requested on your client's behalf by Jane Brown of ABC Insurance Company. You have indicated that you "... never allow companies such as ours to work with your clients. ..."

As you may recall, OPTIONS UNLIMITED is a private consulting firm utilized by ABC Insurance Company and other companies to assist individuals with the problems that may occur following accidents, injuries or illnesses.

Our goal is to insure that your client receives the best results possible from the services that are available and is able to return to a medically stable, comfortable and, hopefully, active lifestyle once again.

Ms. Brown had requested that one of our nurse consultants meet with your client in order to determine how he is recovering from his accident and if he would benefit from our intervention.

Our role is not intended to interrupt or interfere with any care or services he is currently receiving, nor do we provide any "hands on" services. We, hopefully, serve as a resource for your client and his family in resolving and preventing any further difficulties.

Because our services are at no cost to your client, and can only serve to enhance his recovery process, we were hopeful of obtaining your approval; however, we will abide by your refusal.

Should you wish to reconsider or if I can answer questions or concerns you may have, please feel free to call me. Also enclosed is one of our brochures which explain our services further.

Thank you once again for your time.

Very truly yours,

Catherine M. Mullahy
President

CMM:lm
Enc.
cc: William Jones

Courtesy of Options Unlimited, Case Management Services Division, Huntington, N.Y.

catastrophically injured child. A life care plan developed by a case manager will include the probable costs of supporting that child throughout his or her predicted life span (medical services, care providers, improving technologies, and inflation costs are all figured in).

The time taken to perform an assessment depends on the needs of the patient and the severity of the injury or illness. A half-hour might be required to speak to the recovering patient before preparing a two-month postoperative update; a half-hour might be all the time allowable for an easily tired patient in an acute care setting or all the time appropriate for a patient in the last stages of a terminal illness. To conduct a more comprehensive assessment (e.g., for a patient three months into a head injury rehabilitation program following a horrific accident), at least one and a half to two hours should be allotted, especially if the evaluation will include a facility walk-through with a discharge planner. The more providers involved, the more time consuming the assessment will be. Similarly, more recent injuries and singular injuries often require less time than recurring or multiple illnesses. The case manager needs to review the history involved with events in the patient's care plan, because that information will impact the scenario faced today and the plan for tomorrow. From a liability standpoint, the case manager needs to gather sufficient background for a responsible assessment, uncovering everything that will affect her ability to plan intelligently and completely for a patient's anticipated problems and the attainment of the treatment goals.

Factors to consider in estimating the time necessary for an assessment include the line of insurance, the state of health of the patient (a complex medical chart takes time to digest), the site where the interview will take place, the number of people involved (e.g., the patient, family members needing support, discharge planner, physicians, nurses in the unit, etc.). After a case manager determines the amount of time needed, it is important to inform the referral source.

PLANNING

Case management is a process of identifying and solving problems. The first and key issue is whether the treatment is appropriate and being provided in the best possible setting. Given the patient's diagnosis, current medical status, and prior medical history, is the treatment plan attaining the most desirable results? Does it appear that it will lead to an eventual recovery or have there already been too many complications?

Is the treatment plan sound? Is it appropriate, reasonable, and really necessary for this patient? Is it forcing the patient into any undue hardship or discomfort? Case managers might come across situations where treatment may be deemed questionable based on their experience or knowledge. Some cases may be outside the limits of their expertise. In medicine today there are numerous breaking technological advances, therapies, and medications. If the disease is an unfamiliar one, the case manager has a responsibility to become knowledgeable about it. When things look questionable, when results are uncertain, it is appropriate to ask the treating physician or to acknowledge a need for more information. It is also the case manager's responsibility to comment on treatments that, based on her experience, may seem unusual or strange. Of course, tone is vital; no one should blurt out an accusation of mismanagement. The case manager might say, "Listen, I'm familiar with this, this, and this, but I've never heard of this. Is this something new? Is this something that you've had good results with? Why is this patient being referred for this particular therapy? I've seen more situations where patients are treated with another therapy."

If a case manager notes that a patient is in a poor system of care—the physician is not communicating, the patient is having multiple complications, the therapists are unapproachable—part of the case management role is to serve as a patient advocate. The patient's interests definitely should come first. If the patient is not being well served, the case manager can help create a better system of care. Patients do not always have the information they need to see their position clearly. They often are not even aware of what constitutes proper care. They might not know that they can access a second opinion, that they do not have to stay in a hospital where the ministrations are miserable, that they do not have to put up with what is going on. A key tactic is to present information to a patient in a way that does not overtly interfere with the patient-physician relationship but allows the patient to understand that this is not the only "game in town." I have had patients who really did not know that their care was horrible. I have posed questions to lead them to acknowledge that, although perhaps the physician was doing fine, two heads are better than one and they might want to talk to another physician. For example, I might ask, "Don't you feel that maybe you should be getting better by now? Are you concerned?"

When it comes to making recommendations to patients, case managers must protect themselves against the liability that could result from steering them toward particular choices. I would caution case managers not to make direct endorsements but instead to present numerous alternatives to patients. "You have these kinds of facilities to select from; these are physicians who are board certified; these are home health agencies that can provide the type of care you need." Obviously, if a case manager knows a particular physician in the community is absolutely wonderful, there's nothing wrong with saying, "I hear this physician is excellent. Here are two others as well. You are free to select anyone you want." Even though the choice ultimately needs to be the patient's, I would try to select from physicians that I felt were the most qualified. Knowing people's inclination to grab on to the first name suggested, I might tend to arrange the order I present the three options in, but I would never commend one practitioner to the exclusion of all others.

Is the patient in the most appropriate setting for his or her problem? If, for instance, the patient has a rare or difficult disease and is in a small local hospital picked by the patient for its proximity to home, could he or she be better treated in a university hospital that perhaps has an entire department dedicated to that disease? Maybe the patient's treatment would be more medically effective (and more cost-effective as well) if provided by health care professionals who are more knowledgeable about the patient's condition. Is the care setting the most appropriate and most cost-effective? Could care be given any place else? John is in the hospital, his surgery has been completed, and now he is being observed and receiving medication, pain or infusion care services, or physical therapy. Does he have to be in a hospital? Could the case manager arrange for the same kind of services in a less costly and even more appropriate setting? In some cases, a patient may recuperate well at home through the use of support services at far less cost and with better results both emotionally and physically for the patient and with less stress on the family.

It may be that during the acute phase of his illness, John was absolutely in the best possible place, but now he needs rehabilitation and that particular acute care hospital may not be the best for rehab. This is especially true for some traumatic brain injury patients, for spinal cord injury patients, some amputees, and some burn center cases. When the acute phase is over and a patient needs focused rehabilitation, he or she is probably best served in an area or center that has personnel trained and equipment designed to deal with the specific disorder. Acute care hospitals are geared to address the acute phase of a range of conditions, medical problems occurring in episodic fashion. They are not well suited for individual long-term care. Individuals may go from the emergency room to an intensive care unit. After they achieve stability in intensive care, they belong on a medical or surgical floor. At the earliest opportunity, once they can be effectively managed without all the expensive support services of a hospital, they should be moved to a more appropriate and less costly arena for care—the home or another setting.

How motivated are the care provider and the patient in the current setting? Is the provider looking after the interests of the patient or trying to keep beds filled and services going?

During an assessment, a case manager will also be evaluating the money available and the exposure faced. Whose pocket is it and how large is it? Is there a pile of money or are there piles and piles of money? If unlimited dollars are available, should they be spent whatever way the providers want regardless of necessity? Sometimes that attitude does prevail. People will say, "I have $2 million worth of coverage" or "I called my insurance company and they said I have lots of insurance dollars and I don't have to worry." In my mind, it is not responsible in the health care delivery system today to spend money just because it exists or just to line the pockets of providers. I look for the "value-locked dollar"—for a demonstration that the treatment is necessary, reasonable, and will achieve good results and that the treatment plan is the most cost-effective way to provide the requisite care.

What impact will the costs of medical equipment, supplies, and therapies have? During an assessment, one indicator of greater exposure is any ongoing condition requiring home care services, infusion care services, total parenteral nutrition (TPN, which can run from $150–450 per day depending on the provider), pain control medication (for cancer or chronic pain patients), inpatient or outpatient rehabilitation services, or any other intervention that lasts more than a few episodes. Case managers ought to pay particular attention during an assessment where such services are involved because their price, quality, and delivery sites vary so greatly. For example, the intensity and frequency of activity multiplies when a patient is moved from the hospital to a home or alternative care setting. This is because the case manager must contract for bits and pieces of services as well as rent or purchase equipment. The case manager must examine what is already in place, look at ultimate costs, and evaluate where and how her time can be best spent. Can the cost of the facility, of equipment, or of drugs be negotiated or bid to bring it down? The expense in time and energy, however, might make haggling a $100 item down to $75 virtually wasted effort. (Note that case management should never be driven solely by costs. If a case manager starts operating with the mindset that everything is too expensive and that the role of case management is just to save money, then she is laying the groundwork for potential legal action.)

In some cases, cost is not the determining factor. For a patient with a brain injury, an acute care hospital may be the best setting for the first several days or weeks of care. Then the patient needs to be placed in a traumatic brain injury or coma stimulation recovery program. This might not be less costly and in some cases will even be more expensive. The case manager must look at what the patient's needs are and how they can be best met in terms of quality and cost. One factor should never drive the others; there must be an equilibrium among the three. If John is going to be at risk as a result of moving him out of a hospital and bringing him home, with services, obviously the move home is not an acceptable alternative. If he can be moved to a less costly setting where the same results can be achieved in a more cost-effective manner, the case manager should try to get the patient and treating physician to agree to that move.

What is going to happen to the patient and how much is this case going to cost the payer or employer if there is no case management intervention? Is it a good case for such intervention? What can the case manager bring to the table? Is the patient's condition and the patient-family support system going to improve with case management or will case management be just another layer of expense? The system of care already set in place might be good, medically sound, and conservative in its use of care dollars; the patient may be willing and able to follow care instructions, complications may be minimal at present, and the family may be aware of who to call for help. What more could case management offer? In these instances, a case manager must be honest and admit case management has no real role to play.

Sometimes, however, case management, although having no current value, could offer support down the road, when the patient's condition is likely to deteriorate. The medical care required will become more complex, and additional services will need to be coordinated. In the meantime, the case manager does not want to drive up costs by going out to visit the patient every month, but neither does she want to totally pull back and be out of communication, waiting for complications to occur. The lost connection could mean less effective management. In such a situation, the case manager might suggest maintaining contact through regular semimonthly, monthly, or bimonthly phone calls.

In light of the information gleaned through conversations with the patient, family, and members of the care team, what is the most reasonable approach to each problem or issue? What are the alternatives to the current care plan? What are the options for future care? How much will the current or alternative plans cost?

Sometimes there are so many problems that a case manager hardly knows where to begin. Often newer case managers become overwhelmed, thinking they have to identify every single complication or need and come up with all the recommendations for treatment for ever and all time. In reality, a case manager simply must show that there are going to be some long-term problems that eventually will need to be dealt with by the case management plan and that there are short-term needs that can be addressed immediately and resolved. Long-term plans for chronic cases include short-term goals and long-term vision. The case manager's job is to know where everyone wants to go and then, in measurable steps, follow the procedures necessary to ensure that the ultimate goals will be attainable.

REPORTING

As mentioned previously, the nature of the referral source or payer will subtly affect communications from the initial assessment through the reporting stage. The focus should be on client needs at all times, and the information must be balanced to present an accurate picture. A report back to the client should include those things the client is most concerned about. In a disability case where the client is the employer and the case manager goes on and on about the patient's medical condition but ignores return-to-work issues, the case manager has not really met the client's needs. However, when reporting to a claims supervisor or a workers' compensation examiner, a case manager will want to include specific medical information in the form of parenthetical explanations to help the readers properly interpret the medical terms they will see in other case reports regarding the diagnosis or prognosis.

A case manager in a case management company will probably get referrals from different lines of insurance. If the case manager works in an insurance company and the insurance is basically group medical, she will address medical issues for the most part. However, occasionally the case manager might be required to handle a case referred for workers' compensation evaluation or long-term disability evaluation, where focus is not necessarily strictly medical.

In workers' compensation cases, carriers are responsible for both medical costs and lost earnings. There usually is "reserving of dollars," money put aside to pay for long-term expenses incurred in big cases. Most workers' compensation administrators or claims departments will want to know the extent of medical involvement, the severity of injury, the likelihood that there will be some permanent incapacitation, the potential for a full recovery, the length of medical treatment (episodic or continuous), and the need for long-term or enduring medical services.

The first question might be, will the person be able to go back to his or her prior job? If so, at what point is that likely to occur? If John cannot go back immediately, will he be able to go back at some point? In the meantime, can he return to a modified version of his job, perhaps part time (reduced hours or reduced days of the week)? Maybe he could work full time but with one aspect or task taken away? If he cannot go back to the same employer in a modified job (likely in the case of catastrophic injuries), what past vocational and current avocational capabilities does he possess? What is the likelihood that some kind of employment will be possible for him? Did he only possess specific physical skills? Can he use his work knowledge in some other kind of job? Some people lack transferable skills, have only minimal skills, or have transferable skills but no job site in their part of the country where they can be applied. Then the case manager needs to look at other alternatives. Past skills or hobbies often have the potential to be developed into viable job skills.

In long-term disability cases, the payer is mainly concerned with disability issues. Many policies will have HISOCC ("his occupation;" how long he will continue to be disabled for his own job) or ANYOCC ("any occupation;" how long he will continue to be unable to work in any job) provisions. (For a more extensive discussion of HISOCC and ANYOCC, please see Chapter 4.) These issues are critical because, unlike workers' compensation, a long-term disability carrier does not pay for medical expenses. Disability insurance replaces lost wages, period. Therefore, the payer is less concerned with the intricacies of medical problems, even though the medical condition is often at the base of any disability. While focusing on work-related issues, case managers also need to keep long-term disability carriers aware of unresolved medical issues because managing those will often bring a speedier resolution to the lost-wages situation.

Conversely, group medical payers are not particularly interested in return-to-work or socioenvironmental issues. However, from a case management perspective, these issues impact an individual's recovery ability. A group medical carrier may not require a great deal of information but should get some basics (e.g., the injury occurred at work, the claimant is a valued member of the workforce, she is going to be able to go back, her employer has already told her there is a job for her, etc.). These things make a big difference in how a person views him- or herself and are absolutely integrated with recovery from injury or illness.

The frequency and length of case management reports should be confirmed with the referral sources. The nature of the reports is an area of concern for many payers today because of their cost and perceived usefulness.

There are some case management companies specializing in workers' compensation that have a report format that everyone uses for workers' compensation cases. When a group medical case comes in, however, the same report format is used. This format might include a vocational assessment section that calls for a lengthy discussion of work site, transferable skills, return-to-work potential, and so on. As a result, a report on an employee's wife, for example, might include a description of transferable skills and her ability to push and pull and bend. Who cares? Return-to-work issues have no relevance. Someone was on automatic pilot and the group medical payer has been charged for wasted case management assessment time and report-writing time. Case managers must concentrate on the particular situation, the particular line of insurance, the payer, and the particular needs of the patient. There is no all-purpose case management report.

In my opinion, reports should be written at least once a month. All pertinent case activity should be recorded in a specific, regular format. Clients should not be punished with months' worth of case work attached to a large invoice. Most of the discussion will be old news. By reporting in manageable increments of three weeks or a month, case managers gain better control of client files and their cash flow. Significant activity or events requiring clarification should be reported in a timely fashion, first by phone and subsequently through written documentation (within a few days). For example, a case manager who has visited a patient ready for discharge from the hospital and noted that everything is in place at his home does not need to generate another lengthy report on the patient's status. An addendum to a previous report will suffice. This type of reporting will continue for the length of the case and be modified according to the level of involvement.

How extensive should reports be? Some payer organizations have very specific guidelines, limiting initial report writing time to two hours or even half an hour. Others request a verbal report, asking that the case manager not take the time to send a document, even a fax. In this type of situation, the case manager has to educate the referral source. Case management reports have value as documents chronicling case management activity. I know some of our client companies do not read our every report, but the reports do become a matter of record.

Suppose the case manager, during a phone conversation, reports to the payer a previously undocumented call to the patient or the physician. Will either of them remember this exchange of information? What if the case moves into litigation? What if the patient takes a turn for the worse? Especially when planning services, negotiating services, or putting alternate plans in place, case managers need to document decisions and their implementation. This is just good case management administration.

I confronted the issue of reporting in conversation with a client, a third-party administrator, who was seeking to cut administrative costs across the board. I used an example from his own office to make a point. Most claims departments will pay for a surgery. But if a claim comes in for $4,000, it goes unpaid unless that surgical bill is accompanied by an operative report. The claims adjuster does not necessarily understand the medical jargon, but the report is requisite and accepted as documentation for a surgical procedure. I reminded the third-party administrator that he was paying for those operative reports that no one in his office read, yet they were considered a part of good claims administration. I then noted that case managers had procedural guidelines as well.

Just like physicians (who keep notes and dictate reports) or corporations (which maintain minutes of board of directors meetings), case managers need to document their work. Not everyone will read case management reports, but the medicolegal environment surrounding case management and the high cost and high risk associated with typical cases requires case managers to report their activities carefully and comprehensively.

I believe case managers need to explain our position and insist on providing full documentation because it helps validate and legitimize case management intervention. Case management is being requested by payers, and this is key. Case managers, to justify their involvement and demonstrate their contributions, need to be able to document what they did and how it affected treatment outcomes. Simply stated, case managers might be doing important work, but if they do not record it, it did not happen. Reports need to cover not just cost issues, but medical, physician, patient, and family issues as well, and also individuals consulted, actions agreed upon, actions taken, and the results.

Case management needs to put its principles and guidelines on record. I feel that too many case managers go along with every whim of their clients, putting themselves at risk. Far too many people are willing to conduct case management according to someone else's agenda. This is not to say that clients should have no input or be unable to restrict the length of time taken on a report, but case managers must do their job responsibly.

Regardless of the client's (payer's) needs, the report a case manager creates should follow a certain format. It should adequately catalog the generic information and capture the specific nature of the case as well. The case manager serves as an objective observer, weaving the role of case management into the picture. Although most case managers tailor their reports to meet the special requirements of clients, each report will include the same basic information: the name of the referral source, the mailing address and phone number for reporting, the line of insurance, the date of occurrence of the accident or injury, the name of the insured, and the name of the claimant or patient. Each report will also include data obtained from the payer source, the patient and family, medical records, the treating physician, and other medical professionals; a review of the policy coverage and limits; any suggested alternative treatment program; and a discussion of relevant community resources. If an emotional or psychological component of the case is powerful enough to affect other care issues, it must be included as well.

Documentation attached to a report might include copies of the patient's past medical records, consulting reports, reports transferred from another treatment facility, questionnaires the case manager might have sent the treating physicians, letters confirming the agreement of the treating physicians with recommendations made by the case manager—anything that substantiates the case manager's activities and the unfolding of the treatment plan. In addition, the case manager should add information (e.g., brochures on diagnostic conditions, equipment, facilities, etc.) that might help the claims department or plan administrator better understand the patient's condition and needs and should append the patient authorization form affirming the patient's permission for the information to be shared.

I usually suggest to newer case managers that each time they go to write a report, they first ask themselves, "Why aren't I writing my successful closure report today? Why is this case still open?" This can help clarify the case's most pressing issues. The short-term situation should be presented along with solutions or responses, then long-term needs should be cited.

A case management report should present the basics in a brief format using statements that leave room for clarification or follow-up. The first assessment report might be in outline form, but there should be a clause affirming that as the potential for case management involvement becomes more defined or the patient's condition becomes more stable, a more complete report will be filed. Perhaps the client was anxious to receive something on paper for a synopsis to the home office before the case manager was able to speak with the patient or before all medical personnel involved could be contacted. In such cases, the case manager should describe the situation ("This information was gathered in an interview with the family; the patient was unconscious") and add that a broader report will be forthcoming.

The language of reports will be different from phone conversation vernacular. No one would write that a patient's house "was a wreck." Rather, it was "in need of repair." Reports also must consolidate communication. It is impossible to portray the living environment of Crown Heights, Brooklyn to a claims examiner in Kansas City; a few well-chosen words can convey the needed information. Because a range of people might be reading case management reports, they should be understandable to the layperson. Apnea should be described as "the absence of respiratory activity" or "a frequent respiratory distress of infants with an underdeveloped brain center," not as "a low CO_2 level." A report also might be subpoenaed and have to stand up to scrutiny in court, and therefore positive and negative observations should be backed by objective statements. The comment "John is not making progress because he's not motivated" would need to be supported by the fact that John has not attended his physical therapy sessions for the past two weeks even though he had transportation and was fit enough to do so. Hearsay should be avoided.

Developing prompt reports requires knowledge of community resources, service costs, and appropriate medical responses. The presentation of a report is particularly important when recommending an alternative to the existing treatment plan. Suppose the patient is in a hospital. The case manager calls the billing department: "John's been in the hospital for 15 days. I'm the case manager. We're working here with a company that really doesn't have a lot in terms of benefits. Could you tell me what the interim bill is right now, the billing to date? What's it likely going to be?" Then the case manager begins to draft a report taking into account quality of care and cost factors as well as patient and family receptivity to the situation. A day in an intensive care unit in this particular hospital may be $1,400. A physician is going to visit every single day (maybe several physicians every day) at $100 a day, five or seven days a week. Add that. The projected stay in the hospital, if no change is made in the treatment plan, is likely to be another three weeks. The case manager calculates the per diem cost and then, multiplying that cost by three weeks, presents the cost of Plan A.

Then Plan B is described. "I think we could bring John home, but we can't bring him home with anything less than 24-hour care. His wife can take care of him perhaps for the first 4 hours of the morning, but then she has other responsibilities. We'll need to put in a LPN or a home health aide." Knowing that the patient and family will need someone, either an RN or LPN, to provide assistance around the clock, the case manager will investigate the cost per hour of such service in the area and multiply it by 24 hours a day. It may be that that service is not all. John may need physical therapy. The case manager might need to rent equipment (e.g., a hospital bed and wheelchair). In analyzing the second scenario, the case manager must include as many of the variables as can be predicted.

The case manager should present every alternative that seems plausible. One might be to put the patient in a rehabilitation center or a skilled nursing facility at a fixed, all-inclusive, per diem cost negotiated to $200 a day. How does the case manager get that figure? By calling the facility and saying, "I'm trying to draw up a plan so I can submit it to an approval source. The last time I had someone in your facility it was x dollars a day. Is that still in the ballpark? I won't hold you to those exact dollars. I realize that this patient may be different, requiring other services, but this is an employer group and it's the first time they're seeing figures. I'm just trying to give them round numbers on which to base a decision."

Is this report communicated by letter, fax, or telephone? It may need to be communicated quickly, which means telephonically. The case manager gets the client on the phone and relates her findings: "I called up the billing department. It's $1,400 a day, and if we don't do anything, John will be there another three weeks. It will cost $29,400.

"We can move him to St. Jude's Rehab Facility in Yonkers. I had a person there six months ago; the outcome was really good. I was able to get a rate of $375 a day, including physical therapy, for a total of $7,875. Obviously, I will make certain the plan is approved by the treating physician.

"There is another possibility. John wants to come home. That's his preference, but to do it, we're going to have to add 24 hours of care because his wife can only do 4 hours. After we add physical therapy, the costs of bringing him home will be less than keeping him in the hospital but not as economical as the rehab facility, where he will get more services and better results. I have to let you know that home is where he wants to be. However, he and his family will have to look at what they want to do and how they want to use his benefit dollars."

When a report is drawn up and all this information is documented, the tone becomes more formalized and the case manager includes a projected analysis of predictable costs. Noting that these quotes may vary due to a change in the patient's condition or an unforeseen complication, the case manager would list costs for the current Plan A and alternate Plans B and C. A paragraph or two would follow offering the case manager's opinion as to what is best for the patient and why.

The body of a case management report should not include an emphasis on costs. If such a report should go to court, the case manager might have a problem defending what appears to be "bottom-line" health care. It is more appropriate to incorporate financial information by stating that the provider was selected for its quality, ability to meet the patient's needs, and to make the best use of benefit dollars after a review of several providers was conducted. Other financial data, i.e., the range of bids offered by the providers, should appear apart from information on the patient's progress in a Cost Benefits Analysis Report. (See Chapter 10.)

Ultimately, the choice is the patient's, but the case manager can present to the patient and family what she believes will be the best in terms of quality, outcome, ease of provision of services, and cost of services. The case manager can make it clear that John has x benefits but will use a greater proportion of dollars by coming home. She should also portray the realities of home care: "It sounds really great, but if the RN or LPN doesn't show up for a shift or gets sick, it can be complicated." Patients, especially when they are in a known and comfortable situation, are threatened by the thought of having to leave, and some will be more vocal than others. "Is this going to be okay with my doctor? Why would you want to have me moved? I really don't know; this is kind of far away from my family." The more vocal ones might be a problem for case managers who are unused to patients becoming so involved.

Introducing the alternative of a less-expensive but equally proficient facility can cause concern when the patient or family is attached to a care center because of its name or price tag. People may equate "less expensive" with "inferior quality." A case manager should never talk about cost eyeball to eyeball with a patient and say, "It's too expensive here and I've got to get you out." That sets up an adversarial relationship and increases the case manager's liability exposure. Family members might counter, "Well, okay, but if anything happens. . ." When recommending a site change, I use the Taurus/Rolls Royce approach: Everything has a price tag, and it does not necessarily follow that expensive is always good and inexpensive is always lousy.

"Listen, this is a really good center here. I know you're very satisfied. You need to be aware, however, that your wife may need six months of these kinds of services. At $1,200 a day, this only buys us two months of care. Here's another site, where costs will be $500 a day for appropriate services. I'd like your input; I can't mandate that you go there. But I will assist in helping to see that it gets you the results you need, and I will confer with your doctor about it."

Enabling a patient to focus on long-term gains rather than short-term obstacles can help him or her make a decision. "Yes, the new facility is farther away, but even though you'll be away from home for three more weeks, remember that in three weeks you'll be so much closer to returning to life as usual." Giving the patient an example can be beneficial. "I hear what you're saying because of another patient I worked with. This was his situation, but actually when he got here. . ." A patient needs to hear some of the positives to be able to appreciate the case manager's vision. If the patient, by looking at a brochure or going on a tour, can see the facility is really nice and designed to meet his or her needs, he or she will be more inclined to "buy in."

No one is really comfortable with change. A case manager has to help people see the pros and the cons and allow them to voice their concerns and problems. If their objections can be dealt with, the case manager should follow through. If someone says, "Absolutely no, under no circumstances," the case manager should not try to force a change. The case manager should also never create a situation in which she, the employer group, and the carrier are at odds, because the patient will be more tempted to say, "Well you said I had to do this and now look what happened. I'm going to sue you." In addition, it is important to be wary of a patient or family who want to turn over all authority to the case manager, because this also places the case manager at additional risk for a lawsuit. Each patient really needs to be involved in planning and be aware of why decisions were made.

The initial report will sell the case management plan. A report can and should be used to bring something else to the picture—to provide the client with a vision, to demonstrate the more complex uses of case management, or to create new opportunities for case management work. Even a brief report can include underlined or bold sections that emphasize the philosophy behind case management and its role in solving problems. Report-writing at its best includes creative, analytical thinking that anticipates objections in order to win approval.

OBTAINING APPROVAL

Once the case management plan has been devised and the report has been sent to the client, the case manager must then obtain approval to proceed with the recommendations in the report.

Case Manager: Betty, this is Pat Sanders with Professional Case Management. How is your morning going?

Case Manager: You sound very busy. I'll be brief.

Case Manager: I just wanted to make sure you got my last report, which was dated March 14th. [If report has been received but not yet read.] Well, good, I'm glad to know you received it. Since you haven't had a chance to read it yet, can I call you back tomorrow? I just wanted to get your thoughts on my recommendations to see if I should proceed. I'll give you a quick call on Thursday.

[When report has been received and read.] As you may have read in the report, Mr. Williams is considerably improved from the time of my last report. I think our physician change was a good idea; he seems to be responding real well. Did my two recommendations look good to you? One involved a personal consultation with Dr. Friedman, and the second was getting three bids on the hospital bed. If Mr. Williams is going to need the bed for more than three months, we may come out better by a purchase, but I can make some calls on that and let you know.

OK, great, I'll go ahead and get started on this tomorrow, and I'll probably have another report to you in about three weeks. I'll also check on those medications you questioned and give you a call when I have some answers. Thanks for your time.[10]

There are always going to be times when case managers have to use their own judgment and consider who they are representing. A case manager might receive direct communication from an employer or referral source: "I want John out of that facility; it's too expensive." If the case manager feels that the patient is in the most appropriate center and there is no less-costly setting, she cannot allow the client to override her professional judgment. The case manager cannot serve the client first and the patient last; the interests of the patient must always predominate. Case managers are not in the business of slashing away at the federal or corporate health budget at the sacrifice of patients' well-being and safety.

COORDINATION: PUTTING THE PLAN INTO ACTION

Plans are sometimes put in motion as early as the initial evaluation stage. The case manager may not have completed gathering all the information or submitted a report when she gets the go-ahead to put services in place. When a big, involved case has been referred by a client company the case manager has worked with before, the company might request a verbal report from the site. During that telephone call the case manager might say, "This person could go home. I could set up some services. Do you want me to continue with case management intervention?" And the response will come, "Yes, go ahead. Do what you have to do."

Whatever the working arrangement is, whether the case manager is representing an insurer, HMO, PPO, or TPA or is part of an independent case management company, she should be aware of the voluntary guidelines that have been issued to promote consistency in managed care, including case management. Jointly developed by representatives of the American Hospital Association, the American Managed Care and Review Organization, the American Medical Association, the Blue Cross and Blue Shield Association, and the Health Insurance Association of America, these guidelines for the most part cover the conduct of concurrent review (see Chapter 8).[11]

Although the concurrent review guidelines, along with other products such as Care Maps™ [12] are voluntary, such protocols are becoming part of the case management practice and case managers could be held responsible in court for applying and utilizing them. In 1986, *Wickline v. State of California* established that any professional involved in making a health care recommendation could be held liable for damages or harm to a patient that occurs when services in a managed care environment are not provided in accordance with accepted standards of care. Clinical practice guidelines appear in the Clinton health care reform plan as a basic element of utilization and quality improvement, and Congress created the Office for the Forum on Quality and Effectiveness within the Agency for Health Care Policy and Research and gave it a mandate to publish and disseminate national clinical practice guidelines. Cutting across populations, ages, problem areas, and delivery sites, these national guidelines are systematic statements of what is appropriate in specific clinical terms when delivering care to patients. They are accessible on-line through the National Library of Medicine. The first areas of care to be covered include low back pain problems, cardiac rehabilitation, management of cancer-related pain, evaluation and management of early HIV infection, and postoperative pain management. What case manager has never worked on cases involving these areas of care? Another task force at the Agency for Health Care Policy and Research is developing a methodology to translate clinical practice guidelines into medical review criteria—guide-posts that will be used to judge the appropriateness of health care decisions (the criteria are scheduled to appear in 1994). With legal precedent for potentially holding case managers accountable even though they are not hands-on care providers, it behooves every case manager to make herself familiar with these practice guidelines.[13]

FOLLOW-UP

Attention must be paid to each detail. Any time a case manager has any responsibility for making recommendations for services or putting services in place, the case manager owes it to herself, the patient, and the client company who referred the case to make sure that what has been put in place is working and remains quality in nature, cost-effective, and necessary. Obtaining approval for monitoring from a client company can be difficult; managing a case without monitoring it can lead to liability exposure.

Sometimes a client company wants a case manager to make a one-time visit, put services in place, and be done with the case. No one is watching for changes in the patient's needs or tracking and assisting with increases or decreases in services. No one is gauging the continued effectiveness of the physician's treatment plan. What worked well in the hospital may not work at home. After five days, the patient is readmitted to the hospital. What happened? It may be that the patient initially followed the physician's recommendations to the nth degree, then became lax with dressing changes, and now has a dangerous infection. Especially when involved in helping a patient make the transition from one care setting to another, the case manager must make sure that the outcome for the patient will not become compromised.

The monitoring process varies from case to case. It may include semi-monthly home visits by the case manager or periodic phone calls placed by the patient to the case manager. In active cases where multiple services are in place, the case manager must make monthly on-site visits. It may be that there are no services in place but the patient has been discharged and been asked to take specific medications or dress a wound a certain way. The case manager will not go out and watch the patient take pills but will ask for a check-in call to see how the patient is coping. If the patient sounds poor or acknowledges problems, the case manager should call the physician and assess the situation. Perhaps the treatment plan needs to be re-evaluated.

When there are multiple services in place, the patient continues to recover, or the family resists any suggested decrease in service hours, the case manager may need to make an on-site visit to ascertain the true situation. It may be that the family members are not good communicators and things have taken a rapid turn for the worse. Without access, the case manager cannot determine whether continuing to adhere to the treatment plan is in the best interest of the patient.

Continuing follow-up and reports are especially important because they help maintain the case manager's link to the patient and support the case manager's role throughout the case. Rather than simply someone who sets up services or assists with hospital discharges, the case manager is perceived as someone who contributes to the entire treatment plan.

EVALUATING THE PLAN

Along with monitoring the medical treatment plan and its effectiveness, the case manager will evaluate and re-evaluate her own case management plan over the course of the intervention. Is the treatment working? Is the patient cooperating? There will be a flux in case activity and intensity.

Periodically (at least once every 30 days) the case manager should review the treatment plan and the patient's progress. Short-term referrals, which generally run less than three months and are characterized by intense activity at the outset that tapers off as the patient improves, are always reassessed prior to the patient's discharge from a facility or program. Long-term programs, such as geriatric care, are evaluated at intervals of 3, 6, or 9 months, or as in a brain or SCI (spinal cord injury) at one-year intervals. Long-term care evaluations can become challenging because the goal of case management is stability; in some cases, things can hum along for quite a while and there will seemingly be nothing to report.

Further, quality of life is less easily measured than the quantity of money spent on care. Is a continuation of the program warranted? Are the dollars spent on John's care every day worth it? What can the case manager use as a yardstick to measure care progress? Is John experiencing big gains? Perhaps the first month John could not walk alone; this month he walks unaided but his gait needs correction. Or the first month John remained comatose; the second month he was alert but experienced memory loss. As long as improvements are ongoing, the treatment course can be justified.

The patient might be in a facility for a proposed six- to nine-month stay at a cost of $1,000 per day. A monthly visit by the case manager can be extremely effective in monitoring the need for continuing placement. (If the patient has been placed in a facility in another state, the case manager may rely on the facility's case manager to keep her updated rather than making a personal on-site visit.) Treatment might be necessary for a six- to nine-month period, but the patient might not require facility services for the entire time. Although making great strides the first two months, the patient may show no further improvement after three months. Perhaps the patient has hit a plateau and needs a break from the rigorous therapies. This is something the case manager cannot ascertain from facility reports. The case manager might have to decide whether a $1,400 a day facility fee is justified when there is a day program available to the patient that costs $500 per day. The next step might be to place the patient in the day program, then perhaps return him or her to the inpatient facility for another round of more intensive therapy if improvement again becomes noticeable.

Over the course of care, the case manager maintains communication with the treating physicians to share concerns and observations regarding developing conditions. The case manager may need to re-establish ties to a specialist to request assistance. As a treatment facilitator, the case manager keeps in touch with everyone who can make a contribution toward the desired outcome for the patient, including physicians, physical therapists, social workers, employers, and community center personnel.

REPEATING THE PROCESS

Each case will go through modification, redevelopment, and re-evaluation stages. Changes in patient status will require new measures of care.

I do not think a case manager can ever be certain that a case that appears short term is not going to become problematic. Some conditions seem very straightforward, and then, for whatever reason (family dynamics, financial difficulties, new symptoms), the initial diagnosis is changed. Case managers should always allow for extenuating circumstances, unforeseen events, and as much as possible they should try to prevent complications from occurring. Yet, despite the best of care and intentions, short-term problems can become long-term problems.

SPECIFIC CASE MANAGEMENT ACTIVITIES[14]

Throughout the course of care, the case manager will be working in four major areas of activity: medical, financial, behavioral/motivational, and vocational.

Medical Activities

Into this category fall all those activities a case manager performs to ensure that the patient receives the most effective medical and nursing care, including the following:

- Contacting the patient in the hospital, in the rehabilitation unit, or at home.
- Contacting the members of the medical treatment team (the physician, nursing staff, rehabilitation therapists, etc.) to discover the patient's course of progress and needs and utilizing the information in discharge planning and the initial needs assessment.
- Arranging for all services required for discharge or relocation (equipment, home nursing care, therapy, transportation, transfer to another facility, home utilities, etc.); coordinating efforts with the primary RN, discharge planner, or social service administrator to eliminate duplication of service and conserve benefit dollars.
- Visiting with the family.
- Checking the home for safety factors and architectural barriers and arranging for any needed safety aids and modifications.
- On follow-up, re-evaluating equipment, ensuring supplies are replenished, monitoring home nursing services, and arranging for equipment repair; evaluating activities of daily living, home programs, and modifications to treatment.
- Identifying problems, providing health instruction, and referring the patient back to the physician or other health team member when appropriate.
- Identifying plateaus, improvements, regressions, and depressions; counseling accordingly or recommending help.
- Making personal visits or contacting the physician to clarify the diagnosis, prognosis, therapy, activities of daily living, expected permanent disability, limitations, and so on.
- Assisting in obtaining payer authorizations for any modalities of treatment recommended.
- Acting as a liaison between the physician and the insurance company when necessary.
- Sharing pertinent information about the patient with the physician and working together with the physician to achieve the best outcome.

Financial Activities

Some of the specific services a case manager might perform on behalf of a patient are as follows:

- Counseling the patient or family on budgeting and notifying creditors.
- Identifying financial distress and referring the patient or family to appropriate community resources.
- Helping the patient or family sort and prioritize unpaid bills.
- Acting as a liaison between the insurance company, referral source, and patient to alleviate financial and other problems or misunderstandings.

Behavioral/Motivational Activities

Behavioral/motivational activities include these:

- Exploring the patient's feelings about him- or herself and his or her injury or illness and helping the patient with the associated trauma and frustration.
- Monitoring the family's feelings regarding the patient's illness and observing the family's ability or inability to manage under new emotional stress.
- Offering reassurance and information about the patient's condition.
- If qualified, counseling in the areas of marital discord, role reversal, dependency, and sexual problems arising from the injury or illness.

Vocational Activities

Possible vocational activities include the following:

- Obtaining a history of past education, employment, hobbies, and job skills and uncovering vocational interests and future goals.
- If appropriate, overseeing psychovocational testing, work evaluations, schooling, transportation, on-the-job situations, and anything else needed to assist the patient in becoming or remaining gainfully employed.
- Assisting the patient in using the recuperative period in a constructive fashion (studying, upgrading skills, preparing for job interviews, etc.).
- Visiting the patient's place of employment and talking with the personnel director or immediate supervisor about the employer's expectations and the patient's needs.
- Completing a job analysis and discussing the possibility of the patient's return to work in the same job, perhaps after job modifications or lightening of duties.
- Sharing above information with physician at appropriate time.

CONCLUSION

Case managers always need to remember why they are part of the health care system. They are there to empower patients, to involve patients in their own treatment and destiny, to help the very young and the very old live as best they can. During an initial assessment, a case manager might foresee some difficulties in effecting change for the better. The adult children of an elderly patient might be arguing among themselves regarding the best course of care; an HIV-positive patient or a patient with terminal cancer (some companies will not refer a cancer patient until he or she is a hospice candidate) is to be interviewed; a family might be devastated by their child's spinal cord injury. Often the more catastrophic and irreversible the situation, the more strategic the case manager's planning has to be. Can that family remain intact as a unit? In the face of these odds, sometimes the best thing a case manager can do is ask the patient and family, "What is it you want? What do you hope to get from this care? If you could change the patient's care, how would you do it?" By finding out where their heads and hearts are, the case manager can often make an important difference in their ability to cope with a tough situation.

NOTES

1. Terri Mizel et al., "A Win-Win Approach to Case Management," in *Driving Down Health Care Costs: Strategies and Solutions 1992* (New York: Panel Publishers, 1992), 215.
2. "Interpersonal Skills for Case Managers," in *Case Management Practice* (Rolling Meadows, Ill.: Foundation for Rehabilitation Certification, Education & Research, 1993), 118.
3. Ibid., 118.
4. Ibid., 118.
5. Ibid., 120–122.
6. Ibid., 119.
7. Ibid., 119.
8. Ibid., 123.
9. Ibid., 117.
10. Ibid., 169–174.
11. Marilou M. King, "Managing the Business of Case Management," prepared for the Individual Case Management Association, March 1993.
12. Developed by The Center for Case Management, 6 Pleasant Street, South Natick, MA 01760.
13. Alice G. Gosfield, "Clinical Practice Guidelines and Managed Competition: Legal Implications for Case Managers," presented at the Individual Case Management Association Medical Case Management Conference V, Orlando, Florida, September 1993.
14. "Job Descriptions and Standards of Care," in *Case Management Practice*.

CHAPTER

8

Utilization Review: Preadmission and Concurrent Review and Case Management

There are several methodologies available to identify individuals who could benefit from case management intervention. The line of insurance and the structure and sophistication of a claims department affect which "red flags" are used. Some claims departments contract for review services, while others depend on in-house capabilities.

Generally speaking, reviews are either prospective (before the event, called preadmission or precertification), concurrent (during the event), or retrospective (after the event). All these types of reviews are basically forms of utilization review. The purpose of utilization review is to evaluate the necessity, appropriateness, and efficiency of the use of medical services.

Each type of review utilizes certain criteria to determine whether there is a need for further action, decision, or intervention. For instance, an organization that provides retrospective claim review services might review all surgical claims that are over $5,000 and include more than three Current Procedural Terminology (CPT) codes. These factors suggest a potentially unbundled claim, and the action warranted is a review by a utilization review nurse or physician. Another indicator might be an inpatient hospital bill with a disproportionately large pharmacy charge, which suggests a potential overcharge; the action warranted is a hospital bill audit. The review process itself can also be used to identify cases for case management if the organization reviewer is aware of the red flags (e.g., multiple hospital admissions, certain ICD-9 diagnostic codes, claims for apnea alarms, electric hospital beds, infusion care services, etc.).

The problem with retrospective reviews is that the services have already occurred and are now being billed. Occasionally, the best that can be gained is a minimal discount, perhaps for a prompt-pay arrangement (invoices earmarked by the case manager to be paid within two or three weeks). It is always preferable to be positioned from strength, and this is the case if one is aware of services *before* they are implemented rather than after. From a case management perspective, the opportunity to explore alternatives is already absent when the case manager is confronted with a claim for $42,000 resulting from a hospital stay of 28 days. Could the patient have gone to a skilled facility for two of those weeks? Were nursing and other services in the home a possibility? And with these as alternatives, would there have been fee negotiations as well? These are now questions without answers. What to do with the $42,000 bill? Can the carrier get a prompt-pay discount? Was there overbilling? These savings, if possible at all, pale by comparison to what could have been!

Review of services prospectively and concurrently, on the other hand, presents the best opportunity for a successful case management intervention. How this process works will vary from company to company, but in my mind there is no reason to have preadmission or concurrent review other than to identify at the earliest opportunity potentially high-cost cases and then intervene.

It is amazing to me that carriers, third-party administrators, and employer groups often set up a precertification or preadmission review* program without linking it to some kind of case management program. They perform reviews in a management vacuum and then assume that there are no savings to be gained. Several companies have discontinued their use because "they didn't save us any money." And, indeed, they will not, other than those possibly realized through the denial of a few days in a hospital or avoidance of an inpatient stay when a day-op procedure is indicated. (However, day-op procedures at ambulatory surgicenters are often much more costly than an inpatient stay would have been. This is because of the lack of reasonable and customary charges for surgicenter facilities). Without a connection to case management, preadmission review accomplishes nothing more than maintaining a census of inpatient admissions. And preadmission review alone, with-

---

*In my company, we have avoided use of the term "precertification" because it implies approval or denial of the proposed admission and related services and payment for them. The preferred term is "preadmission notification."

out concurrent review, is incapable of reducing lengths of stay or allowing alternative care plans to be considered.

Let us assume that there is an understanding of the value of preadmission and concurrent review and a case management program. Who should provide the services, how should they be provided, and what, if any, should the guidelines and procedures be? Are there standards of practice and what should the results be? Fortunately, there are some established standards and guidelines as well as organizations that continue to evaluate and review existing and developing programs. *Guidelines for Health Benefits Administration,* which is jointly published by the American Hospital Association, American Managed Care and Review Association, American Medical Association, Blue Cross and Blue Shield Association, and Health Insurance Association of America, is a compendium of the recommendations of several member organizations. It is extremely useful for those who wish to start a preadmission and concurrent review program or evaluate the services of an existing provider.

I believe that the maximum opportunity for success exists when one organization provides preadmission and concurrent review along with case management services. Too often one company does the reviewing and another provides the case management. The delays that inevitably occur between identifying a high-cost case, referring it to a case management vendor, assigning the case, and actually managing the case make the system ineffective, rather than an ongoing process of evaluation, identification, assessment, planning, and implementation that *could* be the ideal. The key in case management is how the case manager gets involved and how soon. For example, one has missed an opportunity if a case manager starts working with a spinal cord injured patient 20 or 30 days after the initial hospitalization. Earlier involvement could have resulted in a transfer of this patient to a spinal cord injury treatment center and the prevention of some of the complications that have now occurred, which will be more costly to treat and prolong the period of rehabilitation.

So, let's once again make some assumptions and create the ideal program within one organization. To illustrate how this process could work, let's take a "walk through" the system.

INTRODUCING UTILIZATION REVIEW TO CLIENT GROUPS AND PLAN PARTICIPANTS

Let us suppose that a single organization intends to offer a combination preadmission review, concurrent review, and case management program. The first step in selling and implementing this program is to explain it to potential clients and the plan participants. If these individuals do not understand its purpose, its full benefits will not be realized. Over the years, I have seen various techniques utilized in an effort to implement such programs. These range from mandating cooperation, to penalizing by reducing the percentage of benefit reimbursement, to denying benefits altogether. Although the policy language needs to have some "teeth" to encourage participation, I think proactively positioning the services has a better chance of achieving success in the long run.

In today's environment, where virtually everyone appreciates not just the cost of the health care system but its complexity as well, communicating the concept of a preadmission and concurrent review and case management program is not really difficult. The intent very simply is to identify at the earliest opportunity patients or situations that could benefit from the intervention of a case manager. If concern for patients is seen as the focus, then enlisting cooperation becomes easier.

Case managers should be positioned as advocates and facilitators who have expertise to understand and the ability to effect change. They assist patients by getting information and expediting the delivery of services. To perform their functions effectively, they need a system which allows involvement to occur at the optimum time. Because a seemingly simple admission or "routine" operative procedure can unexpectedly become complex and expensive, each admission needs to be reviewed as it occurs. This does not mean that each will require intervention by a case manager; in fact, most will not. But the strategy of reviewing each will lead to the best outcomes for patients and payers.

Not long ago, I was meeting with two client groups. The first was considering having their claims staff handle all of the preadmission notification calls; they would refer to our case management department those cases they thought would be appropriate for our case management services. The second client group was prepared to suggest to its employer groups that they should notify its preadmission and concurrent review providers only of "serious conditions." It became apparent to me that we, as the case management providers, were going to be disadvantaged by this incorrect perception of the process. Some further education was obviously necessary.

I took a sampling of the first client group's preadmission forms. It was soon apparent that some of the cases it would have identified were not appropriate for case management, whereas others that would have been overlooked required intervention. As an example, one admission for "abdominal pain" turned out to be a malignancy of the pancreas; the patient eventually went home after a three-week hospital stay, with nursing and infusion care services arranged by the hospital (the infusion care services were referred to a physician-owned provider!). Appropriate case management intervention would have served both the patient and the payer in this case.

The second client group, after a similar discussion, soon realized that each individual has a different perception of what constitutes a "serious condition" and that in fact it was not only the "condition" that might signal a problem but other factors as well (e.g., multiple admissions, several seemingly "minor" medical conditions but only one admission, prior history, etc.). Through an education process, both client groups were soon able not only to understand the scope and value of an integrated preadmission and concurrent review and case management approach but to develop an appreciation of its complexity as well, which allowed them to implement a total and integrated system.

Whether by brochure, newsletter, flyer, meetings, or some other format, a program overview needs to be communicated. The sample case presented in Table 8-1 was created for one of our clients to illustrate what would probably occur with and without an integrated system in place. Exhibit 8-1 is a letter designed to be sent to plan participants to explain the advocacy role of the case manager and the nature of the case management process.

THE PREADMISSION AND CONCURRENT REVIEW PROCESS

Each preadmission and concurrent review process differs depending upon client group specifications and the line of insurance involved. For example, a nurse reviewer for workers' compensation may inquire as to the estimated return-to-work date or work restrictions (e.g., no lifting), whereas a nurse reviewer for a group medical plan would not need such information. (However, some information will be requested in both types of review.) It is essential to develop a format to gather the necessary data and organize them so that they will be useful in evaluating and identifying cases with potential for case management intervention. There are software systems (e.g., Certi-Facts by Erisco) that have been developed for this purpose, although an organization might elect to develop its own system.

Each system, manual or computerized, should allow for the input of a professional (nurse or physician). Although standardized questions and data are useful, each patient presents unique problems and symptoms. There needs to be sufficient flexibility to accommodate the differences. If a form or artificial intelligence (computer) system includes only set questions, it is impossible to discover all the situations and variables that might demand special attention. Even some very sophisticated software programs do not, unfortunately, allow for a patient-specific approach,

Table 8-1 Case Sample with and without Preadmission Review, Concurrent Review, and Case Management

Exhibit A	Exhibit B
Mr. Jones enters the hospital as recommended by his physician for diagnosis of pneumonia. As prescribed by his medical plan, he contacts ABC Insurance Co. to advise of his scheduled admission. ABC's representative obtains basic information concerning hospital, treating physician, and possibly the proposed length of stay for this admission (5 days).	Mr. Jones, as prescribed by his medical plan, contacts ABC Insurance Co. to advise of his scheduled admission, and the representative obtains information concerning diagnosis, length of stay, name of treating physician, hospital, etc. This information is then faxed to Options Unlimited, where it is screened for follow-up.
The notification procedure is completed, there is no follow-up of this patient, and eventually this individual will be discharged.	The Options Unlimited nurse contacts the patient and treating physician, and obtains additional information, including prior medical history, other hospital admissions, etc. She is in agreement with the treating physician for length of stay (LOS for this man would be 5 days).
The hospital claim is eventually received by ABC, and it is then noted that the actual stay was for 21 days at a cost of $22,500.	Now on day 5, Options Unlimited nurse contacts hospital utilization review nurse to determine if, in fact, patient will be discharged. Utilization review nurse advises that there was not a good result thus far with current antibiotic and further hospitalization was indicated. Options Unlimited nurse confers with treating physician, who discusses further and hopes that an additional 3 days will result in success.
	Options Unlimited nurse contacts treating M.D. who reports continued lack of response. He will try a different antibiotic, will need perhaps another 7–10 days of hospitalization.
	Due to extended stay, requests for additional days, and uncertain treatment plan, decision made to refer for on-site case management assessment.
	Visit by case manager to patient and treating physician uncovers additional

(continues)

Table 8-1 Continued

Exhibit A	Exhibit B
	problems but result is that M.D. agrees to discharge patient home on I.V. antibiotics (rather than continue inpatient stay).
	The patient is discharged to his home on day 7 of this hospital admission. Antibiotic therapy and nursing services are provided in his home. The Options Unlimited case manager has arranged the services with the input from the M.D., negotiated the fees for these services, and monitored the patient for the desired outcome and eventual discontinuation of these services. Following a 5 day course at home, he is switched to antibiotics by mouth and permitted to return to work.

Results		**Results**	
Action:	Pay claim (obtain discount if possible, audit the claim) of $22,500.00	Pay:	Hospital claim of $7,499.94
Savings:	None	Pay:	Claim for home antibiotic therapy and nursing services of $1,250.00 ($250/day × 5 days).
Questions:	1) Were all the costs necessary?		
	2) Was a 21-day stay necessary?	Pay:	Case management fees of $800.00
	3) Were there other alternatives?	Total:	$9,549.94
		Savings:	$12,950.06
		Questions:	Were the costs appropriate? Yes
			Were the patient and the plan well served? Yes

Courtesy of Options Unlimited, Case Management Services Division, Huntington, N.Y.

---

thereby preventing consideration of the kinds of factors that would indicate the need for additional intervention.

After the basic information is obtained (including admitting diagnosis, length of stay, and treatment plan), there needs to be a determination as to follow-up in the review process. If a length of stay is estimated to be five

Exhibit 8-1 Letter Explaining Case Management to Plan Participants

Employees:
ID (SSN) #:
Claimant/Patient:
Physician:
Hospital:
Date of Admission:
Employer Group:

TO: XXXXXXXXXX
      XXXXXXX
      XXXXXXX, XX XXXXX

We received notification of the above hospital admission on _____.
Please be advised that this is an advisory notice only and does not imply
payment of the claim/bill that will be received for this hospital confinement. It further does not imply payment for any of the services that may be
related to the confinement, i.e., surgeon, anesthesia, etc.

A Nurse Case Manager will be following the patient's progress during the
hospital stay. It is also possible that a nurse case manager may be in contact
with you either via telephone or in person, should this seem appropriate.

All claims received by the plan administrator for _____ will be reviewed and considered and will be subject to the terms of your medical
plan. This includes but is not limited to preexisting conditions, plan limitations and exclusions, cosmetic vs. medical need, uncovered services, etc.,
co-payments and deductibles.

If there are any changes in the case-related information above, please notify
the Nurse Case Manager at 1-800-555-1212. If you have any additional
questions or concerns about this or other medical matters, please feel free
to call us.

Thank you in advance for your anticipated cooperation.

Very truly yours,

_____
Nurse Case Manager, OPTIONS UNLIMITED
cc: File @ J.J.#01481

Courtesy of Options Unlimited, Case Management Services Division, Huntington,
N.Y.

days, there should be a follow-up call on day 4 or certainly day 5 to determine if, in fact, the discharge will occur as planned. If it is scheduled, will there be a need for any further services at home (e.g., nursing visits, physical therapy, or chemotherapy)? How was the hospital stay? Were there any problems or new conditions discovered? Is further testing required? Is a transfer to a different facility now scheduled? Is a follow-up call to the patient or to family members indicated to determine their understanding of the diagnosis or ability to cooperate with the discharge instructions? Were they, in fact, even aware of follow-up care instructions?

This kind of involvement by a nurse reviewer can often prevent a hospital readmission resulting from the patient's lack of knowledge. A follow-up call to the treating physician to share a discovered problem is always welcome and helps establish a productive collaboration between two professionals who want a good outcome for the patient. Necessary services can be arranged with the client group's PPO network or at a negotiated rate. Continued case management involvement additionally provides the ability to oversee treatment effectiveness and continued need.

In situations where the planned discharge will not occur, the nurse reviewer must uncover the reasons for the continued stay. Perhaps the patient developed a postoperative complication or the diagnostic studies have revealed other conditions that need further evaluation. Perhaps the patient remains medically unstable and requires the services and monitoring that only an acute care hospital could provide. For these and many other reasons, continued hospitalization is certainly warranted. Most review groups today inquire at this point as to the expected length of time that hospitalization will be necessary. Again, there are some software programs that have "built-in" norms for typical admissions, and as long as the responses fall within the norms, the stay continues to be "approved" or "certified." For the most part, hospitals and physicians are no longer guilty of overutilizing inpatient stays. There are those patients who for a variety of very understandable reasons do not fall within the "norms." This is where discussion between nurse reviewers and/or physician reviewers and the treating physicians is extremely important. It usually resolves confusion and leads to a better understanding of a complex treatment plan.

Occasionally, however, a continued hospitalization is requested because of factors that could be addressed using an alternate care plan. The patient, for example, may need IV antibiotics or has no one at home to change dressings or monitor medications. Solutions in such situations include arranging for home infusion services, skilled nursing visits, and home health aide services. The expense is considerably less than a continued stay in the hospital. If the nurse reviewer determines the need and proposes an alternative to the treating physician and patient, more often than not it is approved. Knowledge of the case's status at the right time is crucial, however, to the solution and the realization of savings. Without case management review, notification of circumstances might occur but the ability to alter events will be lacking.

I have seen employer or insurer groups that have preadmission and concurrent review and case management programs but also have language in their benefit plans that works against the goal of better management of patient outcomes. For example, a plan might offer unlimited benefits for inpatient stays, payable at 80 percent for the first $5,000 and at 100 percent thereafter, but will limit nursing visits to only 20 per year, four hours per visit, or will allow nursing only if implemented within three days following a hospital stay. Although the group might have intended to prevent overuse of nursing services, its plan language pushes claimants and providers toward overuse of the much more expensive hospital services. A case manager can modify the benefit language and make the best use of a cost-effective alternative but only if she is working with a decision maker who will allow exceptions to the rules. Other groups have preadmission and concurrent review nurse reviewers continue to track a lengthy hospital stay week after week but provide no mechanism for the reviewers to refer patients to case managers who could implement changes.

TIMING CASE MANAGEMENT INTERVENTION

At what point in the review process should a referral be made for case management intervention? There are some basic indicators or red flags to look for and there are other less specific, more individualized considerations. Some indicators may actually be evident during the very first call from a hospital admissions department, treating physician, or patient's family to a preadmission review department or company. A preterm delivery, a high-risk pregnancy, a cerebral vascular accident suffered by a teenager, a spinal cord injury, or a traumatic brain injury with coma are all conditions for which there is a high probability of a lengthy hospital stay, a need for additional care and services upon discharge, high costs, and benefits to be gained through case management. For the most part, it is appropriate to refer any of these as soon as possible to case management.

Other conditions and circumstances would also merit an early referral, not necessarily because of a particular diagnosis but because of surrounding circumstances. For instance, diabetes is not by itself a condition that would prompt a case management referral, but the fourth hospital admission in two months of a patient with diabetes might. Why are these admissions occurring so frequently? Is the patient noncompliant or noneducated? Has the patient been treated in a clinic by a different physician each time? Is the treating physician a retiring family practitioner? Perhaps an endocrinologist is needed? Is it reasonable to wait until there are additional complications? A referral to case management at this point does seem appropriate and indeed should be made.

A patient with an admitting diagnosis of cellulitis may not at first glance seem appropriate for referral to case management. However, imagine that as the patient's stay in the hospital continues more becomes known about this 46-year-old woman: she is also hypertensive, had a coronary bypass two years earlier, is diabetic, and weighs 210 pounds, clearly morbidly obese for her height of five feet six inches. The case is obviously complicated. For one thing, the woman eventually might require a below-knee amputation secondary to her multiple conditions. Doesn't the potential of this occurrence at least warrant an assessment by a case management professional? Patients like this woman would likely be overlooked by a system for case management referral that was driven solely by one ICD-9 code or one set dollar limit. Yet each similar case presents such substantial opportunities for improved outcomes, prevention of complications, and reduction of expenses that *not* referring becomes a costly risk.

When approval for a case management referral is needed, a presentation of all pertinent information should support the request. A claims examiner or other approval source might be inclined to refuse case management for the cases just described, for example, because they do not fit the notion of an appropriate case. To avoid refusal, the case manager should be prepared to outline the problems, the costs that will be incurred if nothing is done, the solutions that could be applied, the approximate costs of the solutions (including case management fees), the length of time intervention will take, and the results that will be obtained. The object is to make the rationale clear, the savings obvious, and the approval much easier to justify.

When preadmission and concurrent review and case management functions are provided by one organization, the transfer of information and concerns is better coordinated and can actually provide ongoing knowledge and improved control of cases. Such coordination can also avoid duplication of involvement, help a claims department manage its workload, assist in the development of prevention and wellness programs, support the evaluation of use of benefits, and expose the need to redesign plans. When a nurse reviewer who has been involved throughout a complicated patient admission can share the background information she has acquired, the case manager is able to "hit the ground running."

As a case manager, I once received a referral from a claims department after it was notified by a provider who had conducted the preadmission review seven weeks prior and noted a diagnosis of cancer of the stomach. The end-of-the-month printout was now in the hands of the examiner, who had also just received a claim for one week of total parenteral nutrition and "other" services costing $10,000. The examiner thought a case management referral was appropriate. And it was, but it came a little too late. The services continued for a second week as arranged. The provider refused to negotiate retrospectively to lower costs; he knew the services were payable at 100 percent. (He knew the patient's benefit plan would pay the full price for his services because he called the claims department and learned this from a customer service representative.) The patient expired following a second and final admission to the hospital. Perhaps the total parenteral nutrition services could have been negotiated more cost-effectively; perhaps a hospice program could have been arranged, allowing the patient to die at home with his family around him; perhaps money could have been saved, too. Perhaps, but the lack of an integrated approach prohibited the pursuit of these options. In this instance, there was preadmission and concurrent review and case management and a benefit plan that would have permitted alternatives, yet because each system functioned independently of the others, in a vacuum, realizing the alternatives was not possible.

It is clear that these utilization review functions (preadmission, concurrent review, case management) need to exist side by side, with cognizance of each other's role and an ability to interact when necessary.

PREADMISSION AND CONCURRENT REVIEW REPORTS

Preadmission and concurrent review summary reports (see Exhibit 8-2) and other documentation of case events constitute an ongoing profile of a case. Case-specific reports (see Exhibit 8-3) help establish a case history and can be used to track the details of a case, which is especially helpful if the case changes from being low risk to being high risk. Produced for all hospital admissions, all scheduled pregnancies, and all emergency cases, case-specific reports incorporate ongoing notes made by nurse reviewers. They are valuable for internal use in a preadmission and concurrent review department, provide the rationale for case management referral, contain the background for the case manager assigned to the case, and are also forwarded to the claims examiner. (The software for the computer-generated report presented in Exhibit 8-2 was developed by Options Unlimited. Not all case management departments and companies have similar computer capabilities, but the form itself is a useful tool whether it is created by a computer or not.)

Exhibit 8–2 Preadmission and Concurrent Review Summary Report

Group # - 001   Third Party Administrator   1/1/93–1/31/93

Date Reported	Emp SS#	Patient Name	Diagnosis	Type	Date of Admission	Date of Discharge	Status
1/2/93	000000000	J. Smith	Fracture	Emerg	1/1/93	1/2/93	Closed
1/3/93	000000000	C. Jones	Norm Delivery	Emerg	1/25/93		Open
1/5/93	000000000	K. Williams	Lump in Breast	Sched	1/8/93		Open
1/7/93	000000000	S. Allen	Myocardial Infar	Emerg	1/11/93	1/18/93	Refer CM
1/12/93	000000000	T. Hans	Herniated Disc	Sched	1/21/93	1/25/93	Closed
1/14/93	000000000	L. Mooney	Miscarriage	Emerg	1/13/93	1/14/93	Closed
1/16/93	000000000	J. Bono	Appendicitis	Emerg	1/15/93	1/18/93	Closed
1/18/93	000000000	N. Strong	Derangement Knee	Sched	1/25/93		Open
1/25/93	000000000	P. Duffy	Depression	Sched	1/28/93		Psych
1/28/93	000000000	I. Grello	Pregnancy	Sched	3/25/93		Open

Total Admissions for Period = 9   Total Discharged = 5   Total Referred for Case Management = 1

TOTAL CASES FOR PERIOD = 10

Courtesy of Options Unlimited, Case Management Services Division, Huntington, N.Y.

Exhibit 8–3 Preadmission and Concurrent Review Case—Specific Report

---

CareWatch ID #: 00676
Date Reported: 08/31/93
Reported by: RENY

Group/Carrier:

Employee Info:
Name: G. Jones   SSN: 123-45-6789
Address: 12 Amhurst St., Mid-Island, N.Y.
Hire Date: 03/01/91   Effective Date of Coverage: 06/01/91
Telephone:

Patient Information:
Name: G. Jones   DOB: 01/25/67   Age: 26
Relation: Employee   Sex: Male
Confinement Type: Emergency
Admission Date: 08/28/93   Length of Stay: 2 Days
Discharge Date: 08/30/93
Procedure: initial hosp. care/eval. and management
Hospital: COMM. HOSPITAL
Address: ROUTE 111
SMITHTOWN, NY 11787
Telphone: (516) 979-9800   Faxphone:

Admitting Physician Information:
Doctor: Dr. J. Kahn
Telephone: 555-1212   Faxphone:
Diagnosis: hemorrhage—cerebral

CASE REMARKS

9/3/93: t/c to hospital, claimant was discharged on 8/30/93 but could not give me any other info. CTR t/c to MD, spoke Evelyn Spencer, who said that the claimant has an app't. with the MD today and she will call me back after he has been seen by the MD. CTR t/c to claimant, who said he felt dizzy and went to the ER, he was admitted to ICU and had a CAT scan, was told he had an elevated BP and is on medication. He continues to feel dizzy sometimes and gets tingling in his tongue. Has an appt. today at 12:30 PM. will f/u on 9/8/. CTR

9/8/93: t/c to claimant - per family member he is having some type of outpt. test today. f/u with claimant 9/9. IK

9/9/93: t/c to MD - told me that claimant was readmitted to hosp. for one day 9/8 to have arteriogram done. Diagnosis is seizure disorder and AV malformation and he was started on Dilantin. Will be referring him to neurologist. Will f/u with claimant. MF

(continues)

Exhibit 8–3 continued

9/10/93: t/c to claimant - still feels dizzy, has appt. with his MD today. Will f/u with claimant 9/14 for outcome and neuro. appt. IK

9/14/93: T/C to claimant - per his father, he has an appt. with neurologist Dr. Kahn (didn't have no.) tomorrow at 1 PM; he still has dizziness and numbness of tongue. f/u with claimant/md 9/16. IK

9/16/93: t/c to claimant - told me that he had appt. with neurologist yesterday and that he referred him to another MD (neurosurgeon?) and that appt. is for next week 9/22. (claimant did not know name of MD offhand). Continues to take Dilantin and continues to feel dizzy, even though he stopped smoking. Claimant mentioned that MD might have to operate on his brain because "there is something wrong with blood vessel in his brain." Obtained Dr. Kahn's phone number 516-555-1212. Will f/u with MD. MF

9/16/93: t/c to MD - not in because of holidays. Will be back in office on 9/21 after 1 PM. MF

9/21/93: t/c to Dr. Kahn - per Sue pt. has AVM, will not be seen again in MD's office until sometime around 10/12, not aware of ref. to another MD, not aware of potential for surg. at this time. f/u with claimant to obtain name and no. of referral MD. IK

9/21/93: t/c to claimant - no answer x 2. IK

9/24/93: t/c/ to claimant - left message on answering machine. MF

9/30/93: t/c to claimant - no answer. Will try one more time tomorrow if no answer or return call, then will close case. MF

10/01/93: t/c to claimant - no answer x 2. IK. MULTIPLE attempts made to contact claimant; per MD office no further therapy scheduled at this time. Case closed. IK

MONITOR FILES FOR FUTURE CLAIMS****************

(continues)

Exhibit 8–3 continued

CareWatch ID #: 00954
Date Reported: 11/08/93
Reported by: BARBARA

Group/Carrier:

Employee Info:

Name:	G. Jones	SSN: 123-45-6789
Address:	12 Amhurst St., Mid-Island, N.Y.	
Hire Date:	03/01/91	Effective Date of Coverage: 06/01/91
Telephone:		

Patient Information:

Name:	G. Jones	DOB: 01/25/67	Age: 26
Relation:	Employee	Sex: Male	
Confinement Type:	Emergency		
Admission Date:	10/30/93	Length of Stay: 4 Days	
Discharge Date:	11/03/93		
Procedure:	initial hosp. care/eval. and management		
Hospital:	COLUMBIA PRESBYTERIAN MED CTR.		
Address:	207ST & BROADWAY		
	NEW YORK, NY 10032		
Telphone:	(212) 305-2500	Faxphone:	

Admitting Physician Information:

Doctor:	Dr. Z. Binder		
Telephone:	(212) 555-1212	Faxphone:	
Diagnosis:	hemorrhage—cerebral		

CASE REMARKS

CASE KNOWN TO OPTIONS FROM PREVIOUS ADMISSION - VERY DIFFICULT TO FOLLOW - CLAIMANT DID NOT RETURN PHONE CALLS.

11/8/93: t/c dr. binder office. MD not available. will have secretary (aline) call me back. vc

11/8/93: t/c to hospital pt info. patient discharged 11/3/93. vc

11/8/93: t/c claimant. no answer. vc

11/8/93: t/c hospital medical records. dept closed (hrs. 9-12, 2-3:45) direct #212-555-1212

11/9/93: t/c to MD - MD is away, per Aline, residents are following claimant. She will get info. from them and return call. MF

11/9/93: t/c from Aline at Dr. Binder's office - told me that claimant is being followed by Dr. Sachs and that I should speak to Pat his secretary for further info. Number is 212-555-1212. Transferred me to that number - according to Pat, MD is away and she could not tell me about hosp. stay.

(continues)

Exhibit 8–3 continued

Claimant does not have a follow up appt. yet, she has to call him this week and set something up. Told me that claimant did not have surgery and during hosp. stay claimant was under the care of Dr. Frank 212-555-1212. MF
11/9/93: t/c to Dr. Frank - not in yet, left message with secretary, Lisa. MF
11/10/93: t/c to Dr. Frank - not in yet; left message with secretary, Lisa, for MD to call-back. BR
11/11/93: t/c to claimant - spoke to man who rents a room from claimant's father. Told me that claimant does not live here anymore. Claimant's father is out right now, he will give him my phone number for him to call me back with number where claimant can be reached. MF
11/11/93: t/c to claims. Renee will pull most recent claims and check on address and call me back. MF
11/11/93: t/c to MD office - spoke to Lisette who told me that she gave the MD the messages. She will speak to him again and try to get info and call me back. Asked if she had claimant's address and phone number and she transferred me to billing to speak to Terry. Per Terry, claimant does not appear to be in computer system at office or with hosp. Check system several times. Told me to call back after 1 PM and speak to Carmen and perhaps she could help. MF
11/12/93: t/c to Dr. Frank claimant had a minor cerebral hemorrhage. Dx. is arterial malformation of the brain; Dr. Sachs is performing surgery at a later date; J(212)555-1212; individual not in any danger; need to contact Dr. Sachs for more detailed info. JG/br
11/15/93: t/c to Dr. Sach's office/Pat: they have been unable to contact claimant; he needs to see Dr. Sachs & then surgery can be scheduled. BR
11/15/93: t/c to claims Renee says claimant admitted to Community Hosp. of W. Suffolk on 11/13
11/14/93: t/c to C.H.O.W.S./UR Dept./Mrs. King - claimant adm. 11/13 via ER with seizures; was in ICU - now on telemetry; under the care of Dr. Zeller, (516)555-1212 has no additional info @ this time. BR
11/15/93: t/c/ to Dr. Sachs/Pat - given above info; she will inform MD to f/u with Dr. Z; BR
11/15/93: t/c to Dr. Zeller's office - informed of pending consult with Dr. S # given; Dr. Zeller in with patient; will call with claimant when finished. BR
11/15/93: t/c from Dr. Zeller, claimant c/o numbness of tongue which MD feels is seizure activity; Dilantin increased - c/o of dizziness; CAT scan WNL; EEG pending; will be disch. tonight or tomorrow; f/u with Dr. S. BR
11/15/93: t/c to claimant; spoke with father; corrected birthdate obtained (12-06-34): will f/u with claimant tomorrow to schedule CM assessment; in rm 254 -, father & son work for the same company. BR
CASE REFERRED FOR CASE MANAGEMENT.

Courtesy of Options Unlimited, Case Management Services Division, Huntington, N.Y.

The review summary report (Exhibit 8-2) shows that only one patient out of ten was referred for case management. One review summary report showed that there was a surprisingly high incidence of admissions for complications of pregnancy for this employer group, consisting mostly of women, and it lead to the development of a maternity screening and management program and the prevention of two premature babies. The savings to the group far outweighed the costs of the managed care program.

ESTABLISHING AN EFFECTIVE PREADMISSION REVIEW, CONCURRENT REVIEW, AND CASE MANAGEMENT SYSTEM

To be effective, a preadmission and concurrent review and case management system or department requires flexibility and cooperation on the part of payers and providers, benefit plan language that supports case management, and a claims administrator who understands the difference between managing benefits and managing cases. As stated previously, the only way case reviewing and case management can become truly potent is when each element is applied as part of a unified system. How should the system be set up? The first step is to look at what is in place in order to determine what is needed. Whether one is working with a third-party administrator, an insurance company, or a self-administered plan, the signs of a benefit and claims system in trouble are the same.

Most health insurance plans today (and with growing frequency, workers' compensation plans as well) have some form of review system in place, especially for hospital admissions. Unfortunately, too often the "notification of an admission" is the only step rather than the first step in an integrated system of review and case management. What value is it to those companies who pay for such services to require individuals to call an "800" number prior to entering a hospital or within 48 hours of an emergency admission? What purpose does it serve and what should be the result of such a notification system? It is interesting how many claims departments, third-party administrators, and employer groups require such a system and put one in place and then have great difficulty describing the results. Over the last several years it's almost become a "we have to have it" kind of service, but run with little accountability, and showing still less in terms of results.

So how can one determine if a company or department needs a better preadmission and concurrent review and case management system? By asking the direct questions listed in the following sections.

Preadmission Review Services

Are patients required to call someone before entering the hospital? If the answer is no, then you know that there is no system in place. The result is that individuals can enter the hospital as often as they or their physicians wish, stay until someone questions the hospitalization, and spend as much as may be available for hospital services.

If a notification call is required, to whom is it made? If it is to a claims department, does a claims examiner or a medical professional take the call? If it is a claims person, is the information intended to be used to decrease lengths of stay or costs, improve outcomes, or identify high-cost, complex cases? If the call goes to a medical professional in the claims department, what is done with the information? Are potential long-term cases flagged for any kind of action? Does the person taking the call have the ability to authorize case management or is there a mechanism established to suggest a referral for case management?

If this kind of preadmission call is directed to a review organization, what are the results? Is the organization simply advised of the admission? Does anyone review the admissions as to their appropriateness? Are patients allowed to remain in hospitals for a fixed number of days, are they allowed to remain as long as their physicians want them there, or is each stay checked after seven or ten days?

Concurrent Review Services

Does anyone review a hospital stay during the confinement? If so, how often are such calls made?

Does anyone from the review group ever speak with the claims department staff? Are reports available to indicate the number of admissions and readmissions and the average stay? Does a review of these reports indicate any problems (e.g., unusually long stays, unusually frequent readmissions, etc.)?

Does anyone authorize continued stays and, if so, what criteria are utilized? Again, some review services have a software program that uses a series of questions; depending on the answers, the system allows or denies extra days. Other review services utilize predetermined medical criteria and a professional reviewer. Use of software systems alone may result in arbitrary decisions and prevent consideration of individual patient needs. The ideal review program assessment would combine industry standards and norms and professional interaction with the patient, physician, and family.

What happens beyond hospitalization, when the patient returns home? Is concurrent review extended? Does anyone track the patient's progress to prevent readmission?

Case Management Services

Assuming that the preadmission and concurrent review services are appropriate, what happens when a "red flag" indicating a possible need for case management is identified? What are the red flags? To whom is the information communicated and when? Is the claims department notified by phone or by report? What then is done with the information?

If there is some kind of notification, is the case referred to case management services? Are the case management services affiliated with the review group or provided by another company?

How long does this process take? Too long an interval reduces the opportunities for timely intervention and cost containment.

How many cases are actually case managed? Does this match the industry standard (3–5 percent of a group have potential for case management) or is the number higher or lower than would be expected?

What kinds of cases are managed? What are the results and the costs? Are any arranged services discounted or are fees negotiated? Are savings reports submitted? What are the costs for case management compared with the savings attained?

Exploring the answers to these questions one at a time will be effective in determining the structure, function, and, more importantly, the results of any cost-containment program. Obviously, when the answers indicate a poorly designed or managed program, they also indicate minimal savings. The lack of savings will place the review group in the unenviable position of trying to justify the costs to their clients without being able to point to significant performance results. Again, this does not mean that these services do not yield savings but they will not produce the savings that a well-designed, well-managed, and fully integrated program will.

Let us assume that the claims department, third-party administrator, or employer group has determined that for whatever reason there is a need to design and implement a fully integrated preadmission and concurrent review and case management program. One question that then needs answering is whether to do the work in-house or hire an outside company or freelance professionals to develop a program to meet specific client group needs.

In-house programs usually offer greater control, but the expense and increased management burden of adding review and case management professionals to existing staff may not be justified. Some considerations for in-house programs include these:

- Who will hire the staff?
- Who will train and supervise the staff?
- Who will define the responsibilities?
- Who will integrate claims and medical activities and responsibilities?

Employer-funded and -administered plans, whether workers' compensation or medical, tend to be better suited for the in-house staff approach. The companies that have such plans have already made the commitment to actively participate in their benefit plans. Larger employer groups are moving steadily toward integrating all of their employee lines of insurance, including short- and long-term disability and workers' compensation insurance, for reasons other than direct control. They are finding that a well-coordinated benefits philosophy and integrated 24-hour coverage are necessary elements of a truly cost-effective care management program. Third-party administrators and insurance carriers are exploring the feasibility of coordinated, in-house programs as well.

For groups that choose not to use in-house staff, collaboration with a full-service managed care organization provides cost-containment capability and the flexibility to design company-specific programs. As employer groups have become knowledgeable about cost containment, they have become more vocal about what they want and do not want for their employees. The ability of a review organization or case management service to be responsive to these requirements or preferences is one factor to consider in designing a program.

PREADMISSION REVIEW, CONCURRENT REVIEW, AND CASE MANAGEMENT CHECKLIST

The ideal program will have the following elements and characteristics:

- Full integration of preadmission and concurrent review and case management services.
- An outside company or an in-house department with nurses, physicians, and clerical and administrative staff who understand each other's role and function, have ongoing interaction, and operate as a unit in pursuit of quality outcomes and cost containment results.
- An established communications link with the claims examiner or claims staff administering the plan.
- The ear of the CEO or a decision maker regarding specific allowances to be made on a case-by-case basis.
- A regular reporting system charting active case management cases by type, duration, expenses, and savings.
- A process of continual evaluation and the capacity to revise the program year to year. If, for example, the program initially included

only one kind of case, criteria might be refocused in the second year to target another specific group. In this way, cases that do not prove cost- or care-effective are taken out of the system.

- A case management cutoff schedule. Only the truly catastrophic cases will have a case manager on board long term. Once a case is stabilized and savings are no longer realized, the case manager should be off it. (The patient and family become in essence their own case managers.)
- A schedule to evaluate the computer systems that are used to capture potential cases or target needy patients, allowing program managers to improve the case selection basis.
- A mechanism to learn from past experience. Has the company or department ever had a preadmission and concurrent review and case management system in place before? If not, there should be a mechanism to track one year's performance against the next and determine how well the program has functioned.

FEES: CAPITATED, HOURLY, OR PER CASE

Once the hurdle of setting up the preadmission and concurrent review and case management system is gotten over, there is another potential stumbling block—the fees. Companies accustomed to buying preadmission and concurrent review services customarily purchase these services at capitated rates (a predetermined per employee, per month cost) ranging from $.85 per employee per month to $1.50 and on up. These become set fees, varying only by the number of employees or covered lives, and have nothing to do with office visits or hospital admissions. Therefore, fees for a group will remain relatively constant if there are 20 or 60 or 200 admissions to a hospital. It is important, therefore, to determine an expected hospital experience for a group prior to establishing fees so that the fees charged will at least meet the expenses incurred in providing services (e.g., payroll, phone, computers, software, etc.).

Some companies, believing that their employee groups (including dependents) are basically healthy, may elect to purchase services on a "per case" basis. Fees may be calculated on an hourly basis for the time each reviewed case would take or on a flat-fee basis (i.e., a set fee is established for each review).

This covers the fees for the "small stuff." When such fees are quoted, they seem almost painless to the client groups. And in fact many client groups consider preadmission and concurrent review services to be case management. They truly believe that "review" and "manage" are one and the same, so discussions about case management fees often generate resistance. If a client group already thinks it is getting review and case management services for a capitated rate of $2.00 per employee per month, then it is necessary to redefine the terms, explain the differences, and determine the services actually being provided. Case management services are usually billed on a hourly basis or deemed "out of contract" or "extracontractual" services. When the services and fees are discussed, the group may decide to forgo them or to use them sparingly, only for catastrophes. ("We've only had one or two of these, thank God, our people are healthy!") Quite apparently, the group needs a little more information about case management, the kinds of cases typically managed, and how case management differs from preadmission and concurrent review.

Case management fees, if billed hourly, do get noticed. A case manager will need to discuss the fee structure and reach an agreement on it with the potential client group or payer prior to invoicing for these services. (Billing guidelines are discussed elsewhere in this book.) Full acceptance of these fees is not automatic, nor is explaining them an easy process. They need to be presented as individualized and time intensive. A description of the kind of work that is involved is helpful and provides an understanding not only of the process but of the time required for visits, arranging for services, negotiating fees, monitoring, and so on. It should be pointed out that if a case is unmanaged, the costs will go unchecked and might indeed prove to be catastrophically expensive. A side-by-side comparison of patients that are case managed and those that are not is extremely valuable in demonstrating potential savings. Because some cases can generate thousands of dollars in invoices, there needs to be a thorough discussion and acceptance of the case management concept before work begins.

Trusting that a payer will automatically perceive the value and accept the costs of case management services is not a risk worth taking. It often results in having to justify expenses after the fact, which places one in the position of "putting out fires." There may be resistance or lack of understanding, but it is better to confront problems before services are initiated than to be well into a program and faced with a client who feels misled.

Because case management is largely intangible, educating prospective or current client groups takes time, energy, and verbal skills. One successful method of education involves the sharing of cost benefit analysis reports. When these reports are reviewed case by case, it becomes evident that the investment in case management is worthwhile. Presenting case management as "the" solution to high cost cases allows even the dubious to consider it, if only on a one-case-at-a-time basis.

Once aboard, "converts" become "zealots" as success after success is documented. Of course, there will be cases that do not yield as large a savings as others, but overall effective case management programs will always result in considerable savings. The bottom line should be that the dollars spent on case management are far less than the savings realized.

Working Effectively with Claims Departments: Case Managers in Consulting Roles

In our current system, there are really very few incentives for providers or anyone other than the payer to watch out for costs. As long as there is coverage available and a claim is accompanied by a doctor's prescription or a letter of medical need, it will be paid because most claims examiners and departments do not have the sophisticated medical knowledge to know whether a procedure is really necessary. Once coverage starts, who in the claims department can say when should it stop? Is the claims staff supposed to decide the beginning and end points in medical care? One would not assume so, but in terms of payments for health care delivery, much has been left in the hands of the providers and claims personnel. Certainly neither individuals or corporations really want to turn over their checkbook, especially in areas where there are no reasonable and customary charges established for medical services, yet they do, daily. When a bill comes in, it gets paid at 100 percent or 80 percent of the submitted amount despite the fact that charges are all over the map; some people are paying what they should be and others are billed far above what is even deemed profitable. So, do we leave everything to the free market—let the buyer beware and hope that care costs eventually stabilize? I don't think so.

Let the buyer beware? Patients are often too weak, too compromised, or too distraught to look out for themselves. Savvy corporate managers, as well as smart homemakers, get thrown into the middle of the convoluted delivery-payment system and cannot begin to act as self-advocates. For one thing, they do not know what questions to ask. Unfortunately for them, the more complex their needs, the less likely it is they will be well served by the system. The more providers involved, the less likely it is that there is one person looking out for the patient. Despite dollars being spent, no one person has the responsibility of trying to ensure that the outcome will be desirable and the services will be quality.

A nurse in a hospital would never decide to get involved in a patient's care just by reviewing the case while sitting at a desk. The nurse would walk down the hall and visit that patient, talk to the physician, and talk to the family. A case manager would do no less. There are too many liabilities and too much at stake. Similarly, shuffling claims (or even speeding claims) through the system for payment is not enough. Patient information is not enough. A physician's operative report is not enough. It is the combination of information and what the case manager does with that information that makes case management a valued service.

Understanding the roles and responsibilities of claims personnel and working in concert with claims staff can help a case manager improve patient outcomes and enhance a payer's bottom line. It can help her build a more successful case management program and achieve a better position in the marketplace. How close a case manager's contact is with a claims department will be dictated by the line of insurance, the entity retaining the case manager's services, and the case manager's position. Some case managers never talk to a claims person, ever. They might converse with the case management department in XYZ insurance company, and that department then perhaps communicates with a claims department. Unfortunately, for far too many companies, the case managers work in a vacuum, with no claims interface at all.

The amount of interaction with a claims department will also depend on the structure of the case management department or company. The individual case manager may have more or less freedom to communicate directly with a claims department, benefit examiner, or claims adjustor. The bigger the company and the more case managers there are, the less likely it is a particular case manager will have ongoing contact with a claims adjustor. Sometimes, the supervisor of a case management company is afraid that a case manager will get too close to accounts and decide to start her own company, taking the accounts along. Case management and claims services are rarely integrated, and both the patients and the program suffer.

In short, the ideal does not exist. Not every case manager has ongoing communication, nor does every case manager who makes a recommendation see it put into place. A report may go to claims supervisor Jane Jones but never past her to the claims examiner. Or the report may go directly to a home office because in this particular company only the home office assigns cases for case management; the local claims department may never see the report or know about it. There is no universal ideal for the interface between case managers and claims departments. However, this does not mean that case managers should ignore the benefits of this liaison or hesitate to establish it. The "norm" does not free a case manager from the responsibility to know claims issues and claims personnel, because whatever work a case manager does is eventually forwarded to a claims department.

CLAIMS DEPARTMENT STRUCTURE AND OPERATIONS

To make the most of their relationships with claims departments and to benefit patients and payers, case managers should distinguish the main players in the claims arena. What are the reporting relationships within the office? How does this person fit into the loop? A person's title may convey how much or how little control he or she has over processing a claim. It is also vital to determine the concerns of the claims staff: What is the real reason a claim was referred for case management? What is the claims manager looking for from the case manager? How can the case manager get timely, accurate answers to her questions so as to be able to address claims concerns? Finally, case managers will want to discover their own process of working with claims staff to get the best for their patients and clients while creating more advocates for case management.

THE PLAYERS

Job functions vary from claims office to claims office. Titles such as *processor, examiner,* and *adjustor* may be interchangeable, or each may denote different jobs with different responsibilities. In general, there are some titles and activities that are fairly consistent across organizations:

- A claims examiner is a claims processor who has the necessary skills to examine claims and make decisions whether to approve, investigate, or deny them.
- A claims processor may not be a decision maker but puts claims into the system. Edits to claim entries may occur after processing. Title usually used in high volume claim environment.
- A claims supervisor is usually in charge of work flow, examiner production, and the first level of management decision making.
- A claims manager usually makes the final decision regarding claims. Directors and vice presidents may be involved in decisions.
- A plan administrator has responsibility for overall administration of the plan and handles appeals and plan design and changes.

These are the people charged with making claims payments and enforcing whatever insurance benefit contract might be in effect. Their responsibilities include the accurate and timely payment of claims in a manner that follows contract language and documents their activities. In most claims offices, there is also a productivity quota that must be met. When working for a self-insured employer group (in-house or self-administered claims), the staff will report to the employer's CFO or CEO. In the case of a third-party administrator, the claims staff answers to the third-party administrator's CEO or vice president. Claims personnel employed by an insurance carrier report to the insurance company's CEO or president.[1]

The expertise and background of claims personnel vary widely. Some claims examiners have minimal experience in claims; some processors are experienced in data entry and are trained as they work their way up the claims staff ladder. In larger companies, an individual may begin as a file clerk, take on data entry, become a processor, and then become, over the course of several months, an examiner adjudicating and paying claims. Most claims personnel have a high school degree at least. Again, the bigger and more established companies tend to have many more in-house people experienced in claims issues. Newer firms and groups often begin their claims operations on a smaller scale, bringing in more expensive, more experienced senior people once their client base is more stable.

Broadly speaking, claims examiners have no background in medical terminology and any experience they do get will come from day-to-day job-site training or from courses they attend in medical benefits administration. There are videos and seminars available covering workers' compensation, liability, and group medical coverage as well as the more complex topics (e.g., copayments, coinsurance benefits, and statutes and regulations) they will encounter as they move up to become senior-level examiners.

Case managers and examiners view each case from totally different perspectives. Whereas case managers view a case globally and consider the patient's entire medical history and experience, claims examiners are presented with cases on an item-by-item basis, checking one ICD-9 or CPT code or R & C charge at a time. Further, examiners are productivity driven. The money that is going to be made by their employer will be made by getting the claims in, getting them quickly and fairly administered, and getting them out. There is not a lot of time to be spent on the phone or deliberating over single claims.

Unaware of this, case managers sometimes get exasperated at the gaps in claims examiners' knowledge of cases. Claims examiners rarely get the opportunity to handle all the claims for one patient, never mind the claims for one entire family.

There is no staffing pattern common to all claims departments, and there may be little true account dedication. A claim comes in and anyone in a room of examiners may process it. Some companies do set up account-specific groups; an insurance company handling 500 different employer groups may have one set of individuals processing claims for ABC, Inc., but they will handle the auto, group medical, and workers' compensation claims for all of ABC's 1,200 employees. Another department may section its staff by procedure; surgical claims staff, dental claims staff, and anesthesia claims staff, for example, will administer surgical, dental, and anesthesia claims for the entire covered population.

The case manager trying to find out "why was this claim paid this way?" might have a long wait, depending on the claims department's line of business. Because it has direct contact with the employer, a third-party administrator will have many more customer service and account representatives right in the claims department. The third-party administrator's representative may be in daily contact with the employer's human resources manager. In a large insurance firm, however, contact may be far removed. The employer group might call its insurance agent or broker, who in turn will call a customer service representative, who will bring it to the attention of an account representative, who will hopefully talk to a claims manager.

The diversity of claims operations makes a case manager's job more difficult; any assumptions she makes about a claims department will usually turn out to be erroneous. Whereas a nurse in a coronary care unit in New York is likely to have had the same experience as a coronary care unit nurse in Nebraska, a claims examiner paying medical claims in a building in Chicago may not have had the same experience as the claims examiner at the next desk. Adding to the challenge for case managers are the reams of claims forms and the computer technology endemic to claims departments.

THE PAPER TRAIL

A claims department is a paper-intensive environment. One claims history can have hundreds of pieces of paper, actual claims submitted by various providers, and, depending on the structure of the department, one claimant may have his or her claims paid by no fewer than 5, 10, or 20 individuals, none of whom may have any understanding of what is going on. Because these pieces of paper relate to only a small segment of the patient's overall condition, and because claims departments can be huge, it is a paper trail that is virtually impossible to track. Who has which claims, how were they processed, and what does this claimant's record look like when it is all assembled? The payment system is convoluted and fraught with regulations; every claim has to be submitted with this attachment and that notice, and because a consensus is lacking on how to handle claims, it takes one person minutes just to decide how to process a claim, which slows down the whole payment sequence. This is what the industry is complaining about, it is what providers are complaining about, and it is what the federal government and the states are complaining about.

And if the payment system is a challenge for the claims industry, it is a source of confusion and anxiety for the patient. For the most part, there is no one person to speak to if a patient has a problem. John Jones says, "Last month I got my claims paid fine, and two weeks later I sent in a claim from the same provider, but now it's been paid differently. Why did that happen?" There do not seem to be any hard and fast rules, and claimants seemingly have no redress. And because of cutbacks in most companies, John can only "speak" to a telephonic mail system. The non-computer-savvy person or the person with a language barrier or a disabling condition is left hanging with no way to resolve major problems.

COMPUTERIZATION

Why hasn't the growing use of computers alleviated some of this mess? Can't claims be keyed into a computer system so a patient's entire claims history could be pulled up on a computer screen? The truth is they can be, but most systems are set up in such a way that the problem has worsened. Claims examiners are no longer looking at actual pieces of paper. A claimant, who has been told to save a copy of everything, might have a copy of the claim but is talking to someone who is looking at a computer screen containing numbers, ICD-9 codes, and that is all. Even if the claimant had attached an explanatory note to the claim, there will be no corresponding explanation on the screen. So the claimant might have gone through laborious steps to clarify his or her situation but no one has recorded it. This is extremely frustrating for everyone involved.

Yet most lines of insurance today, including long-term disability, workers' compensation, and group medical insurance, are administered by software programs. Some insurance company departments and third-party administrators still administer claims by hand, but most large, competitive companies have computers assisting in the processing of claims. Various indicators can be programmed into the software to alert a claims examiner or consultant to a claim that may be problematic. Insurance companies or administrators handling claims for several employer groups need to be able to report back to those employer groups when an individual appears to be filing high-cost claims consistently. This allows the insurance company to control their present claims experience better and also plan for their future benefit needs. Actuarial professionals have been using these same techniques for years, garnering information from software programs to rate groups more appropriately and accurately. These reports also highlight information of interest to risk managers.

Employers in a particular industry purchase insurance at rates based on the industry's experience. In some industries there may be an abnormal number of back injuries or a high incidence of lost-time accidents antici-pated due to the type of work employees perform. Risk managers advise employer groups and insurance underwriters on how to decrease em-ployee risk, prevent accidents from occurring, and contain the associated costs once they occur. Can a different therapy be used to shorten the reha-bilitation period? What preventative or safety mechanisms can be in-stalled to decrease the incidence of injury at that work site?

Most often risk managers are consulted by companies that offer prop-erty, casualty, and liability insurance, yet are rarely approached by group medical carriers. To my mind, it makes good sense to apply risk manage-ment principles to all lines of insurance. I am certain that the trend toward moving patients from high-cost care settings to outpatient settings re-sulted from the examination by consultants of data runs showing the average length of hospital stays. A consultant would look at a benefit plan, see that there was little coverage available for outpatient care, and approach the company on ways to change the plan language to integrate outpatient care and make the whole experience a better one for the em-ployer and insureds alike. In this way, software programs and risk man-agement principles can be utilized for every line of insurance.

In some respects there is an overreliance on software by managers and employer groups, who are understandably impressed by software capa-bilities. But software programs can tell just so much about what is really going on. No matter how sophisticated, software cannot keep up with all the elements involved in claims payment. Sometimes employers rely on software to tell them what the problems are and how to solve them. They create great reports that give the percentage of people who generated a certain percentage of benefit dollars, but the software provides no clues on how to help those people or lower costs.

There is a common misconception that the speed and efficacy of a soft-ware system will now solve the problems that insurers thought they had (e.g., the relatively long time it might take to pay a claim). Now perhaps claims are paid too quickly. Things do get paid faster, but more things fall through the cracks because of the speed. For example, fraudulent claims are less apt to be picked up. Examiners are no longer looking at a claim and saying, "This looks doctored to me." We have lost some of the familiarity and hands-on knowledge regarding problem claims or people who might benefit from a one-on-one relationship with the claims examiner, but we have gained the ability to process the volumes of simple and complex claims that are submitted. Nothing would ever get paid in some cases without the use of software, yet perhaps it is relied on too much in the identification of problem cases. Software alone cannot really tell us what the problems are.

CLAIMS ISSUES

Case managers need to be aware of the concerns of claims personnel. These individuals have their own set of criteria that they must meet on the job, and case managers can create much better relationships by taking the time to understand claims issues. Some of these issues are pre-existing conditions, the funding vehicle (self-insured, fully insured, administrative services only, reinsurance, cost plus), insurance contract language and coordination of benefits (if there are two medical plans in a family). Is COBRA coverage involved? Is the claimant in the midst of an eligibility change: active to retired, active to disabled, active to Medicare eligibility, or active to COBRA? If the insurer is an employee group, return-to-work issues are important to the claims staff, as are ERISA concerns.[2]

INDICATORS FOR CASE MANAGEMENT

Sometimes the best teachers for a case manager are the cases which came to her too late, where she envisions all kinds of possibilities, if only she could have had this case earlier, when the home care first started. Now, it's six months later and she's wondering how to get the family unhooked from their services. Some services are difficult to "undo." By looking back at some of those cases, a case manager can develop her own red flags. The "I could haves" turn into red flag indicators.

Cases that benefit most from case management commonly involve the most expensive services. Use of these services is thus a red flag. Other indicators include a high frequency of admissions in a short period and an unusually long hospital stay. It's traditional for major surgical procedures to require five to seven days hospitalization. (A stay of ten days or longer for a surgical hospitalization indicates multiple problems or complications now and points to problems down the road as well).

This is where a case manager's clinical knowledge comes into play, her feel for what constitutes a big case. Having developed a set of indicators, the case manager then needs to communicate them to claims personnel.

The object is to get them to understand which cases to bring to the case manager's attention so she can at least follow up with a phone call and find out what is being recommended. If the treatment plan includes 12 hours a day of home nursing services or infusion care services for someone with a chronic infection, the result could be 30 days of services at $700 or $800 a day. With negotiation and appropriate service arrangements at the beginning, the case manager can get the patient what is needed and really demonstrate cost savings as the service is being put in place. It is very difficult to renegotiate a bill for $24,000 after the fact.

One new client handed me bills for $24,000 and $50,000 and asked, "Can't you do anything about this?" I informed the client that it is hard to do anything about such bills once the services have been provided. I said that similar cases, however, if referred early on, would benefit from case management and the costs could be reduced. The claims department, for example, was confronted with a claim for payment of monitoring services provided in the home of a woman with a high-risk pregnancy. They were looking at a red flag but did not know it. Instead of asking if the woman was covered, the claims personnel should have been asking if it is normal for a pregnant woman to be monitored at home. I needed to educate the claims department. Fetal monitoring is not usual for most pregnancies, and by informing the claims personnel of this fact, and showing them that abnormal means big costs, I was able to get them to tell me about such cases upfront, when case management could have a more positive impact.

It is important to let the claims personnel know that they really can make a difference. I have tracked a case without case management, run it through the case management process of negotiation and active intervention, then shared the results with the claims staff. I tell the managers of the third-party administrators I work with, "Listen, if you get your people involved, if you give them some kind of incentive, let them become the ones who refer cases, who are given the credit for savings, you will see a marked difference in the reports to your clients." Empowering everyone and giving each person insight into his or her role in the team effort makes for a better claims team and more effective claims administration.

With regard to another service our company provides, claims review, we faced a problem with the wrong kind of incentive. There was an administration quota, and for every claim that claims personnel paid over and above a certain number, they were given a monetary bonus. Obviously, this encouraged them to pay claims quickly. I said, "Do you understand what you're doing here? You're pushing things through the system. It takes your examiners time to pull aside a claim and give it to me for possible case management intervention or review. Yes, you want prompt payment of claims but you don't want to pay everything without consideration. If you can put a monetary incentive in place for those claims examiners who refer claims that actually result in savings, you'll have the proper emphasis. As a third-party administrator, you're absolutely charged with the responsibility to save money, and your people should be rewarded. Not only is it part of their job, but ultimately it will be part of whether or not you get a contract renewed to pay a client's claims again."

The education process continues, little by little, case by case. Exhibit 9-1 is a "tip sheet" I developed for the claims department of one client third-party administrator. It includes red flags for case management intervention as well as indicators for claims review.

Different red flags should be used for different lines of insurance. Looking for case management indicators, a case manager will not apply the same dollar limit per claim in a workers' compensation case as in a group medical case. In workers' compensation, for each lost-time injury there is an established guideline, and if the injured person is still out of work a month beyond the date calculated using the guidelines, then that fact becomes a red flag. (Physicians use the reference *The Medical Disability Advisor: Workplace Guidelines for Disability Duration*, written by Presley Reed and published by LRP Publications, to find out about injuries common to different job descriptions, including typical recuperative periods and return-to-work time frames.) On most workers' compensation claims forms, physicians are usually asked to note the date the claimant can return to work. If a physician has left the space blank or puts down "undetermined" month after month, that is a definite red flag. To my mind, a physician avoiding a return-to-work date indicates a problem. On the other hand, the physician might write in that a workers' compensation claimant should be able to return to work in four to six weeks. Four to six weeks go by, then another four to six weeks, then the patient needs another month of physical therapy three times a week. This kind of extension of treatment also indicates a problem. (Further, if the physical therapy is provided in a physician-owned facility, it may be a red flag.) Other indicators are: if the case continually passes by established goals; if the claimant is going to one doctor, and a month later he's going to another doctor who provides a similar service; if the patient is receiving physical therapy and chiropractic manipulation at the same time. Or the case manager might discover the patient is taking large numbers of pain medications and antidepressant medications, indicating the existence of new emotional components such as depression or lack of concentration, or that a seemingly simple injury has assumed grandiose proportions, with the patient seeing a variety of practitioners.

Also needing watching are cases where a new employee suffers a serious injury. One major concern is that the employer might not feel a com-

Exhibit 9–1 CareSolutions™ Red Flags and AccuClaim™ Red Flags

<table>
<tr><td colspan="4" align="center">CareSolutions Red Flags</td></tr>
<tr>
<td>•Diagnosis:</td>
<td>Cancer
AIDS
Stroke
Transplant
Neuromuscular
Diseases</td>
<td>Spinal Cord Injuries
Alcohol &
Substance Abuse
Cardiovascular
Head Injury
Severe Burns</td>
<td>Hi-Risk
Pregnancy
Chronic
Respiratory
Psychiatric
Multiple Trauma
Hi-Risk Infant</td>
</tr>
<tr>
<td>•Potential Treatment:</td>
<td colspan="2">Ventilator Dependent
IV Antibiotics
TPN/Enteral</td>
<td>Extended ICU
Home Care
Chemo</td>
</tr>
</table>

- •**Frequent Hospitalizations:** 3 Admits Same Year/Same or Related Problem
- •**Cost of Claim:** Same Illness over $10,000 Year-to-Date
- •**Location of Claim:** Complex Care Delivered in Rural Setting, Small Hospital, or Facility w/Poor Outcome History/Diagnosis
- •**Patterns of Care:** Failed or Repeated Surgeries, Hospital Acquired Infections, Malpractice Concerns
- •**Diagnostic Codes:** ICD9CM - Case Management Referral Indicators

042–044 HIV infection	paraplegic, anoxic	765.1 Premature birth
140–239 Neoplasms (cancer)	brain damage	800 Fx vault of skull
250 Diabetes w/ complications	358 Myesthenia gravis (repeat hosps.)	806 Fx of vertebral column w/SCI
252 (possible mult. hosps., coma, renal, eye, neuro)	359 Muscular dystrophy (repeat hosps.)	850–854 Intracranial injury excluding those w/ skull Fx
277 Cystic fibrosis, porphyria, metabolic disorders (mult. hosps.)	430–438 Cerebral vascular disease, car. hemorrhage	860–869 Internal injury of chest, abdomen & pelvis
279 Immunity deficiency disorders (repeat hosps.)	496 COPD 501–503 Asbestosis & silicosis 584–586 Renal failure	870–879 Open wound of head, neck & trunk
286–287 Coagulation defects (repeat hosps.)	644 Early or threatened labor	925–929 Crushing injury (may involve extensive trauma)
290–299 Psychoses	655–656 Fetal abnormality 710 All collagen (SLE+)	948 Burns over 25% of body
300–316 Neurotic personality & other non-psychotic mental disorders	714 Rheumatoid arthritis w/ inflammatory polyarthropathies	952 SCI without spinal bone injury
330–337 Hereditary & degenerative diseases of CNS (Alzheimer's, Huntington's chorea)	740–759 Congenital anomalies, spina bifida, cardiac septal defect	994 Effects of external causes - lightning, drowning, strangulation
340–349 CNS disorders, MS, CP, quadriplegic,	760–763 Maternal causes of perinatal morbidity & mortality	996–999 Complications of surgical & medical care

(continues)

Exhibit 9–1 continued

AccuClaim Red Flags

- **Surgical & Anesthesia Claims:** All provider claims over $1,000.00 & all cases with more than 2 line items should be referred for a medical review. Alert for GYN, Orthopedic, Plastic Surgery. If the surgical claim is referred, corresponding anesthesia claims should be referred also to verify complexity of claimed procedure. Information to obtain: 1) Operative report; 2) Anesthesia time; 3) R&C charges for EACH CPT code.
- **Podiatrists:** All claims that exceed $800.00 should be referred. Information to obtain: 1) Operative report if a surgical procedure is being billed; 2) R&C charges for EACH CPT code.
- **Physical Therapy & Occupational Therapy:** Claims that exceed 6 weeks of treatment should be referred. Information to obtain: 1) PT evaluation; 2) Therapy progress notes that include long- and short-term goals and the range of motion results; 3) Letter of medical need from treating MD w/diagnosis, frequency of treatment, & estimated duration.
- **Chiropractic Care:** Claims that exceed $300.00 should be referred. Information to obtain: 1) Complete copy of the medical records; NO summaries. Include diagnosis, treatment plan, frequency of treatment, estimated duration.
- **Durable Medical Equipment:** This is an area of extreme abuse and overutilization of services and fees. The following claims should be referred: oxygen concentrators & related equipment, hospital beds, wheelchairs, ANY monitors, respirators/ventilators, requests for home modifications (ramps, etc.).
- **Home Health Services:** All claims for nursing, aides, or related services should be referred. Information to obtain: 1) Itemized bills; 2) Nursing notes.
- **Infusion Care Services:** All claims for the following infusion services should be referred: IV antibiotics & other medications, TPN (total parenteral nutrition), chemotherapy, analgesia (pain medications). Information to obtain: 1) MD's prescription; 2) Itemized billing for medications, nursing, & related services & supplies.
- **Any of the following should be referred:** 1) Appeals; 2) Difficult providers; 3) Ambulatory surgical centers; 4) Large hospital bills: over 7 days LOS; to review for LOS, medical needs vs. custodial
- **Procedure Codes:** CPT Accu-Claim Referral Indicators

Integumentary System		Muscoloskeletal	
11000–11044	For cosmetic vs. medical	27590–27598	Amputation
15780–15791	For cosmetic vs. medical	Pulmonary System	
15810–15840	For cosmetic vs. medical	30400–30630	For cosmetic
17304–17310	For cosmetic vs. medical	31300–31660	Laryngectomy-trache-
19318–19500	For cosmetic vs. medical		otomy, etc.
		32310–32545	Lung surgery

(continues)

Exhibit 9–1 continued

Cardiovasular		51550–51597	Bladder (especially for
33200–33220	Pacemaker surgery		cancer)
35450–35458	Vascular vs. cosmetic	Maternity	
37799	Unlisted procedure	59000–59100	High-risk procedures
38999	Unlisted procedure	59120–59140	High-risk procedures
39599	Unlisted procedure	Nervous System	
Digestive		61340–61576	Craniectomy
41100–41155	Mouth, tongue (for	62180–62258	Spine
	cancer)	64999	Unlisted procedure
43600–43630	Stomach (biopsy, etc.)	Eye and Ear	
44100–44340	Intestinal	65771	Radial keretotomy
47100–47135	Liver	69300	Cosmetic
Urinary System		69399	Unlisted procedure
50200–50380	Kidney, incl. transplant	68899	Unlisted procedure

Courtesy of Options Unlimited, Case Management Services Division, Huntington, N.Y.

mitment to get the employee back on the job, especially if modifications are required. New injuries to persons with prior claims for back or other workers' compensation injuries should be treated as red flags. (There is usually a state databank that claims departments can use to research a claimant's prior workers' compensation injuries with other carriers or with other employer groups.) Indicators also include injuries to claimants nearing retirement age, injuries to part-time employees who might also work full time someplace else, or injuries to employees who could do work off the books. The insurer may be paying for an injury that occurred but not on the site the insurer is responsible for, or the claimant might still be able to work his or her main job but not the secondary job. For example, the claimant might work full time as a file clerk in a corporation and part time as a supermarket bagger. While recuperating, the claimant may be able to do filing but not stand for four hours and bag groceries, yet the workers' compensation carrier is still responsible.

Personnel issues can become reasons for people to go on short-term or long-term disability, and case managers need to devote attention to cases involving employees who are nearing retirement age or have both short-term and long-term disability policies (allowing a short-term leave to turn into a long-term leave, which is especially common in departments or companies facing layoffs). Employees who are at risk for being laid off or who have been passed over for promotion sometimes stay on short-term or long-term disability for security, using the insurance payments as a salary replacement. Obviously, the higher the salary replacement within a long-term plan, or the longer the HISOCC clause (see Chapter 4) in a long-term disability plan, the more quickly a case manager should review the claims. On the whole, the higher the policy benefits offered, the more bells and whistles should be going off.

In group medical coverage, the concerns will be different. Group plans cover employees and their dependents, and a case manager might target catastrophic illnesses, premature deliveries, cancer cases, plus other chronic and devastating long-term diseases, like AIDS or multiple sclerosis. Other things to watch for include multiple hospitalizations, multiple physicians, expenses beyond a certain threshold (e.g., $10,000), and particular kinds of services, such as chemotherapy, radiation therapy, and infusion care.

Because most claims departments are not staffed by medical professionals, I encourage case managers to include visual aids or informative material to help illustrate the conditions of claimants when they are first introducing red flags and when they are working on a weekly basis with claims personnel. A case manager can discuss ICD-9 codes and CPT codes until next week and never make the impact that one good picture will create. For example, imagine a case involving body burns. The case manager may say, "There are substantial body burns, but they are confined to the trunk and upper extremities," and then shade those areas in on front- and back-view line drawings of the type supplied by most medical companies. The case manager, without spending much time, has enabled the claims staff to feel they know what the case is about.

I see articles all the time in consumer publications such as *McCall's* or *The Ladies' Home Journal* that can serve as terrific teaching aids. I might tear out a piece on breast cancer or cystic fibrosis and send it along to a claims examiner with a note. I have also purchased medical dictionaries and reference books designed for laypersons and handed them to my claims associates. Specific examples include *The Pill Book* (Bantam Books), *Barron's Medical Guide: A-Z Medical Reference for the Non-Medical Person* (Barron's), and *The Mayo Clinic Family Health Book* (William Morrow and Company).

The more complex and complicated the medical picture, the more user-friendly the explanation has to be. The goal is to get claims personnel to understand the reasons behind the need for case management and the decisions of the case manager. I have gone to the extent of taking a claims representative to a rehabilitation facility. I have also used videos from a rehabilitation facility showing pieces of equipment as well as videos taken by parents showing their child in a walker. I use videos and photos to give a clear impression of a given situation. I do not do this for every case or claim but for those requiring special attention while we try to resolve their problems. Sometimes word pictures suffice: The patient is down a country road six miles from his nearest neighbor, his family is dispersed across the nation, and he lives alone. Word pictures can humanize a case.

I have found all these methods of education extremely beneficial. They not only improve my relationships with referral sources but enable me to do a better job for my patients because I now have the understanding of the people who sent me out in the first place.

THE CASE MANAGER AS CONSULTANT

Claims Software

Working directly with a claims department on specific limit reports, group claims runs, and individual claims runs is a facet of the case manager in a consultant role. She becomes a hands-on team member, sitting alongside the employer group, the third-party administrator, or the insurer, to capture those claimants in need of case management intervention. Using these tools, computer-generated claims runs, and creating the reports that follow from them, the case manager expands upon her case management activities and involvement with clients. These activities comprise the next step beyond noting red flags, but it is not a step every case manager may want to or be able to take (due to restrictions in her job description, the level of her interaction with the claims department, or the lack of computer technology sophisticated enough to generate claims runs). I include it here because I believe such consulting work is a vital part of CM capabilities, profile, and marketing strength.

Specific limit is the term I use to signify a computer-generated report that consolidates a particular type of information or claims run from all the claims experiences of a group of covered individuals. Such reports help pinpoint problem areas where case management can effect a great change in case outcomes and dollar expenditures. If a company's employee base is predominantly female, I might want to see a specific limit report tracking pregnancy-related claims and benefit dollars spent. From this report I could tell if there was a high incidence of problem pregnancies or premature births among these women. Perhaps the company needs to offer prenatal counseling or well mother and well baby seminars. At the least, it needs to make sure its female employees know they should be seeing a physician or nurse-midwife throughout their pregnancies, and it should give them clear information on what their benefit package covers regarding childbirth and infant care.

A case manager or claims manager can set a specific limit "marker" for any time, dollar, or medical treatment indicator. A specific limit report can cover any dollar amount one wants to establish, it can be a hospital report with three admissions or more. Ideally, since everyone is concerned about dollars, the marker will be a dollar amount, but it could also be time or an ICD-9 code. It might be appropriate to spin off a report on everyone in a group who has a diagnosis of cancer. Perhaps the case manager notices cancer cases are typically expensive and, in her role as consultant, wants to see who else in the group is likely to draw substantial benefits.

I might see that I seem to have an unusually high number of diabetes risks. In this situation, I will want to hone my data and look at everyone with diabetes who has spent $5,000, for example. I will want to know if they are in good systems of care. Is there something that should be done? Should the company establish a diabetic management program? Why is there such a high number of cases? This puts the risk management principle into case management, exactly where it belongs.

The object of tracking claims is not to dump a report in an employer's lap that announces that the firm has experienced *x* number of lost-time accidents in the past year, each requiring a recuperation period averaging six months and running up benefit expenses averaging $15,000. The purpose of claims tracking is to assess the information and utilize it proactively to design solutions. Case managers can help employers and third-party administrators create cost-containment claims administration programs to meet their particular needs. Does a company or a community have a particularly high rate of oncology claims, due perhaps to environmental conditions or job-site chemicals? Is a company experiencing an unusual rate of complex pregnancies or premature births? Once the presenting problem is pinpointed, a software program can be created to help find potential cases before complications are manifested.

A case manager consultant looking to interface more directly with claims personnel as a way of increasing cost-management capabilities will first need to understand the client company's claims system and computer and software systems. Five workers' compensation carriers may each have a software program capable of manipulating data in distinct ways and creating various report printouts. Can the system generate a report that breaks out cases with claims totaling over $10,000 or $20,000? Can it separate out all claims paid for lost-time injuries? Can it provide a run (list) of all claims filed by one claimant in the last 18 months?

The person to contact for this type of information is the claims manager. The claims manager may not be the programmer or the in-house computer wiz, but he or she is first in the line of communication. If the company has purchased software from an outside consultant, there may be reports already produced for the client that the case manager can use as a resource. There also may be an in-house capability to design almost any report the case manager might request. The extent of this capability will vary from company to company and from line of insurance to line of insurance.

I sometimes ask to look at a run of workers' compensation cases in which the employee is still on salary replacement after three months, for example, regardless of the injury. Then I often note the amount of dollars that have been spent. If there is an explanation for big dollars spent, everything is fine. It is understandable that someone with a serious injury will be out of work a long time and will have high medical bills. On the other hand, if someone has only claimed a few hundred dollars in workers' compensation medical benefits yet is still off after three months, I want to know what is really going on. So sometimes low dollars can be an indicator. Is the person really being treated? Is the person just sitting out there waiting for someone to say, "Hey, go back to work"?

In group medical coverage, a case manager can ask for a run of all claimants with three or more hospitalizations in a calendar year, all claimants with multiple medical procedures, or all claimants with home health services in place. The marker or specific limit might be a claims total of $50,000 or more (or $25,000 or $15,000). It doesn't take several years for some claimants to reach the $75,000 level; costs of this nature can add up within two or three months, and these cases would be among the ones called up for review.

TRACKING CLAIMS BY GROUP

The real key to consulting in case management is demonstrating to a client that only a small percentage of any employee group is responsible for generating the majority of claims and the bulk of benefit payouts. A case manager cannot attend a client conference, announce this fact, and expect the client to jump on the case management bandwagon. The case manager must be prepared to present concrete and objective information and offer a way to identify the relevant cases and improve the overall claims experience for the entire group. Nothing speaks louder to a client than a report taken from its own group experience. With a claims run, the case manager can show that out of a group of 500, with total claims paid of $200,000, fewer than 20 individuals (4 percent) filed claims totaling 80 percent ($160,000) of that sum. And nothing positions a case manager better than to work with a client as part of a team dedicated to helping better the claims experience.

With documentation, the case manager will work with the claims department or third-party administrator to sell case management to the employer group. Because corporations often assume case managers work on all cases, it is important to emphasize that they focus on just a few; not everyone can benefit from case management. It is also appropriate to remind CEOs that case management is not a punitive investigative process, but a service whose purpose is to recognize and resolve health care delivery problems.

A computer run can be conducted to include all individuals covered by a policy. Perhaps a case manager is working with a company on its workers' compensation coverage. The first step will be to define a benchmark, a worst-case marker, to find the cases in need of case management intervention. The class picked out might include those who have been out of work for two months or longer or those who had a lost-time accident resulting in a year or more of disability leave. (Employers with workers' compensation coverage pay medical as well as lost-wage expenses, so long absences are a big issue for them.) If there are no year-long cases, the case manager will search for absences lasting nine or six months. To create a report, the case manager needs to work with the total number of covered lives, the number of individuals with major claims, and the kinds of injuries typical of the group. Are the injuries often catastrophic, such as traumatic brain injuries, or are they mostly unresolved back injuries? Using the data from a computer run, the case manager can determine that indeed 5 percent of the workers' compensation cases accounted for 83 percent of the claims dollars and that the majority of the individuals filed claims for complex unresolved back injuries.

Exhibit 9-2 is a group claims run, a "hospital claims register," that includes all claims for hospital admissions. This run was requested as a means of focusing in on those patients in need of case management intervention; a broad net (all hospital admissions) was used for the first cast. Such a run could also be conducted using length-of-stay data. The computer run could then be narrowed and patients be better targeted by adding a specific limit (e.g., hospital admission stays of ten days or more only).

Exhibit 9-3 is a report generated from a group run. This type of quarter evaluation report breaks out the high-cost cases over a calendar or fiscal quarter and can be used to demonstrate that only a handful of claimants need case management intervention. If these few cases are properly managed, the whole group will benefit from lower claims costs. In April, 1 percent of the group generated 34 percent of the claims, and in May, 2 percent generated 67 percent of the total. In June, 2 percent of the group was responsible for 73 percent of the benefit dollars paid, and .3 percent (three employees) actually accounted for 44 percent of the total. This run also tracked cases that continued to require costly care from one month to the next. It clearly shows the need for case management.

Exhibit 9–2 Hospital Claims Register

Cert #	Name	Rel	Claim #	Type	Days	Incur	Paid	Paid to Provider	Paid to Patient	Total Paid
11355	M. Gerald	4	1005902919	I/P	4	90/01/12	90/04/05	4,281.66	.00	4,281.66
42093	R. Linda	4	1006501411	I/P	6	90/02/09	90/04/05	3,737.93	.00	3,737.93
62164	F. Kathry	4	1003703222	I/P	4	90/01/16	90/04/05	3,491.34	.00	3,491.34
36894	D. Adrian	4	1004500223	I/P	12	90/01/14	90/04/05	2,773.41	.00	2,773.41
36894	D. Adrian	4	1006600508	I/P	4	90/02/10	90/04/05	4,923.73	.00	4,923.73
47794	S. Debora	4	1003001212	I/P	4	89/12/31	90/04/05	2,786.07	.00	2,786.07
91247	C. Lucy	4	1006502210	O/P	1	89/12/18	90/04/05	813.58	.00	813.58
91247	C. Lucy	4	1006502211	O/P	1	89/12/12	90/04/05	85.00	.00	85.00
42376	D. Donna	4	1006602617	I/P	3	89/12/29	90/04/05	3,306.96	.00	3,306.96
60170	D. Maria	4	1002901123	I/P	3	90/01/07	90/04/05	3,424.97	.00	3,424.97
00136	D. Carole	4	1005701314	I/P	2	89/12/19	90/04/05	1,500.28	.00	1,500.28
00136	D. Carole	4	1006500908	I/P	21	90/01/17	90/04/05	3,780.77	.00	3,780.77
81182	H. Meliss	6	1007200404	O/P	1	90/01/14	90/04/05	198.60	.00	198.60
39464	N. Angelo	1	1004501916	I/P	6	90/01/21	90/04/05	2,975.81	.00	2,975.81
52052	A. Andrae	5	1004400713	I/P	2	90/01/18	90/04/05	2,530.59	.00	2,530.59
67116	D. Lori	4	1002900309	I/P	6	89/12/28	90/04/05	3,766.88	.00	3,766.88
89212	S. John	5	1004500323	I/P	3	90/01/22	90/04/05	1,875.24	.00	1,875.24
11093	B. Jeanne	4	1004400712	I/P	4	90/01/28	90/04/05	2,154.92	.00	2,154.92
62129	D. Lorrai	4	1005901223	O/P	1	90/01/21	90/04/05	307.00	.00	307.00
74120	K. Matthe	5	1005802404	I/P	7	90/02/05	90/04/05	2,866.12	.00	2,866.12
23269	L. Thomas	5	1004400202	I/P	2	90/01/26	90/04/05	1,673.08	.00	1,673.08
88196	A. Daniel	5	1005802408	I/P	5	90/02/06	90/04/05	2,023.55	.00	2,023.55
67198	N. Ronald	1	1006601017	O/P	1	90/02/10	90/04/05	155.00	.00	155.00
43282	A. John	1	1007302218	I/P	2	90/01/10	90/04/05	4,238.52	.00	4,238.52

(continues)

Exhibit 9–2 continued

Cert #	Name	Rel	Claim #	Type	Days	Incur	Paid	Paid to Provider	Paid to Patient	Total Paid
08551	N. Christ	5	1006601523	O/P	1	90/01/05	90/04/05	219.53	.00	219.53
06055	A. Joseph	6	1006701500	I/P	3	90/02/18	90/04/05	1,613.75	.00	1,613.75
06055	A. Dawn	4	1006701504	I/P	3	90/02/18	90/04/05	3,050.40	.00	3,050.40
11038	C. Ann	6	1007302508	I/P	3	89/12/20	90/04/05	1,326.50	.00	1,326.50
46230	P. Georgi	4	1006701400	I/P	3	90/02/08	90/04/05	2,139.82	.00	2,139.82
41144	D. Alfred	5	1007202102	I/P	3	90/02/15	90/04/05	4,282.21	.00	4,282.21
00812	P. Patric	4	1007101011	I/P	4	90/02/09	90/04/05	4,271.95	.00	4,271.95
06326	C. Linda	4	1008102001	I/P	2	90/02/26	90/04/05	1,729.56	.00	1,729.56
21139	J. John	1	1004500309	I/P	11	90/01/11	90/04/05	16,219.06	.00	16,219.06
64552	O. Sharon	4	1006600517	I/P	5	90/01/08	90/04/05	10,707.09	.00	10,707.09
30052	K. Sharon	4	1006600519	I/P	5	90/01/19	90/04/05	5,058.62	.00	5,058.62
52232	L. John	1	1005901124	O/P	1	90/01/12	90/04/05	843.10	.00	843.10
10190	B. Joseph	5	1006600812	I/P	3	89/12/10	90/04/05	1,753.41	.00	1,753.41
10389	F. Meliss	6	1003703010	I/P	2	90/01/16	90/04/05	1,544.32	.00	1,544.32
64984	D. Lawr	1	1004400705	I/P	5	90/01/15	90/04/05	2,725.81	.00	2,725.81
88292	F. Thomas	1	1007300406	O/P	1	90/02/15	90/04/05	65.00	.00	65.00
10083	C. Dawn	4	1005901714	I/P	5	90/01/10	90/04/05	2,563.54	.00	2,563.54
Month Total								119,784.68	.00	119,784.68

Courtesy of Options Unlimited, Case Management Services Division, Huntington, N.Y.

Exhibit 9–3 Quarter Evaluation

MEDICAL CLAIMS—ABC Corporation - April
843 Employees—2,213 covered lives.

Patient Name	Claim Number	Amt. of Claim	Diagnosis
Able, T.	0421160	$3,800	OBS-GYN
Baratii, C.	0743221	2,100	Deceased—in C.M. Ovarian Cancer.
Essig, E. (Wife)	1501617	4,028	Psych—ALC.
Heinz, S. (H)	2214689	3,615	Arthroscopy
Jay, T.	1821041	6,437	OK
Kutner, R.	1847756	4,100	OBS
O'Reilly, T.	1523314	4,580	Vasc. Dis., Diab. in C.M.
Pfizer, J.	1015252	1,800	OK
Renlow, N.	5830764	3,958	Fx Nose
Victor, F.	0962140	9,200	HIP, CVA in C.M.
		$43,618	

Total Claims: $129,575
1% of group generated 34% of claims.

MEDICAL CLAIMS—ABC Corporation - May
858 Employees—2,262 covered lives.

Patient Name	Claim Number	Amt. of Claim	Diagnosis
Ceil, W. (M)	1356602	$2,732	
Childs, B. (W&D)	1516758	5,008	
Dell, A. (M)	2083312	25,571	
Eston, B. (M&S)	4373029	1,881	
Frank, G. (M&W)	0917462	4,923	
Heller, J. M	1503327	3,100	
Hellnick, P. M	2543178	1,644	
Inez, S.	2594622	1,522	
Jonas, S.	1296654	7,521	Referred to case management but pt. declined
Keller, L.	3601744	2,320	
Mort, J.	3237161	1,500	
Neil, B.	5237708	1,646	
O'Reilly, T.*	1523318	3,918	
Ricco, A. (D)	3541006	25,073	We have in C.M.
Sumner, P. (M)	0929763	7,770	
Victor, F.* (M)	0962143	1,800	

Total Claims: $146,800
16 employees (2%) generated $98,100 or 67% of total.
*Also in April report.

(continues)

Exhibit 9–3 continued

MEDICAL CLAIMS—ABC Corporation - June
864 Employees—2,291 covered lives.

Patient Name	Claim Number	Amt. of Claim
Brill, B. (S-Todd)	0543112	$6,417
Brown, K. (W-Gail)	0677896	2,324
Ceil, W.** M	1371818	3,907
Eisner, P. M	5221021	1,459
Glenn, A. M	1147786	17,103
Inez, S.** (W-Heidi)	2594638	2,914
Jay, T.* M	1821053	3,451
Jonas, S.** (M)	1296685	2,675
Miller, M. (M)	1703217	1,690
Mort, J.** (W&S)	1814437	3,085
Mueller, J. W&D	1516992	4,682
Neil, B.** W	5237718	7,525
O'Reilly, T.*** M	1523319	1,452
Ricco, A.** D	3541008	14,632
Sachs, B. M	3202772	2,050
Sortor, A. M	2567131	4,328
Victor, F.*** M	0962144	50,737
Villanez, P. W	5818753	2,280
Zucker, R. (M)	2501763	5,692
		$138,403

Total Claims—$188,704
*in April report
**in May report
***in April, May & June
19 employees (2% of group) expend $138,403 or 73% of total.
3 employees .3% expend 44% of total.

ABC Corporation - 2nd quarter

		Employees	Covered Lives
April	$129,575	843	2,213
May	$146,800	858	2,262
June	$188,704	864	2,291
TOTAL	$465,079		

34 Employees (4% of group) expends $280,121 or 60% of total.

Courtesy of Options Unlimited, Case Management Services Division, Huntington, N.Y.

Regardless of the reimbursement system or type of policy, once the case manager has identified a group of patients who could benefit from case management intervention, the focus turns toward setting up a preventative cost-containment program to reform the group as a whole. After intervening at an early stage in the treatment of a complex unresolved back injury, for example, the case manager, by pointing to the improved outcome, shortened time, and reduced cost, can gain the confidence of the claims department.

INDIVIDUAL CLAIMS HISTORIES

A case manager can also track individual claims histories. In particular, she may want to look at the claims histories of the few individuals responsible for the bulk of the claims for a given period.

In looking at a particular claims history, the case manager may first identify the dollar amount and then fine-tune the review to see if this is a case where case management could make a difference. Suppose the individual has reached the specific limit of $15,000. The case manager might note that the claims were for one hospitalization and one major surgical procedure, a colostomy. The procedure is completed, there were only minor postop problems, so there is no real opportunity for case management to have an impact. Another individual who has reached the $15,000 specific limit may have a series of claims for treatment for an unresolved ulcer of the foot, diabetes, hypertension, and vascular disease. Taken together, these claims indicate a health care time bomb. What is the real problem here? Why isn't the ulcer resolving? Is this person getting appropriate care?

Exhibit 9-4 presents an excerpt from an individual claims report. This report, which breaks out the claims history by ICD-9 and CPT codes, was requested because a set dollar limit had been reached. The question was, what were the charges for? By checking each diagnosis, it was discovered that the medical problems ranged from a stroke to respiratory and vascular difficulties to depression. By reading this history, the case manager is in a much better position to provide assistance.

Another step in the case management consultation process is to review the actual claims in particular files. (Access to files might be possible if the case manager and claims manager have a good relationship.) A computer provides just so much information: coding information, dollars, where the money was spent. By looking at an actual file, the case manager might discover that the patient is on several medications, each prescribed by a different physician. Are the physicians aware of one another and of the other medications the patient is taking? Admissions and complications

Exhibit 9–4 Subscriber History File Accessing Report

Worksheet Inquiry

Group 930656   SUFFOLK CTY (ACTV/RET/COBRA)
Enrollee 123-45-6789   G. DANIEL
Member .... e DANIEL G.
Enter latest incurred to date .... –0/00/1900

Claim no.	Statuses	Incurred dates	Ben	Diagnosis
e 94009618-01	f f	01/11/1994–01/11/1994	M1	CVA/EQU/ ACERMAN MED SUPPLY
e 93051425-11	f f	08/11/1993–12/31/1994	M0	93'RX/X-8 FARMING, FPO PHARM.
e 93099250-02	f f	12/01/1993–12/31/1993	M0	RB/MS/ATLAN- TIC REHAB/CVA
e 93086701-13	f f	12/22/1993–12/29/1993	M0	CVA/PTHD/ ROCHE LAB
e 93086701-12	f f	11/29/1993–12/21/1993	M0	CVA/PTHD/ ROCHE LAB
e 94004825-01	f f	12/20/1993–12/20/1993	M1	GI TRACT DIS/ ERH/KIMBALL MC
e 94004825-02	f f	12/20/1993–12/20/1993	M1	GI TRACT DIS/ INEL 12/KIMB PHY
e 93086701-14	f f	12/01/1993–12/15/1993	M0	CVA/PTHD/ ROCHE LAB
e 94001820-01	h	12/05/1993–12/05/1993	M0	TRACHEST/ ERH/KIMBALL MED CT
e 94001820-02	h	12/05/1993–12/05/1993	M0	TRACHEST/ ERD/KIMBALL EMERDR
e 94001820-03	f f	11/16/1993–12/05/1993	M0	TRACHEST/ VARIOUS PV'S
e 94001820-04	f f	12/05/1993–12/05/1993	M0	TRACH/ INEL#12/MOOSA JAFFARI,M
e 93086701-15	f f	12/01/1993–12/01/1993	M0	CVA/XRAY/ JERSEY SHR MC

Enter worksheet to inquire into, (r)estart or (c)ontinue c
Alt-Z = Help   COM1   9600 8N1 VT102   Printer Off   Online   6:59 pm

(continues)

Exhibit 9–4 continued

Worksheet Inquiry
Group 930656   CTY (ACTV/RET/COBRA)
Enrollee 123-45-6789   G. DANIEL
Member .... e DANIEL G.
Enter latest incurred to date .... –0/00/1900

Claim no.	Statuses	Incurred dates	Ben	Diagnosis
e 93086701-09	f f	11/30/1993–11/30/1993	M0	HEMIPLEGIA/ INEL#69/JERSEY SHORE
e 93099250-01	h	11/26/1993–11/30/1993	M0	RB/MS/ATLAN- TIC REHAB/CVA
e 93086701-08	f f	11/22/1993–11/26/1993	M0	HEMIPLEGIA/ PVIM/AHN
e 93086701-10	f f	11/04/1993–11/26/1993	M0	RB/MS/RUSK INST/ HEMIPLEGIA
e 94004825-04	f f	11/02/1993–11/26/1993	M1	GI TRACT/ XRYD/JERSEY SHORE R
e 93086701-16	h	11/25/1993–11/25/1993	M0	CVA/CON/ LOUIE MD
e 93067106-72	f f	10/07/1993–11/24/1993	M0	VASCULAR/ RDO/NYU RADIOLOGY
e 93086701-11	f f	11/23/1993–11/23/1993	M0	ABDOM PAIN/ SRI/PTI/ASHA MD
e 93094583-02	f f	10/11/1993–11/22/1993	M0	DEPRESS/ MPVO/OLLINS, MD
e 93086701-07	f f	11/08/1993–11/19/1993	M0	HEMIPLEGIA/ PVI/AHN, MD
e 93091059-02	f f	11/16/1993–11/18/1993	M0	CHOLELITH/ PVI/PFEFFER, MD
e 94004825-03	f f	11/12/1993–11/12/1993	M1	GI TRACT DIS/ PVO/PARRY, MD
e 93094583-01	f f	11/02/1993–11/11/1993	M0	DEPRESS/MPVI/ FRANK, MD

Enter worksheet to inquire into, (r)estart or (c)continue
Alt-Z = Help   COM1   9600 8N1 VT102   Printer Off   Online   6:59 pm

Courtesy of Options Unlimited, Case Management Services Division, Huntington, N.Y.

can be caused by interactions between medications. Perhaps the patient is having difficulty describing his or her symptoms or understanding the prescribed treatments and is consequently going from physician to physician. This is the type of case in which the case manager might be able to make a major contribution.

Although helpful information is usually plentiful, a case manager has to know exactly what data are available and how they can be used to help patients, providers, and payers. The claims department should ideally perceive case managers as a tool to better their service, while case managers use the tools of the claims department to help them resolve some case management problems.

MOVING INTO THE CONSULTANT ROLE

I have had terrific opportunities to put these theories into practice in my associations with third-party administrators. As a consultant, I help third-party administrators track claims and increase the efficiency of their administration services. We have become a value-added service in ourselves, and are now part of the third-party administrator's marketing strategy in reaching new clients.

My development and use of claims tracking reports and computer runs was motivated by my frustration at not being able to reach claimants who needed case management in time to make a difference. After convincing the TPA president to allow my company's staff to show how case management can resolve problems and reduce payouts, we were given access to the third-party administrator's claims staff and began training them in case management concepts and delineating the kinds of cases we wanted to see. I created red flags and the claims review tip sheet shown in Exhibit 9-1 as well as a "Request for Service" form (Exhibit 9-5). The claims personnel were to fill out this request form and leave it in my in-box whenever they came across a claim fitting the red flag profile or had a question concerning a case's suitability for case management or claims review. (I made it a practice to be in the third-party administrator's office once a week to review these requests and to be available to the claims staff as an associate and assistant.) When a case is referred to us for case management or claims review, a letter similar to the one appearing as Exhibit 9-6 is sent to thank the claims examiner and to give him or her the name of the case manager assigned to the case. This promotes a more open and communicative association.

How did we convince the third-party administrator's president of the benefits of case management? We selected our trial group by requesting a quarterly report with a specific limit run of $100,000. (This was the stop-

Exhibit 9–5 Request for Service Form

OPTIONS UNLIMITED
HEALTH CARE & DISABILITY MANAGEMENT SERVICES
76 East Main Street, Huntington, New York 11743
(516) 673-1150 FAX (516) 673-8369

DATE

------------- REQUESTED BY: --

NAME	PHONE	YOUR FILE # (SS #)
COMPANY NAME	LOCATION	INSURED
CLAIMANT		INSURANCE COVERAGE & STATE
DATE OF DIS.	DIAGNOSIS	EMPLOYER GROUP

REQUEST FOR

PLEASE CHECK ONE
❑ CareWatch - UTILIZATION REVIEW: PREDETERMINATION, PRE-ADMISSION, CONCURRENT
            REVIEW, IDENTIFICATION FOR CASE MANAGEMENT, SPECIFIC LIMIT REVIEW
❑ CareSolutions - MEDICAL CASE MANAGEMENT
❑ CompSolutions - WORKER'S COMPENSATION
❑ AccuClaim - CLAIMS REVIEW
❑ Other Questions _____

IF NECESSARY, HAVE YOU INCLUDED:

❑ PRE-AND POST-OP PHOTOS	❑ MD/PT OR CHIRO OFFICE NOTES (ATTACHED)
❑ OPERATIVE REPORT (ATTACHED)	❑ R&C CHARGES (LIST HERE):
❑ ANESTHESIA REPORT (ATTACHED)	CPT CODE R&C CHARGE
❑ ITEMIZED BILLING	
❑ NURSING NOTES (ATTACHED)	

CONSULTANT RESPONSE

SAVINGS:

SIGNATURE: DATE:

Send Original and one copy to   REFERRAL SOURCE COPY - YELLOW
                                OPTIONS UNLIMITED COPY - WHITE

Courtesy of Options Unlimited, Case Management Services Division, Huntington, N.Y.

Exhibit 9-6 Claims Contact Letter

Date

_____, Claims Examiner
Third Party Administrator
xxxxxxxxxxxx
xxxxxxxxxxxx

Claimant: John Doe
Insured: Susan Doe
Group: xxxxxx
S.S.#: 999-99-9999

Dear Claims Examiner:
   Please accept my appreciation for referring the above captioned file for case management services.
_____ [Case Manager] will be handling this case. She will conduct an initial evaluation and will contact you with a verbal report to be followed by a complete written report with our impressions and recommendations.
   Should you have any questions about this file, please don't hesitate to call me at (516) 555-5555.
Very truly yours,

President

XXX:xx

Courtesy of Options Unlimited, Case Management Services Division, Huntington, N.Y.

---

loss insurance benchmark for one of the third-party administrator's client companies.) We as case managers were looking for all claims over $10,000, which is our company's own marker. We looked at every month to see if the total number of cases over $10,000 increased and if the same individuals were consistently filing the larger claims. Once we identified several cases, we asked to see the actual claims files. In one instance, we found that the claimant had run up a claims total of $30,000, most of it in pharmaceuticals. There were pages and pages of claims on file for drugs prescribed by different physicians. Reviewing the prescriptions, we searched for drugs recommended for the same or related conditions, side effects, drug interactions, and drug combinations, and we also tried to determine if the drug combinations were contributing to the patient's medical problems. In this case, we found there was reason to be concerned for the patient's safety. Since the third-party administrator fully supported our endeavor, we contacted the individual and his physicians to share our concern, finding that the physicians were unaware of each other and the prescription "overdose." We were then able to establish one primary physician who acted as the sole dispenser of medication. The example proved a perfect one for showing the benefits of case management to both patients and the bottom line.

In another instance, we saw a total of $32,000, but what really caught our eye was the three inpatient hospitalizations. Dollars are a case management indicator, but the truly important factor is always going to be how those dollars are spent. What is driving expenses up? Were those three admissions one long experience or a series of short-stay admissions? When I see three or four admissions within a short time period, I wonder if there is something wrong with the discharge plan or if the individual cannot sustain the level of stability at the time of discharge once he or she reaches home.

Case managers working with claims departments become detectives. Using curiosity, instinct, and a paper trail, they look for items to uncover potentially serious cases. Obviously, the more experienced the entire team, the better they will be at following the paper trail. But any case manager and any group of claims personnel can make a difference, a major difference, for their clients and the covered patients.

NOTES

1. A.C. Reynolds-Meadows and C.M. Mullahy, "Managing Case Management: Claims Issues in Case Management," prepared for the Individual Case Management Association Medical Case Management Conference III, Dallas, Texas, September 1991.
2. Ibid.

Case Management
Administration and Financial
Considerations

10

Cost-Benefit Analysis Reports

Everyone is beginning to flinch at the very sound of the words "the cost of health care." Not far behind the direct costs are the administrative or management expenses that are impacting all of us as we attempt to brake this "running train." While we individually and collectively attempt to grapple with these fees, those of us providing or managing case management services need to realize that our services are an addition to an already costly system. Cost of care is an issue that has to be faced head on. Case managers need to deal with the financial ramifications of care and alternatives. To make recommendations for care that the benefits dollars will not cover is ridiculous, and to not know how costly one facility is in comparison with another is not doing one's job.

If a case manager is going to put together a set of recommendations or alternatives, she needs to cite costs. Further, the case manager needs to involve the patient, family, physician, and other members of the health care team in financial matters. I think we have all been insulated from financial concerns for far too long. At some point early on it is essential to sit down with paper and pencil and a family and say, "If your dad has three more hospitalizations at $1,000 a day, this is how quickly his benefits are going to be eaten up. If we can keep him out of the hospital longer and put services in the home, if you'll be willing to help with some of the care as well, we can get him care and services over the projected length of this illness, which is certainly what our goal needs to be here. We don't want to run out of benefits before he runs out of problems."

Although it would be nice if all consumers and health care professionals perceived the medical and monetary value of case management, unfortunately not everyone does. To avoid being seen as merely part of the "medical-insurance bureaucracy," case managers need to play an active role in communicating the benefits, in health management and dollar terms, of their services. Because most case managers come from nursing or social work backgrounds, they tend to resist talking about the financial aspects of health care.

DOLLARS AND HEALTH CARE

The majority of health care professionals today probably entered the field with a desire to help others. We were the actual hands-on providers of the services deemed necessary. No one questioned our motivation, methods, or outcomes. We were acknowledged as professionals and were generally assumed to adhere to the strictest of practice standards and want only the best for our patients. But then money got in the way, and health care professionals were called upon to balance treatment and cost. Why health care costs became so unmanageable will, I suspect, be left to historians. In any case, there are now so many interest groups that sorting out truth from fiction will perhaps be an insurmountable task. Clearly, the health care system is undergoing profound changes. The system many of us trained in is a thing of the past. Cost is an issue for all of us, consumers (employers and employees) and health care professionals alike. And because cost is an issue, the transition for health care professionals continues to be a struggle. Why is it such a problem?

To develop a better understanding of the current situation, it may help to examine the health care system of yesterday. Those who entered medical and related fields had much in common. They shared, among other things, a desire to help, a need to contribute, and a willingness to comfort and counsel others in distress. They did not share, by and large, an interest in or talent for financial management. In fact, most health care businesses or practice settings have someone other than the physician, nurse, or therapist keeping the books. It was generally accepted that if medical professionals did have responsibility for financial matters, it might influence their decisions and cloud their perceptions of what was best for their patients. For many, many years, it was considered perfectly all right to protect professionals from having to deal with money issues.

Add to this society's idealized view of medicine and health care, and its tendency not to question health care costs. Interestingly, we demand to know the price of almost everything, from houses to cars to airfare to hotel rooms and college tuition. Some of these items, when advertised, have their price tags clearly visible. Other items, such as designer clothing or jewelry, have their price tags more discreetly placed, but the prices are still discoverable through a little effort. This is not the case with health care services, undeniably among the most expensive commodities.

When was the last time you saw a price tag on a MRI scan, or were quoted the fee for a specific surgical procedure, or chose Hospital A or Hospital B because the service was equal but one was more reasonably priced? Although most of us are facing higher deductibles and copayments, we are still not asking the dreaded question, "How much will this cost?"

For example, imagine the case of someone who needs surgery. The medical plan providing benefits will reimburse at 80 percent of the reasonable and customary charge for the procedure. The surgeon selected has quoted a price of \$9,200; the plan has established that the reasonable and customary fee is \$7,500, the reimbursement, at 80 percent of \$7,500, will be \$6,000; and the remaining balance will be \$3,200. Quite clearly, the time to resolve the discrepancy between the price and the payout is before the surgery takes place, not after. What can be done? The person can choose another qualified surgeon who charges less; discuss the matter with the current surgeon, who might be willing to negotiate or reduce her fees; or decide to proceed with the current surgeon despite the additional costs. But at least the decision will be an informed one, with all results and consequences evident.

When I hear providers criticizing case managers for "talking about money" and "asking prices," I realize they may resent having to compete and having to defend their prices. The old days of automatic acceptance of charges are gone forever. And this really is better for all of us. Medical professionals are not unintelligent consumers, and they do know how to make decisions that benefit their patients while at the same time preserving valuable medical resources.

Case management does become involved not only with the outcomes of care but also with the many alternative levels of care and with the financial aspects of care. In fact, to address quality and outcomes and the alternatives without paying attention to the costs is doing a disservice to patients, payers, and, yes, even providers, who will also be losers if costs go unchecked.

Because of its role in cost containment, case management focuses on catastrophically ill patients (acute and chronic) and high-cost cases. As defined and practiced, it addresses costs, but never at the expense of patient safety or quality of care. If case managers do not communicate both its cost-containment benefits and its quality-improvement benefits, case management could well become eliminated as a tool in the treatment of patients.

There are many experienced case managers who initially worked hard to demonstrate their effectiveness to their client companies. Once their clients became believers, the case managers no longer felt the need to push the potential benefits. Case management departments were created, staffed, and supplied with computers and other equipment by major insurance carriers and third-party administrators, and hundreds and thousands of dollars were spent, month after month, until another someone at the senior level closely examined the figures. Then questions were asked: "What does this department do?" "Is it making us any money?" "Does it save us or our clients any money, and if so, how much?" There were no answers because the case managers had stopped documenting their efficacy.

Discussion of fees and costs should be part of any case management program. Financial issues need to be examined and debated before a company implements such a program itself or contracts with a case management provider or before a professional decides to be a provider of case management services. There must be an acceptance of financial accountability for the costs being added to the system. Individuals or departments who are not able to demonstrate cost-effectiveness will not survive, and their demise will be their own doing.

So how do case managers prepare information or reports that will support continued case management involvement? How can they consider or suggest alternative care plans if they do not know the costs involved in the current system of care? How should the subject of costs be approached? What questions need to be asked and to whom should they be directed? Are prices negotiable? Should discounts be requested? How do case managers know what is reasonably priced and, at the other end, what is an exorbitant fee? Does cost have anything to do with quality or outcome? Just as with other products and services, it is best to be prepared with information beforehand. How is this information acquired? By acknowledging that the whole subject of health care costs is uncomfortable, especially for practitioners, and by asking questions over and over to compile provider cost-of-service lists.

There are several ways to obtain pricing information while learning about a company and its services. One of the easiest is to attend local, regional, and national conferences. Most conferences include provider exhibits as well as sessions conducted by provider companies. Such sessions offer marketing and educational opportunities for those who might either have influence on or direct purchasing capabilities. For example, a firm might present a session entitled "Respiratory Management of the HIV Patient at Home." Although the information may be generic, the presenters will typically be available afterward to provide specifics regarding the credentialing of staff, the accreditation of the firm, the location of its offices, the scope of its services, and the cost of its services, plus all of the other "need to know" information, such as, "How much will this cost? Are there additional considerations for all inclusive, for prompt-pay, for volume, for exclusive or PPO arrangements?" (And aren't these questions the same kinds of questions we all ask before making other kinds of purchases? Is anything here "unprofessional"?) Most providers have ranges of fees and negotiating options and are better prepared today than ten years ago to discuss fees. So go ahead, ask!

The larger the conference or the more diversified the subject matter, the more opportunity there will be to meet with multiple providers of a wide range of products and services. A conference titled "The Rehabilitation of the Alcoholic Adolescent" will include presentations on topics of interest, such as "Peer Pressure," "Tough Love," "Family Dynamics," etc. Further, the exhibit hall is likely to feature providers such as in-patient programs, day treatment centers, and residential long-term centers, all utilized in the care of the alcoholic adolescent. If teenage rehabilitation is going to be a strong component of one's practice or department focus, this is an important conference to attend. On the other hand, a conference titled "Managed Care: Health Care Reform and Self-Insured Groups" will provide the opportunity to acquire an incredible amount of information in one setting. Featured will likely be HMOs, PPOs, home care agencies, rehabilitation facilities, head injury programs, pharmaceutical companies, equipment manufacturers and dealers, hospitals, computer software and hardware companies, consulting firms, infusion care services, and so on. This type of conference offers a nonstressful environment in which to learn about the whole range of services and providers available to case managers and, equally as important, to begin discussions about costs. (One way of mitigating some of the anxiety caused by having to discuss fees and other costs is to examine the decision-making process for other purchases and then apply some of the same skills and methods to purchase agreements for health care services. This is a very concrete way to demystify some of the fear and anxiety that has crept into this arena. I believe that this transition is possible if one approaches it in increments of time and information. In the process, our decisions will not only be safe and quality-assuring ones, but will be cost conscious and cost effective as well.)

When the necessary cost information is acquired, what should be done with it? For the small company or independent practitioner, perhaps keeping a separate "provider book" will be sufficient. Dividing the book into sections by provider type or service or location allows easy access to the data. For instance, under "Infusion Care Services" should be listed companies that are quality providers; their strengths, weaknesses, and areas of expertise; special offerings that are of particular interest; and the costs of the services. Other categories might be high-risk pregnancy management, home care, subacute hospitals, durable medical equipment dealers, and so on. The information should be updated continually, eliminating providers that are no longer viable, adding new services, and changing contact names or the location of offices. Provider information needs to be current so that the time spent selecting providers and services is kept to a minimum.

In a larger organization or case management department, serious consideration should be given to putting such information in a computer database. Each case manager would then have access to it and would be able to update and change it according to departmental guidelines, obviously adhering to provider selection criteria applicable to that particular area. The accumulated information would not only be useful in actual case management activities but could serve as the database for cost benefit analysis reports (discussed later in this chapter).

In addition to conferences, there are several other resources that can be utilized in developing provider information: government organizations and publications, travel and professional associations, and periodicals that publish data on costs and trends. *Business & Health, Business Insurance, Hospitals, Medical Benefits, The Wall Street Journal, Medical Economics,* and *The Case Manager* frequently list costs of hospitals per day, average lengths of stay, fees for procedures, and high-cost organizations. They also sometimes publish lists of rehabilitation facilities, skilled nursing facilities, and other types of organizations and evaluate rates, services, and so on.

NEGOTIATING SKILLS

Once armed with information about services and fees, a case manager is better able to arrange for services and negotiate fees. Negotiating is an acquired skill and does require thought, and there are books written on the subject and guidelines developed especially for case managers (see Exhibit 10-1 for a list of gender-related communication problems). William Ury, cofounder of the Program on Negotiations at Harvard Law School, has written two of the definitive books on negotiation: *Getting to Yes: Negotiating Agreement without Giving In* (Houghton Mifflin Company and Penguin Books editions) and *Getting Past No: Negotiating with Difficult People* (Bantam Books). *Getting to Yes* is also available in a video workshop format. The Individual Case Management Association's 1993 Medical Case Management Conference V included a session titled "Telephone Negotiation Skills for Case Managers," which was overbooked five

Exhibit 10–1 Common Female-to-Male Communication Obstacles and Solutions

Problem:	Women tend to take too long to get to the point, using too many details.
Solution:	State your main point up front, using few details. Be brief and precise.
Problem:	Women tend to use soft, tentative, unassertive voices, especially in talking to men.
Solution:	Practice speaking in a firm, moderately loud, confident voice.
Problem:	Women often allow themselves to be interrupted by men in conversation.
Solution:	Try one or several of these: (1) Keep talking in a firm, louder voice. (2) Stop in mid-sentence and wait in silence till the interrupter has stopped. (3) Say politely, "I'll be happy to continue when you're finished."
Problem:	Women often end statements in a questioning tone of voice, with a rising inflection.
Solution:	Speak in firm, declarative sentences that sound like clear statements, not tentative questions.
Problem:	Women tend to seek consensus and agreement by ending sentences with "question tags," such as "don't you agree?" or "am I right?"
Solution:	Drop most of those question tags from your speech, especially when talking to men.
Problem:	Women tend to hedge in conversation instead of stating firm opinions.
Solution:	Mentally define your message clearly, then state it assertively.
Problem:	Women have learned to communicate in a way that builds friendship and agreement, while men are more action-oriented and directive.
Solution:	Be aware of the differences in male-female communications styles and learn to match your communications style to men's when talking to them.
Problem:	Women too often preface remarks by actually asking their listener not to take them seriously. ("This probably isn't a very good idea, but . . ." or "I don't know a lot about this; however . . .")
Solution:	Never apologize or discount what you have to say. Believe in yourself and your statements and speak accordingly.

Source: Reprinted from *Medical Case Management Conference V*, p. 187 with permission of ICMA and Nancy N. Bell, © 1993.

months before the conference. The newsletter *Case Management Advisor* frequently incorporates columns of tips for case managers.

The first thing to keep in mind in negotiating is that there are ranges in price for everything in health care. This does not mean that we aim for the Hyundai category or that selecting a "Rolls Royce" price tag will guarantee excellence—high price tags only guarantee a big bill. The goal is to try to fulfill the patient's equipment and service needs in a cost-justified manner.

The first roadblock case managers and product or service suppliers confront is usually the difference in background, orientation, and industry jargon each party brings to the negotiations. For example, a home medical equipment supplier may be well-versed in the features and functions of the equipment but not understand why certain models are problematic or inappropriate for a patient. The case manager knows the patient's diagnosis and needs but is not necessarily familiar with the technical capabilities of equipment. To overcome this and other snags, it is best to take an honest and open approach to communications.

I have found it helpful to work exclusively with one representative at a durable medical equipment, home medical equipment, or home health care agency. First, this allows me to review equipment, services, contracts, and billing in a single call, and second, it helps me get answers when I need them. Just as I want to know all the options included with a piece of equipment that might assist a patient, I am also interested in terms—lease, rent, rent with option to buy, and outright purchase—and service costs. The various options often affect my decision.

Case managers and product and service providers alike are looking for long-term working relationships. An otherwise good relationship will be undermined if the case manager accepts a price break on a one-year rental agreement knowing the patient probably has only three months to live or if the equipment agreed upon arrives with expensive optional features that were sold to the patient without the case manager's knowledge. In their pursuit of high-quality health care at an affordable cost, both providers and case managers can benefit by serving as resources for each other. Dealers can take the confusion out of techno-speak; case managers can alert suppliers that certain bed features are not recommended for people with a particular back problem. By working as partners with service and equipment providers, case managers will build beneficial business associations and stronger resource bases.[1]

To assist case managers in establishing a negotiating process and evaluating service providers and facilities, the Individual Case Management Association developed two documents: "Service, Equipment and Supplies Placement Guidelines" (Exhibit 10-2) and "Program Questionnaire

Exhibit 10–2 Service, Equipment, and Supplies Placement Guidelines

1. Evaluate client to accurately determine his needs:
   - Personally assess client/family/home.
   - Review evaluations and recommendations of others—PT, OT, physician, etc.
   - Secure physician's order, if required.
   - Recommend or confirm the correct equipment supply or service.
2. Determine whether rent or purchase is more cost effective. Consider:
   - length of service
   - availability and cost of service/maintenance contracts
   - comparative costs of rent/purchase
3. Secure payor authorization (approval or claims professional).
4. Bid equipment, supplies, or service.
   - Requests for bids from providers must be uniform.
     — May be requested by phone (occasionally written)
     —Outline:
       - specific item or service requested
       - date to begin/deliver
       - duration of service
       - means and % of payment from insurer
       - date and time bid will be closed
       - Seek to determine the provider's:
         —ability to deliver service
         —follow-up plan
         —type of supervision
         —teaching support, and
         —reputation for dependability and quality of service
   - Request that providers convey bid figure by phone—with a written confirmation.
   - Vendors should be contacted once only with an accurate and identical description of the item/service needed. Failure to respond by bid closing time will constitute a "no bid."
   - Provided all key issues (service, delivery, and quality) are equal, the business is awarded to the lowest bidder. If not equal, the decision will be at the case manager's discretion/judgement and will be final.
   - Bid information may be available to participants only after the bid is awarded—and only at the case manager's discretion.
   - Providers should be requested not to actively market their equipment or services with case management clients, but rather to forward observations, suggestions, and recommendations to the case manager for consideration and coordination with the medical team and funding agency.

(continues)

Exhibit 10–2 continued

5. Follow-up to insure:
   a. item (or service) is appropriate,
   b. timely response or delivery,
   c. instructions are adequate,
   d. service to equipment is available, and
   e. item (or service) is retained only as long as needed.
6. Summarize bids (and logic behind choice if not lowest bidder), with attention to cost saved in report.

Courtesy of Individual Case Management Association, Little Rock, Arkansas.

and Facility Review for Case Managers" (Appendix 10-A). These were designed to serve as standard tools for selecting providers and vendors and evaluating facilities, and they include criteria to facilitate the making of informed decisions based on the needs of the patient. The forms should be customized by the addition of the case manager's own criteria. Is there one person to contact for financial questions, or one contact for patient updates? This can save a lot of time otherwise spent playing telephone tag or holding on the line while someone who can answer a query is found. Does the vendor return phone calls? What is their level of service? All these elements play into the making of a good service match.

The following negotiating guidelines originally appeared in *HomeCare* under the title "Simple Negotiations." Although designed for home care providers, they are applicable to the type of negotiations case managers engage in:[2]

1. For patients on long-term therapies, implement a reverification process.
2. Negotiate the payment terms. A good general rule is, the deeper the discount offered, the sooner the provider should be paid.
3. Ask if a fax of the claim or other documentation can be sent to speed claims processing.
4. Always confirm verbal agreements in writing. Include in the confirmation letter the effective date of the agreement, the full name of the person who conducted the verbal negotiation, a complete description of the products and services agreed upon, the agreed-upon discount, the agreed-upon payment terms, the net payment after the discount, the agreed-upon type of claims submission form, and notification that the agreement will be considered mutual unless the supplier states otherwise in writing within a certain number of days.

DOCUMENTING NEGOTIATED ARRANGEMENTS

Assuming that a case manager has selected the most appropriate service for the patient and negotiated a different fee structure than the one quoted originally, what is the next step? I believe it is important to document and communicate the terms of agreement that case managers arrange with providers.

It should be re-emphasized, however, that prior to negotiating or arranging for any service, the case manager must have received approval to do so from the payer source. To begin with, the case manager needs to check that there is language in the plan contract that allows case management. Reviewing the details of the plan contract is especially important when arranging for services, selecting providers, seeking discounts, and so on. Will what the case manager arranges for actually "hold up" when the claim for the services finally arrives in the claims department? Will it be paid on a "prompt-pay" basis (i.e., within two to four weeks of arrival at the department)? Will it be paid even though language in the plan may not mention or may even exclude such services? Will it be paid at 100 percent of the submitted charge, rather than 80 percent of what is reasonable and customary? Will it be paid even if the plan maximum for the services has already been reached? Who knew about the services, who approved them, who will pay for them, and if no one else will, is the case manager now responsible?

Failure to get answers to these questions before starting work on a case or for a client company puts everyone at risk—the patient, the provider, the carrier or payer, and the case manager. Acting on mere assumptions in this extremely important area can result in legal consequences for all involved.

When entering into a relationship for the provision of case management services, the case manager needs to describe the scope of the services in sufficient detail to permit a complete discussion of how case management will interface with the department or individuals who will have the ultimate payment responsibility for what could best be described as "alternate care plans." It is essential to lead a potential client group through a typical case, one that will illustrate just how case management works. The presented scenario should include referral, assessment, the care setting, the exposure the group has for this particular area of service within the patient's insurance plan contract, alternative care plans, and the details of the insurance plan contract that apply to these alternatives. For example, the alternatives presented might include sending the patient home and providing round-the-clock nursing care at $40 an hour ($960 a day) or placing her in a skilled nursing facility at a cost of $340 a day. The plan contract allows a maximum of 40 skilled nursing visits of up to four hours each, does not mention coverage for skilled nursing facilities, but does state nursing home custodial care is not covered. The case management proposal is for 30 days of care in a skilled nursing facility at a negotiated rate of $280 a day (not the usual $340) if the claim can be paid within two weeks of receipt. The other option is a continuation of the patient's stay in the acute care hospital at a rate of $1,000 a day, which the treating physician favors and for which there is coverage available. However, once apprised of the skilled nursing facility alternative, the treating physician switches his allegiance, and the patient and family also prefer this option.

The portrayal of a fairly typical case allows a client group to begin to understand the nature of case management and to realize how expensive the restrictions in a given plan contract can be when they prevent certain options from being approved. In the scenario above, the difference between 30 days of hospital care and 30 days of skilled nursing facility care is $24,600. Hopefully, such examples will give client groups the determination, creativity, and sound business/financial rationale to allow the "insertions" of such solutions not just in one case but for as many times and situations where not doing so would be deemed as fiscal irresponsibility.

Case managers need to be able to present this kind of information to client groups in order to create the right environment for case management and the system or pathways that will allow it to be used successfully. Health care cost "problems" are not without solutions. The important thing is to uncover, discuss, and resolve pertinent issues prior to the institution of an in-house case management program or the establishment of a working relationship between an independent practitioner or small company and a client group. There is no point in developing plans that might work "if only." That is why it is imperative that case managers understand and appreciate the various payer systems, plan contracts, and the claims payment process for the various lines of insurance. Inadequate understanding leaves the case manager functioning in a vacuum outside of the system instead of as an integral player within it.

After the case manager has made the client group understand what is required for the implementation and approval of suggested plans, payment issues need to be addressed again. I developed a heightened appreciation for the importance of developing a good relationship with a client's claims department when some claims for services I had arranged and received approval for (from the claims manager) did not get paid and then were "lost." At the same time, other claims were being paid but not at the rate I had negotiated, nor in the desired time frame. This resulted in embarrassment for me, with the provider and with the client group, who questioned the savings I had reported. On closer look, a claim for a higher fee came in and was paid, because it was billed from the provider's regional office rather than from the local office with whom I had "successfully negotiated." For these and many other reasons, I determined that there needed to be a more formal, accountable, and credible way of securing payment arrangements.

To better track and manage case negotiations and claims processing in my office, I designed provider agreement forms to be utilized for each provider and each service. Psychiatric, durable medical equipment, infusion, nursing care, and therapy services all have separate provider agreement sheets (see Appendix 10-B), which are sent with a cover letter explaining their use (Exhibit 10-3). For our staff, I developed guidelines to assist them in filling out the forms and in applying them to different situations (Exhibit 10-4). All these forms are designed to be revised whenever necessary to meet our own needs or the needs of a client company.

These forms can be used for any number of distinct negotiations. They are not used for every x-ray or every piece of durable medical equipment; rather, they are used for high-priced items, for benefit plan exceptions, and so on. Perhaps the payer has a preferred provider arrangement that allows patients to receive a discount, or we have agreed on a prompt-pay discount of 3 percent if I can ensure that the invoice will be paid in two to three weeks (which qualifies as early in claims circles). Especially helpful when an alternative care plan is created, a provider service agreement documents case manager, provider, and payer approval for a specific care procedure so that the claims examiner is not put in the awkward position of having to "authorize" a treatment.

Following negotiations with the provider, the case manager completes most portions of the form, which is sent by fax to the provider for an approval signature. Then a hard copy of the agreement is sent to the provider with a cover letter, which notes that any invoices must be accompanied by the form. A copy of the agreement is also sent to the claims examiner; that particular claim will then be flagged manually or by computer for special handling so that the negotiated price, time frame, or exception is not lost. Given that five or more different examiners or different claims departments might cover one claimant, such tracking is vital.

My company manages the tracking and payment in two different ways. Sometimes the case manager becomes the "clearinghouse" for every invoice received on behalf of a particular claimant and will hand the negotiated claim to an examiner for processing. In other instances, the provider company sends in its customary bill, knowing it will be reduced as per our agreement (e.g., from $410 to $280).

Whatever type of provider agreement format a case manager uses, it should incorporate specifics of the arrangement: the time frame (beginning

Exhibit 10–3 Provider Service Agreement Cover Letter

Date:
Patient:
Insured:
Emp. Group:
S.S.#:

Dear_____,

OPTIONS UNLIMITED is a case management consulting firm utilized by _____, a third party administrator for the above-captioned employer group.

Enclosed, please find a copy of a service agreement form for services arranged with you/your company on _____ for _____.

In order for you to receive payment from _____, you *must* submit *EACH* bill with a *copy* of this service form, using one of the enclosed envelopes. This will insure special handling and payment according to the arrangement, which will be subject, of course, to co-payments, deductibles, and plan limitations.

Any claim/bill received *WITHOUT* this service form will be returned with a message: "Please resubmit with copy of service agreement form."

If there are any problems regarding the information on this form, contact the case manager undersigned immediately.

Claims received for billed amounts greater than indicated in the service agreement form will be reduced to the agreed amount with an EOB message: "Claim reduced to amount agreed to in the service agreement."

Bills for supplies or services not specifically indicated on service agreement forms should be sent to the insured, who will submit a claim to _____ in the usual manner.

Adherence to this procedure will assist in handling and prompt payment; failure obviously will mean delays.

We thank you in advance for your anticipated cooperation.

Very truly yours,

_____

Case Manager
(   )

cc: Claims Examiner, Case Manager File

(continues)

Exhibit 10–3 continued

I have received and am in agreement with the above arrangement and the attached service agreement form.

Name/Title (PRINT) _____

Signature _____ Date: _____

Courtesy of Options Unlimited, Case Management Services Division, Huntington, N.Y.

and end dates), the fees, and any conditions (e.g., "payment at 100 percent" or "payment within 30 days," or "per diem rate is all inclusive; no other charges to be billed"). The information needs to be documented and communicated to the provider and the payer source (claims department). In addition to all pertinent data, such as the patient's name, insured's name, group policy number, social security number, and physician, the form should include a space for the contact person, the case manager, and phone numbers where they can be reached. Each case management department or company will need to develop a method or system consistent with its administrative capabilities and client base. For case management departments in insurance carrier groups, notes entered into a computerized claims system might suffice. Companies working with several carriers might find that mail or fax communication works best. When established, the system should enable accurate payments to be completed in a timely manner and also allow tracking of some of the savings realized by case management.

COST-BENEFIT ANALYSIS REPORTS

Documenting savings from case management intervention is a necessary component of case management work. One method of documentation is to use cost-benefit analysis reports. These are reports which serve to illustrate in financial terms that the costs spent on case management services (and the services that are implemented as part of an alternate care plan) translate into dollar savings, or dollars spent versus dollars saved. Each case management program should have from its very inception a mechanism in place to demonstrate savings to all who will pay for the services. The report format may vary from company to company, and it can certainly be customized or modified to meet client company needs. Report variables may change as a case management program develops.

Exhibit 10–4 Provider Service Agreement Guidelines

Subject: Provider Agreements

Purpose: To document service agreements with providers with the specifics of the arrangement clearly outlined.

Procedural Guidelines

1. Certain cases may require the utilization of specialized services, equipment, and therapies. Through ongoing assessment and in conjunction with the treating physicians, the case manager will identify the needs, select the appropriate services and providers (using the attached guidelines to assist you), negotiate fees and arrangements, and continually monitor.

2. Source of Agreements
   —Nursing (RN, LPN, Home Health Aide)
   —Durable Medical Equipment (inc. apnea alarms, wheelchairs, hospital beds, oxygen, etc.)
   —Infusion Therapy
   —Other Therapies (PT, OT, Speech)
   —Rehabilitation facility, SNF, Psych, and Substance Abuse programs

3. Responsibilities
   —The case manager will fax form and letter of agreement to provider, request their signature to acknowledge acceptance of the terms. When signed, the case manager will send out the hard copy with a supply of envelopes with the case manager's return address.

   —The case manager will receive claims, accompanied by the agreement form, will review for adherence to the agreement, and will forward to the Claims Department for payment.

   —NOTE: Once the services are in place, it is the case manager's responsibility to monitor for quality/outcome and determine on an ongoing basis the need for less (or more) services.

   In addition to requesting the claim for review, any notes related to these services must accompany the claim, i.e., Nurses Notes, PT evaluation and notes, etc.

   It is also the case manager's responsibility to monitor the reevaluation and/or expiration dates of these agreements and follow through with whatever is indicated. You will be in jeopardy of services being discontinued even if still needed, due to failure to renew an agreement.

Courtesy of Options Unlimited, Case Management Services Division, Huntington, N.Y.

A cost-benefit analysis report is so specific that I believe it is best prepared by the case manager who works the case. This individual possesses knowledge about the patient, the problems, and the care plan in place at the time the referral was made. She also identified solutions; prevented additional problems; and selected, arranged for, and negotiated the services that were utilized. As a consequence, she is in the best position to evaluate the intervention's success.

Cost-benefit analysis reports are not extended narratives, nor do they include ongoing documentation. They are concerned with the financial aspects of case management and, in my view, should not be included among the monthly progress reports. Since it is possible for certain cases to be in litigation (in particular, workers' compensation, auto, and disability cases), the financial aspects of case management should generally not be included in the patient-centered reports. While it is expected that costs will never be the focus of case management decisions, there is concern that any mention of dollars (even alongside all the other reasons for a particular treatment decision, such as higher quality care, patient preference, etc.) might be misconstrued or misrepresented by those who view case management intervention solely as a means to control costs.

Some client groups, claims departments, and other purchasers of case management services would prefer to receive reports that deal exclusively with numbers, but it is my contention that this does a disservice to case management. By only portraying savings, one virtually eliminates all of the other contributions of case management. It would seem highly desirable, therefore, to develop a report format that can not only demonstrate savings but also communicate the impact of case management and illustrate the process.

Whatever format is chosen, it is important that each case within a grouping is presented similarly. Following is a list of items that should be included in each case presentation:

1. identifiers (file, case, or social security number; carrier, employer group; date case opened; date case closed; total weeks or months in case management; diagnosis)
2. overview of case management intervention
3. summary of intervention
4. case management fees
5. savings
   - avoided charges
   - potential charges
   - discounts and/or negotiated reductions
   - reductions in services, products, and equipment

6. actual charges
7. gross savings (potential charges minus actual charges)
8. net savings (gross savings minus case management fees)
9. status of case (open or closed)

Exhibit 10-5 is a worksheet that can be used for each case, and Exhibit 10-6 is a set of guidelines that explain how the worksheet sections should be filled in.

A word about hard versus soft savings. Fortunately, there are many opportunities for case managers not only to improve the quality, outcome, and lifestyles for our patients but also, as we perfect our skills and realize our worth, to become better at attaching value to what it is that we do. To cite an example, new case managers may be comfortable suggesting and then arranging for home care as a way of saving money, but experienced case managers know that they can realize additional savings by asking for prompt-pay discounts, reducing levels of care or hours of care through continual assessment of the patient's progress, and so on. Reductions, discounts, negotiated rates, all-inclusive per diem rates, and "freebies" are examples of hard savings.

Soft savings are more difficult to quantify but need to be reported. For instance, a case manager is referred to a patient who, in prior months, had an admission every one or two months for diabetic complications and an emergency hospital stay of five to seven days. At the time of the initial evaluation, the case manager determined that this patient did not understand his diagnosis, was minimally compliant, and in fact frequently ignored dietary restrictions and urine and blood testing requirements. During the three months of case management intervention, the case manager communicated these problems to the physician, referred the patient for formal education and a diet counseling program, and involved the patient in the daily monitoring of his own progress. She successfully resolved what would have been a continuing pattern of admissions and complications. In fact, in the six months of case management involvement, there were no further hospital admissions. This is the kind of soft savings that should be noted in cost-benefit analysis reports.

THE COST-BENEFIT ANALYSIS SUMMARIES

When each client case has been outlined, there needs to be a summary of the case management program for the particular client group—a total financial analysis of dollars saved versus dollars spent for case management services. Examples of such summaries are provided in Exhibit 10-7 Appendix 10-C. The former is a concise summary and the latter is an ex-

Exhibit 10–5 Cost-Benefit Analysis Worksheet

Quarter _____

Re:

File #:

Carrier/Client Group:

Date of Referral:

Date of Closure:

Total Weeks/Months of Case Management:

Diagnosis:

Case Management Fees:

Summary of Intervention:

Avoidance of Potential Charges:

Total of Potential Charges:

Alternate Care and Related Charges:

Total Charges for Alternate Care and Case Management Fees:

Net Savings:

Courtesy of Options Unlimited, Case Management Services Division, Huntington, N.Y.

Exhibit 10–6 Cost-Benefit Analysis Guidelines

Re: Patient/claimant's name here.

File # (SS #): Insured's social security number.

Carrier/Employer Group:

Date Opened: Date opened for case management.

Date of Closure: If applicable.

Total Weeks/Months in Case Management: How long has case been active.

Diagnosis: Major categories only, e.g., Cancer of Liver, Right Side CVA (Stroke). *Remember these will be utilized by "lay" people mostly so keep this understandable.

Case Management Fees: We will insert this figure.

Summary of Intervention:

NOTE: This is not to be a discussion of the patient's entire medical history, symptoms, surgeries. This will have occurred in initial and progress reports and should not be repeated here.

This is a summary of *your* intervention on this case. How did you make a difference, in the quality, eventual outcome, patient compliance, patient and family support, prevention of complications, better/more appropriate use of resources, services, and dollars.

*See example reports for further illustration of this section.

This is the "proof" statement for case management, the justification for it on this case! It is *your* turn to cite *your* accomplishments, and give evidence of the need for our services, and the fees for our services.

Avoidance of Potential Charges: This section will list by specific service *and* possible charges (if there is a range put the range, e.g., $750 per day–$1,000 per day) that *could* have occurred if this *case* did *not* have your intervention. Remember you would not have been there to suggest home IV antibiotics vs. continued stay in the hospital or negotiate rates for services, e.g., fees for home IV and nursing services that could have been charged (and paid for since there is no R & C for these, anything goes!), or reduce RN visits from 3 × per week to 1 × per week to discontinuance. List *each* of these services or hospital admissions for the complications that you prevented or equipment, therapies, etc., that would have occurred and (probably) continued if you did not intervene during this quarter. Your list should look something like this.

1. Continued longer stay in hospital
   5 days @ $850 per day = $4,250
   Additional MD visits while patient in hospital @ $100 per visit × 5 days = $500

(continues)

Exhibit 10–6 continued

2. Home care services—discharge planner & MD request hospital-based home care services following patient's discharge.
RN visits 1 per day × 14 days @ $140 per visit = $1,960
HHA 6 hours per day @ $20 per hour × 14 days = $1,680
PT 3 × per week × 2 months @ $85 per visit = $1,040

Total of Potential Charges: This should be a combined dollar figure for the above charges, e.g., $8,530.

Alternate Care and Related Charges: This is a list of *specific* services and charges for each that *you* put in place, negotiated rates, effected purchase vs. rental, usually instead of the potential charges. For example:

Home care services by community-based, JCAHO-accredited agency at following rates and with MD approval:

RN visits 1 × per day × 7 days @ $100 per visit = $700
then RN visits 3 × per week @ $100 per visit = $300
HHA 6 hours per day @ $18 per hour × 7 days = $756
then HHA 4 hours per day @ $18 × 5 days (family helped on weekends) = $360
PT 3 × per week × 1 month @ $65 per visit = $780
then PT 2 × per week × 1 month @ $65 per visit = $520

Total Charges for Alternate Care or Services:

The sum total of charges compiled from listing above, e.g., $3,410.

Savings: This is a *dollar* figure to be calculated from the potential charges *minus* the charges incurred from the "Alternate Care or Services," e.g., $5,120.

NOTE: Occasionally it will not be possible to claim savings, you may not yet have had an opportunity to reduce the level of care or services, because patient's condition worsened or had to be readmitted to hospital, or you have just put the services in place, no claims are yet in and savings are "to be determined." You may, however, state an approximate dollar figure that you expect will occur.

A word about hard vs. soft savings.

Hard Savings

Fortunately there are many opportunities not only to improve quality, outcome, and lifestyles for our patients but also as we perfect our skills and realize our worth, we become better at attaching value to what it is that we do. To cite an example—experienced case managers may be comfortable suggesting and then arranging for home care vs. continued stays in hospital, but newer case managers may not realize that over and above this there is still an ability to realize additional savings by asking

(continues)

Exhibit 10–6 continued

for prompt-pay discounts, reducing levels of care or hours of care by assessing patient progress and needs frequently, etc. Such reductions, discounts, negotiated rates, all-inclusive per diem rates, "freebies," etc. are *hard* savings.

Soft Savings

This is more difficult to quantify and qualify but *needs* to be stated. For instance, you have been referred a patient who in prior months of referral had an admission of 1–2 months for diabetic complications and the emergency hospital stay was 5–7 days. At the time of your initial evalua- tion, you have determined that this patient lacked the understanding of his diagnosis, had minimal compliance, and in fact frequently ignored dietary restrictions, urine and blood testing requirements, etc. During the 3 months of case management intervention, you have communicated the problems to his MD, referred the patient for formal education, a diet counseling program, and involved the patient in a daily monitoring of his own progress. You have successfully resolved what *would* have been a continuing pattern of admissions and complications, in fact, in the 6 months of case management involvement there have been *no* hospital admissions. The potential charges that *would* have occurred without case management intervention and savings could be stated in the following manner.

Summary of Case Management Intervention:

Case manager during this quarter identified and then implemented solutions for this man who had been referred due to recurrent hospital admissions. Patient was poorly informed and because of this was non- compliant following a diagnosis of diabetes. Further complicating this was prior history of increased blood pressure and angina. Case manager advised treating physician and with his cooperation arranged for diabetic education and counseling program, patient was directed to monitor his own progress and report problems to case manager and MD. Programs were available through community hospital outpatient program with considerable savings and good results. There have been no further admissions during this 3-month period and the patient feels more in control. This man was at absolute risk for increased problems and costs.

Avoidance of Potential Charges:

2 hospital admissions @ 5 days for each × $800 per day = $8,000
MD visits while patient in hospital @ $100 per visit × 10 days = $1,000
Diabetic Management Program @ $1,000 per private outpatient program
Total of Potential Charges = $10,000

(continues)

Exhibit 10–6 continued

Alternate Care Charges:

Diabetic Management Program @ $750 per program = $750
MD visits—1 per month @ $75 per visit = $225
Total Alternate Care Charges = $975
Total Savings $10,000 – $975 = $9,025 plus additional savings over several more months.

The above is an example of what group might determine "soft savings"; *however,* positioned with expertise and stated strongly and authoritatively it becomes highly credible.

NOTE: If there are *no* savings to be claimed, either hard or soft, then state *none* or *to be determined*, with a brief (few word) statement, e.g., patient still in hospital, savings will be realized next quarter.

Courtesy of Options Unlimited, Case Management Services Division, Huntington, N.Y.

---

panded version. Which format should be used depends in part on the needs of the client group and the structure of the case management program, among other factors.

It is recommended that some kind of financial analysis of case management programs be performed on a regular basis, whether quarterly, semi-annually, or annually. Because dollars can add up quickly, especially in very active cases, I believe that preparing cost-benefit analysis reports on a quarterly basis is appropriate. Frequent reporting not only makes the compiling of information a more manageable task but allows on-line case managers and the supervisor or program director to evaluate the effectiveness of services before too much time has passed and too many dollars have been spent. Not all cases will yield savings, and some will be more successful than others. What is important is that a timely evaluation of services (which in essence is what this is all about) allows for earlier recognition of problems and the prevention of bigger ones. If case management fees are high and savings on several cases drop each quarter, the problem may be a case manager who is not utilizing time appropriately or does not know how to capture savings. She may require additional training. It might also be a signal that some cases need to be closed.

Preparation of cost-benefit analysis reports is one of the more difficult tasks for many case managers. For several years, I assumed the responsibility for my staff. However, as business increased, this reporting became a larger part of my job, and what I learned was that I no longer had the

Exhibit 10–7 Concise Cost-Benefits Analysis Summary

March 1, 1993 to June 30, 1993
COST-BENEFIT ANALYSIS FOR CASE MANAGEMENT SERVICES
FOR
COMPANY XXX

Cases Open at Beginning of Period	2
Cases Referred This Period	2
Cases Closed during the Period	1
Total Cases Worked during Period	4
Total Number of Open Cases	3

Total Fees for the Period	$2,562.02
Average Fees per Month	854.01
Average Fees per Case/Period	640.51
Average Fees per Case/Month	213.50

Total Savings for Period	Gross:	$58,016.96
	Net:	55,454.94
Average Savings per Case/Period		$13,863.74
Ratio of Dollars to Savings		1 : 23

NOTE: To evaluate the benefits of a program for a client, we use total fees billed for all cases worked and the savings resulting from our intervention, whether savings were realized in every case, one case, or several.

CASE MANAGEMENT
COST-BENEFIT ANALYSIS REPORT

File #: xxxxxx

Carrier/Client Group: Company XXX

Date of Referral: 4/15/93

Date of Closure: Remains Active

Total Weeks/Months of Case Management: 2 months

Diagnosis: Cancer of the Lung

Case Management Fees: $924.15

Summary of Intervention: Claimant had been receiving chemotherapy until January 1987. Due to adverse effects, treatment was stopped temporarily. Claimant remains at home. Prognosis is poor. Hospice care and coordinator of home care will probably be necessary in time.

Avoidance of Potential Charges:
None to date.

(continues)

Exhibit 10–7 continued

Total of Potential Charges:
To be determined.
Alternate Care and Related Charges:
To be determined.
Total Charges for Alternate Care and Case Management Fees:
To be determined.
Net Savings:
To be determined.

CASE MANAGEMENT
COST-BENEFIT ANALYSIS REPORT

File #:
Carrier/Client Group:
Date of Referral: 11/25/92
Date of Closure: Remains Active
Total Weeks/Months of Case Management: 7 months
Diagnosis: RSD, MPD
Case Management Fees: $632.61
Summary of Intervention: Claimant continues to treat with Dr. May with excellent results. She continues with occupational therapy 3x per week.
Avoidance of Potential Charges:
By referring claimant to Dr. May, surgeries recommended by Dr. Left were avoided. Surgery plus hospitalization would be approximately $12,000.00 or more. Negotiated cost of casting of fingers.
Total of Potential Charges:
$13,800.00
Alternate Care and Related Charges:
Casting - $50.00 per finger. Usually 3 fingers @ 3x per week = $150.00 × 3 = $450.00
Exercise = $40.00.
Heat treatment = $12.00.
Total therapy = $606.00 per week.
Negotiated casting to $100.00 per day.
Total Charges for Alternate Care and Case Management Fees:
$6,104.61
Net Savings:
$7,695.39

(continues)

Exhibit 10–7 continued

CASE MANAGEMENT
COST-BENEFIT ANALYSIS REPORT

File #:

Carrier/Client Group:

Date of Referral: 5/19/93

Date of Closure: Remains Active

Total Weeks/Months of Case Management: 6 weeks

Diagnosis: Preterm labor

Case Management Fees: $943.00

Summary of Intervention: Case referred after physician referred to Care for home uterine monitoring. Negotiated daily rate with Care for more cost effective services. Arranged for services of home health aide to assist claimant with routine daily care activities because of limited mobility and activity restrictions. Monitored for compliance.

Avoidance of Potential Charges:
Hospitalization × 3 for observation and monitoring of premature contractions × 3 days at $800.00 per day = $7,200.00.
Related MD fees @ $100.00 per day = $900.00
Hospitalization for strict bedrest compliance × 43 days @ $800.00 per day = $34,400.00
HHA @ $15.75 = $1,220.00
Uterine Monitoring (non negotiated) = $5,160.00

Total of Potential Charges:
$45,880.00

Alternate Care and Related Charges:
HHA × 20 days × 4 hrs. per day @ $11.50 per day = $920.00
Uterine monitoring = 43 days @ $90.00 per day + $120.00 setup fee = $3,990.00

Total Charges for Alternate Care and Case Management Fees:
$5,853.00

Net Savings:
$43,027.00

Courtesy of Options Unlimited, Case Management Services Division, Huntington, N.Y.

kind of day-to-day knowledge of the cases that allowed for an more accurate capturing of savings. Eventually it was decided that the best person to prepare each individual cost-benefit analysis report was the case manager who was working the case. Instruction in cost-benefit analysis writing is necessary and has now become a part of our training program. (Depending on the size of the case management company or department, preparation of the client group summary would probably be a management task, relatively straightforward if all the case managers' summaries were in hand.)

QUALITY ASSURANCE PROGRAMS

Financial accountability is perhaps the greatest contribution that cost-benefit analysis offers. While the reports are appreciated by clients and are useful as marketing tools, they are also useful as quality assurance tools. Further, the process utilized in the preparation of cost-benefit information becomes an empowering experience. Individuals come to appreciate the real value of case management and recognize their own contribution to each success. In instances of partial failure, they are able to understand the reasons and develop different strategies to meet them. This kind of self-evaluation promotes excellence and allows the ongoing monitoring of case management services.

FEEDBACK FROM PATIENTS

Owing to their lack of understanding of case management services and to their perception that employees might view such services as intrusive or interfering, carriers and employer groups have been concerned about and occasionally have resisted implementing case management programs. When my office began working more directly with corporate decision makers on group health cases, I could better appreciate the employers' position. Although interested in cost containment, they did not want to upset the favorable employer-employee relationships they had established. There was also unease expressed about the potential for liability. Would case managers or treating physicians be directing care? What if something negative happened to an employee as a result of a case manager's recommendations?

Case management requires direct interaction with patients and in some respects does interrupt their access to care and services. Frequently the arrangement for case management services occurs too late for maximum benefits. For instance, one referral to our office was made because over one year postinjury the claimant was still in active medical treatment and had not returned to work. This "reactive" referral by the claims department was viewed somewhat disdainfully by the claimant. Where were we before when he needed us? For the most part, however, case managers have been welcomed by patients and their families. It is important for others to know this.

I first began conducting surveys of patients when I worked primarily in the areas of workers' compensation and auto insurance, prior to my expansion into the group health market. I wanted to be able to improve the delivery of our services not just for our client groups, who were satisfied as long as we were able to save money, but for the recipients of our services—claimants and their families. We developed a questionnaire that was sent at the close of each case; for those cases that remained open for a long time, one was sent out every six months. The questionnaire, which has been revised in light of our increased experience, has helped assure our client groups that case management does make a difference, is well received, and, as a valued employee service, can be used to improve public relations.

The questionnaire is sent with an explanatory letter (Exhibits 10-8 and 10-9). It combines a "check the box" format with blanks where individuals can enter their own responses, suggestions, or criticisms. It does not have to be signed but most are, and we further encourage a response by including a self-addressed stamped envelope.

We provide summaries of the responses to the client groups and usually include actual samples. This has been most helpful, especially with those groups that were initially concerned about the receptivity of their employees. After seeing employee reactions, they soon start calling to suggest cases they now think should be case managed.

Questionnaire surveys are useful not only from a marketing perspective but also in the evaluation of staff members and the identification of problems with service. Many suggestions offered by our patients have become incorporated into our current services. When our case managers are given praise for their assistance, they receive a copy of the document for their records and it becomes part of their personnel file. Criticisms are also taken seriously, obviously allowing for personal preference, personality clash, or a situation that places the case manager in a position of reducing home care services or confronting noncompliant behavior. Criticisms also sometimes point to areas where additional training or supervision might be helpful.

COMMUNICATING SUCCESS

Cost-benefit analysis reports and quality assurance surveys need to be communicated appropriately. They should be provided on a regular ba-

Exhibit 10–8 Quality Assurance Questionnaire Cover Letter

Date

Mr. _____

_____

_____

Dear Mr. _____:

In an effort to improve the quality of our services, OPTIONS UNLIM-
ITED is conducting periodic surveys.

_____, R.N. was assigned to meet with you to provide
case management services as requested by _____.

In order to assess the quality of services and our client's satisfaction, we
are asking that you complete the enclosed questionnaire and return it in
the self-addressed stamped envelope. Your candor and cooperation will
be appreciated.

If you have any question, please call me at _____.

Very truly yours,

Courtesy of Options Unlimited, Case Management Division, Huntington, N.Y.

sis and are ideally presented in personal meetings. Cost-benefit analysis
reports in particular need to be explained, because the information, when
taken out of context or reviewed by individuals unfamiliar with the process or results, can easily be misinterpreted. Certain terms (e.g., *avoidance
of potential charges* and *prevention of complications)* and the method of calcu-
lating savings (gross and net) should be discussed. Reviewing a few or all
of the individual cases within a group is also helpful. It enables a client to
understand the case management process and raise questions regarding
the accuracy of the figures and the credibility of the savings—all important steps. If case managers are not willing to explain and inform, then the
whole purpose of reporting is subverted.

Usually the individual representing a client group in its relationship
with a case manager is the CFO (Chief Financial Officer), an insurance professional, or a human resource professional. In most instances, this individual does not have a medical background and is unwilling to accept everything the case manager feels justified in claiming as savings. To

Exhibit 10–9 Quality Assurance Questionnaire

1. Date contacted by case manager: _____

2. Number of meetings with case manager: _____

3. How would you rate the frequency of contact with the case manager:

   Adequate_____ Too many_____ Too few_____

4. Was the case manager's goals and intervention consistent with your needs?

   Definitely_____ Somewhat_____ Not at all_____

5. Please describe your diagnosis: _____

   _____

6. Has the status of your health/disability changed since OPTIONS UNLIMITED contacted you: _____

   _____

   Please describe: _____

   _____

   _____

7. Check appropriate column for the following:

	Extremely helpful	Somewhat helpful	Help in this area wasn't necessary
• Did you find the services of OPTIONS UNLIMITED helpful in dealing with your medical situation?	____	____	____
• Understanding your diagnosis and treatment?	____	____	____
• Obtaining information from your physician to share with you, e.g., treatment alternatives, instructions to be followed?	____	____	____

(continues)

Exhibit 10–9 continued

- Assisting with arrangements
  for necessary services (nursing),
  treatment, therapy, equipment,
  and supplies? Please indicate
  which one applies.   _____   _____   _____
- Offering support, encourage-
  ment, or assistance in coping
  with your illness/condition
  and/or that of a family
  member?   _____   _____   _____

8. Were there other ways in which the case manager was helpful?

   Please describe: _____

   _____

9. Would you rate the OPTIONS UNLIMITED case manager(s):

   Excellent_____   Good_____   Fair_____   Poor_____

10. Do you feel OPTIONS UNLIMITED intervention came:

    At right time_____   Too early_____   Too late_____ to be effective?

11. Were there other areas of assistance that could have been helpful?

    Please list: _____

    _____

12. How would you like to see our services changed? _____

    _____

13. Would you recommend our services to others in a similar situation?

    Yes_____   No_____

14. Case management services are often part of cost containment programs. It is our hope that while we may contain costs, it should not be at the sacrifice of quality or good outcomes for patients. In general, was our involvement a positive one for you?

    Yes_____   No_____   *(continues)*

Exhibit 10–9 continued

15. If these services were not covered by your insurance, but you could utilize and pay for them as you would other professionals (physician, psychologist, etc.), would you?

Yes_____ No_____

Signature: _____ Date: _____
                    (Optional)

Courtesy of Options Unlimited, Case Management Services Division, Huntington, N.Y.

illustrate, several years ago one of my first major clients was a large health insurance carrier that contracted with my company to develop a case management program for it and its client groups. As part of the program, we obtained early discharges from hospitals, negotiated fees with facilities and providers, arranged home care, and prevented the kinds of complications that would have occurred had case managers not been involved.

Feeling very positive about our services and the results, I looked forward to sharing our first quarterly report with this group. The results were impressive, a 1:23 ratio (i.e., for every dollar that this group spent on our case management services, we were able to save $23). Quite respectable, I thought, especially as we were somewhat conservative in our calculation.

At the meeting, the carrier's representatives included an underwriter, an actuary, the corporate counsel, and the claims director. Not one case manager! I started with the summary page, concise data and the kind of "number crunching" that this group could really get into. Questions began: Where were the actual claims that we got these savings from? If we were saying that they never had claims (avoidance of potential charges), then how could we calculate a savings? How could we prevent a hospital admission or complications? This was going to be harder than I thought. How could I help them understand?

Case by case (fortunately there were only eight that quarter), I led them through the case management process. I described each case at the time we received it, gave the claims history prior to our involvement (three hospital admissions for three-to-five days each on a noncompliant diabetic), reported what we learned at the time of our assessment (this patient had been treated in a city hospital, had a different MD each time, no family MD, was trying to stretch his insulin to last because finances were tight, never did get around to getting his glucometer), and described what the case manager did (referred him to a local endocrinologist, arranged for insulin and supplies to be billed directly to the carrier instead of the patient having to pay first and then wait to be reimbursed, obtained a glucometer at discounted rate, arranged for diabetic training and diet plan by a nurse clinician in a physician's office, and referred him to a local diabetic support group, which he could participate in at no cost).

Finally I summarized the results. There were no admissions during the quarter. With this scenario as described, was there any doubt that without case management intervention, the revolving-door admissions to the hospital would have continued and additional complications occurred due to noncompliance? This overview and walk-through demonstrated the problem, the solutions, and the savings.

We discussed all eight cases and although there was some disagreement over whether something would or would not have occurred, at the end of this meeting all the representatives were enthusiastic about the accomplishments, including the containment of costs. For several quarters thereafter, interest in case management increased and more people attended the meetings, often contributing their own ideas as to what else could have been done and reporting that more of the client groups wanted this case management "stuff." This carrier group became so convinced of the merits of case management that it eventually developed its own department and retained us to work cases it could not handle.

Case managers are experts in assessing and resolving problem cases. Others cannot be expected to understand the case management process as well as we do. It is not enough to manage the case; we need to manage our relationships with clients as well. Educating clients allows them to "buy into" case management and helps avoid micromanagement discussions (e.g., questioning whether the five minutes spent on a phone call was really necessary). To make case management more successful and established as an industry, each case manager needs not only to work effectively but to articulate her achievements—walk the walk and talk and talk.

NOTES

1. C.M. Mullahy, "A Winning Partnership," *Home Health Care Dealer*, March-April 1993, 117–118.
2. L. Thomas-Payne, "Simple Negotiations," *HomeCare*, November 1992, 104.

Program Questionnaire and Facility Review for Case Managers

PROGRAM QUESTIONNAIRE

Name: _____

Address: _____

Phone: _____

Contact Person: _____

Medical Director/Specialty: _____

Number of Beds: _____ Age Range of Patients: _____

Specialty Areas: _____

Per Diem Cost	$_____	Cost varies per program and per individual need. Case managers call the facility for an estimate of cost for care. Following an evaluation of specific need, the facility can issue a letter confirming cost for care.
All Inclusive	$_____	
Room & Board Only	$_____	

Approximate Therapy Cost per 30 Minutes

Physical	$_____	Vocational	$_____
Occupational	$_____	Cognitive	$_____
Speech	$_____	Psychological	
Recreational	$_____	Counseling	$_____
Prosthetics	$_____	Drivers Ed	$_____
Respiratory	$_____	Audiologists (Screening)	$_____
		Therapeutic Recreation Outings	$_____

Comments:

Accredited by: _____ JCAHO _____ CARF

Written Reports Rendered:

Insurance Company Representative included at staffings
_____Yes _____No

Case Manager or Insurance Representative permitted to:
_____Attend staffings _____Participate in staffings

Will the facility provide statistical data on length of
stay, average costs, distribution of discharge
placements? ( ) Yes ( ) No

Will the facility negotiate costs? ( ) Yes ( ) No

Does the facility have fax capability? ( ) Yes ( ) No

    If so, fax #:_____

Will the facility provide written reports no less
often than 30 days? ( ) Yes ( ) No

Staffing

Board-certified medical director? ( ) Yes ( ) No

Physician/psychiatrist team leader? ( ) Yes ( ) No

Is the physician (the team leader) on premises? ( ) Yes ( ) No

Is the physician out-of-facility consultant? ( ) Yes ( ) No

24-hour skilled care available directed by RN? ( ) Yes ( ) No

Team is multi-disciplinary, including representatives
from all therapies? ( ) Yes ( ) No

Do patients have the same therapists and team
members throughout their stay? ( ) Yes ( ) No

Are the majority of employees on staff and not
contracted from an outside agency? ( ) Yes ( ) No

Are therapists registered or certified? ( ) Yes ( ) No

Does the facility have access to consulting
physicians? ( ) Yes ( ) No

Is list of consultants available? ( ) Yes ( ) No

Clinical Care Available

Is a rehabilitation plan tailored for the patient's
specific needs?   ( ) Yes ( ) No

Are team conferences held: _____ weekly   _____ every two weeks

Do all members of the team, including patient,
family, & insurance representative, attend?   ( ) Yes ( ) No

How many hours of therapy/rehab services does
patient receive per day?_____

Are personal hygiene assistance and meals
considered therapy?   ( ) Yes ( ) No

Are the patient's therapy prescriptions appropriate? ( ) Yes ( ) No

Are therapies offered daily, and if patient conditions
warrant, are therapies offered twice a day?   ( ) Yes ( ) No

Weekends?   ( ) Yes ( ) No

Check therapies available:

Physical_____   Speech & Language_____

Cognitive_____   Orthotic Services_____

Occupational_____   Psychological Counseling_____

Recreational_____

Discharge Planning and Coordination of Follow-up

Is discharge planning instituted early in the
hospitalization?   ( ) Yes ( ) No

Is there a tentative discharge date set early in the
hospitalization?   ( ) Yes ( ) No

Is patient/family education ongoing throughout
the hospitalization?   ( ) Yes ( ) No

Does the family education include assisting the
family to realistically consider the client's
long-term physical and cognitive prognosis?   ( ) Yes ( ) No

Is there a prescribed continuum of family ed?   ( ) Yes ( ) No

Is there continuity of care and follow-up after
discharge?   ( ) Yes ( ) No

Will staff perform on-site evaluation for home
modification needs?   ( ) Yes ( ) No

Will equipment and home modification needs be
discussed with insurance representative before
purchase or direction to the family? ( ) Yes ( ) No

Will several bids for DME be acquired if requested? ( ) Yes ( ) No

Will physician team leader refer patient to a local
physician for follow-up and act as a resource
as needed? ( ) Yes ( ) No

Are outpatient services available? ( ) Yes ( ) No

Please detail living arrangements for outpatient program below.

Are patients encouraged to complete trial home
visits prior to discharge? ( ) Yes ( ) No

Will the facility provide a written discharge plan
including: level of care required, number of hours
per day assistance is required, abilities in ADI's,
equipment needs, medications, return-to-work/
vocational potential, specific follow-up care
required? ( ) Yes ( ) No

Additional Comments:

Reviewed by: _____

Office: _____

City, State: _____

FACILITY REVIEW

Does the facility have pre-admission criteria?	( ) Yes	( ) No
Is the facility clean and cheerful?	( ) Yes	( ) No
Does the facility admit only those patients with rehabilitation potential?	( ) Yes	( ) No
Does the facility offer an evaluation program to determine rehab potential?	( ) Yes	( ) No
Does the facility have a designee in the business office to deal with the insurer/case manager?	( ) Yes	( ) No
Do patients look well cared for?	( ) Yes	( ) No
Is there a family education program?	( ) Yes	( ) No
Is there a patient/family information guidebook?	( ) Yes	( ) No
Are there other patients with the same diagnosis? How many?_____	( ) Yes	( ) No
Are there dedicated treatment teams per diagnosis?	( ) Yes	( ) No
Are the facilities and equipment appropriate for the patient's needs?	( ) Yes	( ) No
Do patients have access to dining area, nursing units, grounds, elevators, etc.?	( ) Yes	( ) No
Are there well-defined policies and procedures in place for medical emergencies?	( ) Yes	( ) No
Can the facility adequately treat minor/moderate medical complications on-site?	( ) Yes	( ) No
Will the facility notify insurance representative of upcoming conferences/staffings?	( ) Yes	( ) No
Are goals re-set as patient status changes?	( ) Yes	( ) No
If patient no longer shows significant gains, is discharge proposed?	( ) Yes	( ) No
Is there a staff coordinator or internal case manager assigned to each patient who acts as a liaison for family and insurance representative?	( ) Yes	( ) No
Are there well-defined quality assurance programs in place?	( ) Yes	( ) No
Are there outcome criteria? Is the effectiveness of services measured?	( ) Yes	( ) No

Average Length of Stay:
By diagnosis—the figures for preceding year (if available)
CVA   _____
SCI (NEW)   _____
SCI (OLD)   _____
Referral Procedure:

Courtesy of Individual Case Management Association, Little Rock, Arkansas.

Provider Service Agreements

Initial_____

Renewal_____

CLAIMS NOTIFICATION—PSYCHIATRIC SERVICES

To: _____ Date: _____

Re: Patient: _____

Insured: _____ Group: _____

S.S. #: _____

Physician: _____ Phone: _____

Type of Services:

In-Patient Services_____

Day-Hospital Services _____

Long Term Residential _____

Other _____

Date to Start _____ Date to End or Reevaluation Date _____

Provider: Name _____ Telephone: _____

Address _____ Ext: _____

City, State, Zip Code _____

Contact Person: Service _____ Telephone: _____

Billing _____ Ext: _____

Billing Address, if Different: _____

Fees: Per Diem _____ All Inclusive? Yes____ No____

Per Week_____ If no, state other charges

Per Month_____

Special Arrangements: _____

_____

Claims Person: Name _____ Phone _____

Advised: Yes_____ No_____

Arranged by: Case Manager _____ Phone _____

Accepted by: _____ Title _____

Initial____

Renewal____

CLAIMS NOTIFICATION—DURABLE MEDICAL EQUIPMENT FORM

To: _____ Date: _____

Re: Patient: _____

Insured: _____ Group: _____

S.S. #: _____

Physician: _____ Phone: _____

Equipment:	Purchase Price	Rental Price
Wheelchair: Manual	_____	_____
Electric	_____	_____
Hospital Bed:	_____	_____
Walker:	_____	_____
Commode:	_____	_____
Alarm:	_____	_____
Oxygen & Related Equipment:	_____	_____
Other:	_____	_____

Arrangement Made: _____

Length of Time: _____ Date Started: _____

Date to end or reevaluation date: _____

Discussed with claims department: Yes_____ No_____

Name: _____ Phone #: _____

Provider Agency: _____

Contact Person: _____

Address: _____

Telephone #: _____ Fax #: _____

Arranged by: Case Manager: _____

Company: ___*Options Unlimited*___ Telephone #: _____

Accepted by: _____

Title: _____ Date: _____

Initial_____

Renewal_____

CLAIMS NOTIFICATION—INFUSION SERVICES

To: _____Date: _____

Re: Patient: _____

    Insured: _____Group: _____

    S.S. #: _____

    Physician: _____Phone: _____

Type of Services: Fees: _____

TPN: _____

Chemotherapy: _____

Pentamidine: _____

Antibiotics: _____

Antivirals: _____

Enternal Feedings: _____

Pain Management:_____

Nursing Services Required: (For patient education, site care, etc.)

Describe: _____

Equipment Required: (Pumps, supplies, etc.)

Describe: _____

Frequency of Services:

Continuous: _____Daily: _____Hours per Day: _____

Date to Start: _____Date to End/Reevaluation Date: _____

Provider Agency:_____Phone #: _____

                                         Fax #: _____

Contact: Service: _____ Billing:_____

Address: _____

Arranged by: Case Manager: _____

               Company: ___Options Unlimited___Phone #: _____

Accepted by: _____ Title:_____

Initial_____

Renewal_____

CLAIMS NOTIFICATION—NURSING CARE SERVICES FORM

To: _____ Date: _____

Re: Patient: _____ Group: _____

Insured: _____

S.S. #: _____

Physician: _____ Phone: _____

Type of Service

Nursing:

R.N._____ L.P.N._____ Aide_____ Other _____

Hours per Day: _____ Hours per Week: _____ Fees per Hour: _____

Provider: Name _____ Telephone _____

Address _____

City, State, Zip Code _____

Billing Address, if different _____

Contact Person: Service _____ Phone _____

Fax _____

Billing _____ Phone _____

Note: If more than one agency will be used, enter identifying information

Name _____ Phone _____

Address _____

Contact Person: Service _____ Billing _____

Date to Start _____ Date to End or Reevaluation Date _____

Claims Person: Name _____ Phone _____

Advised: Yes_____ No_____

Arranged by: Case Manager: _____

Company: _____ *Options Unlimited* _____

Phone #: _____

Accepted by: _____ Title:_____

Initial_____

Renewal_____

CLAIMS NOTIFICATION—THERAPY SERVICES FORM

To: _____Date: _____

Re: Patient: _____

      Insured: _____

      S.S. #: _____

      Physician: _____

Type of Therapy:

P.T._____ O.T._____ Speech_____ Respiratory_____ Other _____

Frequency of Therapy: Daily _____ Weekly _____

Fees per Hour: _____ Estimated Duration of Therapy: _____

Date to Start _____

Date to End or Reevaluation Date _____

Name of Therapist(s): _____

Address: _____

City, State, Zip Code: _____

Phone #: _____ Tax I.D. #: _____

Claims Person: Name _____

                      Phone #: _____

Advised?: Yes_____   No_____

Arranged by: Case Manager: _____

Company: _____Options Unlimited_____ Phone #: _____

Accepted by: _____ Title: _____

Courtesy of Options Unlimited, Case Management Services Division, Huntington, N.Y.

Expanded Cost-Benefit Analysis Summary

American Health Insurance Company
Large Case Management Program
Company X
Case Management Analysis
July 1, 1990 to September 30, 1990

Cases Open at Start of Quarter   14
Cases Referred This Quarter   7
Cases Closed This Quarter   7
Active Cases   12
Transitional Cases   2
Total Number of Open Cases   14
Total Fees for the Quarter $16,717.00
Average Fees per Month 5,572.33
Average Fees/Case/Quarter.............................. 1,194.00
Average Fees/Case/Month................................. 398.00
TOTAL SAVINGS for Quarter **247,053.00**
Average Savings per Case/Quarter...................... 17,632.00
Ratio of Dollars to Savings.................................... 1:15

BREAKDOWN OF SAVINGS

Alternate Level of Care................................ $130,398.00
Elimination/Reduction of Unnecessary Services 36,700.00
Review of Bills (overbilling, duplicate charges).............. 15,750.00
Discounts for Services.................................... 13,805.00
Prevention of Hospitalization and Complications 50,400.00
TOTAL $247,053.00

QUARTERLY REPORT—JULY, AUGUST, SEPTEMBER 1990

HCMC #:	12341234
Group:	Company X 123-90
Date of Referral:	4/24/90
Diagnosis:	Ovarian & Colon Cancer
Status:	Open

Claimant was discharged home after lengthy hospitalization with total parenteral nutrition and 6 hours of home nursing care 5 days per week. Reduced rates of $400/d for TPN and $13.00/hr for H.H.A. were negotiated. This home care program was in lieu of acute hospitalization and arranged completely by Health Care Management Consultants.

Patient was hospitalized from 9/9 to 10/2 and again discharged with same services.

Nursing was reduced to 4 hrs/daily on July 28 as claimant's condition stabilized.

Billing errors submitted by TPN vendor were corrected, resulting in savings of $175.00 per day.

Savings reflect difference between potential hospital, pharmacy, and M.D. charges less TPN and nursing charges.

Avoidance of Potential Charges:

69/d × $1,300/d Hospital, Pharmacy & M.D. charges	$ 89,700.00
Plus billing errors $175/day × 69 days	12,076.00
Total Potential Charges	$101,776.00
Actual Charges:	
69/d × $400/d TPN	27,600.00
24/d × 6 hr × $13/hr	1,872.00
20/d × 4 hr × $13/hr	1,040.00
Case management fees:	1,455.00
Total Actual Charges:	**$ 31,967.00**
Net Savings (potential charges minus actual costs):	**$69,809.00**

HCMC #:	4256
Group:	Company X 123-91
Date of Referral:	5/31/90
Diagnosis:	Cirrhosis of Liver
Status:	Closed

Personal contact has been maintained with claimant and M.D. He remains in fairly stable condition and continues medical treatment for cirrhosis and counseling for alcoholism.

Intervention by case manager has reinforced need to maintain sobriety and to follow medical care in order to avoid exacerbation of symptomatology and rehospitalization which had occurred twice in previous quarter.

Savings are reflected in maintenance of outpatient care vs. inpatient hospitalizations.

Avoidance of Potential Charges:

3/d × $900/d	$2,700.00

Actual Charges:

Case management fees	610.00
Net Savings (potential charges minus actual costs):	**$2,090.00**

HCMC #:	4230
Group:	Company X 123-92
Date of Referral:	12/14/90
Diagnosis:	Athetoid Cerebral Palsy
Status:	Open

The father of this 16-year-old severely handicapped boy called TPA with concerns regarding special surgery that was being recommended for his son. There was no 2nd opinion program in place; however, the call was referred to Health Care Management Consultants for assistance. We provided him with the names of several orthopedic surgeons and urged the father to obtain at least one such opinion, and to contact us for any further problems and/or the outcome of the 2nd opinion consultation. He did obtain this evaluation by a physician with expertise in spastic paralysis (which was our suggestion). This physician strongly recommended against this, supported his reasons for this, and offered alternative treatment with braces, wheelchair modifications, etc. The family is in agreement with this, and Health Care Management Consultants will continue to assist with these alternatives.

Avoidance of Potential Charges:

1. Hospitalization for spinal surgery @ $1000/day × 15 days (minimum)	$15,000
2. Cost of spinal surgery	$10,000
3. Related costs—anesthesia, diagnostics, complications	$ 2,500
Total of Avoided Charges:	$27,500

Actual Charges:

Case management fees $ 500

Net Savings (potential charges minus actual charges): $27,000

Note: Other costs including case management fees, equipment will be incurred in the future and additional savings will be realized.

HCMC #:	5742
Group:	Company X 123-93
Date of Referral:	August 14, 1990
Diagnosis:	Malignant Neoplasm of Liver
Status:	Open

This case was identified following a review of pre-cert admissions as well as review of claims for company group. This woman had just had a 14-day admission for malnutrition and dehydration (this admission could have been reduced or even eliminated had a case manager been involved because early symptoms of a complication went untreated). Prior to this was a 3-week admission for surgery to abdomen for cancer of liver and surrounding organs. (This also could have been a shorter stay by providing same services at home.) This is a very complex case in that in addition to diagnosis of cancer, she has arthritis, cardiac disease, hypertension, and kidney disease. She was treated by several physicians and is taking many medications (some of which were contraindicated, specifically steroids). This now has been reviewed and discontinued, preventing further medical complications. Our role is now well understood and accepted by patient, family, and physicians, with patient calling us with concerns or problems.

Avoidance of Charges:

1. Prevention of complications (due to prolonged use
   of contraindicated medication) with resulting M.D.
   visits, diagnostic tests, and treatment $4,500

Actual Charges:

Case management fees $1,720

Net Savings (potential charges minus actual charges): $2,780

HCMC #:	3225
Group:	Company X 123-94
Date of Referral:	9/14/90
Diagnosis:	Coronary Heart Disease
Status:	Open

This case was identified during a review of claims for this group. Although not large amounts of money, it was possible that claimant was involved in an ongoing program for cardiac rehabilitation with no end in sight. There was no language in plan that would allow rejection of charges, nor was it clear as to the duration of services. Initial evaluation indicated claimant had been in program for one year and was planning to continue indefinitely. HCMC has met with claimant, M.D., and has recommended and obtained approval for more cost-effective and appropriate program. This program also contained stress and diet counseling, which was absent from the prior one and clearly indicated.

Avoided Charges:

1. Continuation of cardiac rehab—phase II
   $75/session × 3/week × 52 weeks $11,700.00

Actual Charges:

1. Phase III cardiac rehab program $700/year $700.00
2. Case management fees $1,395.00

Net Savings (avoided charges minus actual charges):   **$9,605.00**

HCMC #:	3226
Group:	Company X 123-95
Date of Referral:	11/2/90
Diagnosis:	Total Hip Replacement—Right Hip
Status:	Open

This case was identified for case management during review of pre-cert intake sheets when this woman was being scheduled for her third surgical procedure on her right hip. We were able to make contact with her and her physician prior to surgery, saw her at the hospital to assist in discharge plans a few days after surgery, and negotiated reduced fees for physical therapy and equipment at home. Early intervention insured timely discharge, a safe environment for recovery at home, and early physical therapy intervention prevented need for continued longer sessions of physical therapy at a later date. HCMC consultant also insured that family could assist in care of patient. This woman will be returning to her job within four to six weeks.

Avoidance of Charges:

1. Hospital discharge—prevention of additional 3 days
   of hospitalization due to our prompt intervention
   and implementing services at $850.00/day $2,550.00

2. Hospital discharge planner had recommended
   3 nursing visits @ $107 each and $321.00
   5 physical therapy visits at $100 each $500.00
3. Hospital recommended equipment via their provider $400.00
4. Extended physical therapy costs $100 × 2/week × 8 weeks $ 1,600.00
5. Prevention of rehospitalization due to fall and reinjury
   7 days at $850 $ 5,950.00
   • There were several hazards in home which HCMC discussed and
     had rectified by family

Total Avoided Charges: $11,321.00

Actual Charges:

1. Physical therapy at reduced fee of $75/visit × 3 visits $225.00
2. Rental of appropriate equipment at reduced rates $150.00
3. Case management fees $1,400.00

Total Actual Charges: $1,775.00

Net Savings (avoided charges minus actual charges):   **$9,546.00**

HCMC #:	3227
Group:	Company X 123-96
Date of Referral:	8/14/90
Diagnosis:	Uterine Carcinoma
Status:	Open

This case was identified during review of pre-cert admission sheets. The client had been admitted to hospital for "maintenance chemotherapy." The HCMC consultant met with claimant and oncologist to arrange for chemotherapy on an outpatient basis rather than inpatient. Both oncologist and patient were agreeable to this. There have been six of these sessions to date. Case management continues to monitor progress, insure prompt intervention in the event of problems, and offer ongoing support and encouragement. The claimant has returned to work part time to insure maximum income and benefits, which are allowing her to care for her 7-year-old son for whom she is the sole support.

Avoidance of Potential Charges:

1. Inpatient chemotherapy (DRG 410)
   $3,457 × 6 sessions $20,743.10

Actual Charges:

1. Outpatient chemotherapy
   $200 every 4 weeks × 6 months $4,800.00

2. Case management fees $2,400.00

Total Actual Charges: $7,200.00

Net Savings (avoided charges minus actual charges): **$13,543.00**

HCMC #:	3896
Group:	Company X 123-97
Date of Referral:	5/16/90
Diagnosis:	Brain Tumor
Status:	Closed

This claimant had surgical excision on benign brain tumor followed by biopsy of benign breast mass.

Health Care Management Consultants has maintained supportive contact with claimant postoperatively. She has recuperated without sequelae and has returned to work in timely fashion. She will continue periodic follow-up with neurosurgeon to monitor potential recurrence of tumor.

Even before Health Care Management Consultant's initial visit, consultant conferred with claimant by phone on several occasions and reinforced M.D. recommendations and health teaching because of past complications. Further complications were avoided and claimant was allowed to recuperate at her sister's home.

Cost savings are reflected in prompt uncomplicated recovery and reinforcement of health teaching.

Avoidance of Potential Charges:

Potential complications with repeat hospitalization
3/d × $1,500 (hospital, physician, & diagnostics) $4,500.00

Actual Charges:

Case management fees $611.00

Net Savings (potential charges minus actual charges): **$3,889.00**

HCMC #:	5428
Group:	Company X 123-98
Date of Referral:	1/29/90
Diagnosis:	Uncontrolled Diabetes Mellitus, CAD, Osteoarthritis, CHF, Thrombophlebitis, Asthma, Hypothyroidism
Status:	Transferred

This claimant has had only one hospitalization this quarter (substantial improvement) for intestinal disorder and abdominal hernia. Surgery was deferred because of claimant's poor medical history. Claimant has had better blood sugar control and other symptom control.

Replacement hospital bed was ordered and delivered at cost $1,777 vs $1,995. Oxygen concentration was rented at $175/month vs $450/month.

Health teaching and reinforcement of M.D. orders have improved claimant's compliance and symptomatology. Use of hospital bed and wheelchair has prevented injury and complications.

Savings are reflected in reduced hospital stays and equipment charges.

Avoidance of Potential Charges:

Potential hospitalization 3/d × $1,000	$3,000.00
Hospital bed $1,995 less $1,777 (negotiated price)	218.00
Oxygen concentration $450 × 3/m = $1,350 less $175 × 3/m = $525 (negotiated price)	825.00
Total Potential Charges:	$4,043.00
Actual Charges:	
Case management fees	1,502.00
Net Savings (potential charges minus actual charges):	**$2,541.00**

HCMC #:	5429
Group:	Company X 123-99
Date of Referral:	2/5/90
Diagnosis:	Bronchopulmonary Dysplasia
Status:	Open

This child has remained home with 12 hours × 5 days/week of R.N. care for persistent respiratory distress and oxygen dependency. Nursing care is necessary in lieu of acute hospitalization. O.T., S.T., P.T. provided by New York State Early Intervention program and arranged through Health Care Management Consultant's direct assistance at no cost to carrier or family.

Referral was made to and child accepted into CARE AT HOME program, a Medicaid Model Waiver program, retroactive to 5/1/90. CARE AT HOME should share costs of continued home care. Budget to be negotiated with vendor.

In worst case scenario, child would be hospitalized indefinitely.

Cost savings reflected in stabilization of medical expenses, coordination of care and supplies to prevent excess billings, and rehospitalization.

Avoidance of Potential Charges:

Potential hospital charge $1,200 × 90 days	$108,000.00
Total Potential Charges:	$108,000.00

Actual Charges:

Medical supplies and DME $2,426 × 3 months (negotiated from $5,000/month)	7,278.00
Nursing charge 12 hours x 60 days × $36/hr R.N. care (5d/wk)	25,920.00
• 30 days of additional nursing charges billed to CARE AT HOME program	(12,960.00)
• O.T., P.T., S.T.—$50/visit x 5/week × 12 weeks— billed to New York State Early Intervention program	(3,000.00)
Case management fees	1,332.00
Total Actual Charges:	$ 34,530.00
Net Savings (potential charges minus actual charges):	**$ 73,470.00**

HCMC #:	5430
Group:	Company X 123-100
Date of Referral:	1/2/90
Diagnosis:	Bronchopulmonary Dysplasia
Status:	Open

This child remains home vs hospitalization. R.N. care is provided 16 hours/day × 7 days plus oxygen and medical supplies. Child has expended $100,000 of nursing charges this year on or about September 10.

Referral has been made and approval granted for CARE AT HOME program retroactive to September 1, 1990. CARE AT HOME will share cost of home care with carrier and family and referral to and approval for this program was through direct and ongoing intervention by Health Care Management Consultants.

Cost savings are represented by prevention of hospitalization, reduced cost for DME and supplies, and stabilization of condition. Parents' requests for increased services have not been deemed warranted.

Avoidance of Potential Charges:

Potential hospitalization 90 days × $1,000	$90,000.00
Cost of P.T., O.T., S.T. $50 × 5/treatments/wk × 12 wk	$3,000.00
	$93,000.00

Actual Charges:

R.N. care 16 hours/day x 7 days @ $520/day × 90 days	$46,800.00
DME and supplies	15,600.00
	$62,400.00
Case management fees	1,072.00
Total Actual Charges:	$63,472.00
Net Savings (potential charges minus actual charges):	**$29,528.00**

HCMC #:	2378
Group:	Company X 123-101
Date of Referral:	8/8/90
Diagnosis:	Recurrent Brain Tumor Secondary to Lung Cancer
Status:	Closed

This claimant was recently diagnosed with recurrent malignant brain tumors and was treated with steroids with some improvement in symptomatology. His condition is terminal. He has been referred to Hospice. Health Care Management Consultants has researched hospice programs and assisted family with care planning based on claimant's specific current needs. Health Care Management Consultants supported family desire and ability to care for claimant at home and to prevent hospitalization. Claimant expired 9/15/91.

Cost savings determined by shortened hospital stay.

Avoidance of Potential Charges:

Potential prolonged hospitalization and ancillary charges 4 days × $1,200 day	$4,800.00

Actual Charges:

Case management fees	1,540.00
Net Savings (potential charges minus actual charges):	**$3,252.00**

Certificate #:	3724
Group:	Company X 123-102
Date of Referral:	8/18/90
Diagnosis:	Substance Abuse and Borderline Personality
Status:	Open

This claimant has been in day treatment at Central Hospital's Community Program.

Cost savings will be projected next quarter.

Case management fees:	$ 513.90

Certificate #:   5198
Group: Company X 123-103
Date of Referral: 7/12/90
Diagnosis: Cancer—Metastatic
Status: Transitional

This claimant has extensive metastatic cancer. Initial assessment was delayed due to claimant's delay in responding to Health Care Management Consultants.

Cost savings to be projected next quarter.

Case management fees $ 667.00

Courtesy of Options Unlimited, Case Management Services Division, Huntington, N.Y.

CHAPTER
11

Becoming Established as an Independent Case Manager

PROS AND CONS

As in other entrepreneurial endeavors, there are advantages and disadvantages in "going it alone," and one should evaluate these carefully before hanging out one's shingle. Thanks to some very important changes, both in health care and our economy, small businesses are on the rise. Although many succeed, some do not fare so well. Being given the opportunity for success will not automatically guarantee it, nor does being a truly excellent case manager guarantee profits.

Why then should one consider taking this step? The benefits are numerous. As the statistics bear out, case management has been and will continue to be one of the most effective tools in the growing array of cost-containment and quality assurance tools in the marketplace today. The large corporate giants are downsizing, and this trend has resulted in the creation and growth of numerous, smaller competitive companies. These companies are facing the same need to contain the costs related to illness and disability and are likely to use the services of smaller case management companies and even independent practitioners. Independents are certainly able to capture a share of this market, as these companies are not necessarily looking for the giants in the case management community.

To case managers who have worked in corporations, hospitals, and health care facilities, some of the problems that characterize large bureaucracies are evident. Too many layers of management, too many meetings, too many delays. ("I'll take that suggestion under advisement," "Let's table that for our next meeting.") Are there reasons for becoming an independent practitioner? Perhaps not, but bureaucratic aggravations frequently lead individuals to at least consider starting their own companies.

Autonomy is one advantage, but there are others. Creating and growing a company provides an opportunity to develop and use talents and skills, including marketing, public relations, financial management, negotiating, risk management, sales, accounting, personnel development, and human resources skills.

Then there are the financial considerations. No longer is it necessary to wait to be given a raise or a promotion, just write a check! Sound too good to be true? It is, but the opportunity for financial gain is most definitely there.

Given all of these wonderful advantages—autonomy, growth, creativity, and opportunity for success and wealth—what reason could there be for not going it alone? Unfortunately, the disadvantages are almost as numerous as the advantages.

Large organizations may have their problems, but they would not exist if they lacked value entirely. Their very size means that many outstanding professionals work side by side and are able to share their knowledge. When case managers leave this type of environment, they usually miss the camaraderie and the sharing.

Those individuals were not only colleagues, but many became friends. Friends to have lunch with, discuss goals and dreams with, commiserate with and have fun with. In addition to those who shared a profession (be it nurse, social worker, rehabilitation counselor), the case managers had other departments and their personnel and resources to draw from while learning and developing an area of expertise. The kind of isolation that comes with independence can truly be overwhelming when cases are not progressing as hoped, when client companies are upset about the time billed on a case, and potential clients, after extensive wooing, select another case management company. These things do happen and sometimes all in one day. Who can one share this with? Not with clients, who would feel anxious if they learned about such problems, nor with colleagues, who may also be competitors. A certain amount of isolation is unavoidable and needs to be addressed. It is easy to keep going when all is well but tougher when it is not.

Although starting a case management company provides an opportunity to create a business from the ground up, it does require learning about things that were of little use before but are now very important. Remember that big company? Aside from the medical staff, it also had departments and services that were probably taken for granted: purchasing, personnel, communications, public relations, and a business office. An independent case manager assumes other roles and performs other functions necessary to keep the business afloat. Remember also the security of knowing that a payroll check will come every two weeks? This, too, is no longer a "given." Neither is a two- or four-week vacation, paid holidays, or a medical and dental benefit package. In short, the financial security of being an employee has been traded for the *opportunity* for substantial gains—an opportunity that may never be realized.

ON YOUR MARK . . .

So much for the pros and cons of becoming an independent practitioner. After consideration of these factors and others, if there is still a determination to take the next step, what should that be? Creating a business plan should be the first move. Just as in case management, the strategy is to gather all of the necessary information, evaluate the situation, and identify the steps that will ensure a successful outcome. Looking at incorporating long- and short-term goals, it is then implemented, progress is monitored, and problems are identified and solved one by one. Why is a business plan necessary and does it need to be a lengthy formal document? Not really, especially if in the beginning the company will essentially be a one-person operation. But a case manager trying to coordinate care and services on behalf of 20–25 cases in different lines of insurance for several different client groups, needs to have the structure. Every business requires some kind of planning—a framework to provide ongoing direction.

DEVELOPING A BUSINESS PLAN

What should a business plan incorporate? Are there key components that every plan should have? Following is a list of important issues to address.

Type of Company. Should it be a full-service company? Should it be restricted to medical case management only? One type of insurance only (e.g., workers' compensation, liability, group medical)?

Location. Will the company provide services in one town or city? In one or several counties? In the entire state?

Size. Some case managers really only want to work cases themselves. They have no interest in taking on partners or hiring and supervising other case managers. Others are willing to make that next and very critical move: becoming an employer. Establishing limitations regarding size and number of cases right at the beginning is extremely important. A case manager with 25 cases might be offered 3, 5, or 10 more. Does she say "No, I don't want any more work," take them and be unable to work them, or be spread so thin that the quality of her work suffers? Or does she start thinking about getting a partner?

Financial Resources. Most small businesses require some kind of budget. In addition to salary, there are other expenses: telephone, rent, utilities, postage, office supplies, equipment, and furnishings. Depending on personal finances, a small business loan might need to be considered. A loan will assist in defraying some of the start-up costs and keep the business going until payments from accounts start coming in. If a large portion of business will be with insurance companies, third-party administrators, and other large groups, payment for services may not be received until 60–90 days after invoicing. This kind of delay can certainly result in financial strain, but it can be planned for instead of coming as a worrisome "surprise." As new accounts are acquired, assessing their financial status becomes as crucial as knowing one's own. To illustrate, one of my accounts is a third-party administrator with a consistently expanding client base. Although I was very excited to learn that all their clients would be using our case management services, that excitement soon turned to anxiety. Two of these accounts went into Chapter 11 (filed for bankruptcy). Another small group had their financial office review each payment before authorizing the third-party administrator to release the checks, and still another only funded its account every 60 days. The combination of lost payments and delays in reimbursement had a definite impact on my business, since I had already paid my staff for the work they had done. This example also demonstrates the need to have not only a financial plan but some contingency plans as well.

Short- and Long-Term Goals. In good case management, it is essential to define goals in order to ensure movement of a case toward a successful outcome. The same applies to business planning. Establish some attainable and maybe some not so attainable goals for the next year and for the next five and ten years. Obviously, changes in the heath care industry and the national or local economy may prevent the reaching of all goals in the planned time frame, but the goals should be set anyway. They will act as "benchmarks" for evaluating and re-evaluating the company's direction. Revising a business plan several times in a year or every few years is not a problem. Not having a plan most assuredly will be.

PRICING THE MARKET

One of the most difficult tasks a new case manager starting a business will have is determining how much to charge for the services provided.

Unfortunately, there are no hard and fast rules for setting prices. Some may believe that undercutting the competition will guarantee business, but this strategy can backfire. It may net a few cases from those who always look for the "cheapest of everything," but more will wonder why the prices are so low. The tendency will be to think services are probably not as good as those provided by other more established companies. Pricing services closer to the competition is actually a more astute business strategy, especially if the goal is to grow.

To illustrate further, let us say the going rate for case management services in your locale is $75 per hour. You are just starting out, working out of your home. You have no secretary (preparing your reports on your computer) and are managing all the cases yourself. You were making $20 per hour plus benefits in a case management company when you left to start your own business. You really want business, so you decide to charge $30 an hour and are looking forward to considerable profit. You also believe that if you charge $30 and others are charging $75, then you will definitely get business. And you do.

You continue and soon are up to 25 cases, cannot work any more yourself, and decide to hire your first staff case manager. She will be perfect, except for one thing: She cannot type. So you also hire a secretary. These two additions to your staff will not be able to work out of your home, so you move into a new office. You have thus, in a short period of time, increased your expenses more than your income. Now what? You need to raise your rates! How do you explain to your new accounts that you will now have to double your rates to $60 an hour or increase even more? An uncomfortable position to be sure—and one indicative of inexperience in business.

Discussions with your accountant or banker will be helpful in deciding a fair market value for your services. Whatever the rate decided upon, it should reflect your costs and allow you to generate a profit. A profit margin is desirable in order for you to continue to be able to upgrade and expand your business, unless, of course, you want to join the not-for-profit organizations or engage strictly in "pro bono" work.

There are various directories and other publications that list companies and provide information about their services and, in many instances, their current rates. The information is fairly reliable, but keep in mind that many of the listed companies may be large, provide several kinds of cost-containment services, or have a national capability, and the costs of any extra services will be built into their hourly rates. So while published rates may be helpful, a company's own rates should really reflect its cost of doing business, rather than being a mirror image of the competition.

LOOKING AT THE COMPETITION

Every case management company and independent practitioner must consider others in the community who are in the same field. This can be intimidating, but it can also provide an awareness that case management is a growing industry.

Competition is good. It keeps case managers on their toes and helps them stretch toward excellence. Also, "breaking into" the marketplace may be easier if there are others who have gone before. Being the only provider of a service does *not* guarantee a company the entire market and may in fact create more problems. Why? Because there is reluctance on the part of purchasers to buy an unknown, no matter how good it may sound. They are inclined to think, "Let the others buy it first, and then we can see how they like it."

Fortunately, case management is already a tried and true service. Others have gone before and have demonstrated its worth. The object, then, is to establish a niche among competitors. Rather than being afraid of what they are doing, learn to seek knowledge about what is already out there.

Knowledge about competitors is not difficult to come by. Attending conferences and visiting the exhibitors area will provide firsthand information. Large companies usually print brochures and other handouts that describe their services and list their office locations, areas of specialization, and occasionally even their fees. Smaller regional or local companies will also have marketing handouts, and these should be reviewed carefully to discover exactly what these companies are selling to potential clients. Similarities and differences in services offered can be utilized to help define one's own corporate identity.

Being knowledgeable about the competition and their various activities is part of being in business. Although "hot off the press" information is not always available, information about changes in competitors' client base, rate changes, and innovative services and approaches can be gleaned from various sources. Of most importance is how the competition responds to change. Changes in workers' compensation programs, employer involvement in benefit plans, wellness promotion, management approaches to high-cost conditions (e.g., high-risk pregnancies, AIDS, etc.), and outcomes research will influence the direction of case management. How each company responds to these changes will obviously be different, and there is much to be learned from the successes and the failures of colleagues.

The successful approaches will eventually be described in articles in industry publications (e.g., *The Case Manager, Business & Health, Business In-*

surance, and *Risk Management),* or in presentations at various conferences. Keeping abreast, therefore, is as easy as attending conferences and reading industry periodicals. Attending conferences, in addition to updating one's clinical and business knowledge, also affords a wonderful opportunity to interact with competitors in a social environment. Sharing experiences and frustrations frequently results in an enhanced ability to view problems and challenges more objectively and move toward resolution.

For instance, in a recent breakout session of a case management conference, there were several case managers representing the national and regional companies as well as independent practitioners. This session was focused on the "business" aspects of case management. There was discussion of billing, including the various approaches used to bill for services and client responses to bills. Interestingly, despite the differences in invoice formats and hourly rates, we learned that we did actually have something in common. Each of us at one time or another had a client who called to question some aspect of a bill. "Did it really take four-tenths of an hour to make that phone call?" "Couldn't you have done it in one-tenth or two-tenths of an hour?" "Company X never charged me for that and you do."

From the conversation, during which we shared the all too familiar "war stories" of client objections, it became apparent that case management is being looked at closely. Our results and our costs are being examined. It also became apparent that the main cause of client discontent over billing was not skepticism about the efficacy of the services or the reasonableness of the bills but rather lack of documentation. By discussing how to prepare cost-benefit analysis reports, we reviewed how to draft documents that demonstrated the benefits of case management intervention as well as its ability to contain costs. This sharing of information among various case management providers uncovered the solution to a very real problem.

Wasn't this "helping" the competition? Isn't that a business no-no? Aren't we supposed to hope competitors fail and then grab their clients? There was a time when I engaged in that kind of thinking. Although not actively hoping that anyone would fail, I had ambivalent feelings about sharing any of my knowledge with the competition. Experience gained over many years has helped me to view the issue of sharing somewhat differently. If the providers of case management services become better at what they do, then the viability of case management is assured. Since sharing information improves the performance of practitioners, it enhances the status of the entire case management industry and makes it more likely any given practitioner will survive.

What about those in our industry who, in our judgment, may be doing it a disservice? This includes those who may have different business practices or who may attempt to garner clients by waging a price war or who may just not be good providers. How should one react when potential clients cite these case managers as the norm? Perhaps a client has had a very bad experience with such a provider and now assumes that all case managers are the same. This certainly is a problem and merely dismissing it doesn't make it go away. We are all part of the good and not so good in this business. Acknowledging that there are good, mediocre, and even bad providers of case management is no different a consideration than in any other product line or area of service. As in other businesses, it is never a good idea to knock the competition. This tactic does not automatically elevate one's own status. When a case manager is confronted with negative comments, her best strategy is to acknowledge the concern without either confirming or denying the information. This enables her to maintain control of the conversation and discuss what must be communicated, that is, her ability to provide competent and appropriate case management services.

In reality, competition should be viewed as just another factor in the world of business. Undue importance given to competitors limits an individual's or company's creativity and ability to survive and excel. There are, of course, plenty of large, well-financed, diversified case management companies, but not every client needs that kind of company. For every big client, there are smaller clients just waiting to hear how a small case management company can help them.

NETWORKING AND THE PROFESSIONAL COMMUNITY

Developing and maintaining contacts in the case management and business community is essential for survival. Having the ability to communicate and share information with members of the professional and business sector will enhance one's capabilities. It is often easy within one's own profession (be that nurse, counselor, social worker, or other) because one shares a common "language" and similar experiences. These become comfortable associations. Reaching outside the case management profession to individuals and organizations not concerned with health care, rehabilitation, or insurance may be somewhat intimidating.

The importance of professional alliances in the workplace is recognized by everyone. In a hospital and other traditional health care setting, a health care provider in one department may need to consult with someone in another department in order to deal with a particular problem. For example, although nurses may possess an understanding of nutritional needs, few would have the extensive dietary education to care for a diabetic without assistance. A call, however, to the dietary department is all that is needed to arrange for a bedside visit, educational materials, and even classes for the patient from a nutritionist or registered dietitian upon discharge. Again, although nurses can assess respiratory function and detect sounds indicative of impending complications, the actual respiratory treatments are most often administered by a respiratory therapist. A social worker on a rehabilitation unit will have as a member of the team a physician and occupational therapist, who will provide the input needed for appropriate therapeutic service and equipment for a post-CVA (cerebral vascular accident) patient. Such associations and contacts are inherent to the multidisciplinary approach in rehabilitation facilities and hospitals.

For case managers, especially those outside traditional settings, professional associations are no less important but perhaps more difficult to establish and maintain. It requires time and research to develop a network and creativity to nurture relationships. Furthermore, the networking process needs to be ongoing. Today one may have two head injury patients in a caseload, but six months from now these cases may be closed. Who should be contacted to assess the needs of the next head-injury patient? Will the neuropsychologist used for the last assessment still be in private practice or will she have joined the staff of a head injury facility two states away?

Given all of the mergers, acquisitions, and closings of health care organizations, keeping key contacts is a never-ending challenge. Interestingly, however, over the years many of the relationships that I established still exist today. Some of these individuals have moved into new companies or now hold different positions yet continue to be colleagues and invaluable assets.

Ten years ago, when I started my own firm, I was feeling somewhat insecure about its standing as a brand-new company. I wondered if any reputable insurance carrier, like Aetna or Travelers, would be "allowed" to assign cases to me. The claims manager with whom I had met must have sensed my concern as I nervously inquired, "Don't you have to get this approved?" and "Will your home office have a problem with an unknown?" In reply, he said something that, over the years, has provided me with the confidence to approach potential clients: "We don't do business with Intracorp or Crawford. We do business with Catherine Mullahy or Jane Doe. Names may get you in the door but they won't sustain a working relationship."

Strong relationships lead to other relationships, and gradually a business network is created and expands. For example, early in my career I was assigned a man who was rendered quadriplegic at the fourth and fifth cervical vertebrae following an automobile accident. When referred to the company that employed me as a rehabilitation specialist, he was on a ventilator in a small community hospital. He had been in its ICU for two months, and the referring carrier requested an evaluation. At the time, rehabilitation facilities were few and far between, and those that would even consider accepting a ventilator-dependent patient were very rare.

This forty-two year old man and his family desperately wanted him home, and the carrier obviously did not relish having him endlessly confined in an ICU. An aggressive pursuit of a pulmonary rehabilitation program began. After endless telephone calls, evaluation of records by various facilities in surrounding states, and one refusal after another to accept the patient, discouragement and frustration surfaced. I could not, however, forget the visit to the hospital with this man's wife and their four children. I prepared them for the fact that we might not be able to find a suitable facility. They would not accept defeat and said they just "knew" I would help. I was willing to keep trying, but how long would the carrier allow my pursuit of an appropriate placement? On my own time, I continued the search. I made numerous calls to other nurses, to physicians with whom I had worked years before, and to spinal cord programs on the West Coast to see if they knew MDs on the East Coast who specialized in this narrow field.

One night on the evening news, there was a feature highlighting a young spinal cord victim who was treated in a facility headed by a physiatrist (i.e., a physician with a specialization in physical medicine and rehabilitation) who was also a pulmonary specialist. Here might be the answer to my problem. The next morning, I called the news station and found out the name of the physician and the facility and crossed my fingers as I made a call. After giving an overview of the pertinent factors and the family situation, I asked if the physician would at least see my patient to determine if our rehabilitation goals were even feasible. Thankfully, he agreed to see my patient personally and accepted him into the facility.

It was a highly successful intervention and my patient eventually returned home, using the ventilator only during hours of sleep. The discharge planning nurse worked closely with me in transitioning this man back to his community and into the care of his wife and intermittent nursing services. The physician was compassionate, dedicated, and of great assistance to me. Over the years he changed hospitals several times but continued to do independent medical exams for me and has been a fellow presenter at conferences and a resource to me in countless situations. And the discharge planning nurse? She, too, has moved several times during these past 15 years. We kept in touch, and 7 years ago she became a regional rehabilitation nurse with a national insurance carrier. A few years later, she was promoted to home office rehabilitation coordinator and became one of my corporate clients. She now refers cases to us for case management services! It is indeed a small and interesting world, and I never dreamed that these associations started so long ago would continue to be so professionally fruitful.

Many professional associations turn into friendships, and, just as in one's personal life, such relationships deserve extra consideration. This does not mean lavish gifts, expensive lunches, or other such gestures, which may be deemed as potential causes of conflict of interest. Sending a note to an associate expressing appreciation and an acknowledgement to his or her supervisor or company are always acceptable and should become a standard networking plan. Additionally, referrals of other patients or colleagues to an associate, as long as there is no monetary payment in return, is a professional way to express recognition of his or her expertise, quality of service, and willingness to work with you in a case management endeavor. Not all case managers have frequent opportunities to refer, but fortunately there are other ways to nurture professional contacts. These include sharing articles of interest, advising associates of seminars, and extending invitations to associates to speak to professional groups or client companies who would welcome their insight. Professional contacts are an important aspect of the case management practice but when viewed as another link in the process leading to success, they can be both rewarding and enjoyable.

THE BUSINESS COMMUNITY

Most case managers today have some interaction with individuals in the business community and are with increasing frequency being recognized for their contributions toward the attainment of the goals of increasing quality and containing costs. Because the business sector pays the largest share of health care costs, a closer alliance between case managers and this concerned group is essential. The object should be not only to improve individual working relationships but to increase the public's awareness of case management in general.

Although most health care professionals know about case management, few business people do, despite its proven success. Interestingly, however, when business people are told what case managers do and the results they obtain, their response is usually extremely positive. They then ask, "Why isn't my company using this kind of service?" "How come there aren't more case managers?" and "Why has this been kept a secret?" Why, indeed?

Part of the answer is that case managers have failed to communicate the benefits of their services to those in the business community. The actual providers of case management services are usually linked to business organizations by individuals who are not case managers. For instance, an employer group needs a package of benefits for its employees. Depending on several factors, including economic feasibility, medical benefits will be provided through a fully insured, partially funded, or completely self-funded (by the group) plan. The group will appoint from within or will contract someone to purchase the kind of plan it feels it can offer and afford. An insurance carrier, a third-party administrator, or the employer group itself will administer the plan and pay the claims. None of the individuals involved thus far in this process is likely to be a case manager.

Soon, as the plan design evolves, there may be discussion of cost-containment techniques, including those of managed care. However, the terms *case management* and *case manager* may never be heard. PPOs, HMOs, and pre-cert, utilization review, and second opinion programs will probably come up in conversation, since they have become relatively well known and well understood. But case management presents a challenge.

Only recently has a standard definition of case management been created—by CIRSC, the regulatory body responsible for the Certified Case Manager designation. Not only were the professionals struggling to define their own role and process, but those who purchased, used, were recipients of, or interacted with case management services were also confused. Is it any wonder, then, that *case management* is not a household word? Add to this the fact that even though case management finally has been defined, those who market case management services are usually from outside the field. They work in insurance, marketing, or finance and tend to tell potential client groups merely that the big cases will be "managed." Unfortunately for the case management professional or company, this kind of characterization is fraught with problems.

Because most managed care tools exist as a system, services are paid for on a capitated basis (per employee per month). Case management services, on the other hand, tend to be billed per hour or per case. If employees and their dependents are unaware of a case management program, then when contact with an employee is initiated through a telephone call or a letter, the response might be, "No, thank you" or "I don't think I need you." The employee may call his or her supervisor or the human resource department, who may not know of the program either. The human resource department may then call the broker or insurance company account representative, who will attempt to sort out the confusion. Wouldn't it have been better for everyone to have known about the case management program right from the start? Most assuredly yes, but even knowledge of the program is not enough. What is really needed is communication from case managers.

For example, case managers need to submit articles to business publications, join community and business group coalitions to address health care concerns, and meet with business and health care leaders to tell them about the advantages of case management programs. Case managers need to be more involved in positioning themselves as part of the solution to the country's health care crisis. As health care reform evolves, many segments of society will be examining the details and looking to see how the changes will impact them directly. The business community, too, will be part of this process. Even in small towns, businesses have formed associations and committees. Such groups frequently look for guest speakers or for experts to join a panel discussion on a health care topic. Open exchanges lend themselves readily to the exploration of problems and solutions.

By calling or visiting the local chamber of commerce, one can acquire lists of member organizations and information about any special health or insurance committees. Because case management today is utilized by most lines of insurance, employer groups need to know that case managers understand their concerns and can help prevent continuing escalation of costs.

Local and regional business periodicals are available by subscription or may be reviewed at the local library. They provide insight into particular areas or issues of concern and afford opportunities to respond, such as by sending letters to the editor, to the authors of articles, and to individuals mentioned in articles. Initiating a correspondence on a topic or issue can lead to an ongoing dialogue and perhaps will create a new client for case management services.

Besides gaining new clients through involvement with the business community, case managers can enhance their ability to manage a business and ultimately achieve success. Because many case managers do not have a business background, relationships with business people are often invaluable. By observing how others resolve business problems, case managers become more comfortable grappling with them. They can also learn about hiring techniques, computers, financial management, recruitment, training, marketing, and legal issues by attending business seminars and meeting with individuals who provide the services necessary for the business operations.

A case management business in reality is much like other businesses and has many of the same requirements. It is necessary to be aware of personal and business limitations and contract or arrange for assistance in dealing with critical day-to-day management issues. Obviously, restrictions (usually financial) may prevent the hiring of the appropriate experts. For example, a public relations or marketing consultant could assist in the creation and expansion of a business, but, especially in the early days, hiring such a person may not be feasible. Growth might be slower than otherwise, but not hiring a consultant is unlikely to create a crisis. On the other hand, a lack of understanding of or comfort with the financial aspects of business can indeed pose a serious threat to the viability of an operation. If expenses exceed income or if taxes or bills are not paid in a timely manner, the consequences can be devastating. In short, whereas some aspects of business can be learned and developed over time, others require immediate attention.

The best place to start finding answers to questions and solutions to problems is right within one's own community. The local chamber of commerce helps businesses to network and is always supportive of new owners. So, too, is SCORE (Service Core of Retired Executives), a group that provides assistance to start-up businesses. The local branch will be listed in the government section of the Yellow Pages. There are myriad government services and resources available to business owners at the federal, state, and local level. Contact can be made by letter or phone or a personal appointment can be scheduled. Private-sector services are also available, often for free or for a nominal fee. Most newspapers have business calendars that list dates, times, locations, and fees for a wide variety of seminars, meetings, and discussion groups. Attending such forums provides an opportunity to explore (without serious financial commitment) services that may be of interest and meet the providers.

Case managers try to empower patients (who are consumers of health care services) by furnishing the necessary background and describing the alternatives so they can make informed decisions. Because owners of case management companies are consumers of business services and products, it makes sense that they should try to empower themselves through the acquisition of information so that business decisions are sound ones. Information empowers one to be a more astute business manager. All the assistance they require to do this is available; they only need to access it.

GENERATING NEW BUSINESS

Because even successful businesses experience peaks and valleys, having a plan to generate new clients is always important. Relationships with good clients can extend over many years, of course, and this is indeed fortunate, because known entities are usually easier for both the provider of case management services and the recipient company(ies) to work with. Owing to the complexity of case management, the number of players involved, and the need to individualize each case management program, it is highly desirable to maintain longstanding associations. This ideal, however, is not always possible. Occasionally, business associations end, even the most successful of associations. For example, a referral source, who is a branch manager of the claims department, and a key contact and focal point of referrals to a case management company, receives a promotion to district manager and moves to a different geographic location. Her replacement is a woman who has had a long and successful association with a different case management group, and it is this company that she will continue to utilize. In this era of mergers and acquisitions, it is also possible that a local referral source (an employer group, third-party administrators, or carrier) may be acquired by another entity which may already have a case management program in place and no need to alter that arrangement.

So what can be done to prepare for the loss of clients? Realize that it can happen tomorrow. Create a plan to generate new business and integrate the plan with the overall business plan. Like the entire business plan, the plan for generating new business needs to be developed thoughtfully, with a budget in mind, expected goals and time frames in place, and a way to evaluate the success of the efforts. The process includes many steps, but the following five are probably the most basic.

Establishing Referral Sources

Who exactly are the referral sources for a case management business? Insurance carriers, employer groups, attorneys, third-party administrators, counties, municipalities, states, the federal government, and individual consumers are current users of case management services. Following the inevitable reform of health care, there are likely to be others.

Various industry and business periodicals provide the names of specific companies that have case management programs. Perhaps there are branch offices or subsidiaries that would be referral sources. Articles citing problems in administering workers' compensation or employee medical plans can be used to identify companies that are probably not aware of the case management solution. It makes sense to get in touch with them and share the good news.

Such an opportunity presented itself to me approximately two years ago. I had sent a packet of information to a start-up third-party administrator in my community. With it was a letter congratulating the new company, wishing them success, and providing an overview of case management. I pointed to the win-win scenario that could be created by adding case management to the company's set of tools and even outlined a high-cost case with and without case management. Allowing the claims administrator some time to review my proposal, I followed up with a telephone call about a week later. He thought it was all "very nice" but felt he was dealing with small employer groups with "healthy employees" and probably would not need case management services. He further stated that he had hospital and physician networks (PPOs) with "great discounts" and thought he was in great shape. Our discussion continued but I was unable to change his mind.

However, several months later, the claims administrator saw an article that I had submitted to a publication for self-insurers and third-party administrators called *The Self-Insurer*. He read it over a weekend, thought it made great sense, and intended to try to contact the author when he got into his office on Monday. He looked at the name, thought it looked familiar, and sure enough found the author was the very same person who had sent him information months ago. He did, in fact, call me, related the story, and admitted that he was now having "some problems," as I had suspected he would. We arranged a few meetings, and we now enjoy a mutually beneficial association. So the direct marketing approach did not initially work, but it did pave the way for an eventual business relationship.

Opportunities like this really are out there and one needs to be prepared to seize the moment. While telephone conversations and articles and letters are all helpful, marketing materials will be important in creating and sustaining an image, which leads us to:

Preparing Marketing Materials

Most case managers will want to contract for assistance in designing and implementing a marketing plan and creating a company image. As with most other aspects in the business plan, marketing will likely be done in stages and within certain financial parameters. A new business will probably not be able to afford multipage and multicolor brochures, yet well-designed business cards and stationery are an absolute must for even the smallest of companies. Selecting a company name and corporate logo is a matter of individual preference, but the advice of a public relations or marketing consultant could be extremely helpful. This does *not* necessarily mean using the largest and most high-profile public relations or advertising firm in one's community. There are many small consulting companies that specialize in the health care market, and they offer many options, even packages of services for discounted fees (e.g., a business card, a corporate logo, stationery, and a simple brochure outlining the proposed services). Purchasing a package of services increases the chance that everything will be well coordinated and focused.

When I first started my company more than ten years ago, I only had enough money for the design of my corporate logo, business cards, and stationery. It was almost two years later before a corporate brochure was created. At that time, my business was restricted mainly to workers' compensation and auto insurance cases; group medical cases were just starting to be referred. It was my feeling the claimants had minimal understanding of case management and frequently did not hear about us until months after an injury, sometimes only after litigation was also involved. For the group medical insurance referrals, case management was a brand-new approach. Because the response to case management by claimants would help make or break us, our first brochure (Exhibit 11-1) was designed specifically for claimants and their families and not the actual payers. However, I also used it successfully to interest potential clients. It was reader-friendly, had an easy-to-understand question and answer format, and showed us to be proactive (something extremely important to me) and cost conscious (something extremely important to our clients). It has been modified over the years but remains an integral component of our marketing package. In general, our marketing efforts and direction have evolved and will continue to evolve in response to the ongoing changes in our industry.

Targeting New Business Goals

Although it is important to maintain current business, it is always necessary to identify potential sources of new business. This is a challenging process, one of discovery and innovation. Determining specific new business targets is accomplished through matching one's strengths and areas of expertise with segments of the business community that could utilize such expertise. To be able to capitalize on the many opportunities, one needs to keep current in one's own practice setting (whether this is oncology, AIDS, high risk pregnancy, etc.) and current within the business community. What are the problems yet to be resolved? How could case management respond? What types of partnerships could be created that would facilitate the provision of services? There are immediate targets for case management services today, and on the horizon are potential users waiting to be identified. This is the excitement of our industry!

Creating and Maintaining Relationships with Referral Sources

Most case management companies initially grow one case at a time and then expand in larger increments as new case management programs are created based on the successful cases. When starting a business, therefore, it is very important to identify and accept the kinds of cases that present the most potential for success, both in terms of medical outcome and savings.

Although we all welcome a challenge and would like to be able to demonstrate that we can do what others cannot, we do not want to attempt the "impossible." Some cases are beyond anyone's capabilities—like that of the patient who is two years postinjury; who has had two surgical interventions, four hospitalizations, ongoing physical therapy, and psychological counseling; whose employer has no light-duty program; and whose union is in a contract dispute with management. And the claims examiner is already demanding that this case be resolved. This clearly is a challenge to avoid.

Exhibit 11–1 Options Unlimited Patient Brochure

WHAT DO I DO NOW?

Call us. Every case is unique and will be considered in a FREE preliminary screening.

If you decide to contract for our consulting services, you can be assured that OPTIONS offers a personalized service and medically knowledgeable people who will deal with you as an individual. With OPTIONS, you will have a friend and confidant, as well as a medical expert.

HEALTH CARE AND DISABILITY MANAGEMENT SERVICES

HEALTH CARE AND DISABILITY MANAGEMENT SERVICES
(516) 673-1150

Catherine M. Mullahy
President

Catherine Mullahy has twenty-six years of experience in health care management in both hospital and corporate settings.

Her diversified nursing experience includes work in multiple trauma, medical/surgical, cardiac, orthopedic and neurologic conditions.

She is the founder and President of OPTIONS UNLIMITED, a health care and disability management company. Her consulting firm possesses national capability, and works with corporations, private carriers, government agencies, and individuals. She has written for national publications, serves as a consultant to insurance companies and providers, and lectures frequently on a variety of topics in the disability management field.

Catherine Mullahy and OPTIONS UNLIMITED offer you a timely and cost efficient program whose specialty is caring.

COST-EFFECTIVE
INDIVIDUAL
CASE MANAGEMENT SERVICES
medical, emotional
and vocational

CATHERINE M. MULLAHY, PRESIDENT
76 EAST MAIN STREET
HUNTINGTON, NEW YORK 11743
(516) 673-1150
FAX 516-673-8369

(continues)

Exhibit 11–1 continued

WHAT IS OPTIONS UNLIMITED?

We are a medically knowledgeable consulting firm that serves the special needs of patients and their families, nationally.

HEALTH CARE AND DISABILITY MANAGEMENT SERVICES

WHAT DOES OPTIONS DO?

We act as the patient advocate to ensure an injured or ill person's return to wellness in the shortest possible time at the lowest possible cost.

HOW DO WE ACCOMPLISH OUR GOALS?

We serve as liaison between the patient, physician, therapist, insurance company and employer, coordinating all facets in order that each patient may return to a productive life.

WHY DO YOU NEED OPTIONS?

When injury or illness strikes, common reactions of the patient and family are shock, panic, and especially, confusion.

They don't know who to talk to, what questions to ask or where to go for help. They are also insecure with the unfamiliarity of medical language at a time when they become completely dependent on the medical community.

A physician simply cannot spend enough time with the family to help them understand the complex problems involved in catastrophic injury/illness cases.

OPTIONS helps the patient and the family to cope with the medical, insurance, social, emotional, vocational and financial problems related to the injury or illness.

SPECIFICALLY, WHAT DOES OPTIONS DO TO ASSIST YOU?

• Secure proper medical care and equipment

• Prevent inappropriate or excessive treatment

• Expedite facility/home placement and care

• Inform insurance company of your condition and treatment

• Help your family to understand and to adjust

• Find community resources to work on your behalf

• Coordinate and provide necessary follow-up treatment

• Remain available to you and your family for reassurance and counseling

WHO WILL PAY FOR THIS SERVICE?

If your insurance company has referred you to us, they will be billed for our services.

If you contact us directly or if you are referred by your doctor or others involved in your care, we will contact your insurance carrier; if there is no coverage, you will be billed. In all cases, we will outline a clear plan for coordinating your care with an easy-to-understand rate schedule.

WON'T USING OPTIONS JUST CREATE GREATER EXPENSE?

Even if your insurance company does not cover case management services, OPTIONS can usually save you money in medical and related costs. We help you get back to the business of living.

DOES OPTIONS SERVE ONLY SEVERE ILLNESS/INJURY CASES?

Although OPTIONS specializes in catastrophic, chronic, and complex medical problems, we have experience in a wide variety of disabilities - pediatric through geriatric.

This does not mean taking only "easy" cases, because the easy ones do not usually require case management and asking for them sets one up for comments such as "Well, this guy probably would have gone back to work without you." There are, however, many cases in between the two extremes. Case managers also have the potential to create opportunities for success by knowing and then communicating the red flags that indicate the need for case management (see Chapter 9).

If one referral has been successfully case managed, it should be relatively easy to obtain others. Likewise, if one good relationship with a referral source in a company has been established, it should be easier to establish others with individuals in the same company. For instance, following positive outcomes and after proving the value of case management to one claims examiner in a workers' compensation department, a case manager could ask if there were other examiners who might consider using case management services. Does this carrier also write auto or group medical insurance? It would also be a good tactic to ask the initial referral source to write a letter of recommendation or allow him- or herself to be used as a reference. Most individuals who are pleased with the results of case management are only too happy to provide an endorsement, giving credibility to a service that in many cases is still an unknown. Because no one wants to be the first customer, a firm endorsement by one person or company encourages others to try the services being offered.

Expressing appreciation for past and current business is important in maintaining ongoing associations and generating new referrals. If such appreciation is not communicated regularly, client groups soon feel less than valued. Sharing information about conferences or articles that might be of interest is one way to expand relationships. So, too, is seeking expert help from associates, perhaps to clarify a claims matter. I have learned most about the complexities of all the lines of insurance our company is now involved with from individuals who started as clients and over the years have become colleagues.

Initially, I had a need to know, and thankfully there were those who had a desire to share their very special knowledge. This collaboration truly was synergistic in that both parties had something to offer and gain from the association; together there was a stronger unit than either possessed as a single entity. With one of these colleagues, I have presented at conferences. She, at my suggestion, was a presenter at a case management conference, and we anticipate coauthoring a book.

All these techniques have helped me to expand my own business, and they are quite viable for the new and even established businesses which want to create new markets or expand existing ones.

Reaching Decision Makers

Even the best marketing plan, impressive marketing materials, and savvy marketing strategies will not necessarily generate business unless the individual who can authorize and pay for case management services can be convinced of their value.

Case management services, unfortunately, are usually placed in the "loss" column by most companies. Most potential clients will be reluctant to pay out additional money for services that, at least until they prove their worth, merely offer the promise of containing costs. Furthermore, the services will not necessarily ease the bureaucratic workload but may in fact require more direct involvement on the part of company staff. Companies are also more inclined to buy products or services that will generate more business and money for them, and case management is not one of these, at least not in the early stages.

Once case management services are established and successful, it is certainly easier to gain work, but what about those first cases? The claims examiner may be a case manager's main contact but will not likely be the individual who can create or allow for the expansion of case management programs. How does one identify and get to the decision maker? By keeping alert, asking questions, and paying attention to the market.

Reaching the individual who has overall fiscal responsibility is not always an easy process but is well worth the effort. Start at the very top—by approaching the CEO or president of the group. If the CEO does not have day-to-day responsibility for health care matters but someone else does (e.g., the chief financial officer, or director of insurance), then this other person will usually be directed to respond to the approach. If one starts at the middle management level, then the person contacted often has to go upwards to obtain an okay. Not only that, but requesting assistance (and money) is often perceived as a reflection of poor management. It puts the individual in the position of having to acknowledge a problem and an inability to solve it alone. Few will voluntarily place themselves in this situation and so the decision to use case management will likely be deferred.

HIRING ADDITIONAL STAFF

Success brings with it new questions and new issues. Growth for many reasons can be troublesome and so requires a good deal of planning. The first issue may be whether to hire another case manager or remain a one-person company. The decision to hire is possibly one of the most difficult for the entrepreneur case manager. It means relinquishing some of the control over case management activities, delegating some of the responsibilities, and, perhaps the most challenging of all, introducing customers to someone who they may perceive as not quite as good as the expert they have become accustomed to working with.

Another possible issue is whether to accept cases in a broader geographical area than previously covered.

Let us assume that a caseload of 18–25 is manageable: the case manager can effectively direct and support elements required for each of those cases. She can stay on top of each case, make enough money to pay the bills, and take regular days off and maybe even some vacation time. Perhaps a few more cases can be handled by putting in a few extra hours or a few extra-long days. But then several "quiet" cases all of a sudden become very active. At this point, a prospective client calls and says he has 8 to 10 cases put aside. (Where was he when the caseload was down to 10?) The time is *now*; a decision must be made. Should the case manager accept these cases and plan to work 15–18 hours a day? Not if she plans to be around for a few years and certainly not if she plans to continue to be able to provide quality, timely interventions and manage cases rather than be managed by them.

Nothing says the case manager must hire staff and build the company. Some case managers are comfortable setting limits, advising customers that 20 or 25 is the maximum number of cases they want, and then suggesting the name of colleagues who might be able to assist. However, there are good reasons to expand—the challenge, the opportunity to provide services to more people in need, the potential to expand use of case management, and of course the possible financial rewards that might be realized.

Hiring individuals who have the necessary expertise and who share the same philosophy, work ethic, and business goals is highly desirable. Finding such individuals, however, is not always easy. One essential step in the process is to clarify just what it takes to be a case manager. Unfortunately, because case management is evolving, it is difficult to succinctly set out all the job's elements.

As already mentioned, there now exists a credentialing process and certification standards (see also Chapter 12), but limiting the search to case managers with the CCM credential would exclude many fine candidates from employment. The credentialing process is a new one, and even experienced professionals, for a variety of reasons, have not yet heard about the process. Examinations are administered twice yearly, and as individuals meet the basic requirements, they will have the opportunity to obtain a CCM.

Experienced case managers who understand all the lines of insurance, have had a diversified clinical background prior to case management, and have worked in a variety of traditional and nontraditional settings would be the best candidates, right? Not necessarily. I have hired case management professionals from competitors and carriers and I have hired nurses who I thought possessed excellent potential but lacked on-line case management experience. For me, it has been easier, though not always trouble-free, to hire and train individuals who have no case management experience. When bringing in individuals with prior experience, I found it was often difficult to convince them to put aside the business practices (billing, need to attain a set number of hours each week) and philosophies of previous employers. Or they had only handled workers' compensation or liability cases and could not keep the return-to-work goal out of our group medical insurance cases. It has generally been easier to train rather than untrain.

Further, professional experience, credentials, published papers, and a multitude of degrees do not guarantee success. I used to be intimidated when applicants would submit incredibly impressive resumés, would know what our salary limitations were (as a small company they were restrictive), yet would want to interview for a position. A few PhDs in particular stand out in my mind. It did not take me long to realize they would fail to make it. These candidates had assimilated all of the theory, could quote studies and statistics, but would not have been able to understand, in my judgment, nor work within the confines of the workers' compensation law of our state. Does this mean that no one with a PhD can be a case manager? Not at all, but it does mean that one has to look beyond credentials, impressive resumés, and accomplishments. At the same time, when I interview individuals who are not experienced case managers, this does not mean they are perceived as people with no experience. In my judgment, case management work is complex, demanding, and challenging. Not every individual can do it, even with training. There are professional attainments and personal characteristics that increase the likelihood of success in this field and personal characteristics that almost preclude success.

Professional Background

The type of professional background staff should have will partly depend on the type of case management services offered. A company that provides a broad range of medical case management services will need staff members with diversified clinical experience. If it works mainly within the group medical insurance area, it should probably hire mostly nurses. This does not mean that only nurses can provide case management intervention; other allied professionals have much to contribute. However, the typical cases referred to case management are high cost and medically complex, and nurses, in my opinion, are better prepared to handle the many responsibilities that are required.

Of course, not everyone licensed to practice as a nurse has the depth and diversification of educational and clinical background that supports good case management. While the length of time that one has been a nurse is important, time and grade alone is not sufficient. Perhaps a nurse has been on a spinal cord unit for eight years or has worked for ten years in pediatrics; the scope of these practice settings is relatively narrow and would ill prepare the nurse to work in most case management departments or companies. Only in very large companies might a case manager only be assigned pediatric cases or patients with spinal cord injuries. It is more usual for nurses to be assigned a wide range of cases. A typical caseload may include a post-CVA patient who needs placement in a rehabilitation facility; a chronic emphysema patient who has become severely compromised; a noncompliant diabetic adolescent; a woman with breast cancer who now, despite aggressive treatment, is a hospice candidate; and a newly diagnosed end-stage renal disease patient who will be on home dialysis. It is evident that a case manager needs a range of experience in order to manage this kind of caseload.

Although clinical experience is important, so too is the setting where the experience occurs. Because case management is involved in arranging alternate care settings for patients, direct knowledge of nontraditional settings is highly desirable. It affords an understanding of what actually happens beyond the walls of the acute care hospital.

Educational Background

Educational background needs to be considered as well. Nurses can be graduates of diploma schools or have associate or bachelor's degrees. Should only those with bachelor's degrees be allowed to be case managers? The answer for now is no. Many nurses who have graduated from associate and diploma programs have continued to broaden their education. They attend workshops and conferences; subscribe to nursing journals, magazines, and newsletters; and may have also taken college courses in pursuit of a Bachelor of Science. On the other hand, there are also nurses who, once they get their degree, virtually shut down their education. This illustrates the importance of going beyond what appears on an application or a resumé, making no assumptions or exclusions based upon education alone.

Life Experience

Professional experience and educational background most assuredly need to be considered when hiring case managers. Another factor that deserves attention, however, is not often mentioned—the experience one derives from living. When an individual loses a child, spouse, or other family member to illness and goes through the stages of caring, then letting go, and then grieving, the entire process can be a sobering and in many ways an enriching experience. Coping with life's travails, surprises, and challenges helps one in ways that education and work alone cannot. Adjusting to divorce, job changes, career hurdles, and family problems while maintaining one's sanity (or a reasonable facsimile thereof) actually prepares one very well for the position of case manager.

Because the kind of cases usually referred for intervention are typically complex and chronic or catastrophic, patients and families will likely have deeply felt and highly personal responses to their illnesses or disabilities. These responses can, if recognition and intervention are lacking, destroy family structures, members, and on occasion the individual himself. A case manager's own life experiences can help her detect and deflect dangerous patient and family responses.

One source of stress for case managers is the interaction that occurs between patients and families, physicians, other health care team members, multiple providers, employer groups, and claims staff. Everyone has his or her own needs, priorities, and personality. Taking on the role of "director" of this drama is not easy, not even for experienced case managers. Novice case managers should probably not even attempt this role. To be credible, a case management professional needs sufficient life experience to strike the delicate balance between empathy and efficiency, negotiating and standing fast, providing support and pushing patients to draw on their own inner strength.

Other Intangibles

When I consider what it really takes to be a good case manager, I am still amazed at how many of the qualities are intangible, including the following:

- a sense of humor
- a strong work ethic
- anger at the system (but not enough to be a hindrance to action)
- a belief in one's ability to make a difference (but not a need for personal power)
- approachability
- optimism
- an ability to look at the positives and build on them, tempered by the right amount of reality to prevent "pie in the sky" plans and goals
- an awareness of the business/financial aspects of health care
- a sense of objectivity
- keenly developed ethical principles
- energy and creativity
- a commitment to professionalism

The interview process should explore a candidate's personal characteristics, although they are admittedly more difficult to uncover and assess than the candidate's professional experience and educational background. Much of the discovery of these personal qualities will depend upon the level of skill of the interviewer and, of course, the structure, philosophy, and goals of the company or department.

THE SEARCH FOR CASE MANAGERS

Before candidates can be interviewed and evaluated, they need to be located and be made interested enough to apply for a job. The usual search methods include posting jobs, running classified ads, and contracting with personnel agencies. There are, however, other viable ways of attracting prospective case managers, some of which require only a minimal financial outlay.

For example, writing an article for a professional magazine or local newspaper that gives an overview of the field helps likely candidates envision themselves in the case management role. Organizations, schools, employer groups, insurance carriers, and health care companies and clinics are always looking for speakers. Although the audience may enter the hall expecting to learn about how to work with case managers, an inspirational presentation may lead some listeners to pursue case management as a career. And sometimes merely "spreading the word" about employment openings will attract candidates, as will inquiring of colleagues whether they know of individuals who might be looking to make a move.

Although more costly in dollars and time, attending job fairs and other conferences can be a fruitful method of finding candidates. At a recent ICMA Medical Case Management Conference, I posted a recruitment form (Exhibit 11-2) when looking to expand our office's nationwide network of case managers. The posting drew a fair response and some good contacts were initiated. Attending conferences may actually serve several purposes besides recruitment, such as advertising services; developing a marketing image; garnering insight into needs of the industry, and generating more business through networking.

To fill a key position, such as manager or director, it may make sense to use a recruiting firm (also known as an executive search firm or "headhunter"). Recruiting firms are highly specialized, and there are several that focus entirely on recruitment for the health care and managed care industries. Although the fees can be substantial (often 25–30 percent of a candidate's first-year salary), such firms can make the hiring process almost painless, and most will refund a fee (at least partially) should the candidate not prove suitable once hired.

Exhibit 11–2 Options Unlimited Recruitment Form

CALLING ALL CASE MANAGERS:

Options Unlimited is a medical case management and benefits consulting firm located in Huntington, New York, with a network of case management professionals nationwide. If you would like to hear more about our company and the opportunities available to you as part of our coast-to-coast case management team, please let us hear from you!

Name _____

Address _____

_____

CM Specialty, if applicable _____

Phone (Day) _____

   (Evenings) _____

Please return your completed form to **Kelly Medwig**
- by posting it on the message board at MCMC V
- by leaving it at the Dolphin's front desk in her name
- by faxing it to Options Unlimited @ 516-673-8369
- by mailing it to: Options Unlimited
                   76 E. Main Street
                   Huntington, NY 11743
   or call Kelly at 1-800-457-7685 after MCMC V

Courtesy of Options Unlimited, Case Management Services Division, Huntington, N.Y.

Balanced against the difficulties of establishing oneself as an independent case manager are the many rewards. Not all case managers will choose the independent path, and some might elect to postpone their decision until a few of the coming major shifts in health care delivery have occurred. Regardless of the exact positions of all the health care players after the nearing legislative and operational changes, case managers are certain to be on the team. Case management is already a proven if not yet integral element of the U.S. health care system. To my mind, this is an exciting time to be a case manager, whether employed by a provider or payer or running an independent company. Being independent just gives one that much more visibility and opportunity to shape and build this young industry.

PART IV

Trends and Opportunities in Case Management

12

CCM Credentialing

In May 1993, 5,000 candidates sat for the first CCM exam offered by CIRSC. Twelve thousand more case managers took the exam in November 1993, and by January 1994, over 14,000 individuals had been credentialed. For the first time in its history, the case management industry had established a set of educational and experiential standards and outlined a knowledge base that delineated the core content of case management practice.

A comprehensive role and function study was conducted in early 1993 to ensure that the examination content areas would "correspond with the competence demands actually experienced in the practice of case management services."[1] Results of the survey, which included two-thirds of those applying for the CCM certification, indicated areas perceived as essential or highly important, such as the role of case management, medical terminology, documentation of case management services, legal and ethical issues regarding confidentiality, identifying cases with potential for high-risk complications, communicating case objectives to concerned parties, and obtaining accurate patient histories.[2] These and a broad range of other pertinent areas were considered in item-writing conferences. Further, after each exam, CIRSC and an examination committee consisting of people representing various areas of case management will review items to determine which will be retained, rewritten, or deleted entirely from the pool of material.[3]

In a 1992 article published in *The Case Manager*, Dorothy Sager, the chair of CIRSC, discussed the future of the CCM exam. She wrote that because CIRSC believes that designation holders should be required to maintain their certification status through a structured program of continuing education, the necessary renewal process will be developed, again using role and function studies to determine appropriate focus areas. Certified practitioners will also have the option of maintaining their status through reexamination. To make certain that the exam can be utilized for initial applicants and those seeking recertification alike, as well as meet the changing needs of the medical delivery system and the case management industry, the role and function studies, item writing activities, and item reviews will be performed on an ongoing basis, with major reviews occurring every five years to preserve validity.

In September 1993, ICMA and *The Case Manager* conducted a case management survey, asking case managers who attended Medical Case Management Conference V for their opinions regarding key issues facing the industry. The respondents ranked case management standards of practice, recognition of case management by payers, ethical standards for case managers, recognition of case management by providers, changes in the U.S. health care system, and the scope of case management as the leading areas of importance.

THE CASE MANAGEMENT PRACTICE SEMINAR

Currently the CCM exam has what would be deemed several core components. These include medical, insurance, and other payment issues; legal responsibilities; ethical considerations; psychosocial issues; and cost-containment strategies. The case management process, including all of its many facets, is the focus of the exam. Although it certainly tests clinical knowledge, the exam is intended to be a tool for the evaluation of the skills necessary for the practice of case management. Factual knowledge is tested, as is the practical application of such knowledge. By having to answer situational test questions, candidates will not be able to merely memorize facts, laws, formulas, and so on, but will need to demonstrate that they have actually engaged in case management activities.

Obviously, those currently in practice will be more comfortable with many of the "hands-on" type of questions, such as the following:

The mental cognitive strengths and weaknesses of a head injured rehabilitation client would usually be assessed by:

   a. psychiatric tests
   b. neuropsychological tests

c. neurological tests
d. intelligence tests

A client has suffered a stroke with resulting left cerebral damage. It is likely that the client will:

a. experience communication deficits
b. begin to use the right hand as dominant
c. require louder than normal voice volume
d. overestimate his/her own language processing ability[4]

The correct answers are *b* and *a*.

Are there ways to prepare for this examination? In an effort to respond to the needs and concerns of those desiring to take and pass the exam, the Foundation for Rehabilitation Certification, Education and Research offers the Case Management Practice Seminar several times a year at various geographic locations. The seminar is interactive, providing knowledge in several key areas with an opportunity to participate in the learning process. It evolved over several years, and although it does not guarantee participants a passing score, it does cover many of the content areas tested in the exam. The foundation does not specifically recommend it as a prep course for the exam but does endorse the content of the seminar as encompassing the core knowledge required for case management and addressing professional responsibilities. The faculty are experienced case managers rather than educators from the academic community. The reaction from attendees has been extremely positive because of the credibility of the presenters and the variety of teaching tools that are utilized throughout, including lectures, videos, slides, group exercises and projects, question and answer periods, and a comprehensive manual.

Having been involved with this seminar from its inception (inclusive of developing some of the content and as one of the core facility presenters), I can attest to its value in the credentialing process. The foundation continually evaluates the responses of the attendees in order to ensure the effectiveness of the content, materials, and faculty. There will no doubt be changes as the industry evolves, but I believe attending the seminar will continue to be a useful method of preparing for the exam.

There are several other conferences, both local and national, that are useful in obtaining the kind of information and insight required to pass the CCM exam. These include the national conferences sponsored by ICMA, CMSA, NARPPS, and other organizations. Presenters at such conferences are often case management professionals, lawyers, physicians, and others who can share their expertise and the kind of hands-on knowledge that is invaluable to prospective test takers.

Currently there is no official study guide for the exam, but several of the works listed in Appendix A will be of help. The information covered in the exam must be contained in published, readily accessible sources.

Although attending seminars and reading will be beneficial, several hours or days of study will not by themselves result in a passing grade. Actual working experience and competence is being tested as well as theory, and although the exam is for entry-level practitioners, it is interesting to note that the average age of those already credentialed is 44.4 years.

Since there are many clinical areas involved in the practice of case management, individuals who have experience in only one specialty area (e.g., neonatology or AIDS) may struggle with certain aspects of the exam. So, too, may allied professionals other than nurses who perform some case management activities but not all or who are members of a case management team but do not have all of the responsibilities. For these individuals, additional preparation may be necessary to round out their knowledge.

In summary, attaining the CCM credential should be the goal of each case management professional, and once it is attained, each professional needs to maintain its currency. Taking the time to get the credential demonstrates both a professional and personal commitment to the case management process and serves to validate its importance for ensuring quality outcomes and the preservation of health care resources. If there are 14,000 CCMs today, how powerful will our voices be when these numbers continue to expand? We will be firmly positioned for the future, helping our patients, their families, the payers, and the providers. As case managers, we know how valuable our work can be, and the CCM credential will underscore and further promote our contributions.

NOTES

1. E. Holt, "Certification for Case Manager Questionnaire, " prepared for the Certification of Insurance Rehabilitation Specialists Commission, March 1993.
2. "Initial Observations from Case Management Study," prepared for the Certification of Insurance Rehabilitation Specialists Commission, June 1993.
3. D. Sager, "From Need to Reality," The Case Manager, July-September 1992, 81–86.
4. CCM Certification Guide (Rolling Meadows, Ill.: CIRSC/Certified Case Manager, 1993), 14–15.

CHAPTER

13

Industry Directions: New Business Opportunities for Case Managers

In a recent address on twenty-first century case management, Jeanne Boling, ICMA's executive director, evaluated the past and speculated on the future of the case management industry. Likening it to a "maturing adolescent," she noted that the formative years of case management are over. The profession has been defined, its value has been recognized, a core knowledge base has been determined, standards of care have been developed, a professional credential has been created, and university coursework at the master's level is beginning to be offered. Case management's focus on the quality and cost of health care has been expanded to include data and outcomes management and reporting. Among issues and topics of current interest, Boling counts leadership for health care reform; advances in case management practice; a growing focus on multicultural needs; outcome-driven case management systems; extended university programs at the master's and doctorate levels; and an increase in health care, business, and academic leadership roles for case managers.[1]

As Boling's thoughts suggest, there is room for continued growth and improvement in the case management industry. And although case management practice will be influenced by changes in health care delivery, legislation, and administration, I firmly believe that case managers themselves must accept ultimate responsibility for the direction the industry moves in.

Case management is mentioned throughout the Health Security Act of 1993, introduced in September 1993 by President Clinton. Discussed under workers' compensation and auto insurance reform, long-term care proposals, Medicaid allowances, and mental health coverage, case management is obviously on the national agenda. But what will be its final form? At this writing, the most optimistic supporters of the new health plan are not expecting a vote on it in the near future and the plan is likely to undergo revision before the final roll call. Also in the hopper are competing plans drafted by reform-minded members of both political parties.

Further, all of these plans might be superseded by bills passed in state legislatures reluctant to wait out the federal reform process. Health reform initiatives are in the works in at least nine states, including bills authorizing citizen access to a basic benefits package (Florida); controls on health costs, a data collection group, and a framework for controlling technology (already passed as part of MinnesotaCare); and a waiver to field-test a managed care program for the Medicaid population (Ohio).[2]

Finally, in addition to the question of when and how to institute reform comes a quiet why? In the late 1980s, employers were faced with annual health benefit cost increases of more than 20 percent. In early 1994, a widely reported survey conducted by benefits consultant A. Foster Higgins & Company showed that for the first time since 1987 health benefit expenses rose less than 10 percent. Nationwide per-employee costs averaged $3,781 in 1993, up only 8 percent from 1992. Gasp! The managed care–managed cost approach is working! (Except in the Northeast, where the average cost per worker was $4,267, up 10.1 percent over 1992 figures.)

Where does all this leave case managers? Right in the center of activity as a force for change and as implementors of effective programs that can be put in place while the nation awaits the final word on health care reform. Case management does not require legislation to be widely accepted and successful; it requires that competent individuals are out there in the field practicing their profession and communicating their success.

Employers, especially self-funded groups, are expecting more from their insurers and third-party administrators. They want to see managed care programs in place and they want to see documented outcomes. If this isn't a business "red flag" for case managers, I don't know what is. Employers and employees are looking for the benefits case management offers, and insurers and third-party administrators will need experienced case managers to meet the demands of their client base. CEOs of small and large companies alike no longer say, "Someone's got to do something about rising health care costs"; they are becoming self-insured, forming buying coalitions, and putting case management to work.

Not only employer groups, third-party administrators, and insurers but also townships, school districts, and unions are seeking new solutions to health care challenges. Beyond broadening their markets, case managers need to consider expanding their range of services. They might do well to offer claims management, employee wellness programs, and medical bill audits. Corporations are looking at total health care-disability management (or "24-hour coverage") as another means of maintaining quality care while better managing costs. Further, there are specialties within case management practice: prenatal, pediatric, elder care, AIDS care, facility-based, and home care case management. The health care field will need case managers who can teach; the cities will need case managers who are bilingual.

When brainstorming on ways to broaden the scope of case management in the worlds of business and health care, it is useful to consider the stories of case managers who have made a difference. Jan Woods, RN, CIRS, CCM, was senior manager of case management services at The St. Paul Companies, an insurer, when she became part of the team that helped extend the application of case management to include general and medical liability cases. Then she went beyond the traditional concept of case management to create St. Paul's liability case management services program. Using concepts and procedures developed by a team of liability claims and case management personnel, the program focuses on evaluating and controlling the damages tied to liability claims. The program proved its efficacy, as utilization of case managers in liability cases almost tripled in three years. Now a claim quality consultant on St. Paul's Claim Quality Implementation Team, Woods is part of a group responsible for designing and implementing structural and procedural changes that will reconfigure the company's entire claims organization.

Working in case management since the 1970s, Karyl Thorn, RN, BSN, MA, CCM, is CEO of Thorn & Associates, a case management firm specializing in conditions that bring about significant changes in lifestyle. HIV management has become a focus of her work, and she is dedicated to enabling HIV-positive individuals to take control, become their own case managers, and live the fullest life possible. She also runs a publishing company, Thorn Publishing, which has published books, newsletters, and workbooks designed for those in HIV-related practices.

Linda Greis, RN, BSN, CCM, built a case management service program as part of a larger business organization. As past director of medical case management, she helped develop the Utilization Management Program of the Atlanta Healthcare Alliance. The alliance is a nonprofit health care coalition of employers, insurers, and providers dedicated to developing and implementing cost-containment strategies. Greis is now Public Affairs Manager at Visiting Nurse Health System, a nonprofit home health agency providing a full array of home care services and products. Her role is to establish a public affairs initiative to win attention for case management and home health issues, to educate legislators, and to increase awareness of Visiting Nurse Health System, which raises charitable dollars for indigent care in addition to serving its insurer-based clients. Greis was also an adjunct professor at Emory University Graduate School of Nursing, where she helped design a graduate-level case management course.

President of Management Consulting & Rehabilitation Services, Patricia McCollom, RN, MS, CRRN, CIRS, CCM, helps individuals and their families deal with the effects of head trauma and spinal cord injury, concentrating on community re-entry, workers' compensation, rehabilitation, job placement, and disability services. She also founded LifeCare Economics, a firm specializing in the medical and legal research required to create life care plans. Life care planning is a systematic appraisal of individual needs at a given time, broadened to encompass projected financial and medical requirements as the individual progresses through his or her life course.[3]

The days of the pure case management company are gone. To be strategically positioned as professionals, case managers will have to provide a range of services, from analysis of a company's potential problematic cases to case management itself to the documentation of outcomes. I believe case managers at this moment have the opportunity to build the industry, to make it an indispensable part of the U.S. health care delivery system, to make *case management* a household term. Challenging times? You bet, but my guess would be that if you have been working as a case management professional already or are just considering a career in case management you are up to the challenge.

NOTES

1. J. Boling, "Initial Report: 21st Century Case Management," presented at the Case Management Society of America Annual Meeting, Chicago, Illinois, February 1994.
2. Ibid.
3. D. Jensen, "Moving with the Market," *The Case Manager,* January–March 1993, 60–69.

Case Management in Action: Cases in Profile

CHAPTER
14

Care at Home

The fact that in most cases home care not only benefits the patient and family but is less costly is reflected in the recent rapid growth of the home care industry. Over the past several years, there has been increasing recognition of the expensiveness of treatment in the acute care setting (cost hikes for inpatient hospital care have averaged 15 percent a year). Consequently, hospitals, employers, and insurance companies have made serious efforts at cost containment while finding ways to provide patients with the services they need in medically sound alternative settings. For the very ill, appropriate settings include rehabilitation centers with specialized programs and skilled nursing facilities. Although the latter are usually looked on, especially by consumers, as residences for the very old, providing long-term custodial care but no real hope of recovery or improvement, recently they have begun to be perceived as appropriate centers for younger ill patients who need a higher level of care for a finite period of time.

Another alternate treatment location is the patient's home. There is strong evidence that recovery tends to occur more quickly and be more comprehensive when the patient is at home. Also, the patient's quality of life usually improves. Being able to participate in decisions about care imparts to the patient a sense of independence and well-being. Specific treatments and medication needs can be integrated into the family's schedule, minimizing disruption to routines and alleviating the patient's feeling of being a burden. An additional benefit of recuperating at home is the decreased risk of contracting a nosocomial illness (an illness from a hospital-borne infection).

The shift from hospital to home care became possible through advances in technology. Home care has become practical as more and more operations and treatments previously offered only in hospitals were provided on an outpatient basis. Dialysis, intravenous antibiotic therapy, blood transfusions, chemotherapy, HIV-related services, preterm labor infusion therapy, and ventilator and pain management programs can all be safely administered in the home setting. In some cases, cost savings can be significant. In a recent issue, *Worth* magazine reported that the home infusion market had grown 30 percent annually since 1982 and that intravenous delivery of medications such as antibiotics and analgesics were being administered in the home for as little as 50 percent of the cost of hospital treatment with no loss of efficacy.[1]

Although technology transfers very well from the hospital to the home, the patient's condition must be relatively stable prior to the switch to home-based care. A patient who is in an acute level ICU or is experiencing one crisis after another is not a candidate for home care. Once the patient is transferred to a floor, home care may become an option, even if sophisticated equipment and services are required. However, there are some situations in which home care may end up costing as much as hospital care or even more, especially when 24-hour-a-day nursing care and very high tech services are needed. In such situations, the benefits and expenses of home care must be very carefully weighed.

Home care is particularly appropriate in certain types of cases. Long-term chronically ill patients—those with chronic neurological problems, such as multiple sclerosis or amyotrophic lateral sclerosis, and those recovering from a complex traumatic brain injury who may still need skilled nursing care while facing a prolonged recuperation—do very well in a home setting. Cancer patients who face the prospect of periodic readmission to the hospital are also home care candidates. Patients undergoing immune system-destroying chemotherapy and AIDS patients with compromised immune systems are highly susceptible to nosocomial infections and may benefit greatly by being transferred to a home setting. Those affected by hemophilia or genetic emphysema can receive replacement therapies at home. Younger children, regardless of the diagnosis, improve well at home, away from the high-tech, impersonal, and often overwhelming atmosphere of a hospital. Even in the case of very ill children, a home setting, all things being equal, is preferable, since it supports the nurturing process and the continuing "childhood" of the child.

For these reasons, a movement developed to keep each patient in the hospital only as long as a coordinated medical team approach is needed and then explore all avenues of removing the patient from the hospital while still providing the quality and comprehensive services needed. Cited as potentially less expensive, home care was tested and proved to be effective for most but by no means all recuperating patients. Even so, what started as a cost-containment measure took on new dimensions—home care was felt to be a healthier and more humane alternative for the critically and terminally ill. According to the National Association for Home Care, the home health care market grew at an annual rate of 10 percent from 1987 to 1991, when payers spent $17.1 billion on home care.[2] The association anticipates a 12 percent annual growth rate for the home care market through 1996, which would place expected expenditures for 1994 over the $24-billion mark.

CONSUMER DEMAND—AND AMBIVALENCE

At the same time that hospitals and insurance companies are demonstrating increased interest in home health care, consumers, often for different reasons, are demanding it more frequently. When an individual is hospitalized, it can be a very disruptive experience for the entire family. First, many patients and families feel intimidated by the hospital setting. Second, practical concerns, such as scheduling hospital visits or conferences with physicians, taking time off from work, and hiring baby sitters, add tension to the worry experienced by the family members. Scheduling difficulties may be especially acute for two-income families with limited time and energy or in situations where the patient is in a specialized facility distant from the home. Consequently, consumers have welcomed care alternatives, especially home care, which for many is the most attractive option.

There is, however, also some uneasiness among consumers about home care. It may not be welcomed by all patients. The hospital environment provides a sense of security. The patient and family alike may well be heartened as recovery progresses and may look forward to the patient's return home, but there is also concern and fear, especially when a life-threatening problem—a stroke or heart attack, for example—is involved. "How am I going to cope? What happens if there is a problem? I can't push a buzzer and have nurses come running. Can I trust this person hired to give me injections?" Facing the loss of their safety net, patients and their families need to be convinced of the benefits and safety of home care through education and the correcting of misconceptions.

Many patients still think of home care simply as consisting of periodic visits by a nurse or other health care provider. They do not perceive it as an ongoing process, a support system that can improve and speed their recovery. In considering and responding to patient reactions, it is important for case managers to remember that patients may receive mixed signals from their families and the medical community. The hospital staff may feel the patient requires a lengthier stay, the spouse may be dreading the responsibility of providing needed care "alone," and the physician might be concerned that he or she will not be kept appropriately informed of the patient's status.

Such fears and concerns are valid and must be recognized and addressed. As stated before, patients often dread the loss of security of being in a hospital and worry about the fact that the physician is not going to be on-site. Many patients, especially older ones, are absolutely bound to this thought: "If I'm sick, I will see the doctor and receive care in the hospital." They worry about the consequences if the doctor is not immediately available. Younger patients, after seeing nurse practitioners and nurse clinicians working with physicians as colleagues, are more willing to consider alternatives. Case managers can play a pivotal role in loosening the hold of long-held beliefs and stereotypes and explaining the benefits of home care.

THE CASE MANAGER AS PIVOTAL LINK

A case manager must approach each case considered for home care very thoroughly and provide the link between the physician, the discharge plan, the patient, the family, at-home service providers, and the payer. The case manager's concerns lie where medical, nursing, and benefit payment issues dovetail.

First, a home discharge must be safe. Although the primary care physician, in cooperation with any other consulting physicians, has responsibility for discharging a patient, all those involved in the patient's treatment plan, including the nursing staff, the case manager, and home care company employees, share in the responsibility and liability for providing appropriate care. The physician writes the discharge orders stating what medications, services, and ongoing care are required. The nursing staff interprets those orders and their implications and develops a detailed discharge plan. The case manager then takes an active role in determining how the elements of the discharge plan can be best implemented. Is a visiting nurse needed twice a week or daily? Should a physical therapist or a respiratory therapist be requested? What equipment is required? What drugs must be administered and by whom? Using her knowledge of the clinical data included in the discharge orders and plan, the patient's status, area home health care providers, durable medical equipment suppliers, and other community resources, the case manager devises a home care plan that meets all stipulations of the discharge plan.

Often this calls for discretion and creativity. Most benefit policies and discharge plans automatically mention RNs as the most appropriate care support, even when other services from within the home care spectrum might provide more effective help. A home health aide, homemaker, or personal care assistant might tend to the patient's needs very well. Some case managers, for example, have revised plans to incorporate baby sitting to provide care for an older child and allow an expectant mother with a high-risk pregnancy to get off her feet and get the rest needed to carry the baby full term. For a small amount of dollars, a homemaker can do laundry, go grocery shopping, and prepare meals, allowing a patient to return home rather than remain in the hospital at a daily rate upwards of $650. Instead of assuming that a benefits plan or a discharge plan is etched in stone, case managers need to argue for solutions not covered by the plan language to create a better solution. By working the system and then articulating the results in dollars and cents, case managers help promote progressive care and optimum outcomes.

Case managers also need to be able to distinguish cases where home care is not the best option. Even if a patient is diagnostically suited for home care and medically stable, the family situation or home layout may preclude home care. Case managers need to be acutely aware of the vulnerability of families as they bring patients home. This is especially true when professional assistance is available only part time. When the patient was in the hospital, the family could come see the patient, perhaps endure a draining visit, but then leave and recharge. Now the patient is home and the family must provide physical and emotional support. Suppose the presence of a home health aide for only a two-, three-, or eight-hour shift can be justified given the language of the policy, which means the family bears the bulk of the responsibility. When evaluating a patient for home care, the case manager should assess the ability of the family to absorb additional stress.

Another consideration is the geographic setting of the home to which the patient will discharged. Is it a rural area, suburban neighborhood, or inner-city area? Each type of location has different levels of access to support and emergency services. Reviewing the setting is especially important for patients needing high-tech equipment and services. What are the rescue squad capabilities? What is the response time to a 911 call? Are emergency vehicles capable of reaching the home in 3 minutes or 45 minutes? If a power failure occurs, can the local electric utility provide back-up generator support for an individual at home on a ventilator?

A personal visit to the home permits the discovery of conditions that may affect the safety of the discharge. The family may have failed to mention that the home is an apartment five flights up with no elevator and is so small that there is no room for oxygen equipment. A visit also allows a case manager to pick up on the emotional state of the family member who will be the primary caregiver. Is he or she verbally expressing a willingness to care for the patient but also exhibiting fear, hesitation, or reluctance?

A case manager must approach each situation individually, evaluating the patient's condition and ongoing needs in consultation with the physician, the family structure, the family member who will be the main care provider, the availability of respite for the care provider, the range of community services, and so on. Home care may not be the best choice; it may be feasible but require ongoing support. Sometimes, a case manager can be put under pressure to move patients from the hospital into a home setting in order to reduce expenditures and establish credibility. It is important to remember that each case is unique and must be evaluated in light of the particular conditions that exist.

CASES IN PROFILE

Home Care is not Always the Answer

As discussed, some medically stable patients may not be candidates for home care because of the family situation. The following case history illustrates this as well as the problems of paying for needed services that don't appear in the benefit plan, and shows the crucial role a case manager can play in achieving an optimal outcome.

Janet Carr, a 59-year-old mail sorter for a self-funded employer group (an insurance company), was contacted by her employer's disability review program after she had been absent from work for seven days without submitting a medical report. She explained she had been suffering from severe abdominal pain but had not wanted to "bother" her physician. The following day the company nurse received a call from a pre-cert utilization review nurse notifying the disability review program that Mrs. Carr had been admitted to a hospital on an emergency basis for a ruptured bowel and acute peritonitis. Extremely ill, she required emergency surgery, which had high risk because of infection and dehydration. Because she was expected to be in the hospital at least ten days and because a physician report cited longstanding emotional and psychiatric problems the patient and possibly her husband suffered from, the employer decided to refer Mrs. Carr for case management intervention.

In an initial brief visit with Mrs. Carr several days after her ileostomy and colostomy, the RN case manager noted her debilitated, critical condition and guarded prognosis. In a subsequent visit with Mr. Carr, she noted that he seemed developmentally impaired and, while able to answer certain questions, was tearful and fearful when talking about his wife, who "takes care of us." Seeking further information, the case manager met with Mrs. Carr's primary nurse and surgeon regarding the Carrs' ability to comprehend the extent of Mrs. Carr's illness. The case manager was also able to contact Mrs. Carr's sister, who confirmed that both Mr. and Mrs. Carr suffered from longstanding comprehension problems as well as emotional and psychiatric problems.

During Mrs. Carr's recovery in the hospital, it became clear that Mr. Carr not only did not understand what type of surgery his wife had undergone or the care she would need but also was unable to perform everyday household chores, such as bill paying and laundry, without his wife's help. He told the case manager that they had no washer or dryer, did not use a laundromat and that he had left the laundry "soaking in the bathtub so she can take care of it when she comes home." Prior to Mrs. Carr's illness, the couple had been able to manage without assistance from outside agencies. It was apparent that this would no longer be true. Mrs. Carr was unable, physically or mentally, to learn anything about ostomy care. Mr. Carr was insistent that his wife return home immediately but "with no outsiders."

Mrs. Carr became medically stable, and her treating physicians felt that continued hospitalization increased her risk for further infection. The consensus among her medical providers was that she would require continuing medical supervision regarding infection control, nutritional status, electrolyte imbalance, and depression for a prolonged period of time. The Carrs had no family physician. Given Mrs. Carr's need for medication administration, ostomy care, dressing changes, and monitoring and Mr. Carr's inability to provide any support, she was a candidate for around-the-clock nursing care.

The case manager here was faced with several challenges. The first was Mr. Carr. Once shown his wife's incisions and ostomies and given a brief explanation of the care she needed, he became willing to consider assistance from outside professionals, although his ability to cooperate was minimal. The next difficulty was Mrs. Carr's medical coverage. She had an indemnity plan funded and administered by her employer, an insurance company, that provided for up to 365 days of hospitalization if required, for skilled nursing care in the home if certain criteria were met, for durable medical equipment and supplies, and for 30 days in a rehabilitation facility. There was no coverage for care in a nursing home or for home health aide or homemaker services. After reviewing discharge needs, alternative services, the family situation, the insurance coverage, and available community resources, the case manager proposed the following options to the benefits administrator:

1. Continued hospitalization, which could be justified because of the need for ongoing care, at a minimum cost of $850 a day.
2. Twenty-four-hour-a-day skilled nursing care at home at a cost of approximately $600 a day. This option lacked homemaker and housekeeping services assistance the couple needed. In addition, Mr. Carr strongly resisted this option.
3. A skilled nursing facility. This option would require demonstration of cost benefits and approval from the benefits administrator. Cost was $105 per day.

Following previous successful experiences with case management services, the employer group had instituted a large case management program that allowed modifications to the basic coverage, limiting exceptions to situations suitable for case management intervention and supported by medical and cost justification documentation. Through this program, the case manager received approval to accompany Mr. Carr to three skilled nursing facilities near the couple's home. Mrs. Carr was admitted to a facility within short walking distance, at an all-inclusive cost per day of $105. For a small additional charge, Mr. Carr was able to join Mrs. Carr for lunch and dinner. The insurance company covered the facility's fees under the large case management provision of its policy in lieu of acute hospitalization. Coordinating with the hospital physicians, the case manager arranged to have Mrs. Carr's medical care provided by the surgeon and then by an internist, who would be the couple's primary physician. Next, the case manager assisted in arranging for disability payments from the employer to the couple, contacted the couple's landlord and utility companies and apprised them of the situation, and helped Mr. Carr record and mail the necessary payments.

Mrs. Carr remained in the skilled nursing facility for two months, returned to the hospital for reversal of the ostomies, and recuperated at the skilled nursing facility for two weeks. She then went home, stronger and healthier and able to care for herself and her husband. This scenario provided the patient with the best care—in this case, not in the home but in an alternative care center—and also resulted in substantial cost savings for the payer. Continuous hospitalization for two months and two weeks would have cost $62,900; 24-hour-a-day nursing care for the same period would have cost $44,400 (at $25 an hour). Care in the skilled nursing facility cost $7,070 and case management services cost $4,800 over a seven-month period. The savings were substantial, the actual amount being $51,030 less than hospitalization would have cost and $32,530 less than home nursing care would have cost. Unaccounted for are the savings resulting from prevention of complications likely to have occurred if the case manager had not intervened on behalf of the patient and her spouse.[3]

A Home Care Case That Succeeded

James was born six weeks prematurely following a maternal infection and premature labor. He developed respiratory distress and was ventilator dependent for several months. After two abdominal surgeries for treatment of an intestinal obstruction and placement of a gastrostomy tube, his condition gradually stabilized, and his parents were given instruction in home care.

Discharged from the hospital at five months, James came home with respiratory equipment and medical supplies, including an apnea monitor, oxygen, an oxymeter, suction machines, an ambu bag, and feeding and additional supplies. His home care program incorporated four hours per day of RN care. Shortly after James returned home, our case manager was called by the family with a request for additional nursing hours.

New to the case, the case manager conducted an initial home assessment and found the parents completely overwhelmed by the emotional and physical demands of caring for six-month-old James, dependent on multiple pieces of sensitive medical equipment, as well as his two siblings, active two- and four-year-old preschoolers. The parents were attempting to maintain home care and keeping in contact with their primary physician, who was 75 miles away at the university hospital, by telephone. They transported James those same 75 miles in heavy traffic to their hospital's emergency room (rather than their community hospital), even during episodes of respiratory distress. Although the parents were pleased with the quality of nursing care provided by an agency, they were dissatisfied with the service and equipment supplied by their home medical equipment dealer. The case manager determined that the care plan was putting James at risk for a respiratory crisis and rehospitalization.

Consulting with all concerned, she presented a number of recommendations. To avoid rehospitalization and to more properly attend the child at home, RN hours were increased to 16 per day. The home medical equipment contract was awarded to a dealer whose personnel are particularly adept at working closely with families and health care professionals. James's oxygen supply system was switched from indoor to outdoor tanks to remove his siblings' temptation to tamper—a potential hazard.

After talking with the family, the primary treating physician, and a local hospital, it was agreed that James would be brought to this nearby facility in an emergency, cutting 60 miles off the one-way commute. The case manager negotiated lower fees with the home medical equipment dealer and the nursing agency, and direct payment arrangements were made with the insurance carrier, avoiding copayment terms for the family and resulting in a significant cost savings to the carrier and family.

Because there were limited health care dollars available for James over his lifetime for home nursing care and other services, the case manager referred the family to the Medicaid model waiver program. Participation in this community-based alternative to hospice or institutional care spread expenses between the family, the insurance carrier, and Medicaid. Funded by federal, state, and county sources, the waiver program for chronically ill children extended James's coverage over his lifetime and provided the family with access to other public funding programs.

Timely intervention by the case manager resulted in the stabilization of James' condition and shortened hospital stays (when they were necessary due to distress or infection). A reinforced emphasis on parent education and increased nursing and supportive services reduced the overall number of hospital admissions, and the use of a more accessible hospital helped prevent a catastrophic event such as respiratory arrest. Further, the case manager, who was on-site for regular assessments, was able to intervene in several crises and provide prompt care in situations where the parents tended to delay medical attention.

Without case management, it is likely that James would have floundered in the medical system and experienced numerous and lengthy hospitalizations at great cost to the family and carrier. His frequent trips to a distant emergency room might well have resulted in respiratory arrest, potential brain damage, and ventilator dependency. Early intervention; referral to physical, speech, feeding, and educational therapies; and enrollment in the Medicaid model waiver program helped prevent developmental delay and mental retardation, optimizing the boy's chances of realizing his full potential.

The care-at-home program has prolonged the life of the claims dollars available for James, and prompt case management is now saving his family, the insurer, and Medicaid upwards of $130,000 annually.[4]

ONGOING SUPPORT AT HOME

When a patient is released to home care, the patient and family need ongoing support, and that requires free and frequent communication between all parties involved.

Once the various elements of home care are successfully established— the necessary medical equipment delivered and set up, the nursing hours arranged, the supplies ordered—regular monitoring and follow-up are essential. The case manager must be alert to the changing needs of the patient, the quality of the care provider service, and signs of family caregiver burnout. Perhaps a family member is providing the primary care with a weekly visit from a nurse to check a catheter. After a few weeks or months, the caregiver will need a respite. A case manager has a responsibility to see that the payer (employer group or insurance company) is convinced of the need and that extra help is temporarily provided, that the primary caregiver is not punished for being willing and able to care for the patient. The problem of caregiver burnout and need for relief is often most acute in situations where the parents are primary caregivers for a seriously ill child and are also trying to do the grocery shopping, get their other children to the dentist or to soccer practice, and continue working at their own jobs.

The case manager needs to be aware that the primary caregiver not only must be willing to provide care for the patient but must have the physical stamina as well—to get the patient in and out of bed or a wheelchair, for example. Does the caregiver have a chronic back problem or predisposition to back problems? A heart condition? Sometimes the case manager may need to bring in additional support services not to overburden the caregiver. Perhaps a wife has agreed to be the primary caregiver for her husband but has a back condition and requires additional support equipment if she is to be able to care for him. It may be difficult to convince the payer, particularly if the husband and wife are on the same insurance policy, that the extra support is requisite. What has to be made clear to the payer in situations like this is that if the extra support is not provided, the caregiver may be the next casualty and the payer will have a second claim to reimburse.

IMPORTANCE OF FEEDBACK AND COMMUNICATION

In her combined role as coordinator, troubleshooter, and problem solver, the case manager should actively pursue and receive feedback from all sources—the health care providers, the durable medical equipment suppliers, the patient (if possible), the family member providing the majority of care, and other family members. Specific parameters for communication must be set up: what to communicate, by whom, to whom, and how often. The case manager may request that the nursing service call in weekly reports or submit copies of weekly nursing notes. This regular feedback allows the case manager to follow the patient's condition and evaluate the need for services. It is unfortunate when a case manager learns from a payer that a patient discharged to home care two months earlier has been back in the hospital for a week because of a deterioration in his or her condition or the failure of the home care setup to function as planned. The case manager must make sure that she is contacted immediately if a change occurs—if the patient's condition worsens, the caregiver service switches personnel or hours, or any family arrangement that can affect the patient is altered. This is not to say that if a sudden emergency or need arises, the home health care provider or family caregiver should not react and do what is called for. If, for example, increased services are required on a weekend and the case manager cannot be reached, the services should be provided. The case manager should then be informed as soon as possible, at which point she can help decide how the patient's differing status can best be accommodated on a long-term basis—in a cost-effective manner appropriate for the patient, the family, and the payer.

What sometimes happens is that, once a discharge plan is devised and home services arranged for, the case manager may be told by the payer (especially if it has an in-house case management service) or the health care provider service, "We'll track patient progress now and contact you if a problem arises." If the case manager feels that her continuing on-site objective assessments are important, she must communicate that message. When turning a case over to a payer's in-house case management service, the case manager should relay all pertinent case information and acknowledge the ability of the payer's case manager to take on the case, but also make it clear that she is available for interim on-site assessments as needed. If a claims examiner decides to continue tracking a case, the case manager should make certain he or she understands the case manager's role in keeping services in place at the appropriate level. She should also suggest that the claims examiner call her if certain complications arise and leave a list of red flags for his or her reference. When a home care provider case management service offers to take over management of a case, the case manager must be diplomatic. Especially in determining the need to increase or decrease home care services, the case manager is likely to be more objective than the home care service provider. She might review her thoughts on the patient's needs with the home care service and make it clear that she is available for on-site assessments as needed should the patient's status change.

Decisions should not be made arbitrarily by one of the parties. A home health care service may not be the most objective judge of when a change in services is needful. Physicians might not be aware of all the details of the home care arrangement. Ideally, the case manager should be the one to adjust the level of services and then discuss all the ramifications of any changes with the provider services and the payer. For example, the health care service that is providing 8-hour-a-day nursing service at home should not arbitrarily increase the hours to 16 or 24 a day. The nursing service can report to the case manager that the patient's condition has worsened and an increase in hours is probably needed, the family caregiver may request additional help, or the physician in charge of the patient may deem more extensive services or medical equipment necessary. In all cases, the case manager should be the pivotal person involved in making the decision and then implementing it.

Follow-up on the use of durable medical equipment is also necessary. Only then will the case manager know if equipment is actually being used and if the patient or caregiver is satisfied with it and comfortable using it. There are cases where equipment remains in the home unused yet is paid for month after month. Perhaps the equipment was part of a standard discharge package, the family caregiver never learned how to use it, the equipment broke, or it was used for a while but is no longer needed. In obtaining information about the use of durable medical equipment, the case manager should speak not only with the health provider but also with the patients and family members.

The case manager must make it clear to the family that if there is a problem with equipment, if they are not satisfied with the health care provider, or if they are overwhelmed, they should call the case manager. A patient or family may be dissatisfied with the health care provider or with the durable medical equipment but be hesitant to complain simply because they do not know what to expect, feel unable to be assertive, or fear that the patient may not continue to get the best service if they mention a problem. It must be remembered that there may be certain things a health care provider would be reluctant to tell a case manager—that three shifts of care providers failed to show up for work one weekend, for instance. Families need to know that there is someone to turn to if a problem arises.

Although follow-up is often conducted over the phone, there are definite benefits to making personal visits. A visit to the home allows a case manager to pick up on emotional states and to see if there is equipment sitting unused in a corner. Are there signs that the patient is being well cared for by the professional health care service and by the family caregiver? Is the patient progressing? If not, why not?

The case manager should be more than an observer. She should be a catalyst for patient progress. This means giving feedback to all parties—not only recording but troubleshooting and devising answers.

As the pivotal person involved in decisions about needed changes in service and their implementation, the case manager must see that everyone is in the loop—the physician, the home care provider, the therapists, the home medical equipment supplier, the patient (if possible), the primary family caregiver, the other family members—and must maintain open communication channels between all involved to ensure that the patient, family, and payer are well served. Only with communication and feedback will come the support that is needed if home care is to be a successful care alternative.

PAYMENT CONCERNS

As stated at the beginning of the chapter, the original impetus for the growth of home care was cost containment. And in most cases home care is less expensive than hospital care (see Table 14-1). However, cost savings are not automatic. Expenses must be calculated, managed, and negotiated intensively.

First, the case manager must determine if and to what extent a benefit plan will allow home care. Today, a provision for home care is included in most benefit plans, but there may be specific limitations. Employers often fear that if too generous a home care benefit is in place, it will be abused

Table 14–1 A Comparison of Monthly Hospital Care versus Home Care Costs

Condition	Cost of Hospital Care	Cost of Home Care	Savings
Infant born with breathing and feeding problems	$60,970	$20,209	$40,761
Neurological disorder with respiratory problems	17,783	196*	17,587
Quadriplegic patient with spinal cord injury	23,862	13,931	9,931
Cerebral palsy patient	8,425	4,867†	3,558
Ventilator-dependent patient care	22,569	1,766	20,803
Nutrition infusions	23,670	9,000	14,670
Antibiotic infusions	7,290	2,070	5,220
Patient requiring respiratory support	24,715	9,267	15,448

*After initial cost of equipment
†In extended care unit of hospital

Data from Aetna Life & Casualty Co.: American Association for Respiratory Therapy: OTA May 1987 report, *Technology Dependent Children: Hospitals vs. Home Care, A Technical Memorandum.*

and some employees will utilize unneeded home care on a regular basis. Therefore, plans include strict restrictions on home care benefits and tough plan language to eliminate the potential for abuse.

Over the last several years, studies have revealed an increased interest in benefit plan design and have demonstrated that a plan's structure can affect the experience of the employer. An employer or benefit manager can, for example, make the plan language so constrictive that individuals are forced to remain in a hospital or other high-cost facility for longer than is necessary if they are to be eligible for any benefits. Or plan language can be flexible enough to allow an umbrella of coverage, with limits designed to prevent abuse.

For example, a plan may provide up to one million dollars in benefits per year but, although covering hospital care up to the limit, may allow only 52 home nursing visits a year. Someone who no longer needs acute care in a hospital but is facing a prolonged recuperation period, say, six months, is going to need two to three visits by a nurse per week and numerous other support services. However, if the plan prohibits that option, the case manager may be forced to utilize the other—in this case, keeping the patient in the high-cost hospital setting.

Or perhaps the plan covers skilled nursing services at home but excludes home health aides or homemaker services. What happens if a patient needs a skilled nurse visit only once a week but cannot manage without the support of a home health aide or homemaker services a few hours each day? Is the patient to stay in the more costly and less desirable hospital setting because the plan will not allow needed ancillary services?

Unfortunately, situations like these arise frequently, and case managers are faced with trying to persuade and negotiate with the payers to allow the other services "out of contract"—to make exceptions to the plan language that will meet the needs of patients and at the same time reduce costs. In this type of situation, a case manager should not feel intimidated but should argue the point with the plan administrators and explain that by allowing a full spectrum of services to be provided at home, they will enhance the outcome for the patient and also save money. By presenting concrete examples of improved care and verifiable savings, ideally including an example involving the employer's own plan, the case manager can strengthen her argument.

Sometimes semantics lies at the crux of an employer's reluctance to permit exceptions. In allowing alternative arrangements, employers and benefit administrators often talk of "out-of-contract" benefits or "contract exceptions," benefits they are not required to provide. Employers need to learn—and case managers should be prepared to do the informing—that alternative arrangements should be viewed as something they do to prevent greater contract exposure. The case manager needs to present the situation clearly, demonstrating that "if you do not allow for and pay for this, then your option is this—which is more costly and may not be the most beneficial step to take." A detailed cost-benefit analysis can be the case manager's most potent tool in presenting the figures.

In addition to investigating and pursuing all of the benefits obtainable through the patient's health plan, the case manager should utilize other resources for providing at-home services to help the patient and payer defray costs. There may be local, county, or state agencies and disease-specific organizations, foundations, or philanthropic groups that can provide services or guidance. The United Way, Meals on Wheels, and "I Can Cope" programs and loaner wheelchairs from the American Cancer Society are examples of available assistance. Easter Seals offers support services on a sliding scale for children and adults with crippling diseases. For help in seeking financing for home care, case managers can contact hospital social workers and discharge planners, city and county health departments, Social Security and public aid offices, community referral agencies such as United Way, senior citizen centers, local councils on aging, the Office for Aging, and the other social agencies listed in the Yellow Pages and community service directories (available at local libraries).[5] In addition, Gale Research annually publishes the *Encyclopedia of Associations*, a resource guide to associations including those established to support individuals with certain diseases or injuries (this guide is also available at local libraries).

Even if a benefit plan allows for a particular service, community and other resources should be tapped. The case manager need not spend plan money just because it is there. A plan might allow for transportation assistance for an at-home patient to travel to and from necessary medical appointments; a local disease-specific society (e.g., the Multiple Sclerosis Society) might also provide transportation services for free. Or, a plan might provide for ambulance costs, yet the local volunteer fire department might offer such services for free. By making a one-time donation to an agency, a corporation might secure transportation or other services for an employee for an indefinite period of time. The key is to be cost-effective and not give away the store. This is especially true if there is a ceiling on overall home care expenses in the plan.

The case manager must also hone negotiating skills in order to deal with home health care providers more effectively. When arranging for a home health agency to provide two shifts of nurses for a patient for an expected two-month period, some negotiation is in order. The case manager need not accept the usual per-diem rate but should suggest an appropriate rate. Assuming services are satisfactory, the provider can look forward to a guaranteed income for a specific duration.

The growth in home care presents great opportunities for case managers. They are the ones to provide that essential and pivotal link between patient and family, health care providers, and payers—or, in other words, they are the ones to make sure that home care works.

NOTES

1. D. Niederman, "Health Care Stocks: A Second Opinion," *Worth*, December/January 1993, 112–116.
2. K. Anderson, "Is It Still Home Sweet Home Care?," *Business & Health*, January 1993, 42–46.
3. C. M. Mullahy, "Just a Few Complications," *The Case Manager*, April–June 1990, 83–87.
4. C.M. Mullahy, "Katie's Exception," *Continuing Care*, July 1991, 22–24.
5. C. Strandell, "Strategies for Financing Home Healthcare," *Home Healthcare Nurse* 9, no. 1 (1991): 5.

Managing a Long-Term Case

Long-term cases present special challenges to the case managers, the payers, and, above all, the patients and families. Among the personal, professional, and business issues for the case manager are explaining the benefits that case management can offer in terms of outcome and cost containment, clearly presenting findings to the referral source, demonstrating concretely how case management can improve the situation overall, and maintaining an objective and encouraging attitude with the patient and family. The single most important contribution the case manager can make is to identify a probable long-term case early on, before numerous services are put in place and before costs start to spiral.

A long-term case is diagnosis driven; long-term care is typically needed for patients with multiple sclerosis, amlotropic lateral sclerosis, cerebral palsy, cancer, brain or spinal cord injury, and multiple trauma (e.g., amputation or burns) and for premature babies. Services may be required for several months or several years. To recognize a long-term case, a case manager refers to the diagnosis, all available medical data, and the prognosis. Through use of this information, supported by prior experience and knowledge of the usual length of time for particular types of cases, the case manager can judge how long a case is likely to be open. Educated speculation on the anticipated length and severity of the case is of interest to the client or payer.

The following are five red flags indicating cases that have a potential to be long term:

1. lack of improvement or complications and setbacks in a seemingly short-term case
2. terminal illness
3. six months of treatment (no matter what the type)
4. multiple medical conditions (e.g., diabetes and hypertension)
5. an increase in complications, indicating possible systemic involvement

INFORMING THE CLIENT

Once she has identified a likely long-term case, the case manager should inform the client company as soon as possible. It is important to be frank and make the client aware that a patient will require care and services for an extended period of time and that consequently expenses on the case will be ongoing. Just as a claims administrator is responsible for "claims reserving" (determining, at the earliest opportunity, the potential for a claimant to require additional monies and earmarking dollars accordingly), a case manager must evaluate a patient's condition and offer an educated guess as to the care that will be required.

Long-term cases—those that require six or more months of case management intervention—are anathema to some clients and payers. A client's perceptions of a patient's probable needs may differ substantially from the case manager's. Therefore, it is very important to clarify the role of case management in long-term cases to the client. Even when the diagnosis identifies a case as long term and the case manager feels that long-term involvement is necessary or advisable, the client may request that the case manager limit her role. To avoid confusion and unnecessary delays in the provision of care, the case manager must be able to spot potential misunderstandings before they occur and inform the client promptly of changing circumstances so as to prepare the client for the possibility of a long-term case as soon as that possibility becomes evident.

The case manager's role is often particularly difficult when a referral source has assigned a case that, based on its information, seems not to be problematic. Suppose that during an on-site visit the case manager discovers a situation that does not mesh with what has been relayed to the referral source over the telephone. The patient's condition or the home dynamics may be much more complex than the referral source realizes. Also, in some cases that at first appear to be short term, unexpected complications or setbacks occur, requiring additional medical attention. A case manager who has established straightforward and forthright communications with the client company and payer will have a stronger foundation to work from when requesting additional funds due to unforeseen circumstances. Such requests become more crucial when specific dollar limits exist in the coverage language or if claims reserving suddenly becomes necessary, as they then have greater potential to negatively impact the case manager's working relationship and ability to put needed treatments in place.

Some case managers, especially those with less experience or those working with a new client or referral source, are reluctant to be totally honest. In an effort to maintain the client relationship, they knowingly overestimate anticipated progress in long-term cases or withhold especially stark information. This strategy can only backfire, diminishing the payer's confidence in case management. By sharing all the information and giving a studied professional opinion, the case manager can help clients appreciate issues of long-term care that they would not otherwise be able to.

LEVEL OF INVOLVEMENT

For a case manager, the type and level of involvement on a long-term case depends on several factors: the diagnosis, patient's age, prior medical history, current medical situation, treatment plan, and services required, among others. One especially important factor is the nature of the benefit plan. The provisions of the plan may severely limit the specific activities and functions that the case manager can offer, even though the case manager may be confronting a long-term problem in need of attention. The amount of family support may also influence a case manager's participation. Is the family willing and able to care for the patient at home? Will they accept use of an alternative setting—a skilled nursing facility, for example? If problems arise with the services as arranged, is there a family member who can handle the situation? As in home care, the patient's geographic setting and the community resources available are other factors that determine the level of case management needed or advisable.

The timing of a case manager's introduction to a case also affects her role. In general, case management involvement is more time consuming and labor intensive in the early stages of a probable long-term case, since incorporating on-site visits, telephone calls, numerous written reports (as required by the client), and written agreements with service providers are required. General tasks include establishing a relationship with the patient, family, care providers, and client; gathering information (e.g., from the physician and hospital discharge plan); assessing patient needs and possible family participation; and arranging for medical care or other assistance.

After the case manager has put the treatment plan into action (i.e., services are in place and the care routine is established), her role usually becomes a less active one. The goal of case management is to enable the people most directly involved with a long-term illness—the patient and family—to live as comfortably and normally as possible. Provided with the appropriate support and the knowledge and resources to manage minor crises (e.g., when a nursing shift fails to show up), the family has been empowered and has become, in effect, its own case manager. The case manager may call once a day in the beginning for purposes of monitoring. After a while, she may touch base once a week. Once the case manager becomes confident that the family is progressing well, she may only check in every other month, having established the conditions under which she should be called, such as when a minor problem threatens to turn into a major problem.

In a long-term case of nine months or two years where there are no major changes in the patient's condition or the care provisions, the need for frequent detailed reports to the client diminishes. This is especially true if follow-up at that point is largely telephonic. Then, reports can take the form of a status update letter or an addendum to a previous report, perhaps submitted monthly or quarterly. A telephone update noted in the client's file might be all that is necessary: "Patient's condition is unchanged since last report three months ago. Care services put into place remain the same and are still working effectively."

IMPORTANCE OF ONGOING INVOLVEMENT

In long-term cases, I believe ongoing involvement is always advisable. It not only benefits the patient and family but also the client, providing increased cost containment since problems are addressed early on. Continuing contact can be achieved in several ways, depending on the client group, its in-house capabilities, the funds available, and other factors. The contact link might be an in-house case manager. When an insurance company is the original referral source, it sometimes hires a field case manager to help set up services in coordination with its in-house case manager. Once the patient's out-of-hospital routine is established, ongoing contact is often managed by the in-house case management service via telephone. The field case manager is only called back in if a problem occurs. While this is not ideal, because on-site visits reveal things not detected through telephone conversations, contact with the patient is maintained. Through experience, a case manager knows which questions will elicit information indicating how the patient's medication and treatment plan is working, whether symptoms are improving or worsening, how the family is coping, and whether there is increasing tension. Picking up on potential trouble spots during phone interviews, the case manager can go back into the field to determine exactly what is going on, what has changed from the original scenario, and what needs to be done to put it all back together before the care plan deteriorates. (Field case managers should make certain they tell in-house case management services that they should be called promptly for a detailed in-the-field analysis of a situation if any hint of change is noted during telephonic contact.)

A case manager working with a self-funded employer group bears the responsibility of communicating to the group or the third-party administrator the importance of keeping a case open. The case manager's contribution might be restricted to moving the patient from hospital to home with appropriate services, thereby "closing" the case. When this occurs, the case manager should carefully explain to the client that she will not be visiting every week or even every month and will not be sending unnecessary or overly detailed reports (and not billing for this level of work) but that regular contact will help keep any small difficulties from getting out of hand. What is important is maintaining a link. Case managers need to articulate this to their referral sources. Examples help to prove the point. The case manager can cite a case (preferably one handled by the same referral source) that was closed, seemingly with justification but prematurely, after which point the claims department suddenly discovered that the patient was back in the hospital. This high-cost situation could have been avoided and the problem handled in a more cost-effective manner if case management had been tracking the case.

As in any home-care case, ongoing case management contact will also improve the relationship between the patient and family and the physician by keeping the physician "in the loop"—informed about the home situation, the patient's progress, and the patient's adherence to medical directives. And again, the case manager can maintain a liaison with service providers, as the need for particular equipment or support may increase or decrease with improvements or setbacks in the patient's condition. Regular on-site visits also enable the case manger to detect caregiver burnout and suggest temporary changes to handle the immediate situation and help make the long-term continuation of care feasible.

Premature closing of cases also jeopardizes the effectiveness of the case manager role. The case manager comes to be seen as a person whose function is merely to set up support services after a patient's discharge from a hospital, which view prevents the case manager from becoming an integral member of the care team and reduces the team's ability to provide needed care for the patient in a cost-effective manner.

CHANGES IN LONG-TERM CASES

Solutions that were once workable and cost-effective sometimes become ineffective over the course of a long-term care case. The case manager should expect to modify her plan or renegotiate prices due to staff changes at selected agencies, service that is no longer satisfactory, or a personality clash between a care provider and the patient or family. As mentioned, a change in service or cost often signals a change in the patient's medical condition. Complications occur. A cancer patient is undergoing chemotherapy and/or radiation, with the disease confined to one organ, the stomach. Unfortunately, the disease metastasizes to the liver and lungs and two months later to the brain. The patient who initially was compliant and cooperative develops breathing difficulties and other complications due to the upset of metabolic processes. She might be in pain, uncooperative, combative, hostile, and later comatose. Through these stages of the illness, the case manager must adjust services to fit the need.

In cases like traumatic brain injury or spinal cord injury, rapid gains and improvements in the beginning of treatment are often followed by long stretches of slower, less evident progress—plateaus. Plateaus present problems for the patient, family, and entire care team. They are disheartening and can be the root of both undue despair and false hope. The patient and primary caregiver feel that progress has halted, that they are stuck right where they were months ago. The claims examiner feels that "no news is good news" and that there are no problems. The referral source sees no need to call in a field case manager because the patient is stable. The case manager finds herself asking, "What can I offer here?"

Through phone contact or on-site visits, the case manager should explain about plateaus and provide encouragement and support. Because she does not see the individual daily, her perspective is key. Although to the family progress might seem agonizingly slow, the case manager can say, "Wow, since last month I can see such change in the strength of his movements, and now he can lift his arm six inches off the bed instead of stopping at two inches." By maintaining a journal herself and encouraging the family to jot down notes, the case manager helps lighten the dismay at the slowness of progress and focus attention on the fact of progress. By making on-site visits, the case manager can also suggest ways in which the care situation might be changed (e.g., recommending equipment that will encourage more movement and giving the family tips on engaging the patient in his own care). This proactive involvement helps keep a family and its support system intact, provides tools and coping skills, and makes it less likely that more expensive services will need to be called in to correct a problem that went unnoticed.

Family situations also change. Initially, a family's ability to cope may be very good, and they will insist that they will do whatever it takes to care for the patient and keep him at home. And in the beginning, this is so; everyone is very energetic and involved. Then, the primary care provider gets burned out. The family then requires support—a homemaker, home health aide, or RN.

Another red flag to watch for is financial difficulty. There are myriad ways in which monetary affairs can change during a long-term case and affect the long-term care situation and the family's ability to cope. Insurance often pays part of the expenses involved in caring for the ill patient while the family funds the rest—and the financial strain can gradually become overwhelming. A number of factors are at play. The primary care giver may have left a part-time job because of the need at home, diminishing family income. The primary wage earner in the family may become unemployed. The patient may be coming to the end of a period of salary replacement but still need several months of care. Continuing longer than expected, the case may hit a benefit ceiling. Throughout the course of care, the case manager must track financial resources and make the best use of them.

The only way a case manager can monitor the patient and family situation and be able to prevent small, moderate, and major problems from becoming catastrophic is to maintain some degree of ongoing involvement in the case.

NEGOTIATING FOR LONG-TERM CARE

When negotiating for long-term services, case managers often overlook a cost-containment tactic available to them: Long-term cases provide a long-term guaranteed income for service providers. Therefore, case managers should address long-term cost issues with the providers upfront, stating frankly that since they will be billing for a set amount over a period of perhaps five or six months, negotiation on costs is appropriate. This is true whether the provider is a skilled nursing care facility, home health aide service, or nutritional supplement manufacturer. The case manager's job is to get patients the level of service they need at the time they need it in the most cost-effective manner. This means negotiating based on need and fair market value and always holding out for the best price available. It is the case manager's responsibility to be familiar with competitive rates and comfortable with challenging costs and seeking deals while always leaving room to negotiate. For example, a vendor or facility representative should never be told the total amount available through a benefit plan; the release of this information would significantly reduce the case manager's bargaining power.

Intensive negotiation is particularly appropriate when a patient's needs and the required levels of services change during a prolonged period of care. An individual brain injury or multiple trauma patient may demand intense skilled nursing and ancillary services at the outset of treatment but will require less and less care during the later stages of recovery. In situations like this, renegotiation is key so that costs reflect the patient's improved condition and reduced need for many services. Further, other services may be requested. For instance, whereas skilled nursing care may be curtailed, physical or occupational therapy may be started. Overall, the case manager should see to it that changes in the levels and types of services being provided to a patient are reflected in changes in costs.

EMPLOYING ALL POSSIBLE RESOURCES

Financial resources for long-term care are always a concern—whether it is for a young long-term patient or for the care of an elderly person. Long-term care insurance policies vary greatly in the type and extent of funding they provide and in the restrictions put on types of services. Resources and benefits may alter as the patient ages, and the family support system and finances may change. In addition to the patient's specific health plan (employer-funded plan, third party administrator, workers' compensation, or other), long-term care policy, or disease-specific policy, all other possible resources for funding and services should be investigated.

As with home care cases, many disease-specific organizations and groups provide or arrange for services. Further, recognizing the long-term needs of patients, disease-specific groups use a sliding scale, based on the patient's financial resources, for determining reimbursement. (A sliding scale arrangement is usually not available for acute, short-term care.) For example, there may be a dollar limit on a plan's psychological benefits. Depending on the need, arrangements can be made for payment on a sliding scale. In this way a young person with an eating disorder may pay a minimum predetermined per-visit rate over a longer period of time. Case managers need to be aware of these types of resources and arrangements, including the funding available through grants, foundations, and other organizations, and use them to supplement and even protect the funding available from the insurance plan so it can be reserved for later use.

Again, community resources should also be tapped. Why pay for transportation to a doctor's appointment or for ambulance service if there are local community organizations providing the service free? Since long-term care is always a financial drain, case managers should make every effort to use whatever resources are available and to safeguard the insurance coverage the patient has at his or her disposal.

LONG-TERM CARE OF THE ELDERLY

Case management can also be applied to manage the long-term care of the elderly—those not seriously ill but requiring support services. This is especially true now that long-term care insurance policies are available and companies are calling on case managers to evaluate the medical and emotional condition of elderly individuals.

Insurance companies are not the only clients seeking to use case management services in the care of the elderly. Adult sons and daughters of aging parents often recognize the need for help in locating community resources, day-care programs, and other services that address the needs of the elderly at minimal cost. These may include senior day activity programs with bus transportation, meal preparation and delivery, housekeeping services, and shopping services. Expanded professional services can be phased in later. Housing situations can also be assessed. For example, an elderly person may benefit from moving from a two-story domicile to a single-level apartment and possibly later to an adult residence where services like transportation, meal preparation, and housekeeping are available.

ADDRESSING THE ISSUE OF DEATH

Death and dying present special problems. This is true whether a spouse is caring for an ill partner, a parent is at the bedside of a child, or an adult is nursing a parent. Sometimes the patient has accepted the situation and is comfortable with dying but the family cannot let go. Often the patient and family do not communicate honestly and frankly, especially when death seems imminent. Such dishonesty is not deliberate; it is caused by a reluctance to address the issue. In a grim situation (e.g., when a patient has cancer that is metastasizing and may spread to the brain), the case manager might be the person most able to introduce the subject by asking, "Have you thought about a living will? Perhaps you want to discuss this with your physician or your attorney?" The case manager can make the patient and family aware of support services; help the patient and family come to grips with the reality of the prognosis; and assist in the completion of an estate will, a living will (Exhibit 15-1), or a health care proxy (a.k.a. medical directive, a document that clearly states the patient's wishes regarding life-prolonging measures; see Exhibit 15-2);

Exhibit 15–1 Living Will

I, *, residing at *, County of Suffolk and State of New York, do hereby make, publish and declare this is my LIVING WILL in manner as follows:

FIRST: I willfully and voluntarily make known my desire that no life-sustaining procedures be used to prolong my dying. If at any time I have a terminal condition certified to be such by two physicians who have personally examined me, one of whom is my attending physician, and the physicians have determined that my condition is irreversible and that my death will occur within a relatively short period of time without the use of life-sustaining procedures which would serve only to prolong the dying process, then in that event, I direct that the procedures be withheld or withdrawn, and that I be permitted to die naturally. These procedures shall specifically include but shall not be limited to mechanical respiration, cardiac resuscitation, blood transfusion, feeding and hydration tubes, or organ transplant. I direct that this advanced directive be liberally construed.

I further direct my physicians to take the same action with the same responsibilities and consequences as set forth above in the event that I should become irreversibly senile. To help my physicians to make such determination, I direct that I be deemed senile if I am unable to communicate either my name, the place where I am, or the names of my immediate family members.

In addition, I make the same directions and relieve the same persons from any responsibility in the event that I am afflicted by an incurable, fatal, or debilitating disease, and have been judicially declared incompetent.

SECOND: This LIVING WILL is intended to include but is not limited to such life-sustaining procedures as machines which act as substitutes for organs, blood transfusions, feeding tubes and surgical operations. It does not include such procedures or medication which would make me more comfortable and relieve my physical pain.

THIRD: In the absence of my ability to give directions regarding the use of life-sustaining procedures, it is my intention that this Declaration be honored by my family and physicians and any health facility in which I may be a patient as the final expression of my legal right to refuse medical or surgical treatment and I accept the consequences from the refusal. In this event, I hereby appoint my wife *, as my irrevocable attorney-in-fact, to communicate to the fullest extent possible all of my directions and intentions declared in this my LIVING WILL, to all necessary persons, including but not limited to my physicians, all other health care providers and all members of my family. This power of attorney shall not be affected by my

(continues)

Exhibit 15–1 continued

subsequent disability or incompetence. In addition, I hereby nominate my said designated agent as Conservator of my property and Committee of my person and property upon the happening of any of the events named herein. In the event my wife predeceases me, fails to qualify, or ceases to act as my said agent, then I hereby appoint my *, *, to act in her place and stead.

FOURTH: I hereby relieve physicians, any hospital or other institution and my designated agents of any liability for damage or death resulting therefrom, directly or indirectly, including any claim of malpractice by me or my Estate.

FIFTH: I direct that if my physician, or my hospital or other institution refuse to obey my wishes in this matter, that my designated agent herein nominated commence suit against such physician and/or hospital or other institution, for all of the hospital costs, drugs, medical expenses, and all other damages flowing from such refusal, and I direct further that neither their bills for subsequent services be paid nor the bills of any other doctors substituted therefor.

SIXTH: This LIVING WILL may be revoked only by personal service of a revocation executed by me upon all persons in possession of the original or to whom any certified copy hereof has been delivered, or known to be in possession thereof, and is otherwise irrevocable. I understand that the Court of Appeals has held that my family or designated agent(s) must show that "as far as is humanly possible" I have not had a change of mind, and I intend that any change of mind must be shown as directed in this paragraph only, and without such written revocation, it is my direction that it must be permitted that I have not had a change of mind, no matter how long a time has elapsed between the execution of this document and the enforcement of this Living Will. An affidavit by the attorney in possession of the original with regard to the issuance and location of certified copies hereof shall be deemed sufficient.

SEVENTH: This document must be executed in the same manner as a Will.

SUBSCRIBED, this * day of *, 1993.

Living Testator

(continues)

Exhibit 15–1 continued

WE, whose names are hereto subscribed, DO CERTIFY AND AT-
TEST that on the date stated above, the Living Testator subscribed his
name to this instrument, in our presence and in the presence of each
of us and at the same time in our presence and hearing declared the
same to be his LIVING WILL and requested us and each of us to sign
our names thereto as witnesses to the execution thereof, which we
hereby do in the presence of the Living Testator and of each other on
the said date, and write opposite our names and respective places of
residence. We do further attest and affirm that at the time of the execution of this instrument by said Living Testator, it appeared to us
that he was a person of sound mind and memory.

_____ residing at _____

_____

_____ residing at _____

_____

Courtesy of Davidow & Davidow, Islandia, New York.

and help arrange for a health care surrogate (a person named by the patient to make health care decisions for him in the event of his incapacitation), cremation, a grave plot, or donation of organs. Information on living wills and health care surrogates is accessible through the media,
hospitals, attorneys, health care organizations, and lay publications.

Case managers not only face the issue of death, they also face issues of
continued "living." How many drugs, unproved treatments, or severe
pain will a patient and family endure? Some patients desire treatment
even when there is only a 1-percent chance of success, whereas others
with a 75-percent chance of remaining alive but facing a different way of
life choose to forgo treatment. In these difficult situations, the case manager must provide the objective viewpoint.

It is important to impress on the patient and family that decisions
should be made in a timely manner; it is too late when the patient is in and
out of a coma and family members start arguing over what to do. It might
be appropriate to suggest a family meeting early on, especially if there are

Exhibit 15–2 Health Care Proxy

(1) I, _____

hereby appoint _____
(name, home address and telephone number)
_____

as my health care agent to make any and all health care decisions for me, except to the extent that I state otherwise. This proxy shall take effect when and if I become unable to make my own health care decisions.

(2) Optional instructions: I direct my agent to make health care decisions in accord with my wishes and limitations as stated below, or as he or she otherwise knows. (Attach additional pages if necessary.)

This Health Care Proxy contains no limitations. I have discussed with my
Agent, and my Agent knows my wishes concerning artificial nutrition and
hydration.

(Unless your agent knows your wishes about artificial nutrition and hydration [feeding tubes], your agent will not be allowed to make decisions about artificial nutrition and hydration.

(3) Name of substitute or fill-in agent if the person I appoint above is unable, unwilling or unavailable to act as my health care agent.

_____
(name, home address and telephone number)
_____

(4) Unless I revoke it, this proxy shall remain in effect indefinitely, or until the date or conditions stated below. This proxy shall expire (specific dates or conditions, if desired):

_____
_____

(5) Signature _____
Address _____
Date _____
Statement by Witnesses (must be 18 or older)
I declare that the person who signed this document is personally known to me and appears to be of sound mind and acting of his or her own free will. He or she signed (or asked another to sign for him or her) this document in my presence.
Witness 1 _____
Address _____
Witness 2 _____
Address _____

Courtesy of Davidow & Davidow, Islandia, New York. Prepared by: Lawrence Eric Davidow, Esq.

several adult children and a dying elderly parent. Families need to be told that patients almost always want to be involved in decision making about their care and their future. The case manager should ensure that the patient knows he or she does not have to consent to all forms of treatment. Everyone should be clear about the arrangements that the patient is going to want and the family is going to be comfortable with.

IMPLICATIONS OF LONG-TERM CARE FOR THE FAMILY

Long-term care has numerous implications for the family, many of them resulting from the patient's illness and prognosis. It is much easier for the family—and for the case manager—when the long-term situation has improvement as an end goal. The more uncertain or grave the future, the more stressful the case becomes. In this type of situation, the case manager cannot say, "It's a bad day; things will get better." When the prognosis is not good, a family may accept the likely death of the patient or refuse to believe the physician's opinion. In most cases, the family sees someone who was once a healthy active member and contributor but is now irreversibly changed.

Attention must also be given to the primary caregiver. Just as the patient should be encouraged to find a disease-specific support group, so too should the caregiver be encouraged to arrange for periods of respite and to talk with people facing similar challenges. There are numerous associations for spouses, parents who have a child with a long-term illness, and for siblings or children of individuals suffering from a long-term illness. The benefits are multiple: for the caregiver, for the long-term patient, and more practically, for the client who will continue to contain costs.

Quite often in long-term cases, whatever strains there were in the family before the illness become exacerbated and the whole situation seems beyond remedy. I call it the "fractured family syndrome." Divorce, alcoholism, emotional illness, overwhelming depression, adolescent rebelliousness, child abuse—case managers see all of these things in such situations. The combination of horrendous health care problems, personal or family stresses, and real or potential financial difficulties can cause unending emotional turmoil. Tension builds, especially in younger families. It is typical for a young mother to be the care provider for an aging and ill parent while fulfilling the roles of wife and parent. Her husband or children may feel neglected. What case managers sometimes see then is resentful and attention-seeking children develop behavior problems or start experimenting with drugs. Or, a spouse may start drinking heavily or become totally involved in work, avoiding the home. In some cases, the family falls apart. The primary caregiver cannot manage it any more.

There are many examples of the spouse of a person with multiple sclerosis, after years of giving caring support and knowing that there are years to come of the same or worse, simply leaving.

What should the case manager do in situations such as these? Following are some tips on helping families through a crisis period:

1. Suggest family counseling.
2. Suggest the primary caregiver join an appropriate support group.
3. Recommend books on coping, such as the *Family Guide to Stroke* (American Heart Association), *Taking Time: Support for People with Cancer and the People Who Care about Them* (National Cancer Institute, National Institutes of Health, U.S. Department of Health and Human Services), *Right to Die* (Group for the Advancement of Psychiatry), *The AIDS Caregiver's Handbook* (St. Martin's Press), *The Caregiver's Journey* (HarperCollins), and *Living with Lupus* (Addison-Wesley). (For pertinent guides, check with national associations, which often put together recommended reading lists.)
4. Remind family members to keep their own appointments and to take care of themselves.
5. Help the family members communicate and achieve some level of comfort with feelings of fear, anxiety, and so on.

Case managers should also remember to get support for themselves through contact with peers. Some case managers try to relive their own experiences through other families, which is detrimental to all involved.

IMPLICATIONS OF A LONG-TERM CASE FOR THE CASE MANAGER

It is important to note that long-term cases have many implications, often hidden at first, for case managers. Case managers react very differently when working long-term cases. The more problematic the case and the more dissolved the family becomes, the greater the burden placed on the case manager. Even though the patient's medical condition may become more stable, other long-term problems occur and the case manager might feel like the only person who is truly attempting to face them. The family may want out and may dump their concerns on the case manager as a way of seeking relief. Frequently case managers become disheartened and burn out.

Some case managers do a very good job of being compassionate and supportive while keeping themselves from becoming too personally involved. However, others cross the line, and that is dangerous because they sacrifice their objective professionalism. There are many reasons or triggers that may lead a case manager to become too personally connected. A 34-year-old case manager working a case where a husband is caring for his 34-year-old wife dying of breast cancer can become too connected. A transference of feelings occurs, and the case manager identifies with the patient. She loses her objectivity and, not realizing it, starts to make decisions based on how she would personally like things done if she were the patient.

There are other circumstances that may obstruct objectivity. Perhaps the husband-caregiver reminds a case manager of her ex-husband, whom she is fighting for child support payments. Perhaps the patient is dying of Alzheimer's and the case manager's mother has just been diagnosed with Alzheimer's. There may be a personality conflict between the case manager and the caregiver, which can obstruct objectivity as much as feelings of empathy can.

There can also be situations in which the case manager has not lost objectivity but simply is no longer effective or useful on the case. At the beginning stages of the case, her energy level was high, she carefully analyzed all parameters, and she devised a workable and cost-effective plan that met the needs of the patient. After a while, changes occurred and everything she tried in response failed. Now the case manager is running out of ideas. The case begins to haunt her, and there is no end in sight. She is no longer a catalyst for improvement.

When no longer objective or effective, case managers need to be honest concerning their own feelings. They must recognize their worth and their contribution or lack of contribution. They need to have open communication with peers and supervisors.

In fact, I think long-term cases require periodic conferences between case managers and supervisors so that the value of the case management process can be continually assessed. Is the case manager making a difference? Is she just reporting to the client, almost like a journalist? Is she acting as a catalyst for change? Or is she identifying the same problems month after month but not coming up with any new solutions? Such reevaluations can uncover the need for a fresh perspective on the case—perhaps that of a different case manager.

Confronting her lack of effectiveness can be very difficult for a case manager, particularly if she has a small one-person business and substantial income may be lost if the she gives up the case. But honesty is absolutely necessary, and if the case manager is not making a difference, for whatever reason, she does not belong on the case. A supervisor in a larger case management unit or company may have to make such decisions, but ideally each case manager will develop an ability to judge her own contributions accurately. Honesty must also extend to the family and client. If a case manager decides that she is no longer effective, she should discuss this with the client, explaining that while the case still requires case management services, she is not the right person for this particular case at this time. Difficult? Yes, but vital if the case manager is to remain effective and provide real help to patients and families in long-term cases.

A CASE HISTORY

Marge Reynolds, a 46-year-old mother of two teens, has a 27-year history of chronic colitis, which she apparently had under control using a combination of medication and diet. In April, she was admitted to the hospital for complaints of abdominal and gastrointestinal distress, vomiting, weight loss, and abdominal pain. Two-and-a-half years earlier, she had developed increasing and unremitting abdominal pains and had entered the hospital at that time for a diagnostic work-up. She underwent a colectomy with anastomosis following the discovery of a partial bowel obstruction, but she elected to forgo a colostomy despite the warnings of her physicians. One week after the surgery, Mrs. Reynolds suffered acute abdominal bleeding. Additional surgery and a colostomy were performed. Her recovery progressed well, and she returned to her normal activities.

The next year, Mrs. Reynolds experienced prolonged vaginal bleeding and was diagnosed as having uterine cancer. Based on her medical history, a complete hysterectomy was done, with additional testing to rule out metastatic disease or ovarian cancer. Her chemotherapy treatments were completed just prior to the onset of the pains and vomiting that led to her hospital admission in April.

Twelve days after her admission and diagnostic work-ups, which incorporated CAT scans and MRI testing, Mrs. Reynolds' surgeon performed exploratory surgery. The operations included a resection of the bowel and stoma, relocation of the stoma site, resection of the abdominal wall, and insertion of a Teflon mesh to replace an excised section of body wall necessitated by multiple tumors of metastatic origin.

Mrs. Reynolds' timely recovery was compromised by her generally weakened condition from previous chemotherapy treatments and further complicated by the need for the insertion of a Porta-Cath to provide nutritional support, as she was experiencing vomiting, diarrhea (related to short bowel syndrome), dehydration, and malnutrition. The hospital social worker recommended that Mrs. Reynolds be kept in the hospital based on the delay in her stabilization, the fact that she required highly sophisticated intravenous TPN 24 hours a day, and her determined resistance to hospice care.

When a hospital extension was first requested for patient stabilization, a preadmission–utilization review nurse red-flagged Mrs. Reynolds' file for case management. One of our independent case managers visited Mrs. Reynolds in the hospital. Finding her too ill to converse, the case manager consulted her chart and reviewed her progress with Mrs. Reynolds' husband, the treating physicians, the nursing staff, the utilization review nurse, and a hospital social worker. From the family physician and Mr. Reynolds, the case manager learned of Mrs. Reynolds' previous hospital admissions, her fight against colon and ovarian cancer, and her recent chemotherapy treatments.

In her initial report, sent to the insurer just short of one month after Mrs. Reynolds entered the hospital, the case manager noted the patient was in a generally weakened condition and was hampered by an underfunctioning ileostomy and episodes of vomiting and frequent diarrhea. The assessment also included detailed descriptions of treatment and medication, the surgeon's planned insertion of a tripe lumen, central venous catheter, or Porta-Cath, and the observation that Mrs. Reynolds was able to get out of bed with assistance and required help with ambulating and hygiene.

During her on-site visit to the hospital, the case manager had been able to discuss the home environment and the potential for home care services with Mr. Reynolds, the hospital nurses, and the social worker. That home care seemed a possibility was welcome news, as Mrs. Reynolds had made it clear that she did not want to be admitted to a hospice. Due to the complexity of Mrs. Reynolds' treatment, the option of home care had not occurred to the treating physician, nurses, or social worker, but the case manager was able to assure the hospital staff and family that home care was a viable alternative for Mrs. Reynolds. In conversation, the case manager confirmed that the insurer would cover the cost of a home health aide, episodic RN attendance, and home IV therapy or hyperalimentation (which was then being considered by the treating physician). The case manager also received word from the treating physicians that home care was a perfectly acceptable medical alternative to hospice care. Discharge was delayed until Mrs. Reynolds' condition improved.

In mid-May, a Porta-Cath was inserted and TPN infusion begun in an effort to stabilize Mrs. Reynolds' condition. She responded well to the nutritional support and experienced less nausea, vomiting, and gastric distress. During the case manager's next visit, Mrs. Reynolds was eating several small meals a day. Working closely with the hospital staff, the case manager continued coordinating discharge planning and home care services.

Mrs. Reynolds' family supported the idea of home treatment but were unable to be at home during the day to administer that care. Accepting bids from the most qualified suppliers and negotiating for the most cost-effective treatment, the case manager arranged for home nursing services (HNS), a home health aide, and TPN services. In early July, less than seven weeks after she arrived at the hospital, Mrs. Reynolds was able to go home.

Instead of continuing her acute hospitalization, she was able to receive treatment at home, assisted by a home health aide who helped with bathing, dressing, meal preparation, and other personal activities. An HNS nurse taught Mr. and Mrs. Reynolds how to hang her intravenous fluids, how to perform tubing changes, how to monitor the electrolyte balance and glucose levels, and what to do in an emergency. From her office, the case manager pushed the insurer to allow her to make a home visit a few days after Mrs. Reynolds' discharge. She wanted to see the program in action and make sure her plan was effective. Her visit was timely.

The infusion company had overstocked the Reynolds' home with supplies, making it difficult to move through the house, and charged for unneeded equipment and fluids that could not possibly be used before their expiration date. Reviewing the invoices, the case manager also found that the firm had charged for a period of 28 days when Mrs. Reynolds was still in the hospital, and it was billing for pump rental and infusion nursing visits that it had previously agreed would be included in the per diem cost. The case manager arranged for immediate credits to the account.

She also noted that Mrs. Reynolds was receiving 24 hours of TPN, unusual for homebound patients because it eliminates any freedom of movement the individual might enjoy. Following conversations with the HNS nurse and family physician, approval was given for Mrs. Reynolds to receive her full prescribed volume of TPN Intralipids over a 20-hour period. The case manager's aim was to allow Mrs. Reynolds to move about her home, increasing her stamina and independence. To boost her mobility, the case manager got carrier approval for a rental wheelchair (no loaner wheelchairs were available from community loan closets). The allowed interruption in infusion therapy and the wheelchair enabled Mrs. Reynolds to attend her son's high school graduation later that month, an important emotional and physical outing that boosted her spirits and reinforced the family's sense of wholeness.

The case manager continued monitoring the home infusion therapy and TPN, Mrs. Reynolds' medical condition, and the need for nursing and home health aide services. In subsequent visits, the case manager noticed that Mrs. Reynolds appeared to have gained strength and a little weight and was pleased with her increased mobility. With her TPN and other infusions now being completed in 18 hours, she was able to take showers, sit outside during good weather, and attend family gatherings. Mrs. Reynolds was also independent in setting up her TPN solutions, tubing, and changing infusion bottles. Her daily life was a far stretch from the acute hospitalization she could well have been experiencing.

Unfortunately, due to the onset of severe back pain and other complications from previous battles with cancer, Mrs. Reynolds was subsequently readmitted to the hospital. With ongoing intervention by the case manager, her hospital stay was of short duration, and she was able to return home. The case manager's continued home visits proved invaluable when the case manager found Mrs. Reynolds in a medical crisis that the attending home health aide was unable to manage. After contacting the treating physician and conducting a re-evaluation of Mrs. Reynolds' home situation in light of her deteriorating condition, the case manager arranged for additional RN support. She also suggested family counseling to help ease the stress felt by Mr. Reynolds and the two teenagers, who were trying unsuccessfully to cope with terminal illness and death.

Through the case manager's early involvement, Mrs. Reynolds was able to experience increased self-reliance and to live the last months of her life at home with her family. Although the wheelchair rental was a very small item in the whole home care picture, it gave Mrs. Reynolds and her family a highlight to remember. Because of the case manager's attention to detail and knowledge of the latest technologies, Mrs. Reynolds received a preferred alternative to hospital or hospice care, and the insurer paid fewer and less expensive claims.

The value of case management to Mrs. Reynolds and her family might be incalculable, but a review of one quarter's cost-benefit analysis report sent by our case manager to the insurer shows exactly what case management meant to the bottom line. Under "avoidance of potential charges," there are 70 days in the hospital at $1,300 per day, plus pharmacy and physician charges totaling $91,000. Total actual charges for case management fees, reduced-rate TPN, and negotiated fees for home health aide and nursing services came to $32,575, for a net savings of $58,425.[1] The case manager also discovered $12,500 in overcharges submitted by the TPN vendor; this amount would have boosted actual charges to $45,075.

NOTE

1. C.M. Mullahy, "Making Case Management Count," *The Case Manager*, July–September 1991, 40–48.

Techniques for AIDS Cases

Case managers working with HIV-positive patients face all the challenges of other types of long-term, catastrophic care cases plus additional elements that don't present themselves in other diagnoses. These include issues of confidentiality, access to information, social stigmatization, prejudice against certain lifestyles, and benefits manipulation.

AIDS carries a social weight attached to no other diagnosis or disease I or my case managers have encountered. There are numerous barriers and roadblocks we run into while trying to reach out to AIDS patients and attempting to gain for them the most benefit from the health delivery system. Without a doubt, the greatest hindrance to our work is the "fear and loathing" that the affliction can generate. Some families and friends remain supportive; others desert those with the disease. In one case our office managed, the family welcomed the patient back into their home only in order to profit from his disability checks. They did not prepare food for him; they did not help attend to his needs. He moved into an apartment and died alone.

A secondary hurdle is the issue of confidentiality. Because of the stigma attached to the disease, concern about confidentiality is understandable. Patients do not want to be shunned at the office or fired. Neither do they want to see their health benefits disappear. Under the guise of preserving benefit dollars for the group (i.e., heeding their fiduciary responsibility), employers have been known to suddenly limit benefit payouts for claims associated with HIV and AIDS. In one instance, we were working on behalf of an AIDS patient whose employer assured us that it valued this person's contributions and planned to take good care of him. Our case manager negotiated in good faith excellent contracts for IV therapy services. Months later, the providers began calling the case manager to report unpaid bills. The claims administrator said that claims were being processed and passed along to the employer for final approval. Too late, we discovered that not only had the employer decided to place a retroactive cap on claims to be paid out for HIV-associated claims but it also had been holding all our patient's claims from the onset of care until costs accumulated to reach that mark. The employer had no intention of "taking good care" of the patient, and unfortunately he lived long enough to get that message clearly, facing the added worry of how his caretakers were going to be paid. (Under ERISA, employers have up to 270 days, or *nine months*, to notify benefit plan members or insureds that their contract has been changed.)

Care providers have been less than forthcoming as well. One doctor absolutely refused to return any calls. In another case, our case manager introduced herself, faxed over her consent authorization, assured the medical records administrator that she knew the patient and the patient's HIV status, yet was denied access to any information until the patient called and said that the information should be released to her.

All such barriers need to be broken down. AIDS is an epidemic that cuts across gender, age, race, and social strata. In nursing school, students are taught to be nonjudgmental; some nurses obviously slept in the day that lecture was given. Prior to taking an HIV-positive case, a case manager should carefully examine her own feelings on the issues. What are her thoughts on gay and lesbian lifestyles? AIDS is not a gay or lesbian disease, but much of the media coverage and emotional reaction to AIDS revolves around the issue of homosexuality. Can the case manager separate the disease from the person she is helping? For so many tangible and intangible reasons, HIV infection seems to stand apart from all other diagnoses. Can she be unbiased in her management of the patient's care? Has she addressed her own feelings about death? Some patients suffering with AIDS are in total denial regarding their demise. Others have accepted the proximity of death but cannot conquer their fear of dependence on others. How will the case manager react when a patient—a person she has been working with for two years, a person who has shared with her intimate details of his life—tells her that he plans to commit suicide if he becomes blind? How does she feel about suicide? Is she prepared for the angry reactions from some family members, the "it's his own damn fault" response that a few feel is appropriate?

I asked my case management supervisors who have worked a number of HIV cases what they would tell a case manager preparing to meet her first HIV-positive patient. They emphasized that the case manager should examine her own response to the prospect of taking the case, and if she has strong adverse feelings, she should explore the option of giving over the case to another case manager. (Once she takes a case on, the case manager should avoid turning over the patient to another person if at all possible; the case manager–HIV patient relationship, more than others, requires stability.) They suggested that she know the diseases related to AIDS very well, gathering information by reading and by attending lectures and conferences. Over the course of her involvement, the case manager should educate the patient, and help the patient become his own case manager. This is a good idea in any case, but HIV patients in particular can benefit greatly by taking an active role in their case management. Many HIV-positive patients are extremely knowledgeable and alert to the subtle changes in their condition that might signal a problem; when accustomed to alerting their case managers and physicians of impending difficulties, their care becomes 100 percent improved and they maintain a much better overall condition and spirit.

The case management supervisors further emphasized that AIDS patients need consistency in the relationship and case managers should develop a strong rapport with their patients. To do this, they will need patience, patience, and more patience. Building trust may be the biggest hurdle. For multiple reasons, HIV-positive patients are wary and skeptical, more so than cancer or MS patients or any other patient group. They are very reluctant to open up and allow themselves to rely on any new person. Sometimes establishing a relationship is a slow process; sometimes it is almost impossible. The case manager needs to be able to approach the patient at the level where intervention becomes acceptable. There might be 30 or 40 things the case manager can suggest that will help; the patient might be willing to listen to only one. The case manager might have to present the options and return to them in three months. In three months, the patient might be willing to discuss certain topics (e.g., a living will, or a medical directive) but be unwilling to act until another three months have passed. More than any other patient–case manager relationship, this one requires continued nurturing and effort.

It should also be said that it is difficult sometimes for case managers to maintain their objectivity in HIV cases because they do become so involved. They learn much about their patients' lives, sometimes more than they expected to ever know about a patient. It can be a tough job to build the rapport needed to help a patient and still be able to step back and assess the patient's condition and needs in an impartial manner.

There are resources that case managers can tap for information and as-sistance regarding AIDS, such as Gay Men's Health Crisis Inc. (in Man-hattan) and the Long Island Association for AIDS Care. The New York State Department of Health sponsors care programs for New York State residents with HIV infection who are uninsured or underinsured. These include the AIDS Drug Assistance Program (ADAP), ADAP Plus, and the HIV Home Care Uninsured Fund. ADAP, designed for people with par-tial insurance or subject to a Medicaid spenddown requirement, provides free medications to treat HIV/AIDS and opportunistic infections. ADAP Plus covers free primary care services at selected clinics and hospital out-patient facilities. Supplementing or replacing medical insurance for AIDS patients, the HIV Home Care Uninsured Fund covers home care services such as home health aides, IV therapy, medications, supplies, lab tests, and durable medical equipment for chronically dependent individuals as ordered by their physicians. Some experimental drugs are available through FDA programs, while nontraditional, nonapproved medications can be obtained via underground AIDS drug networks.

CASES IN PROFILE

A Noncooperative Physician

When he was referred to one of our case managers, Mr. Jackson* had been HIV positive for two years. He was 48 years old, had no AIDS-diag-nosis, and had been hospitalized for dizziness, loss of consciousness, and questionable seizure. Because of his HIV status, his hospitalization claim was marked for case management intervention. His significant other, an alcoholic, had died six months prior. His difficulty in dealing with the death of his significant other, along with his HIV status, had led him to retire. With absolutely no family and no support system, Mr. Jackson had paid a neighbor, Mr. Miller, to serve as his guardian and executor of his will. He lived in a fourth-floor walk-up apartment, and climbing the stairs became a problem as his illness progressed.

Wasting syndrome and fatigue were Mr. Jackson's most visible symp-toms. He also had herpes and chronic fungal infection in his mouth, mak-ing it difficult for him to eat. But the greatest problem with this individual was his physician. The doctor was generally noncommunicative and non-cooperative with every member of the health care team. He did not return phone calls and did not return the case manager's questionnaire. He did not respond to the social worker and was nasty to the nurses on the floor.

---

*All the names in the case histories have been changed.

When reached by phone or met at the hospital and asked a question, he would give only rude answers or no response at all. He would answer no questions about Mr. Jackson and provided no diagnostic information. Although Mr. Jackson was aware of the problem ("I know my doctor won't do anything," he said) and friends encouraged him to change physicians (the case manager even researched and made referrals of other physicians), he would not change. The case manager was new to case management and this was her first HIV case, making the situation a greater challenge to her personally.

The patient gradually started to decline. He became more and more cachexic as a result of the wasting syndrome common to HIV patients, and his fatigue increased. He had limited benefits for a home health aide and nursing visits (40 visits per year). Through research, the case manager was able to get Mr. Jackson into the New York State HIV Uninsured Care Program, which provided for daily attendance by a home health aide and weekly nursing visits. Because Mr. Jackson refused to allow the aide to cook for him, she implemented a Meals on Wheels plan for him. The case manager believed that perhaps dementia was starting to evolve at this point; the patient's responses and attitudes were becoming slightly strange. When she tried to discuss all of these things with the physician, he was completely unresponsive. He never responded to questions about TPN, which would have been appropriate to treat his patient's cachexia. The patient himself also hindered treatment by refusing any drugs or therapies that might have improved his condition, such as AZT. He was willing to go on supplemental oral feedings but was able to drink only one can per day.

For the six months he was in case management, the patient remained very private and enigmatic. When asked if he had told his doctor that he did not want certain treatments, he said, "No, but I won't go on AZT." He had a will but did not have a do-not-resuscitate order.

Four months after initial case management involvement, Mr. Jackson's condition deteriorated. Following a nursing assessment, he was admitted to the hospital suffering from a change in mental status, headaches, disorientation, and neck stiffness. His dementia increased and his temperature spiked to 104; he was diagnosed with meningitis and was treated with antibiotics.

To counteract the lack of a support system, the case manager researched hospice facilities for Mr. Jackson. He expressed a desire to enter the facility in which his significant other had stayed. When the case manager tried to place Mr. Jackson in hospice, the physician did not answer the facility's questions regarding the patient and his diagnosis. Further, the employer, which had affirmed that it would take care of Mr. Jackson's needs, denied that it had said anything of that nature to the guardian, Mr. Miller, when the time came to respond. The employer did not decrease Mr. Jackson's benefits but refused to go out of benefits on the patient's behalf when that became necessary.

As difficult as it was, the case manager talked with Mr. Jackson to plan for the future. He again confided that if his condition worsened, he wanted to be admitted to the facility in which his significant other had died. He could not be sent home because that would have required backup care in addition to the 24-hour nursing service, and Mr. Miller, the guardian, was not willing to be responsible for that care. The physician went on vacation; he did not respond to the case manager, the social worker, or to the facility in which the patient had expressed an interest. The patient remained in the hospital until the day he died two months later. There were absolutely no savings in this case, and the case manager offered her opinion that the physician hastened the demise of his patient.

Turning the Tables

In contrast, Mr. Davis, a 35-year-old man who is HIV-positive, was referred to us when he was admitted to the hospital for diarrhea and abdominal pains. When the case manager met him, Mr. Davis had been HIV-positive for three years, was fairly healthy and active, and was employed as the head of the sales department for a computer company. His employer was and is extremely supportive and has extended his benefit package beyond the plan contract. Surrounded by a family that is both financially and emotionally supportive, he has been welcomed into his mother's home when he needed additional care (his father recently passed away). A sister in particular has been very involved in learning more about HIV and AIDS and has been in regular contact with the case manager concerning her brother.

Approximately a year after the case manager had been introduced to Mr. Davis, he was diagnosed with CMV (cytomegalovirus) retinitis, which destroys the retina and therefore, over time, vision. Treated with high-tech infusion therapy (ganciclovir or DHPG), the patient is able to give himself infusions without assistance. He is very conscious of the costs associated with his care. He has had no nursing visits; he refuses them. In his case, because he is attended by his family and a very compassionate physician, savings through case management have probably been greater than 50 percent.

His physician is very caring and monitors Mr. Davis extremely closely, and although it did take a while to develop a relationship with the case manager (because she was referred by "an insurer"), the physician does respond to her calls. ("He is very soft spoken," she jokes, "but he *does* talk to me.") He is also very willing to work with the case manager to minimize costs. As an example, Mr. Davis has limited home nursing visits available, 40 per year. Those visits could have been used up very swiftly for laboratory draws because Mr. Davis has a central line. When the physician heard about the situation, he allowed the patient to come into his office and have his lab draws taken there. That alone accounts for tremendous savings per year. The physician is also excellent at coordinating Mr. Davis's care with other quality physicians, including an ophthalmologist.

In general, the patient has been stable but does have a problem with CMV retinitis. When relating this case history, the case manager remembered a patient visit that stood out because Mr. Davis, unlike usual, was very depressed. Her skills in creating and sustaining rapport while retaining professional poise were put to the test. The patient–case manager discussion revolved around Mr. Davis's psychological status. She wanted to help pinpoint his fear so they could address it together. She found that death did not threaten him; however, he found blindness unacceptable.

Before he had become sick, the case manager had applied to all potential sources of financial assistance. Mr. Davis made it clear that he was not a believer in the value of psychological counseling. The antidepressant Prozac was suggested. The case manager utilized the New York State AIDS Drug Assistance Program as a supplement to his medical insurance; it covers the copayment and deductible for the patient. Mr. Davis is also already enrolled in the state's HIV uninsured program. He also has 18 months of COBRA coverage on a contingency basis, should he require it.

Continuing to do well despite a T-cell count that is barely perceptible, Mr. Davis is maintaining a more positive attitude, has gained weight, and is staying healthier. He and the case manager decided to ignore his T cells for now; based on the numbers alone, he should not be as well as he is. When he was depressed, he developed more problems. Now on Prozac, he is in better shape overall and has been out of the hospital for seven months. He does have Kaposi's sarcoma the size of a half-dollar on his foot. Due to increasing severity of the CMV retinitis, he has had to stop working. The drugs he is taking for retinitis have severe side effects, decreasing his white blood cell count and making him more susceptible to other infections. His physician has considered admitting Mr. Davis to the hospital to treat him with foscarnet sodium, but because it is a much more toxic medication than ganciclovir and causes additional side effects, they are trying to hold off as long as possible on that decision. Fairly stable, Mr. Davis suffers from fatigue and sweats, but there is no dementia, and diarrhea has diminished.

He and his case manager discuss his change in attitude openly. He knows that psychological problems take their toll, and his health is better when he can live as fully and joyfully as possible. They also periodically discuss the need for a living will and an estate will. Mr. Davis has had a will for his estate drawn up but has not been able to finalize the paperwork. He continues to avoid preparation of a living will, and his case manager has decided to table conversation on that topic for a few months.

On her most recent quarterly cost-benefit analysis report, the case manager noted in her summary of intervention that she had monitored the claimant's medical status via phone and personal visits to the patient and his physicians to prevent complications. She was able to negotiate cost-effective pricing for ganciclovir and filgrastim (or G-CSF) and also negotiated fees for medication changes, resulting in lowered fees for days when medications were wasted. Total potential charges for Mr. Davis during the quarter were $71,128.00. Through alternate care and case management, actual fees were only $28,863.40, for a net savings of $42,264.60.

Significant Support and Lack of Support

Mr. Taylor was a 42-year-old who had never had a major illness prior to his admittance to the hospital in September with a diagnosis of pneumonia. He had been experiencing fatigue, especially after exercise, increasing body aches, and other flu-like symptoms. A sudden shortness of breath brought him to the emergency room. The staff inquired about his HIV status; Mr. Taylor was tested and told that he was HIV-positive.

At the time of the referral, the case manager was unaware of his HIV status; the case was flagged for the diagnosis of pneumonia. Initially, the case manager had a tremendous amount of trouble getting in touch with the patient. The physician who had admitted him was very uncooperative. Following his discharge, Mr. Taylor switched to a physician who was well-known in AIDS treatment circles, and who did cooperate with the case manager, at least when he wanted services put in place. With strong support from his significant other, Mr. Taylor remained well and stable for a few months and lived comfortably at home.

Once the first symptoms appeared, however, the effects of the disease became severe fairly rapidly. The case manager was able to put IV therapy services in place for him at home at a good negotiated rate. (He required no other services—no home health aide or hospice care.) Within three to four months, he was no longer able to work because he was physically unable to be at the job site owing to complications (Kaposi's sarcoma and CMV retinitis). In very poor shape, he was admitted to the hospital in July with pneumonia and required a ventilator. The physician became uncommunicative and never did return the case manager's calls regarding Mr. Taylor's condition. She found out through the medical records department that he had expired.

Unfortunately, the employer group had decided midway through the course of treatment to limit HIV reimbursement to $25,000 lifetime. As it stands now, the company that provided IV services for Mr. Taylor has billed out in excess of $39,000 and has been paid less than $3,000. This was an extremely difficult situation for the case manager, who had negotiated in good faith, and a nightmare for Mr. Taylor. Just prior to his demise, he saw that his bills were going unpaid, and he was visibly concerned about how his caretakers would be paid. It has now become a concern of his estate.

During her course of intervention, the case manager provided support and information, arranged for assistance from compassionate organizations, facilitated initiation of home infusion services to expedite hospital discharge, and renegotiated for infusion services as changes in therapy occurred. Medications applied were Cytovene (ganciclovir) and Foscavir (foscarnet sodium). Without case management intervention, the cost of Cytovene and related services and supplies would have been $10,676.37 (customary charges) and the cost of Foscavir therapy and related services and supplies would have been $50,975.58 (customary charges). At $800 a day, hospitalization expenses for medication adjustments could have been $16,000.00. Total potential charges came to $77,651.95. Because of initial negotiations and renegotiations for IV services, alternate care and related actual charges were only $32,298.88, for a net savings of $45,353.07.

Fear of Living

Mr. Abatale was referred to our office in November 1990. We had received claims regarding AZT prescriptions and the infectious disease specialists that had seen him. Contact with Mr. Abatale was attempted on several occasions; he never replied. A letter was written to him in January 1991, followed by another in March. The case manager continued to request a meeting. She was able to reach him finally by telephone and saw him for the first time in April 1992. At that point, he was living with his parents, Italian immigrants who spoke no English. This was a man who was vice president of a company, traveled extensively, and until very recently had been actively employed and living on his own. An only son, he was his parents' link to society in this country, had handled all their needs for them, and was worried about what would happen to them after he died.

He had been healthy until 18 months prior to first contact with the case manager. For the last 4–5 months of this period, he had difficulty moving, became anemic, and complained of muscle weakness. Having been to several physicians, he was dissatisfied with the medical care he had received; he felt the physicians lacked compassion and that he had been shuttled around. He also went to see a psychotherapeutic counselor and was unhappy with his treatment there. He felt that no one was doing anything to help him.

When the case manager finally met with Mr. Abatale, the first words out his mouth were, "I am just waiting to die." He said he was putting his affairs in order and making arrangements for himself and, as he could, for his parents. Very much a loner, he had been abandoned by fair-weather friends, many of whom did not want to socialize with him once they found out what his problem was. The case manager asked if he had any interests; he responded that he could not pursue any interests due to his fatigue. Unwilling to become involved in any new pursuits or relationships, he did not want to meet people. He refused counseling, saying it served no purpose. He would sleep late in the morning and occasionally go to the physician. He exhibited no interest in doing anything and did not do anything. The case manager was struck by his despondency. "Here was a man who traveled the world and loved it, and he was sitting in his house in the darkness, literally, the drapes were drawn. As far as he was concerned, the only thing left for him was to die."

Ironically, this was a person who had none of the problems and complications customary with AIDS. He complained of minor aches and pains and suffered from poor affect and feelings of depression, but although his T-cell count would drop, he did not develop diarrhea or retinitis or wasting syndrome.

The case manager met with him for a year and a half. Over time, his attitude did change. He expressed appreciation to the case manager for her visits; he said he enjoyed the meetings, that the contact was positive, and that her interest in him made a difference. He began taking small trips, and his outlook improved. Following a vacation in Hawaii with his parents, he traveled to South America to visit old friends. When his file was closed in September 1993 (his company changed claim administrator companies, which unfortunately meant that his case had to be turned over to another case manager), Mr. Abatale was basically stable mentally and physically. The case manager felt the benefits from her involvement were less a matter of financial savings and more in the region of quality of life. Her client had been able to bring himself "back from the dead" and continue to experience a full, fairly active life.

These are only a few examples of the complexities and considerations involved when a case manager is working with an HIV-positive or AIDS patient. What is difficult to relate is the cold indifference of some family members, employers, and providers and the contrasting enthusiastic, steady support of others. There is much that can be done to help prolong and ease the lives of AIDS patients, and case managers have the opportunity to truly make a difference.

ASSOCIATIONS

The ALS Association
185 Madison Avenue
New York, NY 10016
(212) 679-4016

Also: 15300 Ventura Boulevard,
Suite 315
Sherman Oaks, CA 91403
(818) 990-2151

**American Association of
Occupational Health Nurses**
50 Lenox Pointe
Atlanta, GA 30324-3176
(404) 262-1162

**American Association of
Preferred Provider
Organizations**
1101 Connecticut Avenue, NW,
Suite 700
Washington, DC 20036
(202) 429-5133

American Burn Association
c/o Cleon W. Goodwyn, M.D.
Secretary, American Burn
Association
New York Hospital
Cornell Medical Center
525 E. 68th Street, Room L-706
New York, NY 10021
(800) 548-2876

American Cancer Society
90 Park Avenue
New York, NY 10016
(212) 599-8200

American Diabetes Association
1660 Duke Street
Alexandria, VA 22314
(703) 549-1500
(800) 232-3472

American Heart Association
7320 Greenville Avenue
Dallas, TX 75231
(214) 750-5300

American Hospital Association
840 North Lake Shore Drive
Chicago, IL 60611
(312) 280-6511

American Lung Association
1740 Broadway
New York, NY 10019
(212) 315-8700

American Managed Care and Review Association
1227 25th Street, NW, Suite 610
Washington, DC 20037
(202) 728-0506

American Medical Association
515 North State Street
Chicago, IL 60610
(800) 621-8335 (copies)
(312) 464-4706 (information)

Association of Rehabilitation Nurses
5700 Old Orchard Road, First Floor
Skokie, IL 60077-1057
(708) 966-3433

Blue Cross and Blue Shield Association
676 North St. Clair Street
Chicago, IL 60611
(312) 440-6345

Case Management Society of America
1101 17th Street, NW, Suite 1200
Washington, DC 20036
(202) 296-9200

Employee Benefit Research Institute
2121 K Street, NW, Suite 600
Washington, DC 20037-1896
(202) 659-0670

Health Insurance Association of America
1025 Connecticut Avenue, NW
Washington, DC 20036-3988
(202) 223-7836

Individual Case Management Association
10809 Executive Center Drive, Suite 105
Little Rock, AR 72211
(501) 227-5553

National AIDS Hotline
(800) 447-AIDS (specific information)
(800) 342-AIDS (general information, recording)

National Association for Home Care
519 C Street, NE
Washington, DC 20002-5809
(202) 547-7424

National Association of Rehabilitation Professionals in the Private Sector
313 Washington Street, Suite 302
Newton, MA 02158
(617) 558-5333

National Association of Social Workers
750 First Street, NE
Washington, DC 20002
(202) 408-8600

National Head Injury Foundation
1140 Connecticut Avenue, NW, Suite 812
Washington, DC 20036
(202) 296-6443

National Institutes of Health
900 Rockville Pike, Building 31
Bethesda, MD 20892
(301) 496-4000

**National Multiple Sclerosis
 Society**
205 East 42nd Street
New York, NY 10017
(212) 986-3240

**National Rehabilitation
 Association**
633 South Washington Street
Alexandria, VA 22314
(703) 836-0850

**JOURNALS AND
 MAGAZINES**

AAOHN Journal
50 Lenox Pointe
Atlanta, GA 30324-3176
(404) 262-1162

Business & Health
Five Paragon Drive
Montvale, NJ 07645
(201) 358-7200

Business Insurance
740 North Rush Street
Chicago, IL 60611-2590
(800) 678-9595

Case Management Advisor
3525 Piedmont Road, NE
Building Six, Suite 400
Atlanta, GA 30305
(800) 688-2421

The Case Manager
10809 Executive Center Drive
Suite 105
Little Rock, AR 72211
(501) 227-5553

Continuing Care
225 North New Road
Waco, TX 76710
(817) 751-7042

*Group Practice Managed Healthcare
 News*
201 Littleton Road
Suite 100
Morris Plain, NJ 07950-2932
(201) 285-0855

HomeCare
6133 Bristol Parkway
Culver City, CA 90231-3640
(310) 337-9717

Home Care News
519 C Street, NE
Washington, DC 20002
(202) 547-7424

Home Health Care Dealer/Supplier
4676 Admiralty Way
Marina del Rey, CA 90292
(310) 306-2206

Journal of Rehabilitation
1910 Association Drive
Suite 205
Reston, VA 22091
(703) 715-9090

Managed Care Quarterly
200 Orchard Ridge Drive
Gaithersburg, MD 20878
(800) 638-8437

Managed Care Week
1050 17th Street, NW
Suite 480
Washington, DC 20036
(202) 775-9008

Managed Healthcare News
859 Willamette Street
Eugene, OR 97440-2460
(503) 343-1200

Medical Economics
Five Paragon Drive
Montvale, NJ 07645
(201) 358-7200

Modern Healthcare
740 North Rush Street
Chicago, IL 60611-2590
(312) 649-5350

McKnight's Long-Term Care News
2 Northfield Plaza
Northfield, IL 60093
(708) 441-3700

Rehabilitation Nursing
5700 Old Orchard Road, First Floor
Skokie, IL 60077-1057
(708) 966-3433

Rehab Management
4676 Admiralty Way
Suite 202
Marina del Rey, CA 90292
(310) 306-2206

Risk & Insurance
747 Dresher Road
Suite 500
Horsham, PA 19044-0980
(215) 784-0860

Risk Management
205 East 42nd Street
New York, NY 10017
(212) 286-9364

The Self-Insurer
17300 Redhill Avenue
Suite 100
Irvine, CA 92714
(714) 261-2553

Treatment Today
P.O. Box 801651
Dallas, TX 75380-1651
(214) 980-4775

NEWSLETTERS

AAOHN Newsletter
50 Lenox Pointe
Atlanta, GA 30324-3176
(404) 262-1162

AAPPO Journal
One Bridge Plaza
Suite 350
Fort Lee, NJ 07024
(201) 947-5545

The Case Report
CMSA
1101 17th Street, NW
Suite 1200
Washington, DC 20036
(202) 296-9200

*EBRI Issue Briefs and Employee
    Benefit Notes*
The Johns Hopkins University Press
701 West 40th Street
Suite 275
Baltimore, MD 21211
(410) 516-6964

Health Business
Faulkner & Gray
P.O. Box 27758
Washington, DC 20077-1343
(800) 848-1153

Intramural Research Highlights
U.S. Department of Health and
   Human Services
2101 East Jefferson Street
Suite 501
Rockville, MD 20852
(301) 594-1400

Magee Memo
Magee Rehabilitation Hospital
Six Franklin Plaza
Philadelphia, PA 19102
(215) 587-3000

Managed Care Outlook
Capitol Publications
1101 King Street
P.O. Box 1453
Alexandria, VA 22313-2053
(800) 327-7203

Medical Benefits
Panel Publishers
36 West 44th Street
Suite 1316
New York, NY 10036
(800) 562-1973

NAHC Report
519 C Street, NE
Washington, DC 20002
(202) 547-7424

NARPPS Newsletter
313 Washington Street
Suite 302
Newton, MA 02158
(617) 558-5333

NRA Newsletter
633 South Washington Street
Alexandria, VA 22314
(703) 836-0850

O & P Business News
P.O. Box 740247
Arvada, CO 80006-0247
(303) 467-3389

Rehabilitation Review
313 Washington Street
Suite 302
Newton, MA 02158
(617) 558-5333

Research Activities
Agency for Health Care Policy and
   Research
U.S. Department of Health and
   Human Services
2101 East Jefferson Street
Suite 501
Rockville, MD 20852
(301) 594-1364

REFERENCE GUIDES

American Academy of Disability Evaluation Physicians. 1988. *AADEP National Referral Directory.* Arlington Heights, Ill.

American Health Consultants. Updated quarterly. *Common Sense about AIDS.* Chicago.

American Hospital Association. 1992. *AHA Guide to the Health Care Field.* Chicago.

Bantam Medical Dictionary. 1990. New York: Bantam Books.

Benefits Source Book. Updated annually. (Annual guide to research data, products, and services for employee benefit management.) Marietta, Ga.: Employee Benefit News, Enterprise Communications.

Berkow, R., and A. Fletcher, eds. 1987. *The Merck Manual of Diagnosis and Therapy.* 15th ed. Rahway, N.J.: Merck Sharp & Dohme.

Blakiston's Pocket Medical Dictionary. 3rd ed. 1973. New York: McGraw-Hill.

Blum, L. 1993. *Free Money for Health Care: A Financial Aid Directory for Patient Care and Patient Services.* Gaithersburg, Md.: Aspen Publishers.

Carpenito, L.J. 1993. *Handbook of Nursing Diagnosis.* 5th ed. Philadelphia: J.B. Lippincott.

Carper, J. 1987. *Health Care U.S.A.* New York: Prentice Hall.

Castle Connolly Medical Ltd. 1994. *Castle Connolly Guide: How To Find the Best Doctors for You and Your Family.* (New York metro area.) New York.

Center for Consumer Healthcare Information. Updated annually. *Case Management Resource Guide.* Irvine, Calif.

Curaflex Health Services. 1991. *Home Infusion Therapy Resource Guide.* Ontario, Calif.

Darold, T.A. 1994. *Health Insurance Answer Book: 1994 Cumulative Supplement.* New York: Panel Publishers.

Dietrich, H.J., and V.H. Biddle. 1990. *The Best in Medicine: Where To Find the Best Health Care Available.* New York: Harmony Books.

Directory of Pain Treatment Centers in the U.S. and Canada. 1989. Phoenix: Oryx Press.

Driving Down Health Care Costs: Strategies and Solutions 1994. Updated annually. New York: Panel Publishers.

Edelstein, E., ed. 1992. *Blue Book American Druggist: Annual Directory of Pharmaceuticals.* New York: Hearst Corporation.

Field, T.F., and L.P. Norton. 1990. *ADA Resource Manual for Rehabilitation Consultants.* Elliott & Fitzpatrick.

Fiesta, J. 1983. *The Law and Liability: A Guide for Nurses.* New York: John Wiley & Sons.

Fischbach, F. 1992. *A Manual of Laboratory and Diagnostic Tests*. 4th ed. Philadelphia: J.B. Lippincott.

Gaffney, J.B. 1991. *Keys to Understanding Medicare*. Hauppauge, N.Y.: Barron's Educational Series.

Goor, R. and N. Goor. 1992. *Eater's Choice*. 3rd ed. Boston: Houghton Mifflin Co.

Griffith, P.D.M. 1993. *The Managed Care Resource Manual for Obstetrics*. Marietta, Ga.: Healthdyne Perinatal Services.

Guidelines for Health Benefits Administration: Concurrent Review General Administrative Procedures. Chicago: American Hospital Association; Washington, D.C.: American Managed Care and Review Association; Chicago: American Medical Association; Chicago: Blue Cross and Blue Shield Association; Washington, D.C.: Health Insurance Association of America.

HCIA. Updated annually. *HCIA Guide to Hospital Performance 1994*. Baltimore.

Health and Medical Care Directory. 1988. Niagara Falls, N.Y.: Yellow Pages of America.

Health Insurance Association of America. Updated annually. *Source Book of Health Insurance Data*. Washington, D.C.

HealthCare Consultants of America. 1994. *Physicians Fee and Coding Guide*. Augusta, Ga.

Herzlinger, R.E. 1992. *Creating New Health Care Ventures: The Role of Management*. Gaithersburg, Md.: Aspen Publishers.

Individual Case Management Association. 1989. *Competitive Bidding*. Little Rock, Ark.

Individual Case Management Association. 1990. *Health Insurance 101*. Little Rock, Ark.

Individual Case Management Association. 1990. *Report Writing*. Little Rock, Ark.

Inlander, C.B., and K. Morales. 1993. *Getting the Most for Your Medical Dollar*. New York: Pantheon Books.

Isaacs, S.L., and A.C. Swartz. 1992. *Consumer's Legal Guide to Today's Health Care*. New York: Houghton Mifflin.

Junior League of Long Island. 1986. *Life Line: Where To Find Help On Long Island When Life-Threatening Illness Strikes*. New York: Binding Systems. (Consult your local Junior League.)

Karaffa, M.C., ed. 1992. *ICD-9-CM: International Classification of Disease*. 9th rev., 4th ed. Los Angeles: Practice Management Information Corporation.

Kemether, N.A., ed. 1985. *Crisis Management and Catastrophic Care: A Guide for Rehabilitation Specialists.* Richmond, Va.: Vocational Placement Services.

Kirschner, C.G., et al. 1992. *Physicians' Current Procedural Terminology (CPT).* 4th ed. Chicago: American Medical Association.

Krall, L.P., and R.S. Beaser. 1989. *Joslin Diabetes Manual.* 12th ed. Philadelphia: Lea & Febiger.

Larson, D.E., ed. 1990. *Mayo Clinic Family Health Book.* New York: William Morrow.

Lesko, M., et al. 1993. *What To Do When You Can't Afford Health Care.* Kensington, Md.: Information USA.

MacKenzie, L., and A. Lignor, eds. 1993. *The Complete Directory for People with Learning Disabilities.* Lakeville, Conn.: Grey House Publishing.

The Managed Care Yearbook. 1994. Wall Township, N.J.: American Business Publishing.

Medical Interface. 1993. *Executive Managed Care Directory.* Bronxville, N.Y.

Medical Society of the State of New York. 1990. *Medical Directory of New York State.* 62nd ed. Lake Success, N.Y. (Check the local library for state organizations publishing similar directories.)

Melonakos, K. 1990. *Saunders Pocket Reference for Nurses.* Philadelphia: W.B. Saunders.

Mercier, L.R. 1991. *Practical Orthopedics.* 3rd ed. St. Louis: Mosby–Year Book.

National Association for Home Care. 1992. *National Homecare and Hospice Directory.* 4th ed. Washington, D.C.

National Association of Rehabilitation Professionals in the Private Sector. Updated annually. *National Directory of NARPPS.* Brookline, Mass.

National Associaton of Social Workers. *NASW Register of Clinical Social Workers.* Washington, D.C.

National Head Injury Foundation. 1991. *National Directory of Head Injury Rehabilitation Services.* Washington, D.C.

The National Housing Directory for People with Disabilities. 1993. Lakeville, Conn.: Grey House Publishing.

PDR: Physician's Desk Reference. Updated annually. Montvale, N.J.: Medical Economics Co.

PDR Drug Interactions and Side Effects Index. Updated annually. Montvale, N.J.: Medical Economics Co.

PDR for Nonprescription Drugs. Updated annually. Montvale, N.J.: Medical Economics Co.

Pell, A.R. 1987. *Making the Most of Medicare: A Guide Through the Medicare Maze.* New York: Prentice Hall.

Reed, P. 1991. *The Medical Disability Advisor: Workplace Guidelines for Disability Duration.* Horsham, Pa.: LRP Publications.

Rothenberg, M.A., and C.F. Chapman. 1989. *Dictionary of Medical Terms.* 2nd ed. Hauppauge, N.Y.: Barron's Educational Series.

Schwartz, G.E., et al. 1989. *The Disability Management Sourcebook.* Washington, D.C.: Washington Business Group on Health and Institute for Rehabilitation and Disability Management.

Shephard, B.D., and C.A. Shephard. 1990. *The Complete Guide to Women's Health.* 2nd rev. ed. New York: Plume Books; New York: Penguin Books.

Sherman, B.S., ed. 1988. *Directory of Residential Facilities for Emotionally Handicapped Youth.* 2nd ed. Phoenix: Oryx Press.

Sherman, C.D., Jr., ed. 1990. *World Oncology Directory and Source Book.* Milan: World Directories Ltd. Contact Charles D. Sherman, Jr., Highland Hospital, Rochester, NY 14620.

Sherman, J.L. and S.K. Fields. 1978. *Guide to Patient Evaluation.* 3rd ed. Garden City, N.Y.: Medical Examination Publishing.

Springhouse Corporation. 1991. *Cardiopulmonary Emergencies.* Springhouse, Pa.

Springhouse Corporation. 1994. *Chemotherapy Handbook.* Springhouse, Pa.

Springhouse Corporation. 1993. *Physician's Drug Handbook.* 5th ed. Springhouse, Pa.

Springhouse Corporation. 1992. *Professional Guide to Diseases.* 4th ed. Springhouse, Pa.

St. Anthony's ICD-9-CM: Code Book for Physician Payment. 1993. Alexandria, Va.: St. Anthony Publishing.

Stanhope, M., and R.N. Knollmueller. 1992. *Handbook of Community and Home Health Nursing.* St. Louis: Mosby–Year Book.

Substance Abuse Residential Treatment Centers for Teens. 1990. Phoenix: Oryx Press.

Suddarth, D.S., ed. 1991. *The Lippincott Manual of Nursing Practice.* 5th ed. Philadelphia: J.B. Lippincott.

Sunshine, L., and J.W. Wright. 1987. *The Best Hospitals in America.* New York: Henry Holt and Co.

Taber, C.W. 1961. *Taber's Cyclopedic Medical Dictionary.* 8th ed. New York: McGraw-Hill.

Thorn, K. 1990. *Applying Medical Case Management: AIDS.* Canoga Park, Calif.: Thorn Publishing.

Tierney, L.M., Jr., et al., eds. 1993. *Current Medical Diagnosis and
Treatment.* Norwalk, Conn.: Appleton & Lange.
U.S. Department of Health and Human Services. 1990. *AIDS and the
Workplace: Resources for Workers, Managers, and Employers.* Atlanta.
U.S. Department of Health and Human Services. 1992. *Consumer Fraud
Pamphlet: Medicare and Home Medical Equipment.* Washington, D.C.
U.S. Department of Health and Human Services. Updated annually.
1993 Guide to Health Insurance for People with Medicare. Baltimore.
Way, L.W. 1991. *Current Surgical Diagnosis and Treatment.* 9th ed.
Norwalk, Conn.: Appleton & Lange.

SEMINARS

**Annual Stroke Seminar 1994: New Approaches to Care and
Community Reintegration,** Rehabilitation Institute of Chicago,
Education and Training Center, 345 East Superior, Chicago, IL 60611,
(312) 908-6179.
**Caring for Children with Physical Disabilities: A Pediatric
Rehabilitation Perspective,** Rehabilitation Institute of Chicago, 345
East Superior, Chicago, IL 60611, (312) 908-6179.
CMSA Annual Conference and Educational Forums, Case
Management Society of America, 1101 17th Street, NW, Suite 1200,
Washington, DC 20036, (202) 296-9200.
Colorado Brain Injury Symposium, Rehabilitation Hospital of
Colorado Springs, 325 Parkside Drive, Colorado Springs, CO 80910,
(719) 630-8000.
Corporate Leadership and Innovation in Maternal and Child Health,
Conference Development, Inc., 100 Winter Street, Suite 4000,
Waltham, MA 02154, (617) 487-6700.
Disability Management Conference and Exhibit, Washington Business
Group on Health, 777 North Capitol Street, NE, Suite 800,
Washington, DC 20002, (202) 408-9320.
**Eighteenth Annual Interdisciplinary Spinal Cord Seminar: Long Term
Care Issues,** Rehabilitation Institute of Chicago, Education and
Training Center, 345 East Superior, Chicago, IL 60611, (312) 908-6179.
Eighth Annual Review and Update Course in Critical Care Medicine,
Center for Bio-Medical Communication, Inc., 80 West Madison
Avenue, Dumont, NJ 07628, (201) 385-8080.

Fifth Annual Stroke Conference, Magee Rehabilitation Hospital, Six Franklin Plaza, Philadelphia, PA 19102, (215) 587-3424.

First Annual Mental Health Summit, Conference Development, Inc., 100 Winter Street, Suite 4000, Waltham, MA 02154, (617) 487-6700.

Health Care Reform: A Cliffhanger for Medical Rehabilitation, Casa Colina Centers for Rehabilitation, 2850 North Garey Avenue, Pomona, CA 91767, (909) 596-7733.

"Healthcare 2000" and "Keeping Ahead" Seminar Series, Magee Rehabilitation Hospital, Six Franklin Plaza, Philadelphia, PA 19102-9734, (215) 587-3424.

How To Select, Evaluate, and Benchmark Physicians To Achieve Quality Provider Network Management, Institute for International Research, 437 Madison Avenue, 23rd Floor, New York, NY 10022, (212) 826-1260 or (800) 345-8016.

Law of Utilization Management and Quality Assurance, National Health Lawyers Association, 1120 Connecticut Avenue, NW, Suite 950, Washington, DC 20036, (202) 833-1100.

Life Care Planning, Rehabilitation Training Institute, P.O. Box 4116, Winter Park, FL 32793-4116, (800) 431-6687.

Managing AIDS in the '90s: The Healthcare and Business Perspective, Managing AIDS in the '90s, Rehabilitation Management, Inc., 7144 North Harlem, Suite 241, Chicago, IL 60631, (312) 763-5600.

Medical Case Management Conference Series, Individual Case Management Association, 10809 Executive Center Drive, Suite 105, Little Rock, AR 72211, (501) 227-5553.

Nineteenth Annual Rehabilitation Update for the Insurance Industry: Who Is Managing Care? Rehabilitation Institute of Chicago, Education and Training Center, 345 East Superior, Chicago, IL 60611, (312) 908-6179. (Rehabilitation Institute of Chicago also offers seminars such as Traumatic Brain Injury Rehabilitation and Outcomes: Entering the Age of Accountability.)

Sixth Annual National Managed Health Care Congress, NMHCC, 100 Winter Street, Suite 4000, Waltham, MA 02154. (There are also regional managed health care conferences offered throughout the year.) (617) 487-6700.

Glossary

MEDICAL AND INSURANCE TERMINOLOGY

accident and health (A & H). Accident and health coverage is a feature of all group insurance except group life insurance. It is also referred to as *accident and sickness, casualty,* and *disability coverage.* The insurance industry's new general term is *health insurance.*

accident and sickness (A & S). *Accident and sickness coverage,* although sometimes used as synonymous with *accident and health coverage,* usually refers to weekly indemnity insurance (loss-of-time, short-term disability income coverage). See **loss-of-time benefits.**

accumulation period. The maximum length of time an individual has to incur covered expenses that satisfy a required deductible.

active life reserve. Reserve for potential disability claims on currently insured active (not disabled) lives.

The glossary includes terms adapted or reprinted from *Home Care: An Emerging Solution to the Nation's Health Care Crisis,* with permission of Olsten Kimberly QualityCare, © 1993; *CCM Certification Guide,* with permission of the Foundation for Rehabilitation Certification, Education and Research, © 1993; *Health Insurance Answer Book: 1994 Cumulative Supplement* by Thomas A. Darold, with permission of Panel Publishers, a division of Aspen Publishers, Inc., 36 West 44th Street, Suite 1316, New York, NY 10036, © 1994; and *Case Management Practice,* with permission of the Foundation for Rehabilitation Certification, Education and Research, © 1993.

actively-at-work requirement. This is a form of individual evidence of insurability, since the insured's health must be at least sound enough for him or her to be actively at work at his or her usual place of employment on the date the insurance takes effect. Since this definition is impractical for dependents, there is usually a provision that if a dependent is confined in a hospital on the date the insurance would otherwise become effective, the effective date of his or her insurance will be deferred until his or her release from the hospital.

activities of daily living (ADLs). Activities in the nonoccupational environment arising from daily living needs (e.g., mobility, personal hygiene, dressing, sleeping, eating, and skills required for community living).

adjustor. A person who handles claims (also referred to as a *claims service representative*).

appeal. A formal request to reconsider a determination not to certify an admission, extension of stay, or other medical service.

appeal committee. A management group not involved in initial claims decisions; it reviews denials (partial or full) when appealed by the claimant. It is an employee's right (as mandated by ERISA) to have a full and fair review of his or her case when a service is denied. The appeal committee reviews the claims file, the documentation of the denial, and the plan provision that was used to deny. It is the "court of last resort" and requires complete documentation to uphold a denial.

appropriateness of care. Care is considered appropriate if it is the right kind of care rendered in a proper setting.

assessment. The ongoing process of analyzing and integrating data obtained from the patient and family, relevant treatment providers, caregivers, and funding sources in order to identify the present plan of care, current and anticipated needs, and problems or obstacles that may be resolved through case management intervention.

assurance (insurance). Assurance involves the spreading of risk among many, with the likelihood that some will suffer a loss. The term *assurance* is more common in Canada and Great Britain, the term *insurance* more common in the United States.

attending physician. The physician with primary responsibility for the care provided to a patient in a hospital or other health care facility.

authorization to pay benefits. A provision in a medical claim form by which the insured directs the insurance company to pay any benefits directly to the provider of care on whose charges the claim is based.

automatic reinsurance. A type of reinsurance in which the insurer must cede and the reinsuring company must accept all risks within certain contractually defined areas (also called *treaty reinsurance*). The reinsuring company undertakes in advance to grant reinsurance to the extent specified in the agreement in every case where the ceding company accepts the application and retains its own limit.

benefits. The amount payable by an insurance company to the claimant, assignee, or beneficiary under a specific coverage.

bill audit. The review of hospital, physician, durable medical equipment, and health care service provider bills for inaccuracies or overbilling.

business alliances. Groups of business companies allied together to reduce health care costs by jointly purchasing medical services.

capitation. A method of payment for health services in which the health care provider is paid a fixed amount for each person over a specific amount of time regardless of the actual number or nature of services provided to each person.

caregiver. A family member, volunteer, or medical professional charged with providing care in the home setting.

carrier. The insurance company or other entity that agrees to pay the losses. A carrier may be organized as a company (stock, mutual, or reciprocal) or as an association of underwriters (e.g., Lloyds of London).

case reserve. The dollar amount stated in a claims file that represents an estimate of the amount still unpaid.

certification. A determination by a utilization review organization that an admission, extension of stay, or other medical service has been provided and qualifies as medically necessary and appropriate under the medical review requirements of the applicable health benefit plan.

claim. A request for payment of reparation for a loss covered by an insurance contract.

claimant. The person filing the claim to whom benefits are to be paid by the claims administrator.

claims administrator. Any entity that reviews and determines whether to pay claims to enrollees, physicians, or hospitals on behalf of the health benefit plan. Payment determinations are made on the basis of contract provisions, including those regarding medical necessity, and other factors. Claims administrators may be insurance companies, self-insured employers, management firms, third-party administrators, or other private contractors.

claims cost control. Efforts made by an insurer both inside and outside its own organization to restrain and direct claims payments so that health insurance premium dollars are used as efficiently as possible.

claims reserves. Funds reserved by an insurer to settle incurred but unpaid claims; may also include reserves for potential claims fluctuation.

claims service representative. A person who investigates losses and settles claims for an insurance carrier or the insured. *Adjustor* is a synonymous, although less preferred, term.

clinical experience. Expertise gained through professional clinical practice (e.g., any combination of direct patient care in a specialty area, home health, or general clinical area for which the applicant is licensed or certified).

coinsurance. A provision under a health insurance policy whereby the consumer assumes a percentage of the costs of covered services.

comprehensive major medical insurance. A form of major medical expense insurance (written with an initial deductible) that can substitute for separate policies providing basic hospital, surgical, and medical benefits.

concurrent insurance. Insurance of a person under two or more policies providing similar or identical coverages (usually avoided in group insurance).

concurrent review. A form of utilization review that tracks the progress of a patient during treatment; conducted on-site or by telephone.

contingency reserve. A reserve established to share among all policyholders the cost to the insurer of unpredictable catastrophic losses.

coordination of benefits (COB). A method of integrating benefits payable under more than one group health insurance plan so that the insured's benefits from all sources do not exceed 100 percent of his or her allowable medical expenses. Another method, based on a strict benefit-by-benefit (or "carve out") calculation, could result in zero payment by an insurer other than the one that pays benefits first.

copayment. Portion of a claim or medical expense that a claimant must pay out of pocket.

cost-based or cost-related reimbursement. One method of payment of medical care programs by third parties, typically Blue Cross plans or government agencies, for services delivered to patients. In cost-related systems, the amount of the payment is based on the costs to the provider of delivering the service. The actual payment may be based on any one of several different formulas, such as full cost, full cost plus an additional percentage, allowable costs, or a fraction of costs. Other reimbursement schemes are based on the charges for fraction of costs, on the charges for the services delivered, or on budgeted or anticipated costs for a future time period (prospective reimbursement).

cost containment. The control of the overall cost of health care services within the health care delivery system. Costs are contained when the value of the resources committed to an activity are not considered to be excessive.

coverage. (1) The aggregate of risks insured by a contract of insurance; (2) a major classification of benefits provided by a group policy (e.g., term life, weekly indemnity, major medical); (3) the amount of insurance or benefits stated in the group policy for which an insured is eligible.

covered charges. Charges for medical care or supplies that, if incurred by an insured or other covered person, create a liability for the insurance under terms of a group policy.

defensive medicine. The increased use of laboratory tests, hospital admissions, and extended lengths of stays in hospital by physicians for the principal purpose of forestalling the possibility of malpractice suits by patients and providing a good legal defense in the event of such lawsuits.

diagnosis-related groups (DRGs). Groupings of patients by discharge diagnosis to measure a hospital's output. These are used for analysis and monitoring of the hospital's resource utilization performance and costs.

direct contract model. A health plan that contracts directly with private practice physicians rather than through an independent practice association or medical group.

direct costs. Administration costs directly attributable to particular group cases and excluding any share of overhead expenses.

disability. The condition that makes an individual unable to earn full wages by doing the work at which the individual was last employed.

disability benefit. A payment that arises because of total or permanent disability of an insured; a provision added to a policy that provides for a waiver of premium in case of total and permanent disability.

disability income insurance. A form of health insurance that provides periodic payments to replace income when an insured person is unable to work as a result of illness or injury.

discharge planner. The individual who assesses a patient's need for treatment after hospitalization in order to help arrange for the necessary services and resources to effect an appropriate and timely discharge.

discharge planning. The process that assesses a patient's need for treatment after hospitalization in order to help arrange for the necessary services and resources to effect an appropriate and timely discharge.

enrollee. The individual who has elected to contract for or participate in a health benefit plan for him- or herself or his or her dependents.

exclusion. A specific illness or treatment that is expressly not covered by a plan or insurance contract.

exclusive provider organization (EPO). A form of PPO in which any services rendered by a nonaffiliated provider are not reimbursed, and the entire cost must be paid out of pocket by the claimant. EPO providers are usually reimbursed on a fee-for-service basis according to a negotiated discount or fee schedule.

fee-for-service. A form of reimbursement in which physician and hospitals are paid a "reasonable or customary" fee for a unit of service; also a system for the payment of professional services in which the practitioner is paid for the particular service rendered rather than receiving a salary for services provided during scheduled work or on-call hours.

gatekeeper. A primary care provider who authorizes all specialist referrals. Use of gatekeepers is an essential feature of HMOs.

group model HMO. An HMO that contracts with a group of physicians who are paid a set salary per patient to provide a predetermined range of services.

group practice. Three or more physicians who deliver patient care, jointly use medical equipment and personnel, and divide income by a predetermined formula.

health benefit plan. Any public or private organization's written plan that insures or pays for specific health or medical expenses on behalf of enrollees and/or covered persons.

Health Care Financing Administration (HCFA). An administrative body of the federal government that oversees all aspects of health financing.

health insurance. Protection that provides payment of benefits for covered sickness or injury; includes various types of insurance, such as accident protection, disability income, medical expenses, and accidental death and dismemberment coverage.

health maintenance organization (HMO). An organization that provides health care for a geographic area and that accepts responsibility for delivering an agreed set of health maintenance and treatment services to a voluntarily enrolled group. An HMO collects a predetermined periodic payment paid in advance on behalf of each individual enrolled.

holistic medicine. A trend in medicine that emphasizes that the system must extend its focus beyond the physical aspects of disease or particular organs. It is concerned with the whole person and the interrelationships between the emotional, social, spiritual, and physical implications of disease and health.

home health care. Health care provided in the home to aged, disabled, sick, or convalescent individuals who do not need institutional care. The most common types of home care include visiting nurse services and speech, physical, occupational, and rehabilitation therapy. These services are provided by home health agencies, hospitals, or other community organizations.

home health services. Health care services provided to a patient in his or her own home by health care personnel.

hospice. A health care program whose purpose is to provide care, compassion, and support for those patients in the final stages of illness and close to death.

hospital alliances. Groups of hospitals allied together to reduce costs by sharing common services and developing group purchasing programs.

impairment. An inability or lessened ability to perform work duties because of a work-related injury or disease.

indemnity. Security against possible loss or damage; a predetermined reimbursement amount paid in the event of a covered loss.

independent medical exam (IME). Used by insurers to determine an individual's diagnosis, need for continued treatment, degree and permanency of disability, or ability to return to work.

independent practice association (IPA). An HMO that contracts with physicians who see HMO patients in their own private offices. Physicians are reimbursed on a capitated or a fee-for-service basis.

initial evaluation. The assessment conducted by a case manager following case referral. Medical, psychological, social, vocational, educational, and economic factors are explored to ascertain the best course of action for achieving rehabilitation and the feasibility of rehabilitation.

injury. Harm to a worker that requires treatment and/or compensation under workers' compensation.

inside limits. Internal control limits within the structure of overall benefits or the benefit plan; they are utilized to establish a maximum amount for a procedure, service, confinement, disability, calendar year, and so on.

job description. A detailed description of the duties, tasks, and requirements of a job, including specific physical and mental qualifications for performance. A job description is an important tool for analyzing an insured's potential to return to his or her preinjury job and for ascertaining transferable skills.

legal reserve. The minimum reserve a company must keep to meet future claims and obligations as calculated under a state insurance code.

long-term care. Health care provided to individuals who do not require hospital care but who need nursing, medical, and other health care services provided over time.

long-term disability income insurance. Insurance issued to a group or an individual to provide a reasonable replacement of a portion of income lost due to a serious, prolonged illness.

loss control. Efforts by insurers and insureds to prevent accidents and reduce losses through the maintenance and upgrading of health and safety procedures.

loss expenses. That part of an expense (such as legal allocation fees) paid by an insurance company directly to the plaintiff in settling a particular claim.

loss-of-time benefits. Benefits paid to help replace earned income lost through inability to work because of a disability caused by accident or illness. Weekly indemnity insurance is the type of insurance that provides such benefits.

loss ratio. The ratio of losses to premiums for a given period.

loss reserve. The dollar amount designated as the estimated cost of an accident at the time the first notice is received.

malingering. The practice of feigning illness or inability to work in order to collect insurance benefits.

malpractice. Improper care or treatment by a physician.

managed care. A system of health care delivery aimed at managing the cost and quality of access to health care. Managed care is used by HMOs, PPOs, and managed indemnity plans to improve the delivery of services and contain costs.

maximum benefit (overall maximum benefit). The maximum amount any one individual may receive under an insurance contract.

Medicaid. State public assistance programs open to persons of any age whose financial resources are insufficient to pay for health care. Provided under Title XIX of the Social Security Act of 1986.

Medicare. The hospital insurance and supplementary medical insurance systems for the aged and disabled created in 1965 by amendments to the Social Security Act.

modified job. The predisability job adapted for the insured in such a manner that it can be performed within prescribed physical or mental limitations.

modified open panel plan. A service approach to the provision of group legal insurance in which any lawyer who agrees to accept a predetermined fee schedule and other procedural requirements may provide covered legal services to a member of a plan.

network model HMO. An independent practice association of group practices as opposed to solo physicians.

nondisabling injury. An injury that may require medical care but does not result in loss of working time or income.

nonduplication clause. A clause that excludes expenses incurred to the extent that an employee or dependent receives benefits under any type of policyholder-sponsored insurance plan.

nonexempt (nonexempt employees). A classification of employees designating those employees subject to overtime compensation and working time limits under the federal Labor Standards Act.

nonoccupational insurance. Insurance that does not provide benefits for an accident or sickness arising out of a person's employment.

occupancy rate. A measure of inpatient health facility use determined by dividing available bed days by patient days. It measures the average percentage of a hospital's beds occupied and may be institution-wide or limited to one department or service.

occupational therapy (OT). A program of prescribed activities that focuses on coordination and mastery and is designed to assist the insured to regain independence, particularly in activities of daily living.

orthotics. The field that specializes in using orthopedic appliances, braces, and other devices to support weight, prevent or correct deformities, or improve the function of movable parts of the body.

overinsurance. Insurance exceeding in amount the probable loss to which it applies. Overinsurance, which can be a serious problem, is controlled in group medical care coverage by the contractual use of nonduplication of benefits provisions (e.g., coordination of benefits).

partial disability. A condition resulting from an illness or injury that prevents an insured from performing one or more regular job functions.

per diem cost. Literally, cost per day. Refers, in general, to hospital or other inpatient institutional costs for a day of care. Hospitals occasionally charge for their services using a per diem rate derived by dividing total costs by the number of inpatient days of care given. Per diem costs are, therefore, averages and do not reflect the true cost for each patient.

Thus, the per diem approach is said to give hospitals an incentive to prolong hospital stays.

period of disability. The period during which an employee is prevented from performing the usual duties of his or her occupation or employment or during which a dependent is prevented from performing the normal activities of a healthy person of the same age and sex. More than one cause (accident or sickness) may be present during or contribute to a single period of disability.

permanent and total disability. A disability that will presumably last for the insured's lifetime and that prevents him or her from engaging in any occupation for which he or she is reasonably fitted.

physician advisor. A physician who represents a claims administrator or utilization review organization and who provides advice on whether to certify an admission, extension of stay, or other medical service as being medically necessary and appropriate.

point-of-service (POS) plan. Evolved from the preferred provider organization concept, point-of-service plans are customized managed care plans often offered by larger companies. These plans combine employee choice and customized care with tight medical management and local utilization.

preadmission authorization (or precertification). The practice of requiring those covered by a health care plan to telephone a claims department prior to hospitalization, outpatient surgery, or other significant medical procedure. In most cases, a two-week notification period is requested, with allowances made for emergency treatment, where a report within 48 hours of hospital admission is generally required.

pre-existing condition. A physical or mental condition of an insured that manifested itself prior to the issuance of the individual policy or for which treatment was received prior to such issuance.

preferred provider organization (PPO). A system of health care delivery in which a third-party payer contracts with a group of medical care providers who furnish services at lower than usual fees in return for prompt payment and a certain volume of patients. The discounted fee structure is usually of a fee-for-service type.

preventative care. Care directed at preventing disease or its consequences (e.g., through immunization and early detection). Promotion of health through improving the environment or altering behaviors, especially through health education, has gained prominence and is an important strategy used, for example, by HMOs, primary care centers, and others.

primary care. Basic health care provided by physicians, general practitioners, internists, obstetricians, pediatricians, and midlevel practitioners that emphasizes a patient's general health needs as opposed to specialized care. Includes basic or initial diagnosis and treatment, health supervision, management of chronic conditions, and preventative health services. Appropriate referral to consultants and community resources is an important facet of primary care.

probationary period. The length of time a person must wait from the day of his or her entry into an eligible class or application for coverage to the date his or her insurance becomes effective. Also sometimes referred to as the *service period* or *waiting period.*

profile. A longitudinal or cross-sectional aggregation of medical care data. A patient profile lists all of the services provided to a particular patient during a specified period of time. Physician, hospital, or population profiles are statistical summaries of the pattern of practice of individual physicians or hospitals or the medical experience of specific populations. Diagnostic profiles, a subcategory of physician, hospital, or population profiles, focus on a specific condition or diagnosis.

proposal. A quotation submitted to a prospective group insurance policyholder by the insurance company through an agent, broker, or group representative. This quotation outlines the benefits available under the proposed plan and the costs to both employer and employee. This is an important visual sales aid.

protocols. Generally accepted procedures and methods for the delivery of medical care.

provider. A licensed health care facility, physician, or other health care professional that delivers health care services.

rate. The charge per unit of payroll used to determine workers' compensation or other insurance premiums. The rate varies according to the risk classification of the policyholder.

rating. The application of the proper classification rate and other factors that may be used to set the premium rate for a policyholder. The three principal forms are manual, experience, and retrospective rating.

reconsideration. An initial request for additional review of a utilization review organization's determination not to certify an admission, extension of stay, or other medical service. A reconsideration request is called an *expedited appeal* by some utilization review organizations.

rehabilitation. Restoration of a totally disabled person to a meaningful occupation. A provision in some long-term disability policies provides for a continuation of benefits or other financial assistance while a totally disabled insured is being retrained or attempting to resume productive employment.

reinsurance carriers. Insurers for the insurers. See **stop-loss insurance.**

reserve general. (1) An amount representing actual or potential liabilities that is kept by an insurer to cover debts to policyholders; (2) an amount allocated for a special purpose. Note that a reserve is usually a liability and not an extra fund. On occasion, a reserve may be an asset, such as a reserve for taxes not yet due.

retrospective review. Another form of utilization review that allows insurers and employers to maintain records of physicians' practice patterns, hospital length of stay averages, and typical treatment patterns for specific diagnoses and thereby build a database to help analyze "standard and reasonable" procedures and costs.

review criteria. The written policies, decision rules, medical protocols, or guides used by a utilization review organization to determine certification (e.g., appropriateness evaluation protocol [AEPs] and intensity of service, severity of illness, discharge and appropriateness [ISD-A] screens).

second surgical opinion (SSO). When there is a complex medical picture, when questionable treatment is underway, or when elective surgery is recommended, a second surgical opinion is often requested by the insurer, employer, or patient. Some of the elective surgeries leading to an SSO request are often unnecessary, such as the removal of adenoids, bunions, gallbladder, and tonsils or open-heart, knee, or hip surgery.

settlement options. The provisions (stated or intended) in insurance contracts that allow an insured or beneficiary to receive benefits in other than a lump sum payment.

short-term disability income insurance. Insurance that pays benefits during the time a disability exists to a covered person who remains disabled for a specified period not to exceed two years.

staff model HMO. An HMO that employs physicians who operate out of their own facilities or clinics but who receive a salary from the HMO.

stop-loss insurance. Insurance taken by employer groups to cover the financial responsibility of health benefit payments that exceed an established threshold. A company might have health care benefits of $1,000,000 per covered life, with a threshold set at $100,000 with a reinsurer. This means there is coverage for a patient with claims of $150,000 or $250,000, but the company only pays the first $100,000 out of its group coverage and is reimbursed dollar for dollar by the stop-loss carrier for any costs over the threshold up to $1,000,000.

subrogation. In the health insurance context, subrogation is the contractual right of the plan or carrier, where state law permits, to succeed to the rights of the covered person in relation to a claim against a third party. This means that the insured party gives up the right to sue the negligent party. This right is given to the insurance company because it has paid a claim on the insured's behalf. If the insured suffers damages over and above those covered by his or her policy, he or she can sue the third party.

targeted review. A review process that focuses on specific diagnoses, services, hospitals, or practitioners rather than on all services provided or proposed to be provided to enrollees.

third-party payment. Payment of health care by an insurance company or other organization so that the patient does not directly pay for his or her services.

third-party administration. Administration of a group insurance plan by some person or firm other than the insurer or the policyholder.

third-party administrator (TPA). Companies that work with insurance firms, handling all the administrative tasks involved in processing claims. Employers who have become self-insurers, taking on the responsibility of funding their own benefit plans, may use a TPA or they may oversee the payment of claims themselves, via a self-insured, self-administered plan.

transferable skills. The skills an insured has acquired through occupational or vocational endeavors that may be applied with minimal training in another occupation.

usual, customary, and reasonable (UCR). Health insurance plans will often pay a physician's full charge if it does not exceed his or her usual charge, if it does not exceed the amount customarily charged for the service by other physicians in the area, or if it is otherwise reasonable.

utilization. Utilization is commonly examined in terms of patterns or rates of use of a single service or type of service (hospital care, prescription drugs, physician visits). Measurement of utilization of all medical services in combination is usually done in terms of dollar expenditures. Use is expressed in rates per unit of population at risk for a given period (e.g., number of admissions to a hospital per 1,000 persons over 65 years of age per year).

utilization review (UR). UR is the process of reviewing medical services for necessity, appropriateness, and efficiency to ensure that a patient is not given care that exceeds medical need and thereby reduce the number of unnecessary or inappropriate health care services. It includes review of admissions, length of stay, discharge, and services ordered and provided and is conducted on a preadmission, concurrent, and retrospective basis.

utilization review organization. An entity that conducts utilization review and determines certification of an admission, extension of stay, or other medical service.

vocational evaluation. A professional analysis of the insured's work potential, integrating information about physical capabilities, mental aptitudes, interests, personality motivation, transferable skills, and environmental considerations.

workers' compensation. The social insurance system for industrial and work injuries regulated in certain specified occupations by the federal government.

workers' compensation law. A statute imposing liability on employers to pay benefits and furnish care to employees injured and to pay benefits to dependents of employees killed in the course of and because of their employment.

LEGAL TERMINOLOGY

agency. A relationship between two parties in which the first party authorizes the second to act as agent on behalf of the first. It usually implies a contractual arrangement between two parties managed by a third party, an agent.

agent. A party authorized to act on behalf of another and to give the other an account of such actions.

appeal. The process whereby a court of appeals reviews the record of written materials from a court proceeding to determine if errors were made that might lead to a reversal of the trial court's decision.

assumption of risk. A doctrine based on voluntary exposure to a known risk. It is distinguished from contributory negligence (which is based on carelessness) in that it involves the comprehension that a peril is to be encountered as well as the willingness to encounter it.

claimant. One who asserts a right or demand in a legal proceeding.

claims-made policy. A professional liability insurance policy that covers the holder for a period in which a claim of malpractice is made. The alleged act of malpractice may have occurred at some previous time but the policy insures the holder when the claim is made.

compensation. An act that a court orders done (including money that a court or other tribunal orders to be paid) by a person whose acts or omissions have caused loss or injury in order to make the injured party "whole" with respect to the loss.

confidential communications. Certain classes of communications that the law will not permit to be divulged; in general, such communications pass between persons who stand in a confidential or fiduciary relationship to each other (or who, because of their relative situation, owe a special duty of secrecy and fidelity).

cross-examination. The questioning of a witness during a trial or deposition by the party opposing those who asked the person to testify.

damages. Money awarded by the court to someone who has been injured (plaintiff) that must be paid by the party responsible for the injury (defendant). Normal damages are awarded when the injury is considered to be slight. Compensatory damages are awarded to repay or compensate the injured party for the loss that was incurred. Punitive damages are awarded when the injury is found to have been committed maliciously or in wanton disregard of the plaintiff's interests.

defendant. The person against whom an action is brought because of an alleged responsibility for violating one or more of the plaintiff's legally protected interests.

deposition. A sworn pretrial testimony given by a witness in response to oral and written questions and cross-examination. The deposition is transcribed and may be used for further pretrial investigation. It may also be presented at the trial if the witness cannot be present.

disability. In a legal context, the term means incapacity for the full enjoyment of ordinary legal rights.

discovery. A pretrial procedure that allows the plaintiff's and defendant's attorneys to find out about matters relevant to the case, including information about what evidence the other side has, what witnesses will be called, and so on. Discovery devices for obtaining information include depositions and interrogatories to obtain testimony, requests for documents and other tangible evidence, and requests for physical or mental examination.

evidence. Any species of proof or probative matter, legally presented at the trial of an issue, by the act of the parties and through the medium of witnesses, records, documents, tangible objects, and the like, for the purpose of inducing beliefs in the minds of the court or jury as to the truth of their contention.

expert witness. A person who has special knowledge of a subject about which a court requests testimony. Special knowledge may be acquired by experience, education, observation, or study but is not possessed by the average person. An expert witness gives expert testimony or expert evidence. This evidence often serves to educate the court and the jury in the subject under consideration.

fiduciary relationship. A legal relationship of confidentiality that exists whenever one person trusts or relies on another, such as a doctor-patient relationship.

fraud. A false representation of a matter of fact (whether by words or conduct, by false or misleading allegations, or by concealment of that which should be disclosed) that deceives and is intended to deceive another so that person shall act upon such representation to his or her legal injury.

guardian ad litem. A person appointed by the court to safeguard a minor's legal interest during certain kinds of litigation.

imputed negligence. Malpractice due to negligent practice of a person taught.

in loco parentis. Latin phrase meaning "in the place of the parent." The assumption by a person or institution of the parental obligations of caring for a child without adoption.

indemnity. To secure against loss or damage; to give security for the reimbursement of a person in the event of an anticipated loss to that individual.

injury. Any wrong or damage done to another, either to the individual's person, rights, reputation, or property. Consists of damages of a permanent nature.

interrogatories. A series of written questions submitted to a witness or other person having information of interest to the court. The answers are transcribed and are sworn to under oath.

liability. Legal responsibility for failure to act, so causing harm to another person, or for actions that fail to meet standards of care, so causing another person harm.

liaison. A nurse who acts as an agent between a patient, the hospital, and the patient's family and who speaks for the entire health care team.

litigation. A contest in a court for the purpose of enforcing a right.

malfeasance. Performance of an unlawful, wrongful act.

malpractice. A professional person's wrongful conduct, improper discharge of professional duties, or failure to meet standards of care, which results in harm to another person.

misfeasance. An improper performance of a lawful act, especially in a way that might cause damage or injury.

motion. A request to the court to take some action or a request to the opposing side to take some action relating to a case.

negligence. Failure to act as an ordinary prudent person; conduct contrary to that of a reasonable person under similar circumstances.

nonfeasance. A failure to perform a task, duty, or undertaking that one has agreed to perform or that one had a legal duty to perform.

petition. An ex parte application to a court asking for the exercise of the court's judicial powers in relation to some matter that is not the subject for a suit or action, or a request for the authority to undertake an action that requires the sanction of the court.

plaintiff. A person who brings a suit to court in the belief that one or more of that individual's rights have been violated or that a legal injury has occurred.

professional corporation (PC). A corporation formed according to the law of a particular state for the purpose of delivering a professional service.

professional liability. A legal concept describing the obligation of a professional person to pay a patient or client for damages caused by the professional's act of omission, commission, or negligence. Professional liability better describes the responsibility of all professionals to their clients than does the concept of malpractice, but the idea of professional liability is central to malpractice.

professional liability insurance. A type of liability insurance that protects professional persons against malpractice claims made against them.

release. The relinquishment of a right, claim, or privilege by a person in whom it exists or to whom it accrues, to the person against whom it might be demanded or enforced.

remedy. The means by which a right is enforced or the violation of a right is prevented, redressed, or compensated.

res ipsa loquitur. Literally, "the thing speaks for itself." A legal doctrine that applies when the defendant was solely and exclusively in control at the time the plaintiff's injury occurred, so that the injury would not have occurred if the defendant had exercised due care. When a court applies this doctrine to a case, the defendant bears the burden of proving that he was not negligent.

respondeat superior. Literally, "let the master respond." This maxim means that an employer is liable in certain cases for the consequences of the wrongful acts of its employees while the employee is acting within the scope of his or her employment.

right of conscience law. A legal equivalent to freedom of thought or of religion.

right of privacy. The right of individuals to withhold their person and property from public scrutiny, if so desired, as long as it is consistent with the law of public policy.

right to access law. A law that grants a patient the right to see his or her medical records.

right to die law. A law that upholds a patient's right to choose death by refusing extraordinary treatment when the patient has no hope of recovery. Also referred to as the *natural death law* or *living will law.*

settlement. An agreement by the parties to a transaction or controversy that resolves some or all of the issues involved in a case.

standards of care. In a malpractice lawsuit, those acts performed or omitted that an ordinary, prudent person in the defendant's position would have done or not done; a measure by which the defendant's alleged wrongful conduct is compared.

statute. The written act of a legislative body declaring, commanding, or prohibiting an action (in contrast to unwritten common law).

statute of limitations. A statute that sets forth limitations of the right of action for certain described causes (e.g., declaring that no suit can be maintained on such cases of action unless brought within a specified period of time after the right came into existence).

subpoena. A process commanding a witness to appear and give testimony in court.

tort. A private or civil wrong outside of a contractual relationship.

tort-feasor. A wrongdoer who is legally liable for the damage caused.

waiver. The intentional or voluntary relinquishment of a known right.

uniform anatomical gift act. A law of the type existing in all 50 states that allows anyone over 18 to sign a donor card willing some or all of his or her organs after death.

wrongful death statute. A statute of the type existing in all states that provides that the death of a person can give rise to a cause of legal action brought by the person's beneficiaries in a civil suit against the person whose willful or negligent acts caused the death. Prior to the existence of these statutes, a suit could be brought only if the injured person survived the injury.

wrongful life action. A civil suit usually brought against a physician or health facility on the basis of negligence that resulted in the wrongful birth or life of an infant. The parents of the unwanted child seek to obtain payment from the defendant for the medical expenses of pregnancy and delivery, for pain and suffering, and for the education and upbringing of the child. Wrongful life actions have been brought and won in several situations, including malpracticed tubal ligations, vasectomies, and abortions. Failure to diagnose pregnancy in time for abortion and incorrect medical advice leading to the birth of a defective child have also led to malpractice suits for a wrongful life.

ACRONYMS AND ABBREVIATIONS

A & H	accident and health
A & S	accident and sickness
ACCC	Advanced Competency Continuity of Care
ADA	Americans with Disabilities Act
ADEA	Age Discrimination in Employment Act
ADL	activities of daily living
AEP	appropriateness evaluation protocol
ANYOCC	any occupation (used in long-term disability policies)
ASO	administrative services only
CARF	Certification Association of Rehabilitation Facilities
CCM	Certified Case Manager
CIRSC	Certification of Insurance Rehabilitation Specialists Commission
CIRS	Certified Insurance Rehabilitation Specialist
CM	case manager
COB	coordination of benefits
COBRA	Consolidated Omnibus Reconciliation Act of 1986
CPT	Current Procedural Terminology (used in code designations)
CRC	Certified Rehabilitation Counselor
CRRN	Certified Rehabilitation Registered Nurse
DME	durable medical equipment
DRG	diagnosis-related group
EPO	exclusive provider organization
ERISA	Employee Retirement Income Security Act of 1974
HIA	health insurance alliance
HIPCs	health insurance purchasing cooperative
HISOCC	his occupation (used in long-term disability policies)
HME	home medical equipment
HMO	health maintenance organization
ICD-9	International Classification of Disease
ICMA	Individual Case Management Association
IPA	independent practice arrangement
ISD-A	intensity of service, severity of illness, discharge and appropriateness

JCAHO	Joint Commission on Accreditation of Healthcare Organizations
LPN	Licensed Practical Nurse
LTD	long-term disability
LVN	Licensed Vocational Nurse
OT	occupational therapist or occupational therapy
PCP	primary care physician
PIP	personal injury protection (auto policy clause)
POS	point-of-service
PPO	preferred provider organization
PPS	prospective payment system
PRO	professional review organization
PSRO	professional standards review organization
PT	physical therapist or physical therapy
SHMO	social health maintenance organization
SPD	summary plan description
STD	short-term disability
TEFRA	Tax Equity and Fiscal Responsibility Act of 1982
TPA	third-party administrator
TPN	total parenteral nutrition
WC	workers' compensation

Index

403